HERMENEUTICAL APPROACHES IN PSYCHOLOGY OF RELIGION

INTERNATIONAL SERIES IN THE PSYCHOLOGY OF RELIGION

6

Edited by

J.A. Belzen and J.M. van der Lans

Amsterdam - Atlanta, GA 1997

HERMENEUTICAL APPROACHES IN PSYCHOLOGY OF RELIGION

Edited by

J.A. Belzen

∞ The paper on which this book is printed meets the requirements of "ISO 9706:1994, Information and documentation - Paper for documents - Requirements for permanence".

ISBN: 90-420-0041-4 (bound)
ISBN: 90-420-0033-3 (paper)

Printed in The Netherlands

TABLE OF CONTENTS

The varieties of psychology of religion: by way of introduction
J.A. Belzen 7

On basic questions
Cause and meaning, explanation and interpretation in the psychology of religion
A. Vergote 11
Inquiry into the foundations of a hermeneutical psychology — A critique of unpure reason
Th. de Boer 35

On contemporary debates
The real is the relational — Relational psychoanalysis as a model of human understanding
J.W. Jones 51
A theory of gender as a central hermeneutic in the psychoanalysis of religion
N.R. Goldenberg 65
Reconsidering the psychology of religion — Hermeneutical approaches in the contexts of research and debate
K.V. O'Connor 85

On a historizing psychology
Cultural psychology of religion: synchronic and diachronic
J.A. Belzen 109
The hermeneutics of life history — A plea for a hermeneutical psychology of religion, exemplified by the work of Erik H. Erikson
T.H. Zock 129
The obsessional episode in the conversion experience of Ignatius of Loyola — A psychobiographical contribution
J. Corveleyn 155

On interpreting people's stories
A readers guide for interpreting texts of religious experience — A hermeneutical approach
J.M. Day & M.H.L. Naedts 173

Psychology of religion as hermeneutical cultural analysis — Some reflections with reference to Clifford Geertz
U. Popp-Baier 195
Mystical experience and interpretation — A hermeneutical approach
A. Geels 213

On symbols
Between mythology and symptomatology — Thoughts on the psychology of symbols
J. Scharfenberg 233
Symbolic experience: transforming the selfobject relation — A new symbol theory based on modern psychoanalysis
H. Wahl 241
Psychoanalytic hermeneutic and sacramental theology
W. W. Meissner 263

Index 289

The Varieties of Psychology of Religion By Way of Introduction

J.A. Belzen
University of Amsterdam (The Netherlands)

Psychology of religion is alive and well. The number of publications and people involved is ever increasing, networks are being developed, positions being established. Nowadays in academic circles facts like these are regarded as indicators that a field is flourishing. This volume, however, is not going to review these developments. Its intention is to turn to the substance of the enterprise and to expose something of the rich variety of work that is now being done within one of the psychological mainstreams concentrating on the religious phenomena. But first let us say a few words on the enterprise itself. Even though it has existed for more than a century and counts all 'great psychologists' among its contributors (cf. Wulff 1991), to many, psychology of religion is still an obscurity. Either it is considered to be an impossibility — usually because of theological *a prioris* — or it is regarded to be superfluous — often because of personal lack of interest and sometimes even animosity towards religion. On the other hand, there exists outside academic psychology a broad stream of psychology-like approaches to religion and spirituality, which contaminate psychology or use it on behalf of religious 'salvation'. In a way, even an undertaking such as pastoral psychology might be included under this label. Although all these psychology-like approaches deal with religion, they usually are not regarded as psychology of religion in the narrow sense. Despite its frequently being located within departments of religion, the aim and intention of psychology of religion are not salutary. It is more modest and only tries to determine what is psychological about religion. Defining itself as an element of psychological scholarship, psychology of religion, consequently, shares much of the fate of the rest of psychology. While benefiting from the strength of academic psychology in general, however, psychology of religion is threatened by the same dangers. The 'crisis in psychology', which seems to have been an object of discussion ever since Karl Bühler's publication by the same name (1927), has been depicted by Amedeo Giorgi (1976) in terms of lack of unity, lack of relevance and problematic self-understanding as a science. Even if, in this post-modern era, one is inclined to admire psychology's pluriformity, Giorgi's second and third reproaches still seem to hold. The many complaints, from various sides, lamenting psychology's restricted value for a fundamental understanding of human beings, its lack of insight into the peculiarities of the individual, the particularity of its results obtained from middle class white students, and many more are well known and need not be repeated here. In spite of (or perhaps because of) its dealing with small-scale questions, concepts and manipulated variables, and in spite of its ever-increasing refinement of scales and sophisticated statistical techniques, psychology is being criticized for not observing sufficiently, not going deeply enough into the phenomena it wants to explore, especially when it is constructing its 'measuring instruments'. One of the main reasons for this lack of relevance, according to Georgi, is psychology's problematic self-understanding. Because it choses to emulate the natural sciences, it could not solve this fundamental dilemma: either to be faithful to the demands of the life-world and not do justice to science, or to remain faithful to the requirements of science and, precisely because of that, fail to do justice to the life-world. To Giorgi, phenomena have to be approached as they present themselves in the world and therefore "the kind of science psychology should be must be constructed from within the viewpoint of the 'world'. For the world of man, psychology must be a human science" (Giorgi 1976, p. 293).

Very eloquently formulated, pleas like Giorgi's, however, in their turn often have been criticized as being too abstract, too philosophical, not practical enough. Pleading for a different psychology, understood as a human science, these (usually phenomenologically oriented) spokesmen would offer no real alternative. They would complain, but do not show how to do it better. Is this criticism correct? In the years in which Georgi wrote, it may have been true that human scientific psychology was still in the process of understanding and defining itself, but since then much has happened. New and innovative approaches such as social constructionism (Gergen 1985; Shotter 1993a, 1993b), narrative psychology (Brunner 1990, 1992; Josselson & Lieblich 1993), rhetorical psychology (Billig 1987, 1991), discursive psychology (Edwards & Potter 1991; Harré & Gillett 1994), to name just a few, are presenting themselves as viable alternatives which are promising for psychology of religion as well. One should also be wary of exaggeration: in earlier decades there always have been efforts within psychology to approach subjects and phenomena in the plenitude of daily human life, not the last within psychology of religion — perhaps even because the latter was often not located within psychological 'laboratories'.

This volume brings together papers from various corners within the hermeneutical movement. Drawing on older and newer approaches, the authors try to bring a psychological perspective to the study of religiosity. In order to do justice to this evasive human phenomenon, they actively cross their disciplinary boundaries and explore psychology's neighbouring fields. After a general introduction to hermeneutics in psychology, the reader will find studies drawing on psychoanalysis, anthropology, women's studies and philosophy. Historical studies as well as research with contemporary subject are presented; empirical as well as theoretical investigations are reported. Thus, this volume may be trusted to offer a broad representation of the variety that exists within contemporary hermeneutical psychology of religion.

A number of the following studies have been discussed in depth at an international symposium in 1995 at the University of Amsterdam, generously sponsored by the Haagsche Genootschap (Hague Society, founded 1785), one of the 'foster parents' of psychology of religion in The Netherlands. We thank the Genootschap as well as the Delenus Instituut of the University of Amsterdam for having made possible this stimulating intellectual exchange.

References

Billig, M. (1987). *Arguing and thinking: a rhetorical approach to social psychology*. Cambridge: Cambridge University Press.

Billig, M. (1991). *Ideology and opinions: studies in rhetorical psychology*. London: Sage.

Bruner, J. (1990). *Acts of meaning*. Cambridge, MA: Harvard University Press.

Bruner, J. (1992). The narrative construction of reality. In: H. Beilin & P.B. Putall (eds.). *Piaget's theory: prospects and possibilities* (pp. 229-248). Hillsdale: Erlbaum.

Bühler, K. (1927). *Die Krise der Psychologie*. Jena: Fischer.

Edwards, D. & J. Potter (1992). *Discursive psychology*. London: Sage.

Gergen, K.J. (1985). The social constructionist movement in modern psychology. *American Psychologist, 40,* 266-275.

Giorgi, A. (1976). Phenomenology and the foundations of psychology. In: W.J. Arnold (ed.). *Conceptual foundations of psychology: Nebraska symposium on motivation, 1975* (pp. 281-408). Lincoln: University of Nebraska Press.

Harré, R. & G. Gillett (1994). *The discursive mind*. London: Sage Publications.

Josselson, R. & A. Lieblich (eds.) (1993). *The narrative study of lives. volume 1*. London: Sage.

Shotter, J. (1993a). *Conversational realities: constructing life through language.* London: Sage.

Shotter, J. (1993b). *Cultural politics of everyday life: social construction, rhetoric and knowing of the third kind.* Buffalo: University of Toronto Press.

Wulff, D.M. (1991). *Psychology of religion: classic and contemporary views.* New York: Wiley.

Cause and Meaning, Explanation and Interpretation in the Psychology of Religion

A. Vergote
University of Leuven (Belgium)

Psychology of religion is a good testcase for the critical consideration of the scope, principles, competence and limits of psychology in general. It has always seemed evident to me that the distinction between fundamental and applied psychology is only valuable for separating scientific research and the practical use of psychological insights — in education, pastoral work, etc. To consider psychology of religion, psychology of art, and clinical psychology as psychology applied to religion, art, or pathology, is incorrect and sterilizing, for the psychic reality can only be studied in the particular cultural activities of the persons. Well then, a cultural activity is object of interpretation. But psychology does more than interpret, it also explains. The topic proposed to our reflections clearly raises fundamental questions concerning the psychology of religion, because they also partly question the project and scientific status of all psychology. And as I said, religion is a most interesting testcase, for it is the object of many other sciences which are partly hermeneutical: history, philosophy, theology, sociology, cultural anthropology.

In the first part of my study, I intend to clarify in general the relation between psychology and hermeneutics. I will of course have in view religion as a most interesting object for both disciplines. In the second part, I will consider some particular contributions of hermeneutics to psychology of religion.

I. General Thesis: Mutual Inclusion and Difference

Hermeneutics

The name and project of hermeneutics is attributed to Aristotle, and the definition he gave is still valid: hermeneutics is the methodic understanding of human signs, first of texts, then of other human signs. And the interpretation of signs is achieved through the reading of signs according to their meaning and intention: to accomplish the interpretation of reality itself.

Hermeneutics thus evolve, within the complex relationship of the reader interpreting signs, which in turn interpret reality. A continuous shift occurs in the relation between reader and signs to reality, and in the relation reader-reality to the interpreting signs. The word 'reader' here has the most general meaning of the person interpreting signs which bear significance and express human ideas, intentions, feelings, and dispositions. Religion is the object of science in as far as it becomes a phenomenon observable in signs expressing ideas, intentions, etc. There are different kinds of signs: texts, monuments, icons, ritual objects and gestures. The texts themselves are of a very different nature, and a major task hermeneutics accomplished, is to distinguish the different types (*genres littéraires*) of religious texts: oracles, myths, historiographic and poetic texts, rituals, personal prayers of different types, reports and witnesses, apologetic and theological texts. Psychologists of religion should know some essentials of these hermeneutics.

About the present or past signs hermeneutics ask the question : what does — did — the subject exactly intend to express in this organised set of signs: texts, icons, pictures...? This question is examined by consciously placing oneself within the three poles-relation: hermeneutics — sign — reality. The reality can be the world as conceived by the subject, in science or philosophy. It can be the invisible reality as in myths, or the reality can be the imaginary fictional world, natural or/and social, created by the artist as a possible world. It is the task of hermeneutics to clarify what the meaning is of a Greek or Shakespearean tragedy, and of the dramatic fiction as such. Hermeneutics also literally analyze the poem Canticle of Canticles, to examine its meaning when it was inserted in the corpus of the biblical texts to further investigate the interpretations of this text in the Judaic and Christian spiritual, mystical and theological literature.

Reality, in the above definition of hermeneutics, can also be the emotional disposition and connected thoughts expressed in art works. Don't we recall the never ending discussions about the meaning of the smile of Da Vinci's Mona Lisa. At least it makes one aware how difficult it is to interpret a sign expressing emotion. We can even say that an emotional disposition may be overdetermined and is therefore expressed in a sign open to different interpretations.

Religious texts also have overdetermined meanings. Besides the question of the truth intention, specific in different types of literature, the texts which are not fictional are themselves the object of ongoing interpretation. In Christian religion many theologians conceive of theology as being essentially the hermeneutics of the basic Christian texts. At any rate, it is a well known fact that biblical texts themselves partially consist of interpretations of former prophetic texts. Consider the famous story of the Emmaus pilgrims in the Gospel according to Luke. It gives a lesson of Christian hermeneutics of the Old-Testament's prophets. This hermeneutics is not merely a scholarly exercise as is the hermeneutics of the *Iliad*, for it belongs to the essence of Christian belief. If we want to understand something of other religions, we should likewise know the specific way their scholars work with their own basic oral or written texts. Let us not forget that religious myths have often been cited in a sacred ritual setting, they are not just imaginary stories. And to grasp something of the difference between Christian and Islamic religion, we must consider the difference between the conception of revelation in both these religions. The God of Islam is the one who writes a book by dictating it to his 'last prophet'. The God of Christianity is the one who is speaking, to and through the prophets and ultimately through the man Jesus, and so the fourth Gospel identified him as the Word, *Logos*, in the Hebrew *dabar*, meaning 'the spoken creative word'.

PSYCHOLOGY OF RELIGION

Rather than to repeat here the account and defense of my conception of psychology of religion, which I recently presented in the invited essay of the *International Journal of Psychology of Religion* (Vergote 1993, 1995), I will focus here my attention on the kinship with and the difference between hermeneutics. The scope of psychology is to know and understand persons, not texts (or paintings, etc.). Persons are subjectively intimate realities and beings manifesting themselves in activities expressing them by which they become phenomena for scientific research. More specifically we should say psychology intends to know and to understand persons by knowing what is psychological in their activities. This obvious tautological definition of psycho-logy opens awfully intricate questions of which the history of psychology is the impressive and disappointing display.

First of all I would stress that the psychological aspect, also in religion, is an indissociable unity of natural causality and of meaning. I don't agree with the fundamental epistemological principle of the founding theoretician of hermeneutics, the philosopher W. Dilthey. He thought natural sciences elaborate the explanation (*Erklärung*) of the natural phenomena; human sciences (*Geisteswissenschaften*) the interpretation (*Verstehen*). The link which Dilthey makes between *Geisteswissenschaften* (sciences of the spirit, of the mind) and the interpretation shows that he is thinking within the duality of mind and nature (and body as nature). Dilthey conceived of this duality as a philosopher, influenced by the great idealistic postkantian philosophy. He ultimately developed a less consistent philosophy of life, with the hope to elaborate in this way a general hermeneutical philosophy, that would crown the human sciences. However, he failed to formulate stringently his hermeneutical conception of human sciences. I am convinced he was unable to, for his premises, the opposition between interpretation and explanation, do not allow this.

Behaviorism tried to avoid the problem by excluding, methodologically if not theoretically from the theoretical concepts of psychology, the mind and its meaning contents, intentions and emotions. Theoretical behaviorism dreamt of strictly observing objective human facts and of explaining them. This has been an infantile disease of psychology. Infantile by its naive preposterous pretensions, as is e.g. evident in the projects of explaining religion never worked out. A disease, in the sense that it has been an inevitable reaction against too loose introspective psychology. The most interesting elaboration of psychology of religions as explanatory science in the sway of behaviorism, has perhaps been found in the marxist essays where religious meanings are taken as the object of an explanation which still has somewhat the character of a dialectical logic.

The project of elaborating scientific psychology, sometimes superficially opposed to what they call 'phenomenological psychology', can give psychologists a behavioristic mind, even if they do not adhere to behaviorism. They consider human data, also religion, as behavior and they define psychology as the science of human (or animal) behavior. This definition determines in an unhappy way the working concepts. In what follows I intend to elaborate on this definition.

Why use statistics, a challenging question we should ask ourselves and all psychologists of religion. My question does not betray a refusal of statistics. On the contrary, I myself often used them variously and within different scopes. Statistics can be subservient to the right interpretation of religious key-words used by a specific population (therefore I used statistically validated semantic scales: Vergote 1980), or to the knowledge of the determinant influence of age, on religious representations and feelings, in a typical cultural setting. But I cannot agree with psychologists always asking if some proposed research has been repeated and been statistically proved on a socially and developmentally representative population. They have in mind the concept of some laboratory research in natural sciences. They think of religious behavior as a natural object that has some universal permanent characteristics, the so-called basic personality, psychology should identify and isolate from the secondary individual or group traits.

Psychology surely is not purely hermeneutics, although the phenomena psychology is observing and on which it bases its scientific constructions are meaningful signs in the broad sense of the word. Behavior is also expressing intentions and emotions and should be considered as a set of signs. Signs should surely not be reduced to behavior in the behavioristic sense of the term! Psychology however is not purely hermeneutics, because there is an element of nature in the facts psychology is concerned with. That is even true of language, which, according to Saussure, the founder of linguistics, is a combination of nature and culture. Historians following Dilthey and considering historiography as hermeneutics, had to recognize that what happens in human history cannot simply be understood as the development of a logic of meaning. But neither is history a sequence of caused events, as is the natural world; therefore the deterministic basis is mostly failing for making predictions concerning human history. Actually, the valid predictions are mostly the prophecies historians make after the event.

Psychology, as well as history and sociology, although differently, has to use two sets of categories for elaborating understanding in its field: concepts belonging to the realm of meaning: intention, expression, signification; and concepts belonging to the realm of nature: force, pressure, and resistance. Both these sets were the key concepts of Freudian psychoanalysis. Freud very consciously argued that the necessity of this double set of concepts depends on the fundamental nature of the psyche, which is moved by *Triebe*, and are to be distinguished from animal natural 'instincts'. Therefore I propose, following the now largely admitted French translation, to introduce in English the term 'pulsion' as a scientific metaphor which becomes a technical term. By this clear definition of psychology as a combination of interpretation and explanation, Freud laid the basis for a dynamic psychology, the terms of which I will develop in the following points. In psychology I thus interpret religious signs as expressing the subject. But this subject is not monolithic, it is inhabited by forces and always to some degree divided by tensions and contradictions. I stress that the psychoanalytic conception of psychology does not imply neither the reduction of psychology to psychopathology, nor the acceptance of the whole Freudian theoretical system.

A second general characterization of psychology, in my conception, is the following. By reason of its hermeneutic side psychology of religion focuses its attention on religious signs as expressions of the individual subject, but a subject relating to others and to the world. There is no doubt that religion is indissociablely personal and social. A private religion is always a pathological would-be religion. More generally, all psychological facts are individual and social; all psychological processes are intra- and intersystemic. The distinction between personal and social religious psychology is an academic, sometimes useful, often deceptive artefact. Hence, faculty authorities who hesitate concerning the location of psychology of religion with personal or with social psychology, do not find scientific arguments for making a decision.

In the following text, I will consider different aspects where psychology of religion could learn from hermeneutics, precisely because psychology itself is partly a hermeneutical procedure. I will also stress where it differs, especially when I consider the relation between clinical and normal psychology of religion.

II. Application of the General Guidelines

About Some Psychological and Psycho-Religious Terms

Psychology of religion exists because the religious man subjectively produces his religion and expresses it in observable signs. "Production" does of course not mean creation. In this respect the first task of a psychologist of religion is to critically consider the fundamental categories he uses for his first step in organizing his field. Hermeneutics sometimes make us feel perplexed when faced with categories roughly taken over from some ideological trends in psychology or from pseudo-psychological pastoral talks. Psychologists are not aware that in doing so they are already imprisoned in pregiven theoretical schemes of thought. At least, using such categories as self-evident leads to a weak minded mixing of different phenomena.

The definition of psychology as the study of human behavior draws the attention heavily to exterior criteria of 'religiosity', even when psychologists do not adhere to the theoretical priorities of behaviorism. There are psychological studies of religious 'behavior' which make statistics of religious practices as did many sociologists of religion in the years 1920-1950. They also apply questionnaires asking information about belief contents. It's like counting religious noses crossing a bridge each year. The presupposition can be that behavior manifests the strength of the underlying religious need, just as the quantity of eating manifests the intensity of hunger in animals. So, one could establish a map of the presence and intensity of religious needs in various populations.

Psychologists of religion indeed presuppose some dynamic force causing religious behavior. Many identify that secret psychological drive by the term 'need', which is derived from physiology. And physiology is the primary resource for explanatory principles in behaviorism. Applied to religion as to other activities, the term 'need' is nonetheless not to the point nor scientific. For if there are needs, the dynamics in religion as in most human activities cannot be correctly identified with this word. The talk about religious needs is of the family of the *virtus dormitiva* of the medicine of the time of Molière.

If psychologists do not agree with the awkward category of behavior manifesting the intensity (or absence) of religious need, what are their interests in true religious behavior such as ritual practice? I know little literature on this topic. The first thing the psychologist should consider is of course the contextual meaning a religious behavior has in its own tradition. What does it mean for the Buddhist in Rangoon to go in the morning to the temple and to wash a Buddha sculpture? For the Mohammedan to wash his face before entering the mosque? For the Catholic to sign himself with holy water when entering the church? Only with this given hermeneutical understanding in mind is the psychologist competent to formulate interesting questions and working hypothesis, and to elaborate the adequate techniques for research. Questions as these touch on the various facets of the relation between mental content (belief, imagination, emotion), disposition, and expressive behavior. Hermeneutics teach the psychologist that this relation is always multifaceted and evolves through the interaction between disposition and behavioral expression. What conceptions of God (the divine, Buddha, Allah) do the subjects intend to express by their ritual behavior? In what result or effect do they believe? Or is there an unconscious intention? Does regular expressive behavior modify the conception and predisposition? Does regular expressive behavior such as prayer and ritual influence more general ethical and affective dispositions, like feeling of affective well-being, capacity of sympathy and tolerance, and coping with death-anxiety? Research on 'religious behavior' indeed touches on the interesting and intricate questions of psychology of personality, of religion, and of civilisation. Unfortunately one often learns more about this topic from good works of religious cultural anthropology than from psychological studies. Poor psychological concepts elaborating religious sociographical inquiries may obfuscate rather than illuminate intricate deeply personal questions.

Today current religious literature, probably influenced by former psychologists such as W. James, or by phenomenologists such as R. Otto, is inundated with the word 'experience' in all kinds of combinations: belief experience (sic), experience of God, of Christ, of the nirvana, of the divine, holistic experience, experience of guilt; not to mention the so-called 'mystical experience of being lifted out of oneself'. Elementary hermeneutics teach us that words, as well as all signs, are diacritical. They take their meaning through the differences with other signs, within an organized network of signs. So, experience is not identical with belief, faith, perception, imagination, recalling, repression, love, commitment, trust... Pastoral theology likes to use the expression 'religious experience', because it presupposes the immediacy of God's givenness, or the perception of the divine. These pastoral writers and workers indeed fear rather unpleasant questions the word belief may raise, for as such this word opposes emotional and rational certainty; or it evokes conversion and commitment. Psychologists of religion, I think, are perhaps still under the spell of W. James and seek one definite psychological factor ultimately explaining the complex religious structures they meet in civilisations. Doing so, they do as people who take a bud and would make a whole coat with it. I often felt that by reducing religious data to a universal religious experience, some psychologists also hope to maintain a broadminded ecumenism and thus denying the awkward question of the differences between the religions. There is indeed a kind of pastoral democratic mind in some preoccupations with psychology of religion: the will to promote universal tolerance and indifference to differences. This leads to a soft and kind universalism replacing the hard and domineering one of former rationalism.

Historicity of Religion and Process Character of Psychology

Hermeneutics established and variously illustrated a conviction which is of the utmost importance for psychology of religion, as well as for most other branches of psychology: the conviction that all cultural phenomena have a historical character. Before being religious, individuals find religion, just as they find language. They can become religious by virtue of the religion pre-existing to them, in the same way they can become speaker and writer because they are finding themselves within a world of native linguistic and grammatically organized signs. Stating the historical character of religion implies the recognition that the religion encountered by the person and in which — or against which — he is formed, conditions, directs, and limits the religious possibilities available to him. A person of the contemporary West could never become a Shamanist, even if he tried in his fantasy to imitate Shamanism he studied, as did Carlos Castaneda. A Shamanist will never become a monotheist according to the biblical meaning of the word, except perhaps when he meets witnesses of monotheism. As the famous historian L. Fèbvre (1942) has argued, it was practically, i.e. culturally impossible for a person of the 16th century to be an atheist, whereas since the Enlightenment atheism is one of the largely spread and seducing conceptions.

As I often stressed, the historicity of religion determines also the possible scope of psychology. It will never explain religion as such. It doesn't make sense to pretend explaining by psychological factors — force and process — the origin of religion, and thus the religion of the contemporary subjects of research. Too many factors are involved in the religious conviction, thoughts, emotions, and activities. No one creates a personal religion as if he were the first religious person. Psychology studies the processes of subjects existing amidst religious references, ideas, symbols, witnesses, etc.

Secondly, historicity means that the subject is changing, also in the way he involves himself, positively or/and negatively, in, with or against, the given religion. The given religious conceptions, symbols, rituals, ethical laws, models of life..., stimulate the changing involvement of the subject. For every element of his religion is for the subject bearer of a surplus of significations he never can exhaustively grasp and internalize.

I would stress that Christian religion is historical also in the sense that the whole history of theology is a continuous interpretation and reinterpretation of the fundamental data: revelation, creation, redemption. Theology is largely hermeneutics, just as the New Testament is mainly hermeneutics of the biblical prophets. In Christian religion, theology is not only a scientific discipline, for it often had a formative influence on preaching and catechetics, and so on the changing presentation of the same fundamentals of Christian religion.

The history of the changes of the same religion throughout the centuries indicates a process that is not linear. Historical findings contradict two types of linear historicity. First there is the mystical-romantic conception of Mircea Eliade who sees time as the loss of original fullness of being and who interprets religions as striving to save and recuperate the origins referred to by the myths. Secondly there is the opposed conception of philosophers who, in the sway of Enlightenment rationalism, propose the scheme of a straight forward development towards more spirituality, *Vergeistlichung*, says Freud

(1939). For this philosophy the moving force of history is also the *telos*: superior rationality. The German, English and French deisms represent this philosophy of history, which is also a philosophy of religion. The study of history of religion in the West however demystifies this philosophy which has been an interpretation of the past and a prophecy of the future of religion. Hermeneutics manifested the self-deception of the reason-centered interpretation of religion. It also demonstrated why the idea of a linear development must necessarily be falsified. First, as already said, the hermeneutical principle of the diacritical signification of signs brings with it the insight that the signs which constitute the religious messages, symbols, and rituals, are inexhaustibly overdetermined. To focus the attention on some meaningful elements obscures other elements in the same religion. So we observe in the history of Christian religion a steady movement of retrieving original veiled elements and simultaneously 'forgetting' others. This dialectic process — dialectic without the Hegelian idea of a definite *telos*! — goes on in exchange with contemporary non-religious and changing 'values', and partly in reaction against them. The only valuable prophecy about the future of religion is that of historians considering a remote past and foreseeing its near future. When knowing this, we look at the prophecies some sociologists and psychologists of religion like to make, we feel as being in an astrological company.

The lessons of the hermeneutics of history should also awaken the critical mind with respect to religious developmental psychology. Some psychologists like J.W. Fowler (1981) obviously take as model the developmental psychology of Piaget who essentially examined reason functioning in a rational intention and in a mind modelled by science. Transposing the Piagetian scheme, already adopted in ethics by L. Kohlberg, Fowler proposes a similar linear model of faith-development. Research on the complexity of the religious mind and its development convinced me, however, that Fowler's scheme is theoretically forcing the data (Wilde & Vanhuyse 1985). The scheme of linear development constrains, I fear, the far more complex developmental processes so that they illustrate the natural human evolution towards a socially idealised figure of 'psychological and religious maturity'. Besides, I personally often insisted on the pitfalls of the psychological idea of religious maturity by which psychologists have taken over a simple idea of the Enlightenment philosophy, borrowed from physiology. Psychologists then apply the idea to human development, conveying to the word 'maturity' the never considered idea of a uniform predestined finality.

Hermeneutics of history gives the psychologists of religion a second lesson. The present is always and necessarily a way of making the future while interpreting the past. That means that desires operating in the project of the future influence the reading of the past, be it to enlighten or to obscure it. I would stress two processes in the subjective transformation of the past. Narcissism, normal self love, urges to exalt one's past. So each population constructs its legends about its own glorious past. Doing this, the population also draws strength and confidence from its past for the making of its future. An interesting example is the exalted religious interpretation the small group of emigrants, fleeing with Moses, have made of the wading through the Red Sea (Book of Exodus). Similarly, narcissism also urges to forget, or to deny, even to unconsciously repress painful events of the past. Historiography is often the critical recovery of crimes, consciously hidden, or not, by national or religious interests and self-aggrandizement. It is also partly the recognition that former historiography repeated stories of crimes allegedly committed by enemies.

Psychoanalytic experience amply illustrates the psychological functions the memory accomplishes and which distorts the adequacy of its reality. The free association technique in the typical transferential setting is partly a method of recovering hidden memories of the past which are unconsciously active in causing pathological disturbances. Psychoanalytic experience teaches that revealing the truth hidden in present memories, is often a painful and difficult work, because it requires the renouncement to affective representations of the self and of others, involved in the family-romances, in legends about oneself, in hostile representations of others, in the refusal to recognize suppressed anxieties. In this respect psychoanalysis strongly agrees with hermeneutics of history.

Considering insights gained in collective and in personal memory, I would very cautiously adopt the method of narrative psychology of religion, which recently has again been proposed. Actually this method renews the old one of autobiographical story telling. Nowadays, it seems to me, psychologists who adopt the expression 'narrative psychology', borrow it from the recent structuralistic way of analyzing the formal structure of narrative texts: 'narratology'. I wonder whether the interest of psychologists is technically hermeneutical at all. As before psychologists invite people to write a part of their autobiography concerning a certain topic, in order to obtain more personal reports than they could get by questionnaires. They would understand the present by seeing it as the momentary outcome of the past. By this method, it seems to me, the psychologist hopes to reach two results: a better understanding of the present he observes and, by applying the method to a typical population, gather valid information for constructing a developmental psychology of religion. I would not bring into disrepute these new essays of psychology of religion but rather expect interesting results. In the light of the hermeneutical and psychoanalytic observations I will however make some critical remarks.

I do not think that a developmental psychology of religion can be based on the report young or adult subjects make of their own childhood and adolescence. I would however more readily trust the accounts when they enlighten the continuity between some living memories of former religious impressive events and the present religious disposition. In these cases there is probably a kernel of a religious idea and emotion, stirring a disposition, around which a stable attitude (idea — emotion — disposition) has been formed. I would nevertheless be prudent, for the past and still maintained idealisation of a person can be an uncontrollable element of positive religious memories. In other cases, and mostly in negatively colored memories, it seems to me impossible to distinguish the real past event and the subsequent reactive self defensive transformation. I would conclude that developmental psychology of religion can only be based on narrative research done at each age of the considered lifespan. Narrative psychology is more an adequate network for letting speak out in truth the personal *present* disposition than for gaining developmental psychological knowledge.

Besides this conclusion, I would attach a real value to the narrative psychology as a method for bringing into light the tensions, even the conflicts, which underlie the present religious disposition. For the specific object of psychology of religion is essentially the study of the processes in the field of religion. These processes are ongoing inner tensions and conflicts which the subject (or the religious society) is in the process of solving. They differ in different civilisations and religions. The observed religious dispositions are the momentary resolutions of the opposing tendencies. In my book on *Religion, Belief, Unbelief* (1996) I tried to analyze the constituent elements in psychology of religion in the perspective of a dynamic psychology of religion. I just enumerate some of the analyzed tensions: prayer, petition, and trust — disillusion; belief — experience; autonomy — dependence; God's almightiness — evil; judgment — benevolence. Narrative psychology, according to me, has the virtue of letting subjects tell how they now feel and understand the recent experience and thought of conflicts and how they solve it. Processes are events characterized by historicity (*geschehen*: what happens in a time-span) and can best be told in autobiographical story-telling. The so called remote past memories have the virtue of expressing the ideas and feelings which for the telling subject are psychologically recent past which he considers, and in which he tries to organize harmony by his belief — or his unbelief — decision and commitment. As a trained clinical psychologist does, I would not draw from autobiographical accounts inferences concerning the objective truth of the related events, but consider them as the subjective truth. Even more, I would not consider them as relating objectively his subjective past, but as the memory he now has of them. By this method psychology of religion can consequently get insight into processes. Only objective observation is the appropriate method to study real exterior facts influencing the religious disposition.

CLINICAL RELIGIOUS PSYCHOLOGY AND GENERAL DYNAMIC PSYCHOLOGY

As all proper human data, religion is exposed to pathological failures. If religion were just a question of meaning and hermeneutics, there would be no morbid forms of religion. Sick minds can make would-be mathematics, which are not real mathematics, but foolish imitation. Love, religion, sexuality, language-communication can be morbid in their subjective production, while remaining in some sense love, religion, language-communication. I have tried to elaborate on the conception of normal and pathological religion and the criteria for making a reasonable judgment (1988, pp. 12-21). I just like to stress the reciprocal enlightenment which clinical and general psychologies are gaining by the study of normal and pathological religion. The confrontation between them shapes the insight in the interplay between signification and forces, interpretation and explanation.

Anybody sufficiently familiar with the religion he considers can somewhat intuitively understand the observed expressions of religion: rituals, prayers, and utterances about the idea of the divine. Even if the subject does not know the meaning of a ritual fragment, of a symbol or of an icon, he normally is conscious that these fragments have a meaning that could be explained. Moreover, as cultural anthropologists often observed, these symbolic signs have a meaning for them and for their religious activity, without the subject feeling the necessity to formulate it. Pathological forms of religion, rightly called so by clinicians, have no meaning, neither for the subject nor for the religious experts, which could be brought into accordance with the explicitly stated meanings of the religion they refer to. The pathological ways of thinking, feeling and behaving of the subject is strange and he is aware that they are not common to his religious group. If it is not uncanny, at least he has the feeling of some occult meaning.

So, the well educated woman, who worked for a number of years as a high-level prostitute, and who afterwards as schizophrenic patient was treated in a psychiatric institute spent at least ten hours a day standing upright. To the therapist who won her confidence, she finally avowed she was spending her days in "mystical contemplation", "according to the model" of Teresa of Avila she wanted to follow. For her therapist it was clear that behind the exterior imagined posture of ecstasy in her thoughts and emotions there was rather emptiness and absence from herself. The patient was unable to tell anything about her thoughts and emotions in this exterior staging of ecstasy. I will forego the explanation of such a pathological form of religion. What I would stress is that it refers to the meaning some normal, although exceptional religious practices and experiences have. In this case there is even explicitly a would-be imaginary identification with a religious type. The imaginary identification in this case obviously gives schizophrenia a trait of hysterical psychosis. This pathology can be understood when we interpret it as the destructuration of a normal, meaningful and thus interpretable meaningful phenomenon. Destructuration means that occult psychological forces are at work here.

Psychopathology urges the psychologist to adopt the perspective of sorting out *psychological causes*, i.e. forces which are all the more constraining as they are unconscious. This has been the working hypothesis of Freud while listening to his patients. The technique of free association in the ideologically neutral relationship, was the logical practical consequence Freud drew from this first insight in pathology. After some years Freud was convinced a psychological cause — rather a complex causal network — is responsible for the production of morbid psychological phenomena, and not only neurochemical causalities. Freud's endeavor was mainly to understand how psychopathology was a deformation of a culturally normal phenomenon. About the morbid guilt feelings, e.g., and their manifestation in obsessive ceremonials, he said: "It presents a travesty, half comic and half tragic, of a private religion" (1907). This is a magnificent proposition, which concludes a rigorous analysis.

The reader with some clinical experience, who goes through the psychoanalytic analysis of neuroses, is impressed by the fact that pathological forms of religion are far more complex and more difficult to analyze and to understand than normal ones. This is because pathology presupposes the normal phenomena and happens as their unconscious use and distortion. I would clarify this by referring to the similarity of and the difference between linguistic metaphors and lapsus linguae. As Max Black demonstrated, a metaphor is the creation of a new signification attaching it to a familiar word. This creation happens through the interaction of two language-chains, in intentional reference to an object. In the lapsus, on the contrary, there is not an intentional reference. The speaker is under the spell of an unconscious thought breaking through and disturbing his intentional speech. So, in his toast at the official dinner of an international congress of psychology, the president said: "It is a great honor for you to be welcomed by me". Rigorous observation thus contradicts some usual talk in psychology as is the explanation of complex religious ideas by the composition of elementary contents, and of pathology as the breaking down of the composite structure. Pathology carries the psychologist beyond hermeneutics, but not in order to fall back into a positivism where all hermeneutics is absent.

Clinical understanding explains bringing into light hidden mechanisms. Just as pathology this understanding presupposes phenomena whose meaning we interpret. Inversely, the understanding of pathology gives a good insight in the conflictual forces the subject had to harmonize in the process of production of the normal religious phenomenon. Let me illustrate these assertions by briefly analyzing the psychology of guilt and of guilt confession. Freud adequately analyzed the pathology of guilt. However, lacking hermeneutics, he was unable to understand guilt confession and the difference between normal and pathological guilt (Vergote 1988).

Guilt feelings are difficult to accept because they hurt the self-love based on an ideal of the ego. Therefore the subject tends to repress guilt feelings. To avow guilt thus requires that the person overcomes its narcissistic repression which fails in the pathology of guilt. Religious avowal of what is guilt before God, the confession to God requires that the person overcomes not only the narcissistic blow, but also the fear of God. He must harmonize the attribution of two qualities to God that can be felt as conflicting: sanctity and agapè, justice and mercy. Religious sin-confession consequently is far more self-involving than the avowal to fellowmen and, as we may know from experience, the resistance against sin-confession is naturally greater. One cannot understand sin-confession as being merely the expression of guilt feelings. It is a self-involving performative dialogical speech act. This act is expressive of its intention and it performs the resolution of the conflicting tendencies. It is also the restitution of the religious innocence, and of the broken alliance with God. This whole complex procedure is not easily observed in the religious signs of guilt. Psychologists should have a good knowledge of hermeneutical analysis if they want to make some valid research. The psychoanalytical studies teach by contrast that the processes started in pathology but are unconsciously made ineffective. The analysis of this confession as a religious performance permits us already to understand what forces are working in the pathology of guilt called obsessive neurosis. In its turn, the explanation of pathology lets us still more distinctly perceive the forces which are at work in the normal religious activity for producing the meaningful behavior we observe and are able to interpret as religious confession.

I would develop similar analysis for the relation between religious faith and its loss in depression, for true and hysterical mysticism, for rational agnosticism and paranoid atheism.

The Challenge of the Belief-Concept

Hermeneutics of religion and epistemology of science present an impressive account of careful studies of what belief is, considered in different contexts. The reading of these studies puts the psychologists of religion to the test with respect to their usage of the term. When research on religion is done with a popular belief-idea in mind, technical, statistical research can only produce popular psychology.

An observation of paramount importance is that the religious usage of the term belief is specifically biblical. It is even particularly Christian, as exegetical philosophical studies have demonstrated. Since the very origins of Christian religion, its members were called either Christians or believers. Of course the term 'belief' (*pisteusis*) existed and it exists in our common language. A religion does not fabricate a neologism as do physics with leptons and quarks! Hermeneutics teach us precisely that common terms get a specific meaning through the usage in a specific perspective and context: religious, juridical, philosophical. R. Needham, while studying a Borneo population, has to conclude that he "could not confidently describe their attitude to God, whether this was belief or anything else, by any of the psychological verbs usually found apt in such situations." (1972, p. 1). More generally, his finding, after a thorough examination, is "that the concept of belief does not belong among such universal and culturally undifferentiated thoughts" (1972, p. 217). In his study of the Nuer, E. Evans-Pritchard observes that there "God's existence is taken for granted by everybody. Consequently when we say, as we can do, that all Nuer have faith in God, the word 'faith' must be understood in the Old Testament sense of 'trust'... there is in any case, I think, no word in the Nuer language which could stand for 'I believe'." (1956, p. 9). In Greek religion, the key religious word was not 'to believe in the gods', but 'to recognize them' (*nomizein*).

The Old Testament in its Septuagint translation uses the Greek word 'to believe' (*pisteuein*), with the common meaning it has in Greek outside religious usage: to adhere to (a reliable God), to trust. In the Old Testament, the religious man 'believes in God', i.e. trusts in God's lasting fidelity, by reason of what God does. In the New Testament, the object of belief is precisely what God does and which reveals Him. This shows how profoundly Christian religion modified what we call religion in general.

Other kernel words in our psychological language have also got a fundamentally new signification in the modern West, in comparison with our past and with other civilisations: words such as experience, subject, object, covenant, and fear. Such differences and changes convey a world of ideas, feelings, and valuations. When man's mental psychological world and affective dispositions are formed and structured by the language they use, e.g. in the religious context, then it is essential for psychologists of religion to know the multidimensional meaning of the religious key-words.

I think that the construction and application of semantic scales, prepared by interviews and readings of literary works, is a major appropriate way of combining hermeneutics and psychological interpretation. I proposed some research on the meaning and psychology of the God representation with respect to the father- and mother-figure (1980).

I do not mean that all religious and non-religious subjects of a definite cultural area are using their language with the richness of their religious tradition, or even with the exact meaning of that religion. But it is important to know how they use it as well as the richness or poverty of their usage. The unconsidered use of the words by the psychologist distorts the results of his research. We should also be aware of the difficulty for people to define themselves the meaning of such key-words. The amount of penetrating philosophical and theological studies that has been spent in Christian literature to analyze the 'act of believing', e.g. attests to the complexity of the disposition this term indicates in Christian religion. To quickly ask a subject of a research exactly what the term means to him, would be as ridiculous as requesting an examination by a student-physician in Molière's comedy. Only a deep, semi-directive interview could break through to the personal meaning. Let us not forget Wittgenstein's principle, which is exactly that of hermeneutics: the meaning is in the use. "Use" here means the context in which the term is imbedded and which fulfils it with lived meaning beyond the reflexive consciousness of the subjects.

Let me illustrate my assertions by considering some aspects of the meaning, use, and misuse of the term belief. The first remark is that the religious use of the word is grammatically well determined. The Christian says: "I believe *in* God". Before the recent observations by the physicist a scientist could say: "I believe *that* quarks exist", or: "I believe *in* the theory of the quarks". For the scientist, "to believe *in*", had the same meaning as: *that* they exist. The simple comparison between the two uses of the same verb, in the religious and scientific context, shows that we have to do with two significantly different meanings. When a psychologist or an anthropologist says that the ancient Greeks *believed* in different gods, then they use a term which distorts their descriptions and do not add a critical epistemological commentary to their assertion.

It is essential that we understand why *belief* and *to believe* are basic and specific religious terms in Christian religion. A psychologist studying another religion should take this into consideration. The texts of the Gospel leave no doubt about the fact that according to the disciples of Jesus of Nazareth and to the first Christians, Jesus presented himself as accomplishing the prophecies and as being more than a prophet. Without claiming a divine nature, he spoke as having divine authority, and demanded belief in his words and in his person. He consequently stressed and clarified what was already present in the Bible variously but still unclearly and what is the core of biblical monotheism: God is beyond experience and intellectual speculation. He reveals Himself in a personal word (*Yahweh*: I am who I am and shall be). Revealing Himself, He simultaneously and necessarily hides Himself. Linguistics demonstrated that the only definition of the person is: the ego who speaks to the other. And the word 'ego, I' is not a concept, but a grammatical shifter. It is sui-referential. A person can only reveal himself by speaking, and in the process of this self-revelation, the person also manifests that he/she is an intimate, veiled, and personal secret. The genial initiative of Freud has been to grasp these fundamental hermeneutics. So he started listening to his patients, whereas before him the medical attitude transferred on psychopathology was that of looking at.

The ideational and religious history of the term 'to believe in' results in a very specific concept. The hermeneutics of the relation between language, speech-act and personal being, clarifies what the Christian term 'to believe in' signifies. The link with the idea of the personal God, and with the God who reveals Himself is essential.

From the above survey I will draw guidelines for psychology of religion.

1. I stress the distinction between philosophy and psychology of religion. A prejudiced philosophy should at any rate not impose from the start, under the cover of psychology, fundamental theoretical ideas on the facts. This would be a scientific mockery. Psychologists should know what religion their subjects have in mind. In Europe they will not refer to some Indian goddess, or to Zeus, or to the Loys of the possession religion of Santo Domingo, but to Christian, eventually to Jewish religion; some groups to Islam, others to a kind of mixture of Christian religion and a school of Buddhism. The museums they visit and the texts they read make many somewhat acquainted with Egyptian, Greek or Roman religions. But these religions are not for them the religions they refer to for making up their mind with respect to their personal religious or non-religious existence. For most of the subjects the psychologists in contemporary Europe examine, be they believing or not, the Christian religion or at least one of the biblical religions are the reference. Research demonstrated that unbelievers, at least educated ones refer to the Christian God-idea they know rather well. Whatever his own convictions, a psychologist in his research should work as does a psychoanalyst in his therapeutic practice: in strict theoretical neutrality. That means to examine the psychological structures and processes this definite religion awakens and moves. The cultural grafting of religion on man is structuring his psychological dispositions, stirring his desires and imaginations, directing and/or reinforcing his ethical attitudes, provoking conflicts and resistances.

As I said I limit myself to contemporary socio-cultural milieus in Europe, where Christian religion is the main reference. To oppose — as some do — faith to belief, is a hermeneutical nonsense with respect to Christian religion. A philosopher as W.C. Smith (1979) can have the idea, stimulated by a devote but weak ecumenic aspiration and his proclaimed interest in Moon's Union Church, that some fundamental faith is the root of all religions and that beliefs, i.e. the conceptual and imaginary representations, are secondary superstructures. To make such a philosophy the theoretical framework of psychology is to fall back in psychological alchemy. From experience I know that psychologists or philosophers who do not belong to a specific religion but who sympathize with religion, tend to stubbornly oppose to the distinctions I am making. They fear that all belief as I defined it, basing my conceptions on the objective observations of religions, is actually a kind of religious fundamentalism. I feel that out of this fear they develop a theoretical imperialism, I would call *psychological fundamentalism*.

Every non-prejudiced observer must recognize that in Christian religion faith *is* belief in the God who is the God who revealed Himself as the God who He is: the Creator, and not a power imminent within earthly powers as were Greek gods or Baal; the God who as Creator has a fatherly project for humankind. In other words: belief and faith are intrinsically linked in relation to a definite content of the God-idea. And so Christian religion is belief-religion. Researches in psychology of religion, when they are full of prejudices, do not ask the appropriate questions and are no more to the point than armchair anthropology in the past. One of the most self-sufficient prejudices is the a priori identification of belief statements with extrinsicism and authoritarianism.

2. A major topic of psychology of religion in the Christian context — today perhaps also in Judaism — should precisely be that of belief, of course while turning the attention to the intricacies of it. It is proper to this religion to educate in belief in God, and to develop the belief content the term conveys. Before the ritual initiation of baptism, the minister asks: "Do you believe in God?" etc., and one of the important ritual prayers is the confession 'I believe in God' etc. Is it not amazing and significant then that psychologists of religion focus little on that central topic? When it was proposed as topic for the Congress of the European psychologists of religion, held in Leuven 1991, many felt initially embarrassed, not so much because of the difficulties, but because of the fact that it was questioning their own conception of religion and of psychology.

The topic is evidently awfully difficult to study for the psychologist who is ware of its meaning and importance. First of all, we should be conscious that by its very nature 'to believe', in the Christian religious context, is a religious act. The verb, as it is formulated in the grammatical first person in the present tense, is a performative speech act, by which the subject assents to the personal God of the religion proposing the God who revealed Himself. Consequently the expression 'I believe' consequently gets its true meaning only in the specific religious situation where the subject poses himself in the presence of God. This is also the case of the confession of guilt. The psychologist who studies this topic must of course know whether his subject believes religiously. But he cannot reproduce a typical religious setting, where the performative speech act has its true meaning. However, the religious belief-confession has also the meaning of bearing testimony to God, before others. In the Christian tradition, already in the Gospel according to John, the word 'martyr' originally had this meaning. In his study the psychologist can appeal to this meaning element of the word when he asks whether the subject believes in God. When the question is asked in deep-going semi-directive interviews, the answer will of course have more validity than in a sociographical inquiry. For in these interviews the subject can retrace the path of his questioning, hesitation, expression of opposition, and a renewed decision that is truthful at this moment. Such interview is precisely the way to examine the processes of motivation, resistance, transference and its clarification; expectations and disillusionments, renouncements, fears and hopes that are involved in the modalities of belief and unbelief. Naturally, technical systems of content analysis and technical ways of asking the subject to state precisely his ideas are most useful. These considerations are not the object of my present paper.

And what to think of the usage of the expression 'to believe that?' I myself started researches using this formula. The subjects were asked to answer on a simple scale of 5 positions: "I believe that God exists; I believe with doubts that...; I cannot state that...; I do not..., however with doubts; I surely do not...". The correlation with other data was interesting. However I would no more use this formula. By itself it rather expresses the grade of assent to a theoretical truth-proposition. When I say: "I believe absolutely that a neurotic symptom is the ambivalent manifestation of a repressed affective idea", then 'to believe that', is simply equivalent with 'I know'. When I say: '"I believe that to some degree all depression is neurotic and endogenous", then I express a lesser theoretical certitude. At the question whether he believed in God, C.G. Jung answered: "I do not believe, I know"; he obviously gave to 'belief' the theoretical meaning. He showed he did not even have an idea of the religious meaning. I fear that the usage of the neutral, theoretical word, 'to believe that', induces a confusion in the mind and distorts the results; or at least renders them almost uninterpretable.

Are there degrees in the religious belief as there are in theoretical certainty? This simple but important question manifests the intricacy of the religious belief-disposition and -act. It is therefore surely easier to use the theoretical formula. Can a person say: "I believe in God, but I do not absolutely believe"? A little hermeneutics makes clear that this would be as finely contradictory as the avowal of a French politician: "I did tell lies, but I did it quite sincerely" (*de bonne foi*, literally: with good faith). Because 'to believe in' is a performative verb expressing an act of assent and trust, it seems impossible to perform only half of the act. This is possible of course, and it can be continuously observed in human experience. The act of belief is performed in opposition to contrary psychic and intellectual tendencies, in other words: despite the reasons for hesitating or for doubting. It is also possible that man does not perform the belief act despite some forces attracting him to do so, reasons motivating him and desires pushing him, for other motives and reasons can be stronger, induce more fear than desire, etc.

A non-measurable degree of freedom also intervenes in the decision. To believe in God is always, especially in our contemporary Western civilisation, a personal decision which is in more than one way intellectually, affectively, and morally motivated. It is an act that solves a personal set of conflictual tendencies. The same is true of unbelief. Therefore in our cultural setting, all psychology of religion is also psychology of unbelief. Only preconceptions focused the psychology of religion on the religious phenomena alone as if they had to be explained by psychology.

Clearly, hermeneutics of the meaning of the word 'to believe' opens a whole avenue for the most meaningful psychological research on the elements and processes involved in religion originating in the biblical tradition. If psychology could follow this track, it would be beneficial to help sociology of religion to elaborate its own theoretical concepts and hypotheses after having surpassed the often deceiving use of popular psychological concepts ('values', 'needs', 'belief that', 'religious experience', etc.).

Belief and Experience

Shortly after Kant, German romantic philosophy (Fr. Schleiermacher, R. Otto) and American pragmatism (W. James), discovered the importance and multifaceted content of religious experiences. The quoted philosophers thought they should and would enlighten the very sources and values of religion, and so justify religion against an imperialistic and narrow rationalism or positivism. Psychology of religion has been a heir of this philosophy. Substituting itself to philosophy it also had initially often — rarely today — the naive ambition of explaining the origin of religion. The philosophy of religious experience showed one of the paths to follow. In this way I think one may explain the extensive usage psychologists make of the expression 'religious experience'. As already said, some recent pastoral language is loaded with the same expression. I have observed that in pastoral milieus this usage is often a thoughtless cliché. But even then, in the background there is the apologetic preoccupation, sometimes explicitly confessed, to avoid the less seductive and more confronting word 'belief'. In some cases, Catholic pastoral language overcomes the difficulties by joining both belief and experience in the hybrid expression 'faith-experience' or 'belief-experience'. From the context it is clear that 'faith' here means belief in God. Are Christian faith and belief then reduced to experience? Or belief accomplished in experience? Or experience accomplished in belief? In this kind of literature or language, the authors and speakers seem to be in a semi-conscience ambiguity with respect to these questions.

Phenomenological texts and hermeneutics of really mystical experiences have extensively analyzed the structure and conditions of experiences. I myself consecrated an extensive chapter of psychology to the topic of religious experience. I think I could show that experience results from the encounter between signifying language and perception. This encounter requires, in order to happen, some characteristic affective dispositions. Furthermore my contention is that religious experience can be an intervening state between indifference or unbelief and belief. Belief goes beyond religious experience and performs an act of assent to a personal God who is not an object of the religious experience. Once the belief act is performed, it can assume and structure the formerly undetermined religious experience. Then a personal unity is effectuated between the emotional and symbolic perception (of nature e.g.) and belief, and is considered a high moment of personal religion that can result in an almost permanent, religious consciousness. However, such a unity of belief and experience requires education of the mind, of the feelings, and of the sensations, that can be compared with the achievement of love reached by some people, or with the artistic mind some come to.

Religious experience accomplished within the restructuring influence of the belief assent expresses itself in unifying metaphorical language. Metaphorical expressions are abundant in major religious texts. This creates a real problem for young people whose mind is developing and achieving conceptional functional learning, precisely in the period preceding entrance in adolescence, where religion clashes with reason. Psychology cannot observe and analyze the religious conflicts going on in this period in which it clings to the simple concept of faith as a "quality of human living" (Smith 1979, p. 12), or faith that "... does not refer to any particular faith or religion; [but] rather... to the developmental process of finding and making meaning as human activity" (Fowler 1981, p. 1).

At any rate, it is important that first, psychologists should not use the term 'religious experience' without carefully determining it after having considered the topic of experience in general, outside religion as well as in the field of religion. Secondly, that psychology of religion looks at religious experience as a process, involving different psychological components, and evolving between a lesser and a fuller religious qualification; 'lesser' and 'fuller' should of course be understood here in reference to the religion the subject himself refers to when he qualifies his eventual experience as 'a religious experience'.

REFERENCES

Evans-Pritchard, E.E. (1956). *Nuer religion.* Oxford: Clarendon.

Fèbvre, L. (1942). *The problem of unbelief in the sixteenth century: the religion of Rabelais* (transl. B. Gottlieb). Cambridge, MA: Harvard University Press, 1982.

Fowler, J.W. (1981). *Stages of faith: the psychology of human development and the quest for meaning.* San Francisco: Harper & Row.

Freud, S. (1907). Obsessive actions and religious practices. In: *The standard edition of the complete psychological works of Sigmund Freud,* vol. 9 (pp. 115-127) (ed. & transl. J. Strachey). London: Hogarth, 1959.

Freud, S. (1939). Moses and monotheism. In: *The standard edition of the complete psychological works of Sigmund Freud,* vol. 23 (pp. 7-137) (ed. & transl. J. Strachey). London: Hogarth, 1964.

Needham, R. (1972). *Belief, language and experience.* Oxford: Blackwell.

Smith, W.C. (1979). *Faith and belief.* Princeton: Princeton University Press.

Vergote, A. (1980). *The parental figures and the representation of God: a psychological and cross-cultural study.* The Hague: Mouton.

Vergote, A. (1988). *Guilt and desire: religious attitudes and their pathological derivatives* (transl. M.H. Wood). New Haven, CT: Yale University Press. (orig. publ. 1978)

Vergote, A. (1993). What the psychology of religion is and what it is not. *The International Journal for the Psychology of Religion*, 3, 73-86.

Vergote, A. (1995). Debate concerning the psychology of religion. *The International Journal for the Psychology of Religion*, 5, 119-123.

Vergote, A. (1996). *Religion, belief, unbelief: a psychological study.* Amsterdam-Atlanta: Rodopi. (orig. publ. 1983)

Wilde P. de & Vanhuyse B. (1985). *Ontwikkeling van zingeving en geloof tussen 10 en 25 jaar: herwerking van Fowler's analysemap en toepassing op 24 interviews.* [Development of meaning and belief between 10 and 25 years: adaptation of Fowler's notebook of analysis and application of 24 interview]. Unpublished masters thesis, University of Leuven.

Inquiry into the Foundations of a Hermeneutical Psychology
A Critique of Unpure Reason[1]

Th. de Boer
Vrije Universiteit (Amsterdam, The Netherlands)

Introduction

The 'critique' in my subtitle "a critique of unpure reason" should be interpreted in a philosophical way. It has the same meaning as 'critique' in Kant's *Critique of pure reason*. 'Critique' in this sense does not have the ordinary meaning of critique, that is criticism. A critique of psychology in the Kantian sense does not intend to criticize psychology. By the term 'critique' we mean investigation, i.e. an investigation into the foundations of science or an inquiry into the conditions that make science, in particular, psychology possible. A critical psychologist in a philosophical sense is a psychologist who accounts for the presuppositions of his science.

In calling my article a critique of 'unpure' reason I do not suggest that psychologists think uncleanly or unclearly. I mean that psychology as a science always will have some ambiguity. The French philosopher Ricoeur has argued that psychoanalysis is a *discours mixte*, a mixed discourse (Ricoeur 1965, p. 75). I defend the thesis that this is true of psychology in general. Psychoanalysis, according to Ricoeur, is moving between two language games, the "language of forces" and the "language of meanings" and cannot be reduced to either one of them. But psychology as a whole is also a bipolar field. Its field of study encompasses a broad area, with at one extreme physiological explanations, and at the other 'talking cures' like psychotherapy. Man as an ambiguous unity of mind and body cannot be studied by a 'pure' method. Research on automatic reflexes is considered to be within the domain of psychology but so is the study of autonomous reflection. That is the reason why in the history of modern philosophy psychology has been what Husserl called the "battlefield" of philosophical viewpoints, of naturalism and idealism, of the natural-scientific and the hermeneutic approaches to the human sciences. According to the poet Alexander Pope the proper study of mankind, Man, is placed on the "isthmus of a middle state"; he is 'hanging between', "In doubt to deem himself a God or Beast,/ In doubt his mind or body to prefer".

Such an ambiguous being or intermediate entity cannot be studied by any simple, one-dimensional method. In this inquiry I will investigate the presuppositions of two opposite methods, the mechanistic and the hermeneutic; or, put differently, I will inquire into the possibilities and limits of the two main models: the model of man as a machine and the model of man as a text.

I

In my view the broad field of psychology can only be actually covered if one uses both of the two models. In our academic culture, however, the machine model, or the nomological approach, is predominant. This is obvious enough. Books on the philosophy of science as a matter of course deal exclusively with the philosophy of the natural sciences. In introductions to this philosophy many statements are taken for granted which, in my view, are actually prejudices. I will mention six of them here:

1. 'To analyze' means to analyze into logically independent elements.
2. 'To explain' is to explain why something is happening necessarily, according to a law.
3. Description is a preparatory phase to explanation (in the sense of causal explanation: see preceding thesis).
4. Interpretation is a dubious form of explanation which has to be completed by explanation.
5. The unique is inexpressible and consequently cannot be described and explained.
6. 'To test' is to deduce a prediction from a hypothesis and to observe this predicted phenomenon.

In my opinion these commonly held statements in methodology are based on convictions at a deeper level, beneath methodology, at the level of foundations. They should be discussed within a philosophical discipline: the investigation of foundations or ontology. Alas, scientists and philosophers of science are all too inclined to identify methodology with investigation of foundations, or, in the Kantian sense, methodology with 'critique'. So the deeper level remains hidden. I have a *philosophical* dispute here with methodologists. I am defending the hard thesis that the above mentioned presumably self-evident opinions are founded in ontological opinions. It is a hard thesis for empiricist scientists and philosophers precisely because of their empiricism.

It is a part of the *empiricist* world-view to claim freedom of prejudices. Empiricism as an 'ideology' claims to remain true to experience, to obey experience and experience only. It is a bold contention to state that this open attitude is actually bound to ontological convictions. But it is exactly the 'essence' of science which is at stake here. Is this definition self-evident in the sense of the commonly held statements cited above? To answer these questions we are in need of an open-mindedness which goes deeper than the 'experience' within the bounds of the empirical-analytical method. In other words we need a reflection on experience itself. In an investigation of the empirical-analytical method we have to reveal the possibilities and the limits of this approach to the phenomena. The prevailing method of testing therefore has itself to be 'tested' in a philosophical inquiry.

This philosophical way of testing contests the usual methodology of testing since it breaks the monopoly of empirical testing. But the methodology of science cannot be self-sufficient. The contentions of the methodology need to be accounted for, and, as is often demonstrated, an attempt to justify the rules of science by science itself is circular. The testing of the testing procedure cannot follow the rules of the procedure itself. So at the risk of becoming dogmatic the methodology of science has to be open to a broader concept of experience and reason than the scientific procedure. If it does not concede its own limitations, it is an ideology indeed.

I called the investigation of foundations "ontology" since it investigates the relation between method and reality, or better, it investigates the *adequacy* of method in relation to the nature of reality. Does this mean that we can obtain philosophical insight into the nature of reality prior to scientific research? Before answering this question I will try to show that the prevailing methodology, in spite of its empiricism, also implies an ontology and that as a consequence ontology is also inevitable from an empiricist viewpoint.

II

To use the machine model does not mean that man is a machine but that as the Dutch psychologist Linschoten puts it: "the description of man in terms of a machine *just by simplification* produces relevant knowledge" (cf. Terwee 1990, p. 69 ff.). The metaphor of the machine has the function of clarifying one side of human nature or, more exactly, one viewpoint on human nature. The machine model implies that the investigated phenomenon is considered as a system of variables whose values change over a fixed period of time under specified conditions. It enables us to predict, explain and control behaviour. The key terms 'variables' and 'conditions' deserve our attention. The machine model entails that the nature of man can be analyzed in variables, i.e. in logically independent elements, and that these variables have a functional relationship. Some variables are dependent, others are independent. If the independent variable appears the dependent must also appear. The first is called a sufficient condition. This relation is fixed in the law: if p then q. It is essential that p and q are *logically* independent. It is a methodological mistake to connect two variables that are logically dependent. If we suppose a lawlike relation between scrupulousness and sanctity, to use an example from the article of Corveleyn in this book, it is presupposed that there is no internal relation between scrupulousness and sanctity. Or, to quote Von Wright: "the verification of the fact that one of them obtains or does not obtain on a given occasion does not by itself settle the question whether another one of them obtains or not on that same occasion" (Wright 1974, p. 55; 1971, p. 44, 93). If scrupulousness is so defined that it by definition implies sanctity — as something that brings about holy behaviour — than the question of whether sanctity obtains after scrupulousness is settled beforehand, and the lawlike connection is false. Von Wright contends that, for a causal explanation to be possible, to a certain degree the world has to be a "Tractatus world"; it has to satisfy the conditions of logical atomism. In this world all phenomena are instances of causal laws and have no internal relations.

It is the genius of Wittgenstein to have given this world-view its classical formulation in his *Tractatus*. I would stress here that this Tractatus-world is not the world of physics. It is the world that is implied by the prevailing methodology of natural science or, to put it more exactly, that is presupposed by the expositions on method in introductory books on social science. In modern times this world-view seems to be so self-evident that its vocabulary penetrates unnoticed into the language of scientists and in daily life. To explore something implicitly entails making it explorable, that is, defining it in terms of variables and conditions. Decisions on the make-up of the world are made *a priori*, in advance, before the research has started. The term 'object' is not innocent in this respect. In science it does not simply mean 'object of scientific inquiry' but: 'constellation of logically independent aspects tied to one another by causal laws'. In our modern world-view this is taken for granted. In Kant's *Critique of pure reason*, in which the principles of the scientific world-view are formulated, the counterexample of the natural (or better: naturalistic) phenomenon is the dream (Verwey 1985, pp. 44-52). The choice he presents is: causal relation and causally related phenomena, or else phantoms; science, or else magic. This conviction can only be uprooted if we can demonstrate that an alternative is possible, that internal relations (or hermeneutic relations, to anticipate the course of my argument) also exist. Is it true that in our life-world every order or structure is of a lawlike nature? Freud made it plausible that dreams contain hidden meanings and possibilities of understanding which lie outside the natural scientific outlook. Not only in dreams but also in daily life, the vast majority of connections have the nature of meanings. I am reluctant to call these relations 'logical' since this term suggests that the connection is trivial and can be simply deduced. My argument will be that the tracing of internal relations is also informative. It takes time and requires exertion to find them. The results of our efforts are interesting. We are actually doing research but not of a nomological nature. Because there is an internal relation, we not only connect the phenomena of scrupulousness and sanctity in an external, causal manner, but we understand this relationship. We clarify a hidden intelligibility. Max Weber spoke in this context of a "plus of rationality" (Weber 1968, pp. 79, 82).

III

If the world actually had the structure of the Tractatus-world the natural scientific method would be universally applicable. There would be no problems about its adequacy. But there are problems. The most obvious one is that the model cannot be applied to the scientific investigator himself. If the model were universally adequate, science would become incomprehensible. We cannot think about science without presupposing human properties like intentionality, rationality, freedom, the possibility to account for one's acts and thoughts. All of these human characteristics are excluded from the scientific world-model (cf. Boer 1983, p. 39 ff, p. 102).

The problem I mentioned in section II is the problem of the adequacy of the model itself, of the relation between this model and the experienced life-world. In the philosophical literature one can find three solutions to this problem.

1. The first is a pragmatic one. The model is a would-be model, a fiction. We only pretend, for the time being, that the model is adequate. Science in this conception is a game, albeit a very effective game. The problem is not solved here but avoided since the question of truth is evaded.

2. A second solution is to weaken the method. The strait-jacket of the empirical-analytical approach in this case is loosened. In recent times the method seems to have become very elastic, especially under the influence of the popularity in social science circles, of the

Kuhn/Feyerabend position. I am not an admirer of this move to the left wing of neo-positivism. After all it is and remains a philosophy of natural science, be it a sceptical one. The natural scientific framework remains the frame of reference of this viewpoint. So the relevance of this method is presupposed by this anarchism. It is not a strong point for social scientists to make an appeal to the weakness of the natural scientific method. If anything goes — as the popular reception of Feyerabend would have it — a loose, human scientific approach to human phenomena must also be permitted; but permissiveness is no philosophical virtue. I think Karl-Otto Apel is right in characterizing this way of thinking with the dictum: "because they don't understand the difference between scientism and science, they reject science". But a human scientific approach too, has to be strict, i.e. scientific.

3. The third solution tries to make a distinction. One part of the human being, the 'lower' part, corresponds to the model, another part does not and is free. This solution also remains unsatisfactory as long as the division of labour is not philosophically argued. The method and its implicit model as such have universal pretensions. In the natural scientific approach itself there is, in principle, no inherent limitation to its application. It claims to be able to comprehend everything. Of course you can test the appropriateness of the method and judge it in the light of the results, but this too is a pragmatic and philosophically unsatisfactory solution. So we need what I have called "an investigation of foundations" in order to assess the adequacy of the method. This solution refers to philosophy and demonstrates the insufficiency of empiricism.

I do not propose to relativize or, for that matter, to knock scientific method. To make a progress in this problem of adequacy we have to take a step beyond methodology. The possibilities and limitation of the prevailing scientific method can only be judged in a 'critique' in the Kantian sense. Only if we transgress the boundaries of methodology can the adequacy of method be evaluated. In the case of human science we need a philosophical anthropology. In the last two parts of my exposition I will give the main lines of the 'make-up' of man. In this case we also have to ask how this model can produce relevant information about man *by simplification*, in Linschoten's words and in order to judge this simplification we need a philosophical outline of the nature of man. I will do this after an investigation of an alternative model, the 'text model' described in section IV.

IV

The art of reading texts, traditionally called 'hermeneutics', is older than science in the modern sense. It is as old as philosophy itself. Before evaluating the adequacy of the text-model in the human sciences, we shall first summarize some characteristics of texts and of their interpretation.

I will draw your attention here to two points:

1. The coherences 'analyzed' in the interpretation of texts are not the external, logically independent relations of science. These relations are not contingencies but relations of meaning. The relation of a meaning to another meaning is internal. It is not necessary nor possible to define these meanings or meaning-units as independent elements. In the interpretation of works of literature the concept of 'density' is sometimes used. Compactness of meaning is an artistic quality. It is achieved by the cumulative effect of different interacting semantic properties. The text is a texture, a knot of interwoven meanings that can be analyzed but not in an empirical-analytical way. Coming back to the six self-evident statements in the ordinary philosophy of science, in the first paragraph, we can affirm that the first — to analyze is to analyze in atomic elements — is indeed a prejudice. We are all familiar with another kind of analysis in the interpretation of texts.

2. My second point is that interpretation is no generalization and is not supported by generalizations. In interpreting we do not use nomic connections, universal quantifiers or principles of inference. We explain by referring to the context which is always unique. A text is a unique complex of meanings linked with other unique complexes of meaning (cf. Steiner 1974, p. 154 ff.). We justify an interpretation by referring to the context, we do not need general laws.

These two remarks have important consequences. A first implication is that unique phenomena too, are explainable. There *is* a science — *id est* a rigorous way of knowing — of individuals, contrary to the generally held opinion — the commonplace, rather — that this is impossible. This prejudice — the fifth in my enumeration — has a metaphysical background in philosophy in general and is strongly enforced by the domination of the natural scientific method in modern times. In the scientific world-model every phenomenon, in a self-evident way, is conceived of as an instance of a general law. The unique in this world-view is indeed a ghost in the machine.

If the unique were indeed unexplainable, or even ineffable or inexpressible, as long tradition has had it, the human condition would be a miserable one. Individual persons would be unable to express themselves and would not understand each other. Humankind would be struck with dumbness. If the individual were nothing more than a bearer of universals (as in Russell's ontology) and if concepts and words always had a universal meaning, than the individual would indeed be condemned to silence.

A further consequence is that not every determination is a causal determination. Without coherence a science is impossible. We cannot satisfy ourselves in the human sciences with description or simple enumeration. It is, in my opinion, a false concession to the prevailing method to hold that human science is not explanatory but only descriptive. This would affirm the third prejudice mentioned above. Every science presupposes understanding and every understanding presupposes coherences. An apparent description is sometimes revealing because it contains implicitly explanatory connections, for instance when we label a demonstration as a 'revolution' or a 'civil war'. These descriptions seem to answer to a what?-question but are in fact interpretations and offer an answer to a why?-question. Clifford Geertz speaks in this context of a "thick description", a method which according to him defines the whole enterprise of cultural analysis (see Popp-Baier's article in this volume). Thick descriptions contain interpretations of the actions of other people and of the web of significance human beings have spun.

The structural analysis of texts in semiotics exemplifies that coherences are not always of a causal nature. Hermeneutics is another example of a science which analyzes complexes of meaning. (I will not deal here with the problematic relation of these two sciences of meaning. Cf. for this problem Ricoeur 1984, p. 49 ff.).

The most important implication, however, is that interpretation is an autonomous, independent, 'scientific' activity with its own criteria and standards of evaluation. I call a science every form of rigorous knowing (German: *Wissenschaft*) having the capacity of criticism and refinement. There is no reason to discredit interpretation as a dubious explanation that has to be completed by causal or nomic explanations (Groot 1969). The process of interpretation does not need to be tested by external procedures but has a built-in ongoing process of confirmation and falsification.

V

Earlier in this article I discussed the two models used in the sciences of man. I made a plea for the necessity of investigating foundations in order to assess the adequacy of the models. One of these models is predominant in human science. It is a part of the accepted empirical-analytical view. I tried to undermine this monopoly in two ways. Firstly I indicated the inherent problems of the scientific world-view. Secondly I confronted it with an alternative model: the model of a text. In this paragraph I will dig a bit deeper by carrying out a piece of foundational research. I will try to find an answer to the problems of section III. In order to evaluate the adequacy of a model, I argued, we have to compare it with reality; we have to do ontology. In order to assess the relevance or pertinence of the machine-model and the text-model in the study of human behaviour we have to investigate the nature of human behaviour or the nature of human acts. We are in need of a philosophical anthropology that can function at the same time as a foundation for science.

I indicated in my remark on Kant's *Critique of pure reason* that a main problem in our understanding of reality is the predominating idea in modern times, based on the success of natural scientific method, that reality is a compound of 'facts' (logically independent elements) related by causal laws or nomic connections. This almost seems to be self-evident in our commonsense conception of reality. To happen is to cause and to be caused, to be an element of a chain of events. Nothing is happening at random, though we do not know the causes.

We can notice the influence of this prevailing conception of reality in the philosophy of action. The difference between an action and a physical movement is that the former is motivated by an intention. It is an expression of a meaning or a reason. But not every intention leads to an act. What is the difference between a mental intention and an act? The difference is that the act is a realized intention. But what does the realization add to the intention? What is reality? Reality is conceived of as effectivity. An act can bring about changes in reality. Intentions, words do not. So we are inclined to think that the thing added to intentions to make them actions is causality. Action is intention plus causality (just as communism is Soviet councils plus electricity, according to Lenin). It seems as if the dominating conception of reality excludes the possibility that reality is an incarnation or embodiment of meaning. It is, apparently, very difficult to think of reality as something to which rationality is *inherent,* i.e. as an action.

Take for instance the ascription theory in the philosophy of law (Hart 1949; Lenk 1978). In this theory an action in reality is a movement of the body but in society certain properties are *ascribed* to it. By doing so the movement is elevated to the juridical status of an action. So responsibility, in this theory, is a kind of floating property without any basis in reality. Action here is a product of interpretation or, rather of introjection. Ontologically there is no difference between an action and a physical movement. I consider this theory as an artificial construction to salvage prejudices about reality.

My second example is a famous problem in the philosophy of human science. There are philosophers who, opposing the natural scientific approach, defend an intentionalistic or teleological method in psychology and sociology. In this debate, a central argument of the opponents of this method of 'understanding' is that this explanation does not explain why something *must* happen. A rational explanation, they argue, only can indicate what could be rationally expected, but it cannot explain why something happens necessarily, i.e. is necessitated by causal circumstances. The nomic connection is lacking. So according to the proponents of causal explanation, the well-known schema of a rational explanation (as given for instance by William Dray) has to be rewritten if it is to reproduce genuine (i.e. nomological) explanation. A statement must be added to the scheme about a disposition of the actor, a disposition to act rationally. This would make the explanation a true account of what must happen and afford a basis for prediction (cf. Boer 1983, p. 75 f.). But what are we to understand by this 'disposition to act rationally'? According to my 'world-view' such an actor does not act rationally, but irrationally. Someone acting rationally will deliberate his course of action when he finds himself in a certain situation. He will ponder his line of conduct and weigh the arguments one against the other. If he has 'the disposition to act rationally' this rational way of acting would be superfluous.

In my view the answer to the objection, that in a rational explanation the necessity of the act is not demonstrated, has simply to be that this is not a disadvantage but an advantage. If actions are realized intentions, i.e. realities in which an intention is *inherent* than these realities are, indeed, never necessary. The opponents are right. But it would be contradictory to say that an action is necessary. An action is by definition an expression of freedom. To demonstrate its necessity would destroy it as an act.

I conclude that the argument would be valid only if the 'scientific' world-view (the Tractatus-world) were valid, i.e. if reality were by definition natural, causally determined reality. The possibility and validity of rational explanation is not at stake here but the concept of reality is. It is an ontological discussion taking place under the guise of a discussion on the logic of science. But ontological questions can only be decided by philosophy.

An adequate philosophy of human action can only be based on the only authority we have: experience. The experience of human action is the instance to judge the nature of human actions 'as they are'. In our own experience we do not find any phenomenon whatsoever to support the idea that the transition from an intention to an act is executed by adding to the former something like an effective force, for example a movement of muscles which is in turn caused by processes in the brain. If physical movements turn up, acts of the will are not realized but frustrated; I intend to raise my hand and at the same time it is lifted by an external force. The act of doing it is incompatible with being moved. But the only evidence we have, in experience, is that we *are* doing it. So it follows that reality, in spite of Kant, cannot be defined as being caused by laws of nature. We have to amend our concept of reality and our concept of methodology, not our concept of action. When I act after a well-reasoned decision the result is not a movement of my body added to an intention but the embodiment of a reasonable will. Causes may play a role in this process but it is a subordinate role.

We see the 'reality' of these actions everywhere in everyday life and social exchange. Fellow human beings induce me to something. I receive an order or a piece of advice. A conversation can change my life. All these influences or incitements are not causes added to meaning. Realities that actually have the capacity to change me, i.e. to convince me, are meaningful events, actuating meanings, influences to which reason is inherent. Counselling is not conditioning.

I want to stress here that it makes sense to ask what a desire means though a desire is not a sentence (see, for the opposite opinion of Searle, Popp-Baier's article in this volume). The desire does not speak but is expressible, e.g. in a dream report. We enunciate the meaning embodied in the desire. The meaning component distinguishes a motive from a cause. A motive 'works', though not by causality. Subconscious desires, too, have meaning, and we can speak of a 'semantics of desire' as Ricoeur does.

After this little bit of ontology (or philosophical anthropology) I come back to the question of adequacy. I do not contend that the nomological approach is entirely inadequate. To comprehend man, the information obtained by the machine-model can be very important and is sometimes indispensable.

The relevance of nomological psychology can be summed up in two points:

- This psychology is necessary to acquire knowledge about the conditions of our normal functioning, e.g. of our capacity for vision and speech.
- There is an intermediate zone in the human being where quasi-causes can be transformed into reasons and causal connection

> into rational coherences. The discovery of laws is a preparatory stage here. I elaborated on this problem elsewhere (cf. Boer 1983, pp. 142-168).

In both cases — explanation and quasi-explanation — explanation is imbedded in understanding. Explanation serves understanding but in two different manners.

Finally I want to make a comment on my statement, at the beginning of this section, that we have to compare models with reality. Do I suppose here an obsolete correspondence theory of truth? Do we have an immediate access to reality beyond language and discourse? I cannot give a complete theory of truth here but I will make some remarks. In science and in human science we cannot do without concepts like objectivity, correspondence, and the like. In every branch of knowledge we make a distinction between truth and illusion. The same is true of philosophy. In philosophical arguments we try to find an adequate kind of discourse for a given domain, e.g. the unconsciousness. What should we use here a language of forces or a language of meanings? What is the proper frame of reference for actions? A language of physical movements or a language of intentions? Trying to answer these questions we are led by our intuitions, our sensitivity to reality. Reality is not accessible outside language, but language is not a screen, nor is reality a fixed object behind it. In using language we can 'listen' to reality, permitting reality to 'speak'. These metaphors are permissible because language is a medium which reveals reality. We clarify our thoughts by trying to match these to our experience, a proces which Husserl called "fulfillment". Contrary to what is often believed by human scientists, this attitude towards reality requires distance, not participation; or, to put it more exactly, this detachment is, like in psychoanalysis, a kind of concentrated attention. It is part of the training of the analyst to acquire this attitude (cf. Boer 1994, p. 37 ff.).

VI

In section IV we discussed hermeneutics as the science of texts and we contended that it is an independent autonomous science. But a human being is not a text. What are the differences? What about the adequacy of the text-model? I think there are three important differences.

1. The first fundamental dissimilarity is that a text is a linguistic phenomenon, while human actions are embodied meaning. I elaborated on this point in the former section. The next two differences are consequences of this basic difference.

2. In the second place a text is a closed, completed entity; the human being is open to an unknown future. In a certain respect his past is also open because it can be reinterpreted in the light of later experience. The difference is the existence in *time*. In a book there is also a time order in the story (in the science of literature this is called the 'history'), but the order is fixed. Of course, our interpretation of former parts of a book can be influenced by the reading of later parts but the book itself cannot be changed. When finished it is a *momentum aere perennius*. The human being, however, is changeable, a circumstance that makes psychotherapy possible.

In existential philosophy the human being is called a 'task of being' or a 'longing for being' (*désir d'être*, Sartre). The meaning — which is fixed in a work of literature — is 'at stake' in the human being (Heidegger). I prefer the definition of man as a being that wants to express himself, he is a longing for articulated language (in the sense of *langage*, not *langue*).

For a human being it is possible to say: "I was not myself". We can deplore or renounce our own utterances as inadequate expressions of our 'true self'. This is not to be understood as a moral condemnation but as an existential judgement. The psychotherapist, too, is not a moralist. His intention is not to amend or to correct reality in the light of norms but to help the client to express his reality, to complete reality. In this sense the human being is perfectible. There are 'grades of being', to use an old neo-Platonic term. For a human being as a longing for being, it is obviously possible to exist in a deficient way.

3. A third difference, closely connected with the second is that *contingency* plays a role in human existence. In a piece of art the contingency is reduced as far as possible. According to the dictum of a Dutch novelist, in a novel no sparrow may fall from the roof without consequences. Another writer wrote: I am fond of life that approaches me as a book. There is a ring of nostalgia resounding in this statement. If life could be a book, it would have more coherence, more significance. In a good book every detail has a meaningful place in the whole of the book, but real life is full of loose connections. Even in a book that intends to depict the lack of sense, the expression itself of meaninglessness tries to remove meaninglessness. If you wanted to write an unreadable book, you would only have to write about life 'as it is'. So to consider human life as a text is a kind of idealizing it. In reality human life is full of incidents, accidents, disturbances and sometimes chaos.

These differences, however, do not imply that the metaphor of text is inadequate to understand the human being. It implies merely that the application has its limitations. It cannot be a coincidence that the metaphor of the text is so deep-rooted in daily life. Sometimes we can 'read' a face as if it were an 'open book'. Some people have 'dark pages' in their life history or 'blanks'. We can 'turn over a page' in our life or begin with a 'clean sheet'. The model of a text can be legitimized because human acts embody meaning, as we argued before in section V.

This is the reason why we can understand a person by a reconstruction of his motives, by 'rational explanation' (I refer tot the development of this notion by Dray, Winch and Von Wright; cf. Boer 1983, p. 130 ff.). The 'factors' explaining his behaviour do not have the status of causal determinants but of circumstances, or of contextual incitements. We do not need nomic connections to understand him.

Man's existence in time, in a certain sense an imperfect presence of meaning, does not detract from the applicability of the text-model. The relations between his past and his future are relations of meaning. The coherence of his life is an object of interpretation, of an interpretation that is open-ended, like every psychotherapy. Because of the fact that human reality is an embodiment of meaning, a therapy as 'talking cure' makes sense. In this respect the fact of 'grades of being' mentioned before is of decisive importance. They are grades in the realization of meaning in human life. The longing for expression is a longing for adequate expressions, for a *parole pleine* (Lacan). In the striving for an 'authentic existence' we recognize a pursuit for the unity of life; a unity that is not given but that we strive for.

In all these respects the model of a text seems to be very fruitful. The human being can be interpreted. We find here the famous hermeneutical circle but in a living form. In understanding man, vague preconceptions can be made more articulate and distinct; former interpretations can be re-interpreted. The difference from the interpretation of texts is that the activity of interpretation has an impact on the interpreted entity itself. This is the condition of possibility of psychological consultation and of every significant dialogue.

The third difference, too, does not make the application of the text-model impossible. Indeed, in contrast with a text, human life is full of non-sense. It is a 'text' with mutilations and gaps, i.e. unconscious, hidden intentions. This means that in a hermeneutic psychology there is room for psychological interpretation of the kind we find in psychotherapy and especially in psychoanalysis. Psychoanalytical interpretation, inappropriate in the case of a text, is appropriate — sometimes — in the case of the author of a text — and ... of the reader.

But reader and author, I would say, are not in the same position. In the latter instance we have to keep in mind our paradigm: the interpretation of texts. We have to respect the autonomy of the text. The biography of the author is relevant only when it produces hypotheses for a better, more complete understanding of the text. Unless he is a patient, but we never know that. It is conceivable that readers are sometimes patients, the *raison d'être* of psychotherapy.

NOTES

1. A first version of this text was published in *The Husserlian foundations of phenomenological psychology* (pp. 57-70). Pittsburgh: Duquesne University, 1993. (Tenth Annual Symposium of the Simon Silverman Phenomenology Center).

REFERENCES

Boer, Th. de (1983). *Foundations of a critical psychology* (transl. Th. Plantinga). Pittsburgh: Duquesne University Press. (orig. publ. 1980)

Boer, Th. de (1994). Philosophical foundations of a hermeneutical psychology: a defence of objectivity. In: S. Miedema et al. (eds.). *The politics of human science* (pp. 37-50). Brussels: VUBPress.

Groot, A.D. de (1969). *Methodology: foundations of inferences and research in the behavioral sciences* (transl. J.A.A. Spiekerman). The Hague: Mouton. (orig. publ. 1961)

Hart, H.L.A. (1949). The ascription of responsibility and rights. *Proceedings of the Aristotelian Society*, *49*, 171-194.

Lenk, H. (1978). Handlung als Interpretationskonstrukt. In: *Handlungstheorien interdisciplinär. Vol. 2, part 1* (pp. 279-551). München: Fink.

Ricoeur, P. (1965). *De l'interprétation: essai sur Freud*. Paris: Seuil.

Ricoeur, P. (1984). *Temps et récit. Vol. 2: La configuration dans le récit de fiction*. Paris: Seuil.

Steiner, G. (1974). Whorf, Chomsky and the student of literature. In: *On Difficulty and other essays*. Oxford: Oxford University Press, 1978.

Terwee, S.J.S. (1990). *Hermeneutics in psychology and psychoanalysis*. New York: Springer.

Verwey, G. (1985). *Psychiatry in an anthropological and biomedical context: philosophical presuppositions and implications of German psychiatry 1820-1870* (transl. L. Richards). Dordrecht: Reidel. (orig. publ. 1980)

Weber, M. (1968). *Methodologische Schriften: Studienausgabe*. Frankfurt am Main: Fischer.

Wright, G.H. von (1971). *Explanation and understanding*. London: Routledge & Kegan Paul.

Wright, G.H. von (1974). *Causality and determinism*. New York: Columbia University Press.

The Real is the Relational
Relational Psychoanalysis as a Model of Human Understanding

J.W. Jones
Rutgers University (New Brunswick, NJ, U.S.A)

In the *Nichomachean ethics*, Aristotle takes the man of practical reason as his model for philosophy, a suggestion which recurs in the contemporary focus on praxis (Schrag 1980). For the logical positivists of the early twentieth century, the Baconian scientist was the perfect philosopher: philosophy consisted in following a strict rule-governed methodology. In *Human understanding*, Stephen Toulmin suggests the lawyer as the correct model for the philosopher-scientist. Harkening back to Aristotle's man of practical wisdom, for Toulmin science and philosophy require deliberation and judgment. John Dewey and the pragmatists suggest the man of action as the model philosopher. Science and philosophy prove their truth in action. The purpose of this paper is to argue that the practicing psychoanalyst is perhaps the best model of philosophical and scientific endeavor. In doing so we will stand a current controversy on its head. Psychoanalysis has been plagued since its beginning with controversy about its scientific status, a controversy recently up-dated by the polemics of Adolph Grünbaum (1984). Whereas such polemicists argue that psychoanalysis must conform to the canons of Baconian science in order to be legitimate, I will argue that philosophy and science, in reality, conform to the interpretive methods of psychoanalysis.

Interpretation in Relational Psychoanalysis

Freud, as we all know, made interpretation the defining act of psychoanalysis. Interpretation enlarges the rational ego's power over the irrational id and so enables the ego to win the "civil war" going on inside the patient. "Where id is, let ego be" was Freud's central maxim. Interpretation expands the hegemony of reason over previously uncolonized regions of the mind, or, as Freud says gives the ego of the patient "once more mastery over the lost provinces of his mental life" (Freud 1949).

For Freud, psychopathology arises from wholly intrapsychic factors: the conflict between instinctual drives and the demands of social and moral reality represented intrapsychically as the superego. In his significant revision of Freudian theory Heinz Kohut makes painful interpersonal relations rather than conflicted intrapsychic structures the root of later problems. Kohut asserts that "All forms of psychopathology .... are due to disturbances of selfobject relationships in childhood" (1984, p. 53). Since psychopathology results from the empathic failures of childhood which block the development of selfhood, if experiences of empathy are provided later on, the process of self development can resume. The image that guides Kohut's theory of treatment is of "thwarted and remobilized self development" (1984, p. 142). Therapy, then, provides a developmental second chance.

This leads to a radical transformation of the nature of interpretation. In answer to the question contained in the title of his book *How does analysis cure?* Kohut suggests that the analyst provides the patient with the selfobject experiences needed to grow new psychic structures. Interpretation then is curative not because it expands the domain of reason but rather because it conveys to the patient an experience of being understood. Not insightful interpretations but empathic ones hold the key to cure. Psychoanalytic healing takes place through "the opening of a path of empathy between self and selfobject, specifically the establishment of empathic in-tuneness between self and selfobject" (1984, p. 66).

The Newtonian wish for knowledge of a world totally distinct from all observers became the cornerstone of traditional analysis - the 'reality principle' - a metaphysical claim transformed into a diagnostic rule. Such a principle was crucial to the classical understanding of the interpretation of the transference, for the patient had to be persuaded by the analyst that he or she was distorting the 'reality' of the analyst by his or her projections of childhood material. Of course, any comments at all about the analyst were, of necessity, projections and distortions since the 'reality' of the analyst was presumably that of a blank screen. Merton Gill is clear that no such separation of analyst and analysand is possible.

> No matter how far the analyst attempts to carry this limitation of his behavior, the very existence of the analytic situation provides the patient with innumerable cues which inevitably become his rationale for his transference responses...[Thus there is an] inevitable intertwining of the transference with the current situation....If the analyst remains under the illusion that the current cues he provides to the patient can be reduced to the vanishing point, he may be led into a silent withdrawal .... The patient's responses under such conditions can be mistaken for unconscious transference when they are in fact transference adaptations to the actuality of the silence (1979, p. 271).

For Gill transference is always interaction. It is a myth that the analyst's behavior contributes nothing to the patient's response.

Thus, according to Gill, transference interpretations should be primarily focused on the interaction of patient and therapist, not the projections of genetic material onto a supposedly blank screen. Analysis becomes examining the actual patterns of interaction between patient and analyst in the "here and now" (1979, p. 273).

Gill has broken the spell of the myth of the objective observer under which classical psychoanalysis (see for example, Greenson 1967, p. 39; see also Brenner 1955; and Fenichel 1941) has labored. Especially in the interpersonal sphere (although quantum mechanics suggests this is also true of the physical world) there is no knowledge of reality apart from our relationship to it and our relationship impacts on the reality we are observing. Shorn of the myth of objectivity, analyzing the transference shifts from uncovering reality to interpreting it. Interpretation, then, becomes a collaborative effort in which "analyst and patient engage in a dialogue in the spirit of attempting to arrive at a consensus about reality" (1979, p. 274).

Interpretation, then, is an ongoing cybernetic process in which Gill recognizes that "transference interpretations ... have an effect on the transference" (1979, p. 277). This line of thinking moves Gill away from the Newtonian model of an inert analyst observing a self-contained, intrapsychic interplay of forces called the patient, towards conceiving of analyst and patient as a parts of a single reciprocal system of interpretation called the transference.

This moves Gill towards the camp of those who seek to redefine psychoanalysis as a hermeneutical discipline in which a coherent account of a patient's experience replaces correspondence to objective reality as the guiding interpretive principle (cf. Spence 1982; Messer et al. 1988).

Interpretation in Natural Science

Richard Bernstein (1983), in a book whose title *Beyond objectivism and relativism* captures the problem, summarizes the findings of contemporary philosophy of science (a similar discussion can be found in Jones 1981). After describing the work of Feyerabend, Rorty, and especially Kuhn, he argues that modern philosophy of science "emphasizes the role of ... interpretation" in scientific understanding (1983, p. 157). Instead of the empiricist model of reason as a set of universal rules, scientific rationality (and by extension reason in general) requires "imagination, interpretation, the weighing of alternatives, and application of criteria that are essentially open" (1983, p. 56).

In a similar vein Harold Brown reviews what he calls the "new philosophy of science" which represents a shift from a rule-governed empiricism to a view of science constituted by "perception, theory and commitment" (Brown 1977). Science uses rule-governed and impersonal procedures but these are embedded in, and their use governed by, larger, paradigmatic contexts which are created not by an infallible methodology but through "judgments on the part of scientists and debate within the scientific community" (1977, p. 167, slightly altered). Changes in scientific theory then involve "a restructuring of experience akin to a gestalt shift" (1977, p. 167). Such a restructuring in our understanding of science is, Brown suggests, itself a paradigm shift in the philosophy of science.

Nelson Goodman (1984) in *Of mind and other matters* insists that all cognitive activities, especially "knowing, acting, and understanding in the arts, sciences, and life in general involves the use - the interpretation, application, invention, revision - of symbol systems" (1984, p. 152). Art and science share a "common cognitive function," and can both be "embraced within epistemology conceived as the philosophy of understanding ... Since science and art consist very largely in the processing of symbols" (1984, p. 146).

Another argument for the essentially interpretive nature of all human knowledge can be found in a book authored jointly by a cognitive psychologist and a philosopher of science. Michael Arbib and Mary Hesse in their 1986 book *The construction of reality* insist that "all language is metaphorical" (1986, p. 150) and apply this maxim to psychology, religion, and the philosophy of science. A careful analysis of scientific work leads them to reject the empiricist's "view of language as an ideal static system with fixed meanings which are dependent upon ... rules" (1986, p. 148). Rather, language systems in the sciences and humanities are a "complex web of semantic interactions in which there is no rigid distinction between the literal and the metaphorical" (1986, p. 146). Changes in scientific theory or moving from the sciences to the humanities involve primarily a change in categories. New theories in science or scientific and artistic models achieve a "metaphoric redescription" of experience (1986, p. 156).

Inevitably a view of knowledge as mediated (rather than passively imprinted on our brains) leads them to a constructivist and interactional model of human knowing, in which knowledge comes only "through our dialogue with the world" (1986, p. 181). "There is", they write, "an essential interaction between the knowing subject and the world, both in terms of the linguistic categories brought to the world in describing it, and in the activity of the subject in physical relations with the world"

(p. 159). Natural science is no different in this regard than the humanities or theology for "scientific theory provides constructed models of scientific reality" (1986, p. 159).

> Scientific models are a prototype ... for imaginative creations or schemas ... Symbolic worlds all share with scientific models the function of describing and redescribing the world; and for all of them it is inappropriate to ask for literal truth as direct correspondence with the world ... We do not suddenly put on a different hat with regard to 'truth' when we speak of the good or God from that we wear for natural science (1986, p. 161).

In another jointly authored book, a physicist and a philosopher of religion arrive at a similar conclusion. Using a multitude of examples from both theology and science Mary Gerhart and Allan Russell (1984) show how both fields gain their understandings through the construction of metaphors.

In their 1980 book, *Metaphors we live by*, Lakoff and Johnson provide one of the most powerful arguments for the inevitability of interpretation in natural science and all forms of human understanding. All sciences are linguistic systems. This linguistic inevitability means we have no unmediated access to reality. All data is, in the words of a virtual cliché in contemporary philosophy of science, "theory laden." The characteristics we attribute to objects in our world "exist and can only be experienced relative to a conceptual system" (1980, p. 154).

Lakoff and Johnson call these basic conceptual networks "metaphors". Metaphor "pervades our conceptual system and is a primary mechanism for understanding" (1980, p. 196). Our reality - that is the world of our lived experience - is shaped by the metaphors through which experience is mediated, and so it is no exaggeration to say that metaphors "create realities" (1980, p. 156). This is because

> we define our reality in terms of metaphors and then proceed to act on the basis of the metaphors. We draw inferences, set goals, make commitments and execute plans, all on the basis of how we in part structure our experience, consciously or not, by means of metaphor (1980, p. 158).

Metaphors stand conceptually between objectivity and subjectivity, involving discursive reason and creative expression. Our most rule governed activities like the scientific method depend upon metaphors which "unite reason and imagination" (1980, p. 193) for all "human conceptual systems are metaphorical in nature and involve an imaginative understanding" (1980, p. 194).

They call their approach "experientialism." Knowledge arises neither from the external world impressing itself on our passive minds or from the projection of our subjective ideas onto a blank screen, instead "we understand the world through our interactions with it" (1980, p. 194). Thus we might call theirs an interactionalist hermeneutic since "understanding emerges from interaction, from constant negotiation with the environment and other people" (1980, p. 230).

These authors all concur that science, the model of human understanding for modern culture, involves interpretations which arise out of our 'dialogue' with the world of our experience.

RELATIONAL HERMENEUTICS

Dilthey (1900) described the hermeneutical process as a relationship - an interaction between reader and text. When understanding a text, an interpreter, of necessity, reads the text in the con-text of her own lived experiences. A living understanding means connecting the text to one's own life experience. Otherwise the text remains dead. But understanding also means standing-under (*verstehen*) the giveness of the text. Thus a true reciprocity is established between the conscious reader and the integrity of the text.

My contention is that a similar dialectic takes place between analyst and patient. On one hand the analyst, at least in the Kohutian school of self-psychology, seeks to enter empathically into the experience of the patient, to see the world through his eyes, to grasp the truth of his life story. And the patient seeks to internalize the experience of the analyst, her interpretations, her understanding, the empathic give and take of their relationship. On the other hand, at least in the relational school of psychoanalysis, the therapist acknowledges the impact of the patient upon her. His struggles may re-evoke her struggles; his passive-aggressive behavior may frustrate her; and she will share his joy in changes made and new directions taken. Rather than being pathologized as countertransference distortions, such reactions on the therapist's part are important clues to the interactional patterns and the affect that accompanies them in which the patient may be trapped.

If the therapeutic alliance is to be therapeutic, it must be genuine and mutual within the constraints of a professional relationship. It must contain authentic mutuality which acknowledges the reciprocal impact of therapist on patient and patient on therapist and their common struggle towards new understandings of each other and themselves.

This reciprocal desire for self understanding and the understanding of another drives therapy and, I am suggesting, all interpretative activity. The hermeneutic passions are the desires to know another and to be known by them. In Kohutian terms, empathy means both understanding others on their own terms and bringing them within the orbit of one's own experience. This, I gather, is the meaning of Kohut's maxim that empathy is "vicarious introspection". In an empathic encounter the other's integrity is preserved as the truth of their experiences is respected on its own terms *and* the other's experiences are brought into conjunction with one's own experiences.

While clearest in terms of the relationship of two people, especially patients and therapists, such an empathic dialectic also operates in relation to a text. Dilthey spoke of empathically entering into a text. In a living interpretation of a text, the reader both appreciates the text on its own terms and relates the text to her own experiences.

Envisioning interpretation as a relational activity gets us past the dichotomy of objectivity and subjectivity which has so bedevilled modern attempts at understanding understanding in both the natural and human sciences. As Lakoff and Johnson argue, an interactionalist or relational epistemology preserves both the giveness of the Other (the essence of objectivism) and the inevitability of interaction shaping our knowledge (the essence of subjectivism). While there are many historical examples of psychoanalytic understanding consisting of analysts imposing the hegemony of their categories on the other (one thinks of Freud and Dora), there are also many examples of analysts listening to the other empathically (one thinks of the work of Stolorow, Brandchaft, and Atwood) or mutually interacting with the other (Gill). In the empathic interrogation that characterizes relational psychoanalysis and, I would argue, all human understanding, the integrity of the other is not lost by confining the other to prefabricated categories nor is the role of the knower denied in the name of a false objectivity (Mitchell 1993, 1988).

RELATIONAL HERMENEUTICS AND THE MEANING OF INTERPRETATION

I have suggested that a relational process of interpretation unites psychoanalysis and natural science as common hermeneutical disciplines, or as Nelson Goodman says, both are "embraced within epistemology conceived as the philosophy of understanding." Such a claim stands in the tradition of hermeneutical philosophy by making the category of interpretation central. But it also goes against the grain of those hermeneutical philosophies (for example Dilthey; see also Spence, Bernstein, and Messer et al.) which have traditionally been designed precisely to radically distinguish the natural sciences, centered on causality, and the human sciences, centered on the interpretation of meaning. The proponents of this position must surely feel that I have here stretched the term 'interpretation' far beyond any substantive meaning.

This difference may reflect two different approaches to the philosophy of science and, secondarily, to the relations between science and religion. The philosophers of science and writers on the relations between science and religion cited above, as well as Barbour, Rolston, and myself, tend to focus on the *process* of scientific understanding. Hermeneutical philosophers who follow Dilthey tend to focus on the *contents* of scientific theories and science's reliance on the language of causality rather than of intentionality or meaning. The first position tends to stress the continuities between the sciences and the humanities and religion, the second compartmentalizes them as different forms of knowing.

In contemporary discussions (e.g., Spence) of psychoanalysis as a hermeneutic enterprise, interpretation tends to denote making something meaningful by fitting it into a larger, often narrative, framework. So, for example, psychoanalytic interpretations are said to cure by enabling the patient, at the end of analysis, to tell a reasonably coherent narrative of his or her life. Interpretation makes dreams, feelings, and behaviors meaningful by fitting them into a coherent account. The same thing can be, and often is, said of scientific theory - that it provides a coherent account of certain phenomena by fitting the phenomena into a larger, theoretical schema.

This analysis does *not* entail that there are no differences between empirical methodologies and the interpretation of texts or the work of psychoanalysts or theologians. Rather it allows us to form a more nuanced account of exactly where the similarities and differences among disciplines in fact are to be found (for an extended discussion of the differences as well as the similarities between science and religion, see, for example, Jones 1981, 1984; Barbour 1990; and Rolston 1987). A more nuanced account would neither privilege science or dichotomize science and all other ways of knowing (as modernity has done) nor compartmentalize all fields as totally separate and disconnected. Nor does this analysis deny that empirical science relies on the language of causality and a full account of human experience requires not only the language of causality but also the languages of intentionality and self-reflexiveness. But both kinds of accounts ('causes' and 'meanings') arise from a constructive interaction between knower and known.

Feminist Hermeneutics

The centrality of relationality for the process of understanding forms the core of certain schools of feminist philosophy which begin from the writings of Chodorow and Gilligan, Baker Miller, and others. According to this model the effects of being parented primarily by a woman fall differently on men and women. In order to establish their own identities and identifications, men must separate from the mother, often through the mobilization of aggression. This act of breaking connections becomes, on this view, the core around which all other masculine activities are constructed. Thus "the basic masculine sense of self is separate" and so "masculinity develops a more reactive and defensive quality than femininity" (Chodorow 1989, p. 184). Aggression against woman becomes the foundation of masculine identity.

Women, on the other hand, develop their identities by remaining in connection to their primary object. They are more oriented towards "care" (Gilligan) and "relationship" (Chodorow). Such a view "stands the traditional Freudian understanding on its head" and "revalorizes the woman's construction of self and makes normal masculinity extremely problematic" for women become, on this view, "repositories of "affiliativeness, relatedness, empathy, and nurturance" (Chodorow 1989, p. 185). Fox Keller applies this analysis to natural science and argues that when this masculine drive for separation and distance becomes sublimated into the drive for knowledge the result is the Cartesian dichotomies of objectivity and subjectivity, thought and feeling, mind and body. Keller is quick to note that these Cartesian dichotomies parallel the dichotomy of masculinity and femininity whereby the real and the rational are gendered masculine and the subjective and emotional gendered feminine. When institutionalized as critical philosophy and natural science, such an "a-relational masculinity" is transformed into an uncaring homage to technical reason and the subjection of nature.

Toril Moi criticizes this approach as an example of "feminist essentialism" (1989, p. 191) which idealizes the mother-child bond and reduces the feminine to the maternal, fails to find a role for the father and the law thereof in human development, and cannot account for those male philosophers who critique Cartesian rationalism and argue for the centrality of relatedness. Except for Melanie Klein, the object relations theorists for whom relationality is central and whom Chodorow et. al. extoll were all men (e.g., Fairbairn, Guntrip, and Winnicott). Such a valorization of the feminine as intrinsically relational cannot account for antagonisms between women or cooperation between men (and men and women) except as socially, not psychodynamically, derived.

Moi also hears in this theorizing a tendency to transcend dichotomies and so collapse all differences and distinctions, a move she rightly regards as extremely problematic. This brings us back to our main point. Such absorptive union is one model of relatedness (one might think of Hegel or some schools of romanticism) but, I would argue, that is not the model which predominates in object relations theory and contemporary psychoanalysis. Fairbairn, Guntrip, and Winnicott certainly did not theorize a kind of relationality in which identities dissolve. To the extent that contemporary relational psychoanalysis draws upon these British Middle School theorists as well as the infancy research of Stern and others which speaks of the "interpersonal world of the infant," identity is not "sublated" (as Hegel envisioned) but rather redefined as a relational construct (Jones 1991a, 1991b).

In relational psychoanalysis the drive to know is neither the drive to dominate nor to absorb but rather to relate to. Ideally, differences are not dichotomized or dissolved but understood and respected. In the psychoanalytic dialogue, understood relationally, there is difference without domination. In, for example, Gill's discussion of transference there is neither object or subject but two participants in a common interaction. In such psychoanalytic knowing, dialogue replaces domination.

This model envisions relational connections neither as undifferentiated unities nor as loose collections of unaffiliated atoms. Rather than equating unity and uniformity, such a model uncovers reciprocal interactions which preserve both interconnection and individuation (Jones 1991b). Such a model may be fruitful across a variety of domains. For example, the relationship between disciplines such as psychoanalysis and theology may be theorized as one in which connections between the disciplines remain evident in a way that separate fields are not collapsed into or reduced to each other (for a further discussion of the application of this model to the relationship between disciplines see Jones in press).

Having rejected object relations theory, Moi arrives at similar epistemic conclusions by a different route. She also notes two other characteristics of psychoanalytic knowing which are relevant for our purposes. In psychoanalysis the non-rational, represented by feelings, dreams, and intuitions, is not denounced or denied but is rather listened to. Thus psychoanalysis, in spite of Freud's commitment to Newtonian rationalism, deconstructs the dichotomy of thought and feeling. And, psychoanalytic dialogue reaches no permanent closure. An analysis ends but the process of analysis goes on. Dreams are continually reconsidered, early events are revisited time and time again from different perspectives. In contrast to the linear view of understanding they often bring to therapy, I often tell patients that therapy is a little like getting a problem surrounded, that is looked at from a variety of different perspectives. In a similar vein, Moi writes:

> There is, then, in the psychoanalytic situation a model of knowledge which at once radically questions and displaces traditional notions of subject-object relationships and deconstructs the firm boundaries between knowledge and non-knowledge. As this situation of knowledge offers no firmly established binary opposites, it cannot be gendered either masculine or feminine, thereby offering us a chance to escape the patriarchal tyranny of thought by sexual analogy. As feminists in search of new ways to think about objectivity, knowledge, and modes of intellectual activity, we can ill afford to neglect the model offered by psychoanalysis (1989, p. 198).

RELATIONAL HERMENEUTICS AND THE PSYCHOLOGY OF RELIGION

We have argued that the open-ended, interactive, relational interpretations of psychoanalysts are a cogent model for human understanding in the arts and sciences. What are the implications of this for the psychology of religion? At the end here, I would briefly mention two. One involving the relations between psychoanalysis (and science in general) and religion; the other involving the psychoanalytic approach to religious material.

First, the relations between psychoanalysis and religion. Freud denoted religion as feminine (Van Herik). Under the dichotomous epistemology of modernity, this linked religion to the emotional, the subjective, the infantile, the irrational, to what was not knowledge. And that is how religion has been treated during most of the history of psychoanalysis. We have argued that, ironically, psychoanalysis undercuts the very dichotomous empiricism in whose terms Freud originally cast it. Such an epistemological transformation ramifies beyond psychoanalysis into philosophy and even our understanding of natural science. In an epistemic framework that refuses to dichotomize thought and feeling, reason and intuition, and insists on remaining open to both, the conflict between religion and science loses much of its force.

Second, regarding the treatment of religious material. I and many others (Jones 1991a, 1991b; Sorenson 1990, 1994a, 1994b; Meissner 1984) have argued this point extensively elsewhere and so it need not be repeated again here. Simply put, a heuristic process built around interaction, dialogue, open interpretation, and the importance of affect and intuition, is potentially able to approach religious material openly and empathically as well as critically and analytically. Rather than necessarily pathologizing the forms in which religious experience is embodied (ritual, meditation, ecstatic states, moral reflection), such a hermeneutic impels psychoanalysis into dialogue with the kinds of knowing found in humanity's religious and spiritual traditions.

REFERENCES

Arbib, M. & M. Hesse (1986). *The construction of reality*. Cambridge: Cambridge University Press.

Barbour, I. (1990). *Religion in an age of science*. San Francisco: Harper & Row.

Bernstein, R. (1983). *Beyond objectivism and relativism*. Philadelphia: University of Pennsylvania Press.

Brennan, T. (1992). *The interpretation of the flesh: Freud and femininity*. New York: Routledge.

Brennan, T. (1989). *Between feminism and psychoanalysis*. New York: Routledge.

Brenner, C. (1955). *An elementary textbook of psychoanalysis*. Garden City, NY: Doubleday.

Brown, H. (1977). *Perception, theory, and commitment*. Chicago: University of Chicago Press.

Chodorow, N. (1989). *Feminism and psychoanalytic theory*. New Haven: Yale University Press.

Dilthey, W. (1900). *Dilthey: selected writings* (transl. H. Rickman). Cambridge: Cambridge University Press, 1976.

Fenichel, O. (1941). *Problems of psychoanalytic technique*. Albany: Psychoanalytic Quarterly Press.

Flax, J. (1993). *Disputed subjects: essays on psychoanalysis, politics and philosophy*. New York: Routledge.

Flax, J. (1990). *Thinking fragments: psychoanalysis, feminism, and postmodernism in the contemporary West*. Berkeley: University of California Press.

Freud, S. (1949). *An outline of psychoanalysis*. New York: Norton.

Gerhart, M. & A. Russell (1984). *Metaphoric process*. Fort Worth: Texas Christian University Press.

Gill, M. (1982). *Analysis of transference, vol. 1*. Madison, Conn: Internatonal Universities Press.

Gill, M. (1979). The analysis of the transference. *Journal of the American Psychoanalytic Association*, *27*, 263-288.

Gilligan, C. (1982). *In a different voice*. Cambridge: Harvard University Press.

Goldenberg, N. (1979). *Changing of the gods: feminism and the end of traditional religions*. Boston: Beacon Press.

Goldenberg, N. (1990). *Returning words to flesh*. Boston: Beacon Press.

Goodman, N. (1984). *Of mind and other matters*. Cambridge: Harvard University Press.

Greenson R.R., (1967). *The technique and practice of psychoanalysis, vol. 1*. New York: International Universities Press.

Grünbaum, A. (1984). *The foundations of psychoanalysis: a philosophical critique*. Berkeley: University of California Press.

Hare-Mustin, R. & J. Marecek (1990). *Making a difference: psychology and the construction of gender*. New Haven: Yale University Press.

Herik, J. van (1982). *Freud on femininity and faith*. Berkeley: University of California Press.

Jones, J. (1981). *The texture of knowledge: an essay on religion and science*. Lanham: University Press of America.

Jones, J. (1982). The delicate dialectic: religion and psychology in the modern world. *Cross Currents*, *32*, 143- 153.

Jones, J. (1984). *The redemption of matter: towards the rapprochement of science and religion*. Lanham: University Press of America.

Jones, J. (1986). Macrocosm to microcosm: towards a systemic theory of personality. *Journal of Religion and Health*, *25*, 278-290.

Jones, J. (1989). Personality and epistemology. *Zygon*, *24*, 23-38.

Jones, J. (1991a). *Contemporary psychoanalysis and religion: transference and transcendence*. New Haven: Yale University Press.

Jones, J. (1991b). The relational self: contemporary psychoanalysis reconsiders religion. *Journal of the American Academy of Religion*, *59* (4), 501-517.

Jones, J. (1992). Knowledge in transition: towards a Winnicottian epistemology. *Psychoanalytic Review*, *79* (2), 223-237.

Jones, J. (in press). *Toward a relational psychoanalysis of religion*.

Jones, J. & N. Goldenberg (1992). Transforming psychoanalysis: feminism and religion. Monograph published by *The Journal of Pastoral Psychology*, *40* (6).

Keller, E.F. (1983). *A feeling for the organism: the life and work of Barbara McClintock*. New York: Freeman.

Keller, E.F. (1985). *Reflections on gender and science*. New Haven: Yale University Press.

Keller, E.F. (1992). *Secrets of life, secrets of death: essays on language, gender, and science*. New York: Routledge.

Keller, E.F. & J. Flax (1988). Missing relations in psychoanalysis: a feminist critique. In: S. Messer, L. Sass & R. Woolfolk. *Hermeneutics and psychological theory*. New Brunswick: Rutgers University Press.

Kohut, H. (1971). *The analysis of the self*. New York: International Universities Press.

Kohut, H. (1977). *The restoration of the self*. New York: International Universities Press.

Kohut, H. (1984). *How does analysis cure?* Chicago: University of Chicago press.

Kuhn, T. (1972). *The structure of scientific revolutions*. Chicago: University of Chicago Press.

Lakoff, G & M. Johnson (1980). *Metaphors we live by*. Chicago: University of Chicago Press.

Meissner, W.W. (1984). *Psychoanalysis and religious experience*. New Haven: Yale University Press.

Messer, S., L. Sass & R. Woolfolk (1988). *Hermeneutics and psychological theory*. New Brunswick: Rutgers University Press.

Miller, J.B. (1976). *Toward a new psychology of women*. Boston: Beacon Press.

Mitchell, S. (1988). *Relational concepts in psychoanalysis*. Cambridge: Harvard University Press.

Mitchell, S. (1993). *Hope and dread in psychoanalysis*. New York: Basic Books.

Moi, T. (1989). Patriarchal thought and the drive for knowledge. In: T. Brennan. *Between feminism and psychoanalysis* (pp. 189-205). New York: Routledge.

Rolston, H. (1987). *Science and religion: a critical survey*. New York: Random House.

Schrag, C. (1980). *Radical reflection and the origin of the human sciences*. West Lafayette: Purdue University Press.

Sorenson, R. (1990). Psychoanalytic perspectives on religion: the illusion has a future. *Journal of Psychology and Theology*, *18*, 209-217.

Sorenson, R. (1994a). Ongoing change in psychoanalytic theory: implications for analysis of religious experience. *Psychoanalytic Dialogues*, *4*, 631-660.

Sorenson, R. (1994b). Reply to Spezzano. *Psychoanalytic Dialogues*, *4*, 667-672.

Spence, D. (1982). *Narrative and historical truth*. New York: Norton.

Spence, D. (1987). *The Freudian metaphor: toward paradigm change in psychoanalysis*. New York: Norton.

Stern, D.N. (1985). *The interpersonal world of the infant*. New York: Basic Books.

Stolorow, R., B. Brandchaft & G. Atwood (1987). *Psychoanalytic treatment: an intersubjective approach*. New York: Analytic Press.

Toulmin, S. (1960). *The philosophy of science*. New York: Harper & Row.

A Theory of Gender as a Central Hermeneutic in the Psychoanalysis of Religion

N.R. Goldenberg
University of Ottawa (Ontario, Canada)

Matters of Preface and Definition

Even though I have been using it as a principle of interpretation for my work in the psychology of religion for over two decades, I feel that I have only recently begun to comprehend the extent that gender influences religious traditions. The fact that gender is the primary focus, or, perhaps, one might say, the obsession of my analysis of religion reflects a conviction I share with the anthropologist Howard Eilberg-Schwartz who writes that "... gender is not just another subject that intersects with religion, but is central to the work that religion accomplishes ...." (1994, p. 5). Gender is an obsession of my work in the psychology of religion because I believe gender to be an obsession, perhaps a *raison d'être*, of religion itself.

As a preface to the argument I will advance here, I will discuss my understanding of three terms — gender, religion and psychoanalysis — in order to present the shape and limits of the conceptual tools I will be using. Then, I will describe the attitude that characterizes my approach to both religion and the psychological analysis of it.

I use the word 'gender' to refer to the social practice of dividing human beings into two categories — male and female — to which everyone is obliged to relate. Deeply impressed by the work of the philosopher Judith Butler (1990, 1993), I think of gender as a complex system of relationships in which we are always immersed. Like language in which the meaning of the words we use intelligibly is determined by history, tradition and multi-faceted social contexts, we experience gender as fixed yet somewhat malleable.

The norms of gender reside in established cultural contexts that can and do change over time. Forever negotiating our maleness and femaleness amidst shifting contexts, we are compelled to act in plays whose scripts are continually being rewritten. Occasionally, we can *ad lib*. Often, we believe in gender the way many of us believe in religion — that is, we believe that the parts we are playing come to us naturally, inevitably. At other times, we are aware of the social conventions that oblige us to dress and perform as actors and actresses in a daily, ongoing drama. In this paper, I hope to convince you that the sets of discourses and social practices that we recognize as religions, have been and continue to be primary constructors of our ideas about gender. Although I will concentrate on Jewish and Christian ideology and practice, I suspect that my argument has relevance beyond these two traditions.

I suppose that in regard to religion, the label 'secular Jew' would apply to me quite well. It might also be fair to say that in regard to psychoanalysis, 'devout Freudian' might have some value as a descriptive phrase. A friend who had been a member of a psychoanalytic study group in which I took part for over ten years once answered a query about her religion by answering "Freudian". Like her, I admit to this affiliation. However, although Freud's thought continues to be a profound influence on my way of understanding human culture, I do not feel that I am either unaware or uncritical of the master's limits. Furthermore, I do not consider psychoanalysis to have privileged access to any truth that could exist outside of linguistic and cultural practice. Along with the philosopher Ann Pellegrini, I understand psychoanalysis to be "a powerful cultural narrative" that "provides patterns of order and interpretation for telling and making sense of life experiences" (1994, p. 4).

In this paper, I will draw on psychoanalytic theories that derive from the work of Freud and some of his followers. I have been strongly impressed with the work of Melanie Klein, D.W. Winnicott, W.R.D. Fairbairn and other post-Freudians who have developed Kleinian and object relations approaches to psychoanalysis. My appreciation of this branch of analytic theory has been enhanced by having the opportunity to work and study with Drs. Ben Esrock, Dean Eyre and Ann Mully, three British-trained analysts who practice in Ottawa.

MATTERS OF ATTITUDE, PERSPECTIVE AND BELIEF

In regard to my own attitude to religious belief, I concur with Freud, another Jewish atheist, who, in 1901, described his belief in religion like this: "In point of fact, I believe that a large part of the mythological view of the world, which extends a long way into the most modern religions, is nothing but psychology projected into the external world" (1901, p. 258). The two words that can be misleading in Freud's sentence are 'nothing but'; it would be wrong to interpret this phrase as minimizing the impact of religious myths . As we all know over the next thirty-eight years of his life, Freud would say a great deal more about the power of the phenomena which in 1901 he seems to be dismissing.

For me, to believe in religion the way Freud did, raises an important question: how does religious psychology project itself into the external world? Or, to put it differently, what are the ways in which certain psychological wishes and fears become the mighty constructors of culture we name religions? Maya Deren in her 1970 study of voodoo writes something akin to Freud's statement. "Myth", she says, "is the facts of the mind made manifest in a fiction of matter" (1970, p. 21). Her definition leads me to frame my question in another way: how does myth shape the matter of collective social and political behavior? Or, rather, how does religion make itself true?

To approach the issue of how that which is, or appears to be, individual and psychological becomes that which is collective and social, in relation to religious belief, I find it helpful to make use of some of Judith Butler's thinking about performance. In reference to acts of speech, Butler says "... a performative [action] succeeds ... only because that action echoes prior actions, and *accumulates the force of authority through the repetition or citation of a prior, authoritative set of practices*. What this means, then, is that a performative 'works' to the extent that it draws on and covers over the constitutive conventions by which it is mobilized. In this sense, no term or statement can function performatively without the accumulating and dissimulating historicity of force" (1993, pp. 226-227). I think that the doctrines and practices of religious traditions operate analogously to Butler's concept of speech acts. Her work encourages me to think of religion in terms of sustained, elaborate and repeated social performances that derive power from continued citation of the mystified authority of texts, rituals and institutions.

The frequent and ubiquitous repetition and re-enactment of scriptures, rituals, prayers and parables as well as the replication and reinterpretation of sacred stories and dramas in literature, film, theater, architecture and visual art give what we term the 'great traditions' an enormous force of historicity. What might have begun long ago within the psychology of particular people or amidst the history of particular circumstance has now accumulated as a thick sediment produced and maintained by seemingly infinite individual and institutional reiteration and incantation.

I understand this process to be circular: that is, in relation to religion, I consider the cultural sediment to be part of the clay that forms and reforms our particular psychologies and histories, whether or not we would describe ourselves as religious. Even for atheists, there is no escape from thousands of years of religious history and practice. After all, this history is repeated day after day in subtle and obvious forms not only in religious institutions, but also in secular domains of culture that reflect the structures and assumptions of religious traditions.

In a practical sense, I believe in religion much as I believe in the days of the week. That is, as I write this, I know today is Monday because an extensive, long-standing and ongoing consensus establishes this particular twenty-four hour block of time as Monday. While there is no essential, supernatural or biological quality that undergirds this consensus, I feel that it is perfectly natural for today to be Monday. The script of my life will be shaped by a wholly social agreement that is as pervasive as it is invisible.

Should I choose to behave as if today were not Monday, I would eventually run into conflicts with other people who would be following a Monday script. I might prefer to live as though today were Friday, Saturday or Sunday — but, since everyone else would be performing their Monday activities, I would be continually reminded that I am deviating from a norm. As long as I remain in contact with my culture, I will have to be conscious of others' belief in Monday.

Similar principles operate in regard to religion. Because the scripts of doctrines, rites and imagery permeate culture, they affect everyone whether or not she or he willingly adheres to the directives of any tradition. Government, education, art, literature and entertainment all have roots in religious practices and institutions. Even the idols of pop culture derive from religious precedent. Madonna's transgressions seem especially naughty because of her reference to the nomenclature and teachings of Catholicism (Downing 1993). And, for many people, Elvis the King still lives, like Christ the King for many more.

Although it is risky to generalize about the varied, elaborate and shifting psychological and social scripts that the major traditions of the West authorize, I believe it is accurate to say that gender is an abiding, central concern of each one. And, in regard to Judaism, Christianity and Islam, I think it is accurate to state that men, male divinities and masculine behavior are the primary foci of texts and rites.

The preoccupation of Jewish and Christian traditions with men was apparent to the first feminists who, in 1882, set about analyzing every part of scripture that made reference to women. The American suffragist Elizabeth Cady Stanton writes in her memoirs that although her group was warned about the magnitude of the task, she and her "revising committee" soon discovered that "these texts [about women] composed only one-tenth of the Old and New Testaments". Thus, the work did not seem to be "a difficult or dangerous undertaking". Stanton and her friends were eager to comment on every Biblical passage that could possibly be construed as mentioning women: for example, they include an entry on Balaam's ass because the animal was female (1898, p. 467).

Perhaps one effect of the richness, range and productivity of feminist scholarship in the last several years has been to obscure the importance of Stanton's first insight about religion — namely, that men are its chief subjects. Although I applaud and encourage the excellent gynocentric research that has brought to light the hidden history of women in the great traditions; and although I feel certain that feminist work in theology and religious philosophy will significantly modify the basic concepts and orientations of these traditions, I want to return to the problem that provides that initial impetus for feminist activity. I would like to use psychoanalytic theory to help explain why maleness is at the heart of the religious enterprise.

FREUD'S VERSION OF THE MALE DRAMA OF RELIGION

According to Freud, a male tragedy is central to both Judaism and Christianity. The last sentence of *Totem and taboo* — *"Im Anfang war die Tat"* — states his major premise about the origins of religious belief and practice (1913, p. 161). The deed, as we all know, was the murder by a primal father by a horde of primal brothers who wanted access to the women of the tribe. In Freud's account, religion is a system that codifies men's reactions to the killing of the father. Celebration is accompanied by periodic rituals of feasting and permissiveness, while remorse is expressed by instituting elaborate taboos around almost everything connected with the memory of the father and his reign.

Taboos concerning the women of the tribe are especially strict since the father was initially killed so that the brothers could gain possession of the females. Thus taboos around social contact between opposite sex members of the same tribe serve to maintain the rules of the father. The ambivalence between the sons' love for the father and their hatred of him can be used to explain most significant religious phenomena. Freud emphasizes that "in the course of the later development of religions the two driving factors, the son's sense of guilt and the son's rebelliousness never became extinct" (1913, p. 152).

The role of the father and his relationship to the sons is the theme of both Freud's major works on the history of religion — *Totem and taboo* (1913) and *Moses and monotheism* (1939). If we place the two works side by side, we can see that the later work, *Moses and monotheism*, is actually a continuation of the earlier work begun in *Totem and taboo*. In *Moses and monotheism*, Freud points out that his analysis of primitive religion in *Totem and taboo* links Judaism and Christianity to what he terms "the forgotten event of primeval times" (1939, p. 89). He combines both religions into one tradition whose dominant characteristic is its preoccupation with a slain father figure:

> The killing of Moses by his Jewish people, ... thus becomes an indispensable part of our construction, an important link between the forgotten event of primeval times and its later emergence in the form of the monotheist religions. It is plausible to conjecture that the remorse for the murder of Moses provided the stimulus for the wishful phantasy of the Messiah, who was to return and lead his people to redemption and the promised world dominion. If Moses was this first Messiah, Christ became his substitute and successor, and Paul could exclaim to the peoples with some historical justification: "Look! the Messiah has really come: he has been murdered before your eyes!" Then, too, there is a piece of historical truth in Christ's resurrection, for he was the resurrected Moses and behind him the returned primal father of the primitive horde, transfigured and, as the son, put in the place of the father. (1939, pp. 89-90)

The father figure, then, is resurrected in Moses who is resurrected in Christ. Moses and Christ are figures who represent "The Great Man", the primal father whom Freud sees as having an immense influence on the thought of his followers (1939, pp. 107-111). This great man is none other than the murdered primal father — the "Supreme Being" who, according to Freud in *The future of an illusion* and other writings, prevents those who believe in Him from commitment to "reason and science", the intellectual path promising the best hope for the future of humankind (1927).[1]

Throughout Freud's essays about religion, Judaism and Christianity incur his disfavor to the degree that he sees them as posing obstacles to the free exercise of thought. Freud says that the initial intellectual advancement of Judaism is cancelled out by a maze of rules and restrictions that arise from guilt over the original parricide. As Judaism evolves, Freud thinks that its directives and regulations become "ever stricter, more meticulous and even more trivial" (1939, p. 134).

Although Jewish legalisms hampered the growth of the intellect, Christianity did greater damage by cloaking the ancient crime with the mystifying concept of original sin. This idea made the deed even more difficult to recognize: "the fact of the parricide ... was ... obliged to submit to a more powerful distortion. The unnameable crime was replaced by the hypothesis of what must be described as a shadowy 'original sin'' (1939, p. 135). While Freud concedes that it was an advance in culture simply to depict the murder of God through the image of Christ's execution, he believes that the vague abstractions of its theology made Christianity a "severe inhibition upon the intellectual development of the next two thousand years" (1939, p. 88).

By applying psychoanalytic method, Freud tries to counteract the limitations on thought imposed by religions of the Father in all of his works about the history of religions. His goal is to unravel the chain of events that have led to what he considers to be the neurotic belief in a Supreme Being. "As though the world had not riddles enough," he writes, "we are set the new problem of understanding how these other [religious] people have been able to acquire their belief in the Divine Being and whence that belief obtained its immense power which overwhelms 'reason and science'" (1939, p. 123). His answer to the riddle of religion lay in revealing the crime that both Judaism and Christianity disguise in their texts and rituals.

Freud's insistence that the sons' murder of the Father is the basis of religion never falters. He metes out harsh criticism to any "philosophers" who compound the repression of the crime by dissimulating about the true nature of the Father-god:

> It is ... humiliating to discover how large a number of people living today, who cannot but see that this religion is not tenable, nevertheless try to defend it piece by piece in a series of pitiful rearguard actions. One would like to mix among the ranks of the believers in order to meet these philosophers, who think they can rescue the God of religion by replacing him by an impersonal, shadowy and abstract principle, and to address them with the warning words: "Thou shalt not take the name of the Lord thy God in vain!" (1927, p. 74)

The father of psychoanalysis is uncompromising on the point that God must be seen as an anthropomorphic male figure. It is only by calling God His true name that Freud believes people can arrive at an understanding of religion and throw off its yoke.

The role of women in Freud's version of the history of religions is minor. In *Totem and taboo* and seven years later in *Group psychology and the analysis of the ego*, he conjectures that "mother deities" arise for a brief period in human history when the sons are not yet ready to assume leadership. According to Freud, mother imagery predominates for a time because the murderers of the father are paralysed by the fear and guilt generated by their crime. He thus understands the reign of goddesses as a drama reflecting the emotional conflicts and fratricidal tendencies of the primal sons (1913, pp. 152-153; 1921, p. 135).

At no time in this schema do women take an active role in religious development. Freud discounts any legends and stories that depict a female figure as an initiator: "In the lying poetic fancies of prehistoric times, the woman, who had been the prize of battle and the temptation to murder, was probably turned into the active seducer and instigator to the crime"(1921, p. 136).

History vs. Dream

Although in most of his writings Freud seems to believe that his historical conjecture reflects real events, occasionally he admits that, like a 'just-so story' his hypothesis might not be literally accurate (1921, p. 122). However, even as a just-so story that, for example, purports to explain how the leopard got its spots, Freud's imaginative rendering of humanity's religious past has value as a descriptive account that emphasizes a dominant characteristic of his object of study. To understand religion, I think we ought to follow his central hermeneutic principle by stressing the masculinity of God and the maleness of the traditional drama. In our continuing work in the psychology of religion, we would do well to remember that for Freud, religion was all about men.

Freud's effort to uncover what religion is hiding stops with the crime. To go further, perhaps we should look at his own work as continuous with the religious traditions he analyzed. By merely glancing at women in his account of religious history, Freud is repeating a religious pattern. Because he did not ask why women should be given a minimal role in the manifest content of religious text and performance, he constructed an argument that diminishes women yet again.

Captivated by the *Sturm und Drang* of the sons' conflict with the father, Freud winds up writing himself into a similar script: the father of psychoanalysis slays the father god of religion and establishes another priesthood with revised doctrines, texts and rules. Instead of the collective murder of the primal father that supposedly founds religions, each individual's struggle through an Oedipal conflict constructs a foundation for psychoanalysis.

Since our cultural circumstances differ from Freud's, we are not compelled to follow exactly in his footsteps. While he hypothesizes a hidden history that mirrors the dominant masculinity of religions, we might draw from another sphere of psychoanalytic theory. I suggest that we treat the religious performance of maleness as we would the manifest content of a recurring dream. Although the dream keeps saying that various male figures — Yahweh, Christ, Mohammed — are the initiators of everything of value in the world — sacred texts, sacred children, commandments and laws — as interpreters we can look for a latent meaning behind this bravado. As Freud taught us to do when we think about dreams and other imaginative constructions, we might suspect that the manhood trumpeted by religious texts and institutional practices is a displacement of its opposite — i.e. womanhood. We might wonder whether the outward unimportance of women in the world's religions might be an attempt at what Freud calls negation and Melanie Klein terms denial. Both concepts describe a refusal to recognize that upon which a subject actually depends.

Homoeroticism and Religious Imagination

In his recent book, *God's phallus and other problems for men and monotheism*, Howard Eilberg-Schwartz argues that worship of a sole male god cultivates intense homoerotic feelings in men. He thus, in my opinion, implies that the manifest masculinity of religion rests on latent femininity. Eilberg-Schwartz points out that Freud recognizes the connection between homoeroticism and male divinity in the case studies of Dr. Schreber and the Wolf Man as well as in the essay "A Seventeenth-Century Demonological Neurosis": in each instance Freud discusses how images of God (or the devil) function as expressions of conflicted homosexual wishes (1911, 1918, 1923).

Eilberg-Schwartz says that Schreber's fantasies of "being unmanned and sexually desired by God" show that the troubled doctor "was able to think the unthinkable and thus express what traditional theology has always been afraid to face" — namely, a deep longing for intimate union with a divine father (1994, p. 137). *God's phallus* shows the various ways in which this "dilemma of monotheism" is addressed throughout the history of Judaism. Often the body of God is hidden or denied so that the desired paternal phallus can not be imagined literally. At other times, both God and men are feminized in order to cloak male-to-male love in more acceptable heterosexual metaphors. And, in several biblical and rabbinic stories, men are threatened or punished with castration or death because they wish for a too-explicit homosexual union with God.

Eilberg-Schwartz sees Jewish ideas about the production of sacred text as linked to homoeroticism since in Judaism only men's creative activity with one another is said to increase Torah. Images that depict the genesis of text as resulting either from mouth-to-mouth male congress or from male-to-male transmission of semen are key to Eilberg-Schwartz' argument that "torah production was the cultural equivalent of physical reproduction" (p. 214).

Although his work does not attempt a full analysis of homoerotic longings in Christianity, Eilberg-Schwartz thinks that similar desires and their concomitant ambivalences move through Christian theology. For example, he believes that "the homoerotic love of men for Christ is avoided by speaking collectively of the Christian community as a woman". Thus, when Paul says that a man stands in the same relationship to Christ as a woman to a man, he imposes a heterosexual metaphor of desire on what is in fact a male-to-male association (p. 237).

I look upon Eilberg-Schwartz' work both as an invaluable contribution to feminist theory and as an important correction to it. Up to now, feminists studying gender in religious traditions have understood male images of divinity as providing rather unproblematic benefits to men. In *God's phallus*, Eilberg-Schwartz' analysis of the dilemma posed by the repression of homoerotic desire within monotheism reveals that the masculinity constructed for men by the dominant western traditions is unstable and fraught with contradiction. He compels us to ask: how do men function in religions that preach heterosexuality and decry homosexuality yet enjoin their followers to crave intimacy with a male God and fantasize about a loving, creative union with Him?

Eilberg-Schwartz' book challenges those of us who are interested in gender and religion to expand our theories so that we may take better account of the conflicted masculinity presented by the traditions we study. Paradoxically, I suggest that one way to explore the dynamics of what could be termed religious masculinity is to focus on what our dominant traditions do about femininity.

Eilberg-Schwartz believes that the fear of imagining male-to-male intimacy too literally prompts the production of religious texts that ascribe feminine qualities to men and to God. He considers the guilty repression of homoerotic desire as leading to the appropriation of female traits and capacities by male religious subjects. Homosexual feelings, he writes, do not necessarily feminize the men who have them, but can occur "in [homosexual] men who by all criteria are as masculine as heterosexual men". He finds Freud's theories of same-sex desire "wrongheaded" in this regard (p. 37).

In the less restrictive systems of religious symbols that Eilberg-Schwartz briefly outlines in the concluding chapter of his book, men would be freer to envision close, loving relationships with their divine father. He implies that this decrease in homophobia would make religions less likely to feminize both human and divine fathers and sons.

I doubt that religious doctrines and symbols could ever be purged of their associations with feminine images. In a religious context I think that the dynamics of fantasy always lead one member of the divine-human couple to adopt female traits. To put it another way, I think that within religious systems visions of male-to-male intimacy must always allude to women.

Because claims about creation are of central concern to religions, the inflated masculinity that characterizes the dominant traditions must either appropriate or deny feminine qualities in order to make reference to the phenomenal world. Religious texts describe the beginnings of heaven, earth, foundational laws and supernatural leaders and then proscribe the continual recitation and reenactment of their originary hypotheses. Males — whether human or divine — can claim the major role in this all-encompassing generative drama only if they subsume women or negate female existence.

The psychoanalyst Janine Chasseguet-Smirgel writes that denial of the fact that intercourse between a man and a woman is necessary for human reproduction characterizes fantasies about same-sex creativity (1985). She sees the refusal to acknowledge generative union of parental figures as a motivating idea in imaginative literature, in art and in the theater. Because the negation of heterosexual coupling inspires elaborate imaginal ruses, Chasseguet-Smirgel identifies it as an important force in culture. She thinks that artistic productions that ignore sexual truths and deny human differences are pleasurable because, from time to time and in differing degrees, we all like to escape reality.

Chasseguet-Smirgel restricts her analysis to cultural phenomena that are generally recognized as based in fantasy. However, the dynamic she discusses flourishes in sacred texts as well. In Genesis, for example, both creation stories deny the facts of biological reproduction so that men can be portrayed as the sole genitors of the human race. In the chronologically earlier version, a male God pulls Eve out of male flesh and thus achieves an instant conception, pregnancy and delivery. Man gives birth to woman in this imaginative reversal of the facts of life.

Prior to the birth of Eve in Genesis 2:7 we read that "the Lord God formed man of the dust of the ground, and breathed into his nostrils the breath of life; and man became a living soul". This is another example of the male wish to conceive without needing a woman. Man's nostrils substitute for a female vagina; God's breath substitutes for semen; and, I believe, the "dust of the ground" connotes excrement that is magically crafted into a son by skilled male hands. The image of soil being transformed into a baby brings to mind Freud's observation that children often equate babies with faeces that both men and women can produce (1909, pp. 74-75 passim).[2]

Genesis 1:27 is often cited as an egalitarian text in contrast to the version discussed above. To many feminists, the lines — "So God created man in his own image, in the image of God created he him;

male and female created he them" — undermine sexist interpretations of creation because God seems to be both male and female. However, this reading ignores the contradiction that the God who creates male and female is still referred to as male in both the original Hebrew and in all subsequent translations. Thus, this text is another rendering of the same theme: males contain females within themselves and thus do not need women to reproduce.

THE MONOGENETIC THEORY OF PROCREATION

The New Testament modifies but nevertheless extends the idea that women are ancillary figures in relation to reproduction and nurture. Even though Mary is ostensibly important as the mother of the divine son, God bypasses all physical contact with her female body to reproduce himself. He is the necessary agent in the generative process; she is the container whom he does not have to touch to impregnate. The anthropologist Carol Delaney writes about how the Christian story of the Virgin Birth exemplifies what she terms "the monogenetic theory of procreation". Instead of reading the story as a statement about the creative independence of Mary, Delaney thinks the Virgin Birth champions man as the determinative agent of human reproduction. She believes that Christian imagery around this theme supports a widely promulgated notion that man is the true parent of the child: he magically deposits his "seed" in whatever female he chooses to function as his "soil" (1986, pp. 494-513; 1991).

I agree with Delaney that the monogenetic theory of procreation illuminates important assumptions about gender imbedded in Christian texts. For example, when Jesus instructs his followers to honor the "the word of God" over "the womb which bare thee and the paps which thou hast sucked" (Luke 11: 27-28), he is teaching that the father's directives are of greater significance than maternal flesh. God the father is thus presented as the source of that which is truly formative for the community, namely, "the word".

Likewise, Jesus' statement (Matt. 12:48-50) that "whosoever shall do the will of my Father which is in heaven, the same is my brother, and sister, and mother", stresses that adherence to the laws of the father determines bonds of both sibling and maternal affiliation. His answer to the questions "Who is my mother? And who are my brethren?" reiterates the claim that loyalty to the father's word establishes social groupings more effectively than does sharing the same mother. Paternal directives usurp maternal ties and the monogenetic theory of procreation is recited once again.

Ritual Repetition as a Foundation for Secular Ideas about Gender

In Judaism and Christianity, ritual activities directed by a male hierarchy continually displace women's agency and creativity as baptism and circumcision supersede the importance of physical birth. In Judaism, a boy's reading from the Torah at his *bar mitzvah* both mimics and suppresses the importance of a girl's initiation into her adulthood through menstruation (Bettelheim 1962).[3] In Catholicism, symbolic feeding from a male body during mass is infused with social meaning, thereby eclipsing the value of any nursing and nourishment provided by women (Raab 1991). Incessant repetition of such rites continually reasserts the basic religious principle that men are the primary agents of creation.

The rituals of androcentric religion work effective magic. Because many of our secular intellectual traditions stem from religious institutions, the primacy of male procreative power is insisted upon within secular spheres of culture. For example, some scholars suggest that the origins of Western science reveal a male interest in making women irrelevant to the important work of creation. According to Sally Allen and Joanna Hubbs, alchemical images express a desire to bring the wonders of maternity under male control. They write that, instead of recognizing an equitable conjunction of male and female opposites, the alchemical opus works to displace the female part in biological creation through a male-directed technology (1980).

This line of thought is continued by Carolyn Merchant (1980) in her work on the death of nature and more recently by David Noble in his book, *A world without women: the Christian clerical culture of western science* (1992). In his study of the influence of monastic culture on medieval science, Noble points out that monks would cultivate an ambiguous gender identity by imagining themselves as females in maternal roles. For example, in the twelfth century, Bernard of Clairvaux entreats his fellow abbots to "show affection as a mother would .... Be Gentle, let your bosoms expand with milk not swell with passion". Similarly, Francis of Assisi is said to have encouraged his associates to address him as mother (p. 284). Noble believes that science is permeated by the clergy's desire to make women unnecessary and to dominate the creative forces of a nature imagined to be 'mother'. He is not alone in suggesting that the most recent expression of this wish is men's efforts to control new reproductive technologies.

MALE ENVY AND THE PSYCHOLOGY OF RELIGION

A psychoanalytic hermeneutic that can help to further describe and illuminate men's imitation and appropriation of women both in our sacred traditions and in the secular practices that derive from them is Melanie Klein's theory of envy. I will draw on Klein's presentation of her controversial concept in the 1957 essay titled "Envy and Gratitude" in order to argue for a connection between Kleinian psychoanalysis and what I like to call the divine masquerade.

"Envy", writes Klein, "is the angry feeling that another person possesses and enjoys something desirable — the envious impulse being to take it away or spoil it" (Klein 1975, pp. 176-235). She traces the etiology of envy to early experiences of taking in nourishment either from a mother's breast or from a bottle. If this basic activity goes well, the foundation for the adult ability to take satisfaction from life will be established. She says "this mental and physical closeness to the gratifying breast in some measure restores ... the lost prenatal unity with the mother and the feeling of security that goes with it" (p. 179).

It is important to stress that in Klein's thought, as in psychoanalytic theory in general, particular early experiences with breasts or bottles are resonant with meaning that unfolds as a person's life progresses. "We find in the analysis of our patients," writes Klein, "that the breast in its good aspect is the prototype of maternal goodness, inexhaustible patience and generosity, as well as of creativeness. It is these phantasies and instinctual needs that so enrich the primal object that it remains the foundation for hope, trust, and a belief in goodness" (p. 180).
Because envy is a primary force that erodes the capacity to take pleasure in life and find value in experience, mitigating it is considered a significant goal of Kleinian therapy.

Although an infant might develop aggressive feelings from frustrations that arise while she or he is trying to satisfy hunger, Klein thinks that the destructive wishes that characterize envy are directed toward the beloved source of nurture mainly because it is felt to be outside the baby's control. Thus, the good mother and her representative in bottle or breast is hated for being both absolutely necessary for her child's well-being and completely independent of her child's will. Klein believes that as adults all of us tend to experience some degree of envy in reference to people we love and admire because we know that their beauty, wealth or talent is separate from us. Guilt about wishing to damage what we love and appreciate often accompanies our envy. In her view, we can measure our sense of peace by the degree to which we can enjoy goodness and success that exists apart from ourselves. "Whereas envy is a source of great unhappiness," she writes "relative freedom from it is felt to underlie contented and peaceful states of mind — ultimately sanity" (p. 203).

What makes envy so destructive and uncomfortable is that it threatens to hurt that which it wants and needs most. Klein says "there are very pertinent psychological reasons why envy ranks among the seven 'deadly sins'. I would even suggest that it is unconsciously felt to be the greatest sin of all, because it spoils and harms the good object which is the source of life". She agrees with Chaucer, who, in *The parson's tale*, says "it is certain that envy is the worst sin that is; for all other sins are sins only against one virtue, whereas envy is against all virtue and against all goodness"(p. 189).

In a general sense, creativity can be considered to be the target of envious feelings. Klein says "though superficially ... [envy] may manifest itself as a coveting of the prestige, wealth, and power others have attained, its actual aim is creativeness. The capacity to give and to preserve life is felt as the greatest gift and therefore creativeness becomes the deepest cause for envy" (p. 202). She thinks that both sexes envy one another; each wants "to take away the attributes of the other sex" so that creativity could be wholly within male or female control.

Klein believes that excessive envy in men extends to all feminine attributes, "in particular to the woman's capacity to bear children". In a man who is psychologically mature, "compensation for unfulfilled feminine desires" can be derived from "a good relation to his wife or lover and by becoming the father of the children she bears him ... the feeling that he has created the child counteracts the man's early envy of the mother's femininity" (p. 201).

The last sentence of the quotation above rewards close attention: "the feeling that he has created the child counteracts the man's early envy of the mother's femininity". How do men come to believe that they create children? Since the male role in procreation is always somewhat theoretical — i. e. children do not emerge from male bodies — linguistic customs such as stamping mother and child with a male surname have evolved to reassure men of their utility. Initiation rituals are thought to serve a similar purpose. As Bettelheim writes, the history of anthropology is rife with theories that analyze male puberty rites in pre-literate cultures as efforts of men "to take over the functions of women" (p. 18).

Male anxiety about procreation and dependence on women has implications far beyond so-called primitive rituals.[4] I think that men's concerns about their marginality in relation to reproduction and nurture give rise to religious systems. What makes these systems problematic is that instead of mitigating the envy of femininity that Klein describes, religions aggressively diminish women in order to glorify men. Male envy is thus both denied and promoted. Please consider this hypothesis as I juxtapose religious themes that correspond to four of the mechanisms that Klein identifies as defenses against envy.

Klein writes that "a frequent method of defence is to stir up envy of others by one's own success, possessions, and ... good fortune, thereby reversing the situation in which envy is experienced" (p. 218). I see this technique manifested in overblown praise for the power, majesty and omnipotence of male god figures. Often the claim is made that all creativity issues from male divinity. In Job, for example, God praises himself with a long inventory of his abilities and achievements in order to deflate mankind. However, in addition to privileging divinity over humanity, I read God's grandiose rhetorical questions — such as "where was thou when I laid the foundations of the earth?" (Job 38:4), "who divided a watercourse for the overflowing of waters, or a way for the lightning of thunder?" (Job 38:25), and "who provideth for the raven his food" (Job 38:41) as evidence of the father god's insecurity about his role as sole creator of the world. The insistence that everything issues from the male godhead both masks and reveals the anxiety about generativity that seems basic to biblical religion.

Splitting the desired object into parts that can be separately idealized and despised is another way to cope with envy. Kleinians theorize that imagining the bad object as entirely different from the good one has the psychological goal of keeping whatever is loved safe from aggressive wishes. However, since hatred for the bad object is not allowed to be lessened by any tender feelings, splitting can encourage distorted views that lead to destructiveness.

In Judaism and Christianity, images of women tend to appear in pairs that are split: one is virtuous with a "price far above rubies" (Prov. 31:10) ; while another's "end is bitter as wormwood, sharp as a two-edged sword" (Prov. 5:4). As stories about women unfold in the traditions, the good women tend to get better while the bad ones get worse. The case of Esther and Vashti provides an interesting example. Even though Queen Vashti initially does nothing more than refuse to appear before her drunken husband, she is vilified in rabbinic literature (Gendler 1976, pp. 241-247). Esther's glorification seems to require the denigration of her predecessor. Similarly, as Christian myth continues through the centuries, Mary's purity is increasingly extolled over Eve's duplicity. Mary is put forward as the Second Eve whose role is to serve as an antidote to the vileness of her ancestor. Such images encourage both sexes to think of women in terms of caricature, as beings who either embody perfection or evil. The persecution of witches is a dramatic tragedy that was made possible by the willingness of large numbers of people to see women in unrealistic ways.

Klein writes that the aim of envy is often "the destructive introjection" of what the subject needs (p. 181). Greek myth presents us with a graphic image of this when Zeus swallows Metis, Athena's mother, and gains the ability to give birth through his head. Although the appropriation of women by men in Judaism and Christianity is more subtle than this, I think the Jewish and Christian imitation and appropriation of women express the same envious wish that motivated Zeus. By masquerading as women in texts and rituals, men imaginatively eliminate the separate existence of women and put creativity and the capacity to nurture wholly under male control.

Primary and Secondary Motivations

I realize that my analysis appears to be one-sided. By now, my readers are probably impatient to ask where are the women in my argument: how do religions express women's desires? My answer to the imagined query is this: on the basic level of symbol and image, contemporary mainstream religions of the world are constructed to reflect men's fantasies, not women's. Although women are often enthusiastic followers of the world's major faiths, I believe this participation reflects the wish to be within institutions that are relevant and socially significant. Women support religious performance even though the psychological content of the symbols arises out of male alienation. To use a bit of American slang, in regard to religion, masculine need determines "the only game in town".

By arguing that the symbolic foundation on which religion rests is that of the male imitation of women, I am not arguing that this is all religion is. Religious traditions are also concerned with facets of behavior, law and social organization that have little to do with gender. Furthermore, the motives of both women and men who participate in religion are complex. Habits, customs and rituals learned in childhood carry a strong emotional valence throughout life. Religious organizations can provide a sense of order, community and psychological comfort that derive from their long-standing institutional presence in human history. Many people join the clergy in order to be part of groups that are actively trying to improve the world in conjunction with a structured ideology. In addition, many members of congregations enjoy the sensuality and drama of religious services: music, pleasing architecture, and the theater of ritual can enrich both male and female lives.

Nevertheless, although I recognize the secondary gains that can accrue to people who engage in religious practice, I maintain that the underlying dynamic of the primary symbols of all major contemporary faiths involves the male appropriation of female qualities. In my most ambitious moments as a theorist, I would go as far as to claim that religion is a totally male form of ideation and practice that allows men to transform themselves into women. This, I suggest, is the goal of the "transcendence" proposed by theologians: it is the contingency of masculinity that men want to escape. I think that rituals and texts involving an afterlife, rebirth, second birth or miraculous birth address the male issues I have outlined in this paper. Likewise, I see religious interest in the transformation of one thing into another and ritual concerns about separating objects and people into categories of rigid difference as reflections of two poles of a dilemma concerned with both being and not being male. Expanding this line of thought further will be a goal of my future work.

NOTES

1. See also Freud's arguments in *New introductory lectures*, e.g.: "Of the three powers [art, philosophy and religion] which may dispute the basic position of science, religion alone is to be taken seriously as an enemy" (1933, p. 160).
2. In other mythological systems, a male creator forms human beings out of the dirt he finds under the claws of a water animal such as an otter, beaver or muskrat. I think that such stories also reflect the anal theory of birth discussed by Freud.
3. Bettelheim's work provides a general discussion of the imitation of women in male rituals of initiation.
4. In the last twenty years, psychoanalytic theorists like Nancy Chodorow and Dorothy Dinnerstein have argued that contemporary ideas about child-care and the separate roles of the sexes reflect fear of female maternal power. Their careful and nuanced work has led many to look more closely at child-rearing arrangements.

REFERENCES

Allen, S. & J. Hubbs (1980). Outrunning Atalanta: feminine destiny in alchemical transmutation. *Signs, 6*(2), pp. 210-221.

Bettelheim, B. (1962). *Symbolic wounds: puberty rites and the envious male*. New York: Collier.

Butler, J. (1990). *Gender trouble: feminism and the subversion of identity*. New York: Routledge.
Butler, J. (1993). *Bodies that matter: on the discursive limits of "sex"*. New York: Routledge.
Chasseguet-Smirgel, J. (1985). *Creativity and perversion*. London: Norton.
Chodorow, N.J. (1978). *The reproduction of mothering*. Berkeley: University of California Press.
Delaney, C. (1986). The meaning of paternity and the Virgin birth debate. *Man, 21*(3), pp. 494-513.
Delaney, C. (1991). *The seed and the soil: gender and cosmology in a Turkish village society*. Berkeley: University of California Press.
Deren, M. (1970). *Divine horsemen: the voodoo gods of Haiti*. New York: Dell.
Dinnerstein, D. (1976). *The mermaid and the minotaur: sexual arrangements and human malaise*. New York: Harper and Row.
Downing, M. (1993). Understanding major issues in the field of women and religion. In: G. Finn (ed.). *Voices of women, voices of feminism* (pp. 29-41). Toronto: Fernwood Press.
Eilberg-Schwartz, H. (1994). *God's phallus and other problems for men and monotheism*. Boston: Beacon Press.
Freud, S. (1901). *The psychopathology of everyday life*. (*The standard edition of the complete psychological works of Sigmund Freud, vol 6*; transl. & ed. J. Strachey). London: Hogarth, 1962[2].
Freud, S. (1909). Analysis of a phobia in a five-year old boy. In: *The standard edition of the complete psychological works of Sigmund Freud, vol. 10* (pp. 5-149) (transl. & ed. J. Strachey). London: Hogarth, 1964[5].
Freud, S. (1911). Psycho-analytic notes on an autobiographical account of a case of paranoia (Dementia paranoides). In: *The standard edition of the complete psychological works of Sigmund Freud, vol. 12* (pp. 3-82) (transl. & ed. J. Strachey). London: Hogarth, 1964[3].
Freud, S. (1913). Totem and taboo. In: *The standard edition of the complete psychological works of Sigmund Freud* (transl. & ed. J. Strachey). *Vol 13: 'Totem and taboo' and other works* (pp. 1-161). London: Hogarth, 1964[4].
Freud, S. (1918). From the history of an infantile neurosis. In: *The standard edition of the complete psychological works of Sigmund Freud, vol. 17* (pp. 7-122) (transl. & ed. J. Strachey). London: Hogarth, 1964[4].
Freud, S. (1921). Group psychology and the analysis of the ego. In: *The standard edition of the complete psychological works of Sigmund Freud, vol. 18* (pp. 69-143) (transl. & ed. J. Strachey). London: Hogarth, 1964[4].
Freud, S. (1923). A seventeenth-century demonological neurosis. In: *The standard edition of the complete psychological works of Sigmund Freud, vol. 19* (pp. 69-105) (transl. & ed. J. Strachey). London: Hogarth, 1964[3].
Freud, S. (1927). The future of an illusion. In: *The standard edition of the complete psychological works of Sigmund Freud, vol. 21* (pp. 5-56) (transl. & ed. J. Strachey). London: Hogarth, 1964[2].
Freud, S. (1930). Civilization and its discontents. In: *The standard edition of the complete psychological works of Sigmund Freud, vol. 21* (pp. 64-145) (transl. & ed. J. Strachey). London: Hogarth, 1964[2].

Freud, S. (1933). New introductory lectures on psycho-analysis. In: *The standard edition of the complete psychological works of Sigmund Freud, vol. 22* (pp. 5-182) (transl. & ed. J. Strachey). London: Hogarth, 1964[2].

Freud, S. (1939). Moses and monotheism. In: *The standard edition of the complete psychological works of Sigmund Freud, vol. 23* (pp. 7-137) (transl. & ed. J. Strachey). London: Hogarth, 1964.

Gendler, M. (1976). The restoration of Vashti. In: E. Kottun (ed.). *The Jewish women: new perspectives* (pp. 241-247). New York: Schocken.

Klein, M. (1975). *Envy and gratitude and other works 1946-1963*. New York: Delacorte.

Merchant, C. (1980). *The death of nature*. New York: Harper & Row.

Noble, D. (1992). *A world without women: the Christian clerical culture of Western science*. New York: Knopf.

Pellegrini, A. (1994). *Performance anxieties: staging gender/'race'/sexuality (through) psychoanalysis*. (unpublished Ph.D. diss., Harvard University, Cambridge, Mass.).

Pellegrini, A. (1995). *Performance anxieties: psychoanalysis and "race"*. New York: Routledge.

Raab, K. (1991). *When the priest becomes a woman*. (unpublished Ph.D. diss., University of Ottawa, Ottawa, Canada).

Stanton, E.C. (1898). *Eighty years and more: reminiscences 1815-1897*. New York: Schocken, 1971.

Reconsidering the Psychology of Religion Hermeneutical Approaches in the Contexts of Research and Debate

K.V. O'Connor
University of.Sydney (Australia)

Introduction

Recent debate across many disciplines but especially in the human or social sciences, has been characterised by a questioning of so-called objectivist and mechanistic approaches to scientific enquiry. Increasingly within psychology, researchers have highlighted the limitations and disadvantages of a too narrowly conceived scientific approach based on the natural sciences, and have turned to European philosophy, and to 'interpretative' or 'hermeneutical approaches' for alternative theoretical conceptualisations within which to reconsider and reframe psychology and its methods (cf. Messer et al. 1988; Faulconer & Williams 1990). The psychology of religion has not been impervious to these recent developments. Indeed, throughout its history, the psychology of religion evidences ongoing and recurring debates concerning its purposes, its appropriate limits and boundaries, and the advantages and disadvantages of traditional scientific methods in pursuit of its object of enquiry. Accordingly, efforts to reconsider and reframe its foundations in theory and method have characterised the discipline and its discourses from its inception, a fact often overlooked by contemporary researchers.

Currently, however, the evolving critique of science and of the nature of understanding itself, has led to new approaches to interpretation and to doing science that could quite possibly have far-reaching implications for the ongoing development of the psychology of religion. The current resurgence of interest in, and application of, 'hermeneutical approaches' in the psychology of religion raises important questions for consideration. Do such approaches constitute a substantive or fundamental re-emphasis and/or reframing of the psychology of religion in the late Twentieth Century? And if so, what might be some of the implications or consequences for researchers and for the discipline? In order to appreciate and evaluate the importance of these new 'hermeneutical approaches' in the psychology of religion and their possible implications, it is necessary to situate them in the historical and current contexts of research and debate out of which they have arisen and in which they are co-located and mutually influenced. These will be reviewed briefly before looking at their possible importance for the psychology of religion as a whole.

THE HISTORICAL CONTEXT: A PLURALITY OF ORIENTATIONS AND APPROACHES

From the turn of the century, psychologists of religion based their theory construction and research on the presupposition that 'religion' could be investigated by the same scientific approaches and methods used to study other aspects of human behaviour. A survey of research internationally suggests that, although there have been serious attempts to formulate appropriate research paradigms, an inevitable diversity characterises orientations and approaches to research in the psychology of religion in the late Twentieth Century. Some have suggested that the psychology of religion has become so diversified that it might be more apt to speak of "psychologies of religion" (cf. Pruyser 1987). This diversity arises from a number of interacting sources and factors. These include: the early dependence upon, and different perceptions of, its relatedness to other disciplines concerned with a study of 'religion' (e.g. philosophy, cultural anthropology, history, sociology and theology); the different understandings of psychology as a science, and of 'religion' as a object of enquiry; the variety of theoretical perspectives and methodological orientations within mainstream psychology itself (e.g. psychoanalytic, behavioural, humanistic-existential, cognitive, and social); the complex of applied interests and influences (e.g. philosophical, educational, pastoral and clinical); and the fact that focal centres of study and research have developed, most often independently of each other, in different institutional settings (e.g. universities, seminaries, applied training institutes of teaching), in different academic departments (e.g. Schools of Psychology, Philosophy, Religion and Theology), in different countries with different theoretical and research traditions. Issues inherent in some of these factors are elaborated further.

Despite consistent attempts to delineate the nature and scope of the psychology of religion (cf. James 1902; Allport 1950; Dittes 1969; Godin 1967; Vergote 1993), continuing pluriformity can be partly attributed to the lack of clarity and consensus, and perhaps more recently some active resistance to defining its appropriate limits and boundaries *vis-à-vis* other systems of knowledge. As attempted resolutions over the past 30 years in particular, some psychologists of religion for example, argued in favour of a theological-psychology of religion (e.g. Homans 1967; Spilka 1976); some proposed a social-psychology of religion (Giles et al. 1975; Loewenthal 1975; Hunsberger 1980); while others advocated an all-inclusive interdisciplinary or multidisciplinary perspective (Strunk 1970; Lans 1977; Harris 1978; Francis 1979). Recently, consistent with postmodern thought and developments, others see the blurring of boundaries as inevitable or congenial to their more diverse interests and alignments, psychologically and religiously.

Other issues are more directly related to the existence of a plurality of theoretical perspectives and methodological alternatives within psychology itself. One central issue identified by psychologists of religion, concerns the preparadigmatic nature of psychology as a science (in the Kuhnian sense) and the fact that no one overarching paradigm exists to unify it various perspectives. It is obvious however, that whatever the subjects studied, the focal area of research, or the methods of enquiry adopted, a resulting investigation will be directed by one or more of the existing systems of psychological theory. Accordingly, in the past, attempts at redefinition and the development of coherent research models, led some psychologists of religion to argue in favour of its 'unique emphasis' within the psychological tradition (Strunk 1957, following James 1902); it led others to put a case for a humanistic-existential psychology of religion (Royce 1962, 1967; Strunk 1970; Morris 1980); a normative psychology of religion (Palma 1978); or a psychoanalytic psychology of religion (Meissner 1984), with their respective methodological implications.

There is no doubt that specific interdisciplinary and disciplinary interests will remain a feature of the psychology of religion for the future. Similarly, it is evident from the historical record that a fundamental rethinking and reframing of the psychology of religion is not exactly a new feature of its development. Psychologists of religion have continually looked to different theoretical orientations and approaches to ground and inform their projects. Perhaps what they have not been so precise about, is a delineation of the presuppositions and assumptions underlying their preferred or posited research frameworks.

Another focal point of debate and divergence from its origins concerns the object of the psychology of religion (Dittes 1969; Thouless 1971; Vergote 1969, 1986, 1988, 1993; Lans 1986). As a consequence of the Cartesian subject-object dichotomy, religion tended to be regarded as either an inner, or alternatively an outer, phenomenon of human experience or expression. Accordingly, the tendency was either to attempt to reconstruct the origins and constituents of religion on the basis on inner elementary religious experience as Schleiermacher and Otto had attempted to do, or to focus primarily on the observable manifestations of religion in ritual, church attendance, and other social manifestations and behaviour. This latter project appears to have been an especially barren enterprise in understanding a phenomenon as complex as religion. How informative from a psychological point of view have been the efforts of those who focused on inner religious experience is perhaps equally debatable. From the early studies of Starbuck, Coe, James, and Hall, to the mid century revival of interest by Clark and Glock, and the more recent work of Hood and Hay, outcomes have been somewhat meagre in terms of ongoing theory development from a psychological viewpoint. More importantly they have raised serious questions about the appropriateness of certain empirical approaches and about the measurement paradigm itself in the psychology of religion (cf. Hood 1986).

Researchers have also been critical of the respective limitations of idiographic and nomothetic approaches which, like the unfortunate juxtapositioning of phenomenological and empirical distinctions, were also characteristically viewed as opposing orientations. Some psychologists of religion, for example, argued that the idiographic mode, which limited its object of investigation to origins and solitary experiences, or to events which had special psychological salience, led to a narrow compartmentalisation of 'religion' and 'the religious', and placed unnecessary limitations on the discipline (cf. Capps 1974). Others maintained that nomothetic approaches, which more often applied statistical measures in pursuit of correlations between psychological traits and manifest examples of religious behaviour, were often indiscriminate and goalless and contributed little to the knowledge of religious phenomena as such, that is, to what could be considered as specifically religious (cf. Godin 1967). Where some psychologists of religion advocated and envisioned reconstruction in the discipline at the theoretical level, others proposed a radical rethinking of its too narrow empiricism which had come to be characterised by a paucity of basic items and a mechanistic approach to causation and interpretation.

Based on a more flexible and expansive understanding of 'religion' and 'the religious', encompassing not only its derivative status, but its embeddness in ordinary human phenomena, and its interwovenness in the total complex of meaning, the former, that is those critical of descriptive and phenomenological approaches, argued that the proper object of investigation in the psychology of religion "is the very multidimensionality of religion which its research methods assume but which traditional theoretical constructs undermine" (Capps 1974, p. 48). The proposed quest for a congruence between a broadly construed empiricism and an expanded conceptualisation of religion, found its locus in the 'multidimensionality' of religion, proposed by Glock (1962) and Smart (1969), as a 'new' theoretical construct, and is evident in approaches based on the categories of religion such as beliefs, attitudes, values, experience and behaviour or combinations of these. It is not inconsequential that this 'new' impetus provided researchers, primarily in the social psychological tradition in America and Australia, with a 'new' paradigm for research and discourse (cf. Brown 1966, 1987; Rokeach 1969; Gorsuch & McFarland 1972; Batson & Ventis 1982). Yet others in the social psychological tradition seeking a basis for theoretical reconstruction, looked to mainstream psychology, especially attribution theory, to effect a 'new' orientation (cf. Spilka et al. 1985).

By contrast, those critical of the shortcomings of a restrictive and reductive empiricism which often neglected the signification of language and behaviour, sought for a deeper comprehension of religious experience and expression, religious symbols, texts and rituals, that is of the meanings attributed to religious phenomena by the experiencing subject 'from within'. For researchers more sympathetic to phenomenological approaches which took into account both the world of experience and the mind/person experiencing the world, and emphasised a descriptive analysis of the essential structures of experience on the one hand and of subjective processes on the other, the appropriate scientific task was the location and understanding of religious meanings within human experience. Accordingly, the understanding and elaboration of the human factors and substructures upon which the religious attitude is built characterised such approaches and provided what can be identified as an alternative research orientation in the psychology of religion. It is most closely associated with European researchers and those working out of a psychoanalytic paradigm in areas such as religious experience, religious belief and unbelief, religious psychopathology and clinical practice (cf. Godin 1967, 1985; Vergote 1969, 1988; Meissner 1984). What is significant about these approaches is the incorporation of hermeneutical thinking and the delineation of interpretative criteria.

The historical legacy of these ongoing, if somewhat unrelated efforts at reconstruction, was a growing consensus during the 1970s and 1980s that the psychology of religion had indeed "come to a fundamental impasse in its development as a science of religion" (Capps 1974, p. 36). In the 1990s evidence in the research literature suggests that the impasse deepens as psychologists of religion continue to seek to clarify and to consolidate their positions, often in academic settings either somewhat unsympathetic to religion on the one hand (e.g. psychology), or to scientific approaches on the other (e.g. schools of theology or religion). The focal dilemmas, however, remain primarily concerned with theoretical reconstruction on the one hand, and with reviewing assumptions implicit in the empirical tradition on the other. Several current research trends are worth noting in response to this situation. Where in the so-called empirical tradition in previous decades, the categories of religion or theories derived from general psychology provided a basis for theoretical reconstruction, currently, the categories of psychology and its theories are being revisited. This emphasis is substantially accounted for by the varied applied and academic interests and investments of psychologists of religion in the late Twentieth Century. In research areas, current perspectives and emphases on cognition, the emotions, biology and the body illustrate this trend, as do recent studies on personality traits and correlates, religious development in children and adolescents, including cross-cultural studies, and those employing attachment theory as an explanatory basis. Across the board, but especially in the psychoanalytic tradition which has been somewhat more amenable to phenomenological and hermeneutical approaches in the psychology of religion, issues concerning the relationships between religion, personality and mental health, have also emerged as focal concerns.

Central to these issues in the psychology of religion throughout its history are ideological differences between psychologists with respect to conceptualisations of psychology as a science. In general, these differences stem from fundamental ambivalences about its status as a science. Differences were characteristically framed as contrasting polarities, inherently in conflict, namely: that the object of psychology is to build abstract concepts and construct models — alternatively, that concepts and models must express reality and should be applicable to the concrete; that the object of psychological science is explanation — description; that the object of investigation is external behaviour — inner consciousness; that a principle purpose is theory construction — application; that epistemologically, scientific knowledge represents the most legitimate approach to scientific truth — knowledge by acquaintance; that the methodology of psychology more appropriately be empirical — phenomenological; that approaches to data collection be nomothetic — idiographic. Perhaps the central contradiction inherent in the psychology of religion has been the attempt to produce at one and the same time an objective science (in the natural science sense), as well as a science of human persons (in the human or social science sense), a science which seeks to formulate laws and at the same time to understand the significance of human experience and behaviour. In many respects these dilemmas remain, and psychology continues to be characterised both by uncertainty and shifts in emphasis concerning its goals, its metaphysical bases, its epistemological status as a science, and the appropriateness of its approaches and methods. However, the situation is not entirely bleak, and there is growing evidence of a significant current reconsideration of psychology as a science (cf. Faulconer & Williams 1990). Nor is the picture entirely pessimistic for the psychology of religion even if it does share some of the same uncertainties and ambivalences of mainstream psychology. The multiple recurring polarities evident in its models and methods, the swing of the research pendulum between the categories of religion and those of psychology, and the diversity of methodological approaches and influences discernable in its history, have in fact been generative tensions in its development. What is equally evident from its history, however, is that significant development has occurred in the psychology of religion only when researchers have been prepared to go beyond narrow conceptualisations and restrictive methods. It is argued that the foment of questioning and change discernable across different disciplines and within psychology itself at the present time, provides both a stimulus and a framework for the development of alternative approaches to theory construction and to methodology, and that may effect substantive change and development within the psychology of religion for the future.

THE CURRENT CONTEXT: A MULTIPLICITY OF OVERLAPPING DISCOURSES

For some time now, philosophers and historians, natural and social scientists, theologians and literary theorists, artists and poets, have called for a radical response — a 'silencing' or 'overcoming' of Enlightenment assumptions concerning human existence and human understanding (cf. Polkinghorne 1990). At the core of Enlightenment thinking, or modernism, was the idea that formal reasoning applied to sense data provided a foundation for certain knowledge, a notion which became an unquestioned supposition of its discourses and methods of enquiry. Critics have endeavoured to expose the limitations and errors of this notion and "have sought to deconstruct Enlightenment discourse by showing that its foundational principles are merely ungrounded assumptions" (ibid. p. 93). Within philosophy especially, this process of deconstruction appears to have been taking place in many overlapping conversations, all of which in one way or another, are influencing psychology and the psychology of religion. One is a general discourse about human existence and the recasting of metaphysics. An object here appears to be to find an alternative to both ancient and modern metaphysics and a radically different starting point for thinking about explanation, causality and understanding (cf. Faulconer & Williams 1990; Schrag 1990). Radical participants in this discourse emphasise "the error of seeking a foundation to assure the truth of our epistemological beliefs and call for us to be comfortable living without certainty" (Polkinghorne 1990, p. 93). A related discourse focuses more specifically on the philosophy of science and its methods, particularly on the breakup of the Enlightenment consensus about science. Participants in this discussion "talk about the ways in which a "postempirical" or "postpositivist" science might be practised" (ibid.). As a consequence of the breakdown of Cartesian-empiricist epistemology, thinking about the very "laws of nature", the methods on which the natural sciences were based, and the cultural-academic communities they gave rise to historically, have been radically loosened-up and reframed. As a result of this process of deconstruction, not only has the Cartesian ideal of objectivity been exposed and found to be inadequate and erroneous (particilarly the relationship between the observer and the observed and the dominant dualistic distinctions between subject and object, parts and wholes etc.), but there has been a radical reconstrual of science "as a way of knowing" (cf. Moore 1993), "as a pattern of perception" (cf. Jones 1982), as a human endeavour, subject like any other to the historical, communal and intentional contexts in which it is carried out (ibid. p. 149). In the human or social sciences especially, this rethinking of epistemology and of traditional empiricism, has led to a recognition and rehabilitation of metaphoric-symbolic forms of knowledge within human understanding (cf. Ricoeur 1960; Vergote 1960; Royce 1967; Olds 1992). For psychology, and for the psychology of religion, the restoration of the symbolic and metaphoric to their discourses and to their projects enables them to address the fulness of subjective experience in ways that certain empirical approaches have excluded or discounted in the past.

Another aspect of contemporary philosophical discourse of special relevance to psychology and the psychology of religion concerns the relationships between consciousness and nature, between interiority and exteriority, and between subjectivity and knowledge. Freudian, Lacanian and Feminist psychoanalytic perspectives in particular have disrupted and challenged many "assumptions about knowledge and subjectivity common to the social sciences and humanities as well as in everyday life" (Grosz 1990, p. 2). Where Freud upheld the primacy of consciousness with his postulate of the unconscious, Lacan performed his own inversion (ibid.). Grosz maintains for instance, that "more than any other post-Freudian, Lacan questions the taken-for-granted interpretations of Freud's texts, subverting the centrality accorded to the ego in ego-psychology by affirming the language-like operations of the unconscious" (ibid., pp. 2-3). While agreeing that the later perspective provides arguably the most sophisticated and convincing account of subjectivity, contemporary feminist theorists have argued "that psychoanalysis itself is nevertheless phallocentric in its perspectives, methods and assumptions" (ibid., p. 3), and challenge these accordingly. Characteristically in the past, however, feminist discourse tended to address assumptions concerning women as the objects of knowledge, by alternatively focusing on them as the subjects of knowledge, and the subjective processes whereby women understand, create and use knowledge (cf. Crowley & Himmelweit 1992). Unhappily, however, this appears to have been as dualistic a position as the one it opposed. By contrast, by beginning with a fundamental presupposition, not of a Cartesian dualism of mind and body, or subject and object, but of their necessary interrelatedness, has enabled some recent discussants to integrate corporeality generally and to develop a basis for reconfiguring the body in terms of perception and the connectedness of consciousness (cf. Grosz 1994, following Merleau-Ponty 1962, 1963). Newer emphases on notions of the 'lived body', on the explanatory power of the body as well as the mind, on bodies in their concrete specifications and cultural contexts, and subjectivity in terms of corporeality, not only redress the dualistic reactivity of some feminist discourse, but have the "added bonus of inevitably raising the question of sexual difference in a way that mind does not" (Grosz 1994, p. vii). In effect, questions "of sexual specificity, questions about which kinds of bodies, what their differences are, and what their products and consequences might be" (ibid.), can be raised in ways that are nondualist as well as nonreductionist, a position congenial to many contemporary psychologists, and one which enables a discourse about the body and the experiences of women and men to develop in the psychology of religion in ways perhaps hitherto stymied or negated.

Another discourse that impinges directly on the psychology of religion concerns the issue of religious experience. At basis, this discussion appears to centre on the interplay between cognition and feeling in religious understanding. Within Christian theology, as an example, some theologians (cf. O'Collins 1977; Fletcher 1982) have tended to see the 'crisis in theology' as arising from the over-emphasis on cognition at the expense of theories of experience. This emphasis, they point out, arose primarily from excessive caution and suspicion concerning personal knowledge and experience (cf. Watts & Williams 1988). Accordingly, they see the tasks of reconstruction to reside in the rehabilitation of 'experience', that is, of inner, personal, non-cognitive, and non-institutional experience. Conversely, this project has been rejected by those theologians critical of the implied dichotomy between cognition and feeling in experience, and of the attempt to find a new and personal ground for religion by some considered to be at odds with Christian doctrines and Church institutions (cf. Vergote 1985). Similar dichotomies and dilemmas are evident also within contemporary Christian Theology in the prevailing (cf. Dulles 1983), and newly proposed models of Revelation and God operative in the discipline, such as the 'New Cosmology' and 'Process Theology'. The issues appear to revolve around the dichotomies of immanence-transcendence, and subject-object. Accordingly, models old and new can be distinguished one from the other by the swing between a focus on the "object" and "subject" of revelation on the one hand, or by a different directionality, that is, either from above down, or from below up, on the other. These differences appear not strictly 'theological' but reveal different philosophical assumptions and conceptions of knowledge, reality and the relationships between them (cf. Ormerod 1990). What appears exceptional about the Process models of Christian philosophy as well as theology, is their opposition to a static metaphysics. Alternatively emphasising the notion of creative becoming, and of the relatedness and interrelatedness of reality, such models permit of change and interaction, and highlight the reciprocal and interactive nature of intercausal connections between the various elements of reality, in ways that linear causal models of explanation cannot accomodate.

A preoccupation with change and causality has also been a feaure of contemporary discourse in the social sciences (cf. Bateson 1979; Watzlawick et al. 1974; Lyddon 1990). Here the search for basic principles and proceses of change have been accompanied by inquiry into the nature of change itself, especially as it underlies developmental and psychotherapeutic frameworks in psychology. Similarly, in studies of religion, despite the efforts of theorists to develop models of faith and religious development, and the seductiveness of these conceptualisations and typologies for practitioners in fields like religious education and religious formation, within the psychology of religion it appears necessary not only for its future development, but for the application of research to applied domains, that researchers go beyond naive observations *that* change happens.

The common concerns of these overlapping discourses are the relationships between experience and knowledge and the construction and development of models of understanding. It is here that hermeneutics and hermeneutical approaches can be situated since these concerns have been central to their projects. In the lacunae between the multiple recurring dichotomies that have characterised metaphysics, epistemology and scientific methodology, 'hermeneutic approaches' provide an alternative to modernist approaches and a radically different starting point for thinking about human existence, knowledge and understanding. In psychology, and in the psychology of religion, 'hermeneutic approaches' not only provide new ways of thinking about meaning and change and significance, and about psychological interpretation and explanation, but have methodological implications for the ways in which scientific enquiry might be carried out. These issues are explored in following sections in terms of their relevance for the psychology of religion.

HERMENEUTICAL APPROACHES

By contrast with its Aristotelian conceptualisation and its biblical applications as a science or theory of literary interpretation, the term 'hermeneutics' is used today in so many different contexts with such different meanings, that it appears no longer to have a generally accepted definition. Currently it represents "not so much a highly honed, well-established theory of understanding or a long-standing, well-developed tradition of philosophy, as it does a family of concerns and critical perspectives" (Wachterhauser 1986, p. 5). Despite differences amongst exponents, however, hermeneutical theories appear to converge around a number of important issues. Central to these is a resistence to the notion that reality can be grasped 'in itself', and in the stance that language and history are always both conditions and limits of human understanding (ibid.). In the work of hermeneutical thinkers such as

Dilthey, Heidegger, Merleau-Ponty, Gadamer, Habermas, Ricoeur, Foucault, Lyotard, and the contemporary advocates of Liberation, Black and Feminist hermeneutics, these themes of history and language continually occur as interacting and distinguishing leitmotifs (cf. Wachterhauser 1986; Thiselton 1992). Also central to hermeneutical theories of understanding, and arising out of the interplay between history and language, is the concept of 'historicity' (with concommitant ontological implications) on the one hand, and an emphasis on the linguistic mediation of understanding on the other. The former notion refers not just to the fact that "we live out our lives *in* time, but that who we *are* is through and through historical" (Wachterhauser 1986, p. 7). The latter notion identifies language as "a principle vehicle by which the past is transported into the present and carried over into the future" (ibid., p. 9). Hermeneutical thinkers also appear less interested in definitive understandings founded on certitude, than on evolving understandings that are consequent on changing historical and linguistic conditions. Underlying this position is a desire and tendency to take change seriously. For the hermeneuticist, interpretation and understanding is not static.

The focus and emphasis on language and history among hermeneutical thinkers, and on the finite, conditioned and situated nature of all understanding, result in a 'holistic' or 'contextualist' theory of meaning. Effectively, "the meaning of any phenomenon or proposition depends on the 'whole' of which it is a 'part'" (ibid., p. 12), that is, it depends on the 'context' in which it is located and in which it has a function. The contextualist theory of meaning has several important implications. First, it implies that "all understanding will necessarily be an understanding relative to the standpoint of the enquirer" (ibid., p. 13). Second, it implies the impossibility of achieving the rationalist ideal of foundationalism, that is, the discovery of 'foundational' truths which would ground the certainty of knowledge. By contrast, hermeneuticists see historicity and linguisticality as the transcendental conditions of all understanding, and, since these are continually changing and shifting, all understanding is "a finite grasp of something from a relative perspective and never a complete or otherwise final vision of things" (ibid.). Accordingly, all understanding involves interpretation, and the attribution of meaning is an interpretative act. What emerges from hermeneutical discourse in general, is the notion of "a historically situated, linguistically mediated, contextualist and antifoundationist theory of understanding" (ibid., p. 16), one that gives priority to interpretation as an inherently human activity.

In addition to these general philosophical and theoretical issues concerning human understanding, of special relevance for the social sciences and for psychology are the methodological alternatives to natural science approaches that hermeneutics poses for researchers. In the context of the social sciences, 'methodological hermeneutics' places emphasis on the understandings and meanings people give to their experience and to their activities in the concrete socio-historical settings of their lives. What is emphasised in such hermeneutical approaches is "the inseparability of fact and value, detail and context, and observation and theory" (Messer et al. 1988, p. xiv). A principle objective of methodological hermeneutics is to understand individuals in their historical and cultural contexts, that is, to understand the intentions, plans, goals and purposes of persons in the total contexts of their lives. These elements of human activity, hermeneuticists point out, are "inescapably enmeshed in a web of meaning" (ibid., p. 8). In this sense the meanings that people attach to their experience and actions "cannot be removed from (their) explanations without irretrievably losing the essence of these phenomena" (ibid., p. 9), that is, of what is essentially human about them. Accordingly, explanation is possible without recourse to laws as in the objectivist model of science. Indeed hermeneuticists have claimed that the contextual description of phenomena may lead to several types of explanation, including as Terwee (1989) summarises, narrative (Gergen 1986), teleological (Taylor 1971), motivational (Peters 1958) and contextual (Terwee 1983) explanations. In that hermeneuticists believe in the possibility of knowledge and understanding outside the realm of formal laws and operations, their aims may be seen to be in direct contrast to objectivist approaches which tend to decontextualise facts and are more interested in generating universal laws concerning human action and behaviour. Within psychology, their claim is that "there is no need for empirical psychology to reduce reality into abstract variables and to search for laws" (Terwee 1989, p. 3). Following on from this, the common tendency in hermeneutical approaches in psychology is to favour and utilise qualitative description, analogical understanding, and narrative modes of exposition, and to see these methods and approaches as 'empirical' in the broad sense of the term, that is as grounded in experience and based on rigorous observation, rather than on speculation or theory most often imposed *a priori*.

IMPLICATIONS FOR PSYCHOLOGY AND FOR THE PSYCHOLOGY OF RELIGION

That the psychology of religion is presently undergoing a major reconsideration is evident. That the bases of research models in the psychology of religion require broadening also appears evident from the historical record. What is not so clear at this time in its development is the manner in which this will be achieved and what the outcomes will be. It seems certain, however, that the psychology of religion will be characterised by a diversity of approaches. Indeed, we have no reason for supposing that either psychology in general, or the psychology of religion in particular, will ever develop one all-inclusive framework within which all psychological phenomena will be understood, even if some strict empiricists still argue a case for a unified psychology (cf. Terwee 1989), and some psychologists of religion continue to speculate about such a possibility (cf. Paloutzian 1983). For those who look at the situation from a hermeneutical perspective, the problem appears entirely different, perhaps non-existent. For as Terwee recently pointed out, "Hermeneuticists don't expect unity. They are familiar with the never-ending debate on the basic questions of philosophy, they will point out the rhetorical nature of human reality, and keep faith in the rational character of the enterprise as long as a dialogue remains possible" (Terwee 1989, p. 32).

This is not entirely to suggest, however, that some psychological orientations and methods might not be more appropriate for specific purposes in the psychology of religion, that is, they might be more appropriately matched to the aspects of 'religion' being investigated, as some researchers have argued (cf. Meissner 1984; Watts & Williams 1988). As has been the case throughout the history of the psychology of religion, it seems certain that researchers will also continue to look to ancillary disciplines particularly philosophy, theology, history, anthropology and sociology, and perhaps increasingly to biology, literature, semiotics and feminist theory for insights and methods. Again, that this collaboration is inevitable is one thing, the ways in which it will be achieved and the possible outcomes are altogether other issues. What is evident in the late Twentieth Century, is that the psychology of religion, like psychology itself, is being forced to look seriously at the relationships between its theoretical conceptualisations and goals and at its methods of enquiry in more consciously critical ways, ways it is argued, that will substantially affect its future. These tasks are both provoked and aided by hermeneutical thinking and 'hermeneutical approaches' to human understanding. Some implications are considered, first of a general nature, then of a more specific kind related to some central issues in the contemporary psychology of religion.

Within psychology and the psychology of religion, the traditional stance has been to portray 'objectivist' and 'hermeneutical approaches' as alternative, more often mutually exclusive, orientations. This divide appears evident in some contemporary perspectives. As a consequence of the 'either-or' position, advocates of 'objectivist approaches' have appeared somewhat defensive with respect to their claims of scientific objectivity and legitimacy. Conversely, hermeneuticists have appeared somewhat reactive in their antifoundationalism and critique of modernist epistemology. It would seem an unfortunate option within the psychology of religion if this position/divide prevailed, and where generative energy was expended in developing more convincing rhetoric, than more illuminating research. Currently, however, several alternatives also present themselves.

One suggests that the two different approaches may simply "be seen as alternatives which may co-exist peacefully" (Terwee 1989, p. 4), or as complementary approaches to the tasks of studying human experience (cf. O'Connor 1983). Hermeneuticists in the psychology of religion actually appear not to deny the possibility of objective research or the place of science-based approaches that concentrate on regularities in human behaviour which may be observed and measured. But while they acknowledge the legitimate character and place of such research, they are cautious about the possibility of reductionism inherent in it, and generally of its inability to deal with internal relations (and with interactive causality) that are as much a part of human experience as is externally observable behaviour. In these areas, 'objectivist approaches' appear limited and inadequate. They simply do not adequately take into account the very complexity of human nature, human events and experience, and the complexity of 'religion' itself, and more often respond by decontextualising persons and abstracting aspects of behaviour or traits that might be regarded as religious, or were linked to religion in particular ways. In consequence, results have often been artifacts of the very ways and means by which psychologists of religion construed their research enterprises, their concepts and their methods. Results were often by-products of the psychologists own limited horizons and epistemic styles, rather than genuine understandings of the meanings and significations of persons in relationships, in families, in faith communities, and larger contexts, and of the interpretative frameworks of understanding (cultural, religious and psychological) which informed those meanings and attributions. To understand the religious significance of a persons 'being-in-the-world', an understanding is required of the unique contexts and patterns of relatedness, the individual's internal processes and styles of knowing, construing, and of relating to their world, their interpretative frameworks and metaphors, their patterns of 'coming-to-terms-with' their experience, and their dispositions towards change. No single model of psychology, or approach, can adequately conceptualise and address the complexities involved. In effect the second position clearly acknowledges the legitimacy of both approaches for specific purposes.

A final position, evident in the stance of researchers influenced by theorists such as Gergen (1982, 1985) and Danziger (1985) is premised on the recognition that even traditional objectivist research is based on implicit interpretations. All research in the social sciences, they point out, even the most exacting, is dependent on fundamental choices that researchers make about, for example, theoretical frameworks, particular subjects or subject groups, methods of research and even modes of analysis of data. In other words, "even the most objective research is dependent on interpretative choices, which are often left implicit" (Terwee 1989, p. 4). Following from this, a general implication for psychologists of religion concerns the explication of their presuppositions and assumptions, their research prejudices and proclivities. In this way the psychology of religion can be carried out on a broad basis, one that recognises the potential complementarity and utility of different approaches on the one hand, and the essentially interpretative nature of science on the other. In consequence, the psychology of religion, like a renewed psychology, would operate "more like a humanities discipline than like a natural science discipline, and the kind of validity its conclusions would have would be more like the valid interpretations of literary expressions than like the valid conclusions of logical and mathematical deductions. Although it would retain a capacity to use the tools of formal science, these tools would be understood to be aids to description rather than means for prediction and control" (Polkinghorne 1990, p. 112).

Another important implication for the psychology of religion arises from the recovery of hermeneutical reasoning as the principal means by which human beings understand reality (cf. Heidegger 1972, 1985), and the expanded notion of rationality that grounds knowledge, not so much in intrasubjective, but in intersubjective interaction (cf. Habermas 1978).

By emphasising the hermeneutic reasoning of subjects among its approaches to human experience and action, the psychology of religion would approach the latter "as the expressions of hermeneutic understandings that are planned and informed according to configured and linguistic schemes, such as narratives and stories" (Polkinghorne 1990, pp. 111-112). The importance, and utility of narratives and stories lies in the fact that they are representations of how people actually view their life experience and life course, their "own knowledge, beliefs, interpretative schemata and principles of action and judgement" (Waele & Harré 1979, p. 177). They are hermeneutic in the sense that they incorporate the phenomenology of persons themselves, the meaning-laden character of social interaction and behaviour, and the contextual nature of knowing. By incorporating human intentions and goals, and the attributions of meaning and significance that people give to their conduct and actions, the narrative mode "allows for the use of connotative as well as denotative meanings in its forms of description and often employs metaphor, similie, and other rhetorical devices" (Woolfolk et al. 1988, p. 9). Theorists such as Ricoeur (1981), Gergen (1988), Schafer (1981) and Spence (1988), emphasise the role of the narrative mode, as distinct from objective or scientific forms, in psychological, especially psychoanalytic understanding. They highlight notions and processes, such as the generative nature of metaphor, of "narrative unfolding" and "narrative revision" which not only account for meaning, coherence and unity in the descriptions of peoples lives, but allow for ways narratives change and develop over time, and of their implications for credibility, continuity and the intelligibility of the relationship between past and present. Other theorists such as Goolishian & Anderson (1987) and Hoffman (1990), working out of a social constructionist perspective, emphasise the systemic connection between language and meaning, meaning that is influenced by history and culture. They point out that meaning is intersubjective, interactional, local in nature and is always changing. Human systems are primarily language- and meaning-generating systems, problem-determined and conflict-solving systems. Not only do people live out their lives in terms of their interpretations and attributions of meanings, they are collaboratively engaged in their constructions and deconstructions, in communicating their meanings, and in processes of mutual influence. Understanding the life, not only of an individual but of a human community, involves not only the presupposition that meaning is intersubjective, but that change takes place through conversation or communicative exchange, and through the solving and re-solving of conflict. While language involves the dialogical creation of intersubjectivity, it is not simply representative. It is "the transformation of experience, and at the same time it transforms what we can experience" (Goolishian & Anderson 1987, p. 532).

Narrative modes and the exploration of metaphor provide rich possibilities and potential for the ongoing development of theory and research in the psychology of religion, and for collaboration across different orientations. For example, they provide a basis for tracing the contours of religious belief and unbelief as life-long processes and outcomes of working through intra- and inter-systemic conflicts over belief in particular historical situations and religious traditions and in cultures which produce particular religious representations and belief dispositions in individuals and in groups (cf. Vergote 1984; Corveleyn & Hutsebaut 1994). Hermeneutical approaches also provide a stimulus, and methodological alternatives to investigating and understanding such processes and outcomes in religious organisations, and in religious traditions other than Christianity. Similarly, the incorporation of hermeneutical phenomenology, metaphor and narrative analysis, have aided the identification of religious psychopatholgy in counselling and psychotherapy, especially in terms of the particularised interplay between intrapsychic, systemic and cultural influences. Much innovative work has been achieved, for example, in understanding the psychological and religious determinants of pathology in people, including historical figures, using clinical and psychohistorical approaches (cf. Vergote 1988; Belzen 1991). Contemporary interest in exploring and detailing the interaction and impact of particular socialisation processes, gender, and sexual and cultural determinants, both as sources and expressions of pathology (cf. O'Connor in press), may be further informed by hermeneutical approaches for the future.

In the areas of moral and religious development, the incorporation of hermeneutic understanding and narrative methods, provide alternatives to those models based on classical stage-based theories and traditional conceptions of development premised on linear causal explanations and invariant, hierarchical sequences. As attractive and aesthetically appealing as they might appear, such approaches are reductive, they fail to deal effectively with the complexities of human and religious development, they overlook the importance of situational and contextual influences, and typically incorporate troublesome value premises (cf. Steenbarger 1991). Conversely, in hermeneutical approaches, development is framed in contextual and relational terms. It is seen as a function of complex person-situation interactions, "with individuals and their contexts reciprocally determining one another in a continuous process of change" (ibid., p. 289). In this sense too, actions and events such as moral judgements and actions, life choices and decisions, cannot be said to have an identity apart from the contexts that constitute them, issues which Day (1991, 1993) has been exploring in interesting ways in relation to identity, voice and gender in religious experience. More importantly, within a hermeneutical and contextual framework, development **is** change and does not necessarily carry the troublesome connotations of growth and maturation. This stance obviates reference to notions like 'religious maturity', conceived of and used in such a variety of ways in the psychology of religion as to render it of doubtful validity, but still one envisaged as the goal of religious development in traditional approaches. While psychologists of religion are challenged to account for those aspects of 'integration' and 'development' in which change is cumulative, change is a central feature of human existence and religious experience. Accordingly, in the processes of reconsideration taking place within the psychology of religion at the present time, researchers need to start with, rather than simply presume, the processes and the content, the contexts and the mechanisms, and the critical determinants of religious change and development in individuals and systems. We need to know, for example: How people and systems change religiously? What changes? How people and systems solve and re-solve (or alternatively, fail to and why?) significant conflicts and questions? What is the direction of the change? — towards belief, or unbelief? What determines the direction? What are the significances and the consequences of the change? — for the individual? — for relationships? — for groups and systems? Are the changes sustainable? Under what conditions? and so on.

If religious experience and religious change were looked at in some of these ways, that is, informed by hermeneutical approaches, it would facilitate an exploration of the meaning of belief and unbelief, and enable an understanding of how and why some people and systems change and others do not. More importantly, it would permit the generative interaction, collaboration and integration of psychoanalytic and social constructionist, cognitive and affective, and developmental and clinical perspectives in the psychology of religion. These would seem to be important issues, projects and possibilities for a contemporary psychology of religion.

REFERENCES

Allport, G.W. (1950). *The individual and his religion.* New York: Macmillan.

Bateson, G. (1979). *Mind and nature.* New York: Dutton.

Batson, C.D., & W.L. Ventis (1982). *The religious experience: a social-psychological perspective.* New York: Oxford University Press.

Belzen, J.A. (1989). *Psychopathologie en religie: ideeën, behandeling en verzorging in de gereformeerde psychiatrie, 1880-1940* [Psychology and religion: theory, treatment and care in reformed psychiatry]. Kampen: Kok.

Belzen, J.A. (1991). *Rümke, religie en godsdienstpsychologie: achtergronder en vooronderstellingen* [Rümke, religion, and psychology of religion: backgrounds and presuppositions]. Kampen: Kok.

Brown, L.B. (1966). The structure of religious belief. *Journal for the Scientific Study of Religion,* 5, 259-272.

Brown, L.B. (1987). *The psychology of religious belief.* London: Academic Press.

Capps, D. (1974). Contemporary psychology of religion: the task of theoretical reconstruction. *Social Research, 41*, 362-383.

Corveleyn, J. & D. Hutsebaut (eds.) (1994). *Belief and unbelief: psychological perspectives.* Amsterdam: Rodopi.

Crowley, H. & S. Himmelweit (eds.) (1992). *Knowing women.* Cambridge: Polity Press.

Danziger, K. (1985). The methodological imperative in psychology. *Philosophy of the Social Sciences, 16,* 241-262.

Day, J.M. (1991). The moral audience: on the narrative mediation of moral 'judgement' and moral 'action'. In: M. Tappan & M. Packer (eds.). *Narrative and storytelling: implications for understanding moral development.* San Francisco: Jossey-Bass.

Day, J.M. (1993). Speaking of belief: language, performance, and narrative in the psychology of religion. *The International Journal for the Psychology of Religion, 3*(4), 213-229.

Dittes, J.E. (1969). Psychology of religion. In: G. Lindzey & E. Aronson (eds.). *Handbook of social psychology. Vol. 5* (pp. 602-659). Boston: Addison-Wesley.

Dulles, A. (1983). *Models of revelation.* Dublin: Gill & Macmillan.

Faulconer, J.E. & R.N. Williams (1990). *Reconsidering psychology: perspectives from continental philosophy.* Pittsburg, Pennsylvania: Duquesne University Press.

Fletcher, F. (1982). *Exploring christian theology's foundations in religious experience.* Melbourne: College of Divinity.

Francis, L.J. (1979). The psychology of religion: beyond revival. *Bulletin of the British Psychological Society, 32*, 141-142.

Gergen, K.J. (1982). *Towards transformation in social knowledge.* New York: Springer.

Gergen, K.J. (1985). The social constructionist movement in modern psychology. *American Psychologist, 40,* 266-275.

Gergen, K.J. (1986). Narrative form and the construction of psychological science. In: T. Sarbin (ed.). *Narrative psychology: the storied nature of human conduct*. New York: Praeger.

Gergen, K.J. (1988). If persons are texts. In: S.B. Messer, L.A. Sass & R.L. Woolfolk (eds.). *Hermeneutics and psychological theory* (pp. 28-51). New Brunswick, NJ: Rutgers University Press.

Giles, H., S. Jones, M. Horton & J. Lay (1975). Towards a more dynamic social psychology of religion. *Bulletin of the British Psychological Society, 28*, 47-50.

Glock, C.Y. (1962). On the study of religious commitment. *Religious Education Research Supplement*,98-110.

Godin, A. (1967). The psychology of religion. *Insight: Quarterly Review of Religion and Mental Health, 5*(4), 1-6.

Godin, A. (1985). *The psychological dynamics of religious experience*. Birmingham, Alabama: Religious Education Press.

Goolishian, H. & H. Anderson (1987). Language, systems and therapy: an evolving idea. *Psychotherapy, 24*, 529-538.

Gorsuch, R.L. & S.G. McFarland (1972). Single vs multiple-item scales for measuring religious values. *Journal for the Scientific Study of Religion, 12*, 53-64.

Grosz, E. (1990). *Jacques Lacan: a feminist introduction*. Sydney: Allen & Unwin.

Grosz, E. (1994). *Volatile bodies: towards a corporeal feminism*. St. Leonards, NSW: Allen & Unwin.

Habermas, J. (1978[2]). *Knowledge and human interests* (transl. J.J. Shapiro). Boston: Beacon Press. (orig. publ. 1968)

Harris, D. (1978). The psychology of religion: run silent, run deep? *Bulletin of the British Psychological Society, 31*, 130-131.

Heidegger, M. (1972). *On time and being* (transl. J. Stambargh). New York: Harper & Row. (orig. publ. 1969)

Heidegger, M. (1985). *History and the concept of time: prolegomena* (transl. T. Kisiel). Bloomington: Indiana University Press. (orig. publ. 1979)

Hoffman, L. (1990). Constructing realities: an art of lenses. *Family Process, 29*(1), 1-12.

Homans, P. (1967). Towards a psychology of religion: by way of Freud and Tillich. *Zygon, 2*, 97-119.

Hood, R.W. (1986). Mysticism in the psychology of religion. *Journal of Psychology and Christianity, 5* (2), 46-49.

Hunsberger, B. (1980). Problems and promise in the psychology of religion: an emerging social psychology of religion? *Canadian Journal of Behavioral Science, 12*, 64-77.

James, W. (1902). *The varieties of religious experience*. Glasgow: Collins Fountain Books, 1960.

Jones, J.W. (1982). The delicate dialectic: religion and psychology in the modern world. *Cross Currents, 32*, 143-153.

Lans, J. van der (1977). Religious experience. an argument for a multi-disciplinary approach. *The Annual Review of the Social Sciences of Religion, 1*, 133-143.

Lans, J. van der (1986). Two opposed viewpoints concerning the object of the psychology of religion: introductory statements to the plenary debate. In: J.A.

van Belzen & J.M. van der Lans (eds.). *Current issues in the psychology of religion: proceedings of the third symposium on the psychology of religion in Europe* (pp. 76-81). Amsterdam: Rodopi.

Loewenthal, K. (1975). Psychology and religion: comments on Giles, Jones, Horton and Lay. *Bulletin of the British Psychological Society, 28*, 349-350.

Lyddon, W.J. (1990). First- and second-order change: implications for rationalist and constructivist cognitive therapies. *Journal of Counselling and Development, 69*, 122-127.

Meissner, W.W. (1984). *Psychoanalysis and religious experience.* New Haven: Yale University Press.

Merleau-Ponty, M. (1962). *The phenomenology of perception* (transl. C. Smith). London: Routledge & Kegan Paul. (orig. publ. 1945)

Merleau-Ponty, M. (1963). *The primacy of perception.* Evanston: Northwestern University Press.

Messer, S.B., L.A. Sass & R.L. Woolfolk (1988). *Hermeneutics and psychological theory: interpretive perspectives on personality, psychotherapy and psychopathology.* New Brunswick: Rutgers University Press.

Moore, J.A. (1993). *Science as a way of knowing: the foundations of modern biology.* Cambridge, Mass.: Harvard University Press.

Morris, J.E. (1980). Humanistic psychology of religion: steps towards reconciliation. *Journal of Religion and Health, 19*, 92-102.

O'Collins, G. (1977). Theology and experience. *Irish Theological Quarterly, 44* (4), 279-301.

O'Connor, K.V. (1983). *The structure of religion: a repertory grid approach.* (Unpublished Doctoral Thesis, University of New South Wales, Australia).

O'Connor, K.V. (in press). Religion and mental health: a review of Antoine Vergote's approach in *Guilt and Desire. The International Journal for the Psychology of Religion.*

Olds, L.E. (1992). *Metaphors of interrelatedness: towards a systems theory of psychology.* New York: State University of New York Press.

Ormerod, N. (1990). *Introducing contemporary theologies.* Newtown: Dwyer.

Palma, R.J. (1978). The prospects for a normative psychology of religion: G.W. Allport as a paradigm. *Journal of Psychology and Theology, 6*, 110-122.

Paloutzian, R.F. (1983). *Invitation to the psychology of religion.* Glenview, Ill.: Scott, Foresman & Co.

Peters, R.S. (1958). *The concept of motivation.* London: Routledge & Kegan Paul.

Polkinghorne, D.P. (1990). Psychology after philosophy. In: J.E. Faulconer & R.N. Williams *Reconsidering psychology: perspectives from continental philosophy* (pp. 92-115). Pittsburgh, Pennsylvania: Duquesne University Press.

Pruyser, P.W. (1987). Where do we go from here? Scenarios for the psychology of religion. *Journal for the Scientific Study of Religion, 26* (2), 173-181.

Ricoeur, P. (1960). The symbol: food for thought. *Philosophy Today, 3/4* (4), 196-207.

Ricoeur, P. (1981). *Hermeneutics and the human sciences* (ed. and trans. J.B. Thompson). Cambridge: Cambridge University Press.

Rokeach, M. (1969). Value systems in religion. *Review of Religious Resarch, 11* (1), 3-23.

Royce, J.R. (1962). Psychology, existentialism and religion. *Journal of General Psychology, 66*, 3-16.

Royce, J.R. (1967). Metaphoric knowledge and humanistic psychology. In: J.F.T. Bugental (ed.). *Challenges of humanistic psychology* (pp. 21-28). New York: McGraw-Hill.

Schafer, R. (1981). *Narrative actions in psychoanalysis.* Worcester, Mass.: Clark University Press.

Schrag, C.O. (1990). Explanation and understanding in the science of human behaviour. In: J.E. Faulconer & R.N. Wiliams. *Reconsidering psychology: perspectives from continental philosophy* (pp. 61-74). Pittsburg, Pennsylvania: Duquesne University Press.

Smart, N. (1969). *The religious experience of mankind.* New York: Scribner.

Spence, D.P. (1988). Tough and tender-minder hermeneutics. In: S.B. Messer, L.A. Sass & R.L. Woolfolk (eds.). *Hermeneutics and psychological theory: interpretive perspectives on personality, psychotherapy, and psychopathology.* New Brunswick: Rutgers University Press.

Spilka, B. (1976). "The compleat person": some theoretical views and research findings for a theological-psychology of religion. *Journal of Psychology and Theology, 4*, 15-24.

Spilka, B., P. Shaver & L. Kirkpatrick (1985). A general attributional theory for the psychology of religion. *Journal for the Scientific Study of Religion, 24*, 1-18.

Steenbarger, B.N. (1991). All the world is not a stage: emerging contextualist themes in counselling and development. *Journal of Counseling and Development, 70*, 288-296.

Strunk, O. (1957). A redefinition of the psychology of religion. *Psychological Reports, 3*, 138.

Strunk, O. (1970). Humanistic religious psychology: a new chapter in the psychology of religion. *Journal of Pastoral Care, 24*, 90-97.

Taylor, C. (1971). Interpretation and the sciences of man. *Review of Metaphysics, 25*, 3-51.

Terwee, S.J.S. (1989). *Hermeneutics in psychology and psychoanalysis.* Amsterdam: Centrale Drukkerij Universiteit van Amsterdam.

Thiselton, A.C. (1992). *New horizons in hermeneutics.* London: Harper Collins.

Thouless, R.H. (1971[3]). *An introduction to the psychology of religion.* Cambridge: Cambridge University Press.

Vergote, A. (1960). The symbol. *Philosophy Today, 4*, 53-72.

Vergote, A. (1969). *The religious man* (transl. M.-B. Said). Dublin: Gill & Macmillan. (orig. publ. 1966)

Vergote, A. (1984). *Religie, geloof en ongeloof: psychologische studie.* Antwerpen: Nederlandsche Boekhandel. [Transl.: *Religion, belief, unbelief: a psychological study*. Amsterdam: Rodopi, 1996]

Vergote, A. (1985). Experience of the divine, experience of God. In: A.T. de Nicolas & E. Moursopoulos. *God: experience or origin?* (pp. 77-90). New York: Paragon House.

Vergote, A. (1986). Two opposed viewpoints concerning the object of the psychology of religion: introductory statements to the plenary debate. In: J.A.

van Belzen & J.M. van der Lans (eds.). *Current issues in the psychology of religion: proceedings of the third symposium on the psychology of religion in Europe* (pp. 67-75). Amsterdam: Rodopi.

Vergote, A. (1988). *Guilt and desire: religious attitudes and their pathological derivatives* (transl. M.H. Wood). New Haven, CT: Yale University Press. (orig. publ. 1978)

Vergote, A. (1993). What the psychology of religion is and what it is not. *The International Journal for the Psychology of Religion, 3* (2), 73-86.

Wachterhauser, B.R. (ed.) (1986). *Hermeneutics and modern philosophy.* Albany: State University of New York Press.

Waele, J.-P. de & R. Harré (1979). Autobiography as a psychological method. In: G.P. Ginsburg (ed.). *Emerging strategies in social psychological research* (pp. 177-224). New York: Wiley.

Watts, F. & M. Williams (1988). *The psychology of religious knowing.* Cambridge, NY: Cambridge University Press.

Watzlawick, P., J.H. Weakland & R. Fusch,(1974). *Change: principles of problem resolution.* New York: Norton.

Woolfolk, R.L., L.A. Sass & S.B. Messer (1988). Introduction to hermeneutics. In: S.B. Messer, L.A. Sass & R.L. Woolfolk (eds.). *Hermeneutics and psychological theory: interpretive perspectives on personality, psychotherapy, and psychopathology* (pp. 2-26). New Brunswick: Rutgers University Press.

Cultural Psychology of Religion Synchronic and Diachronic

J.A. Belzen
University of Amsterdam (The Netherlands)

Psychology in the Plural

Since modern psychology is a very pluralistic enterprise, let us just briefly consider what kind of psychology we could rely on to come up with relevant conclusions when studying religion. The fact that religiosity is always diverse — and sometimes highly diverse in terms of time, culture and individual — can facilitate an initial screening of the many divergent psychologies and mini-psychologies. In theoretical psychology, or in the philosophy of psychology, the diverse domain of theory formation in psychology is usually subdivided into two or three groups. People refer to mechanistic, organistic and hermeneutic theories which exhibit successive levels of mounting complexity as a result of the increasing historico-cultural determinacy of the object and results of the research (Sanders & Rappard 1982; Strien 1993). While in mechanistic and organistic theories the tendency is to disregard the historico-cultural determinacy of human reality as much as possible, in hermeneutic psychologies this is deemed both impossible and undesirable. Therefore, hermeneutical psychology seems the obvious ally in studying religiosity.

These and other philosophy-of-science divisions of the different psychologies stem from an older but not entirely dated bipartite division. The distinction between the natural and the human sciences, a distinction put forward around 1900, is admittedly no longer adhered to today in its rigorous form: the related distinctions between explaining and understanding, between nomothetic and idiographic research, could no longer be very strictly maintained. Virtually nobody today, for example, professes belief in the value-free character of the natural sciences. Still, in these terms there was and is a reference to a problem which played a large role in psychology, in the past as much as in the present. The question is: must psychology be conceived and practiced in the manner of the natural sciences or should it study its object in the manner of the human sciences?

Wilhelm Wundt, who is regarded as the founder of the natural-scientific approach in psychology, stated in his day that psychology would have to be plural. Psychology can only turn to experiment as an auxiliary method if it seeks to examine the "elementary psychic processes"; but if it seeks to study the higher psychic processes it has to consult other sciences for orientation (Wundt 1900-1909). His own suggestion was that psychologists should consult history. Since Wundt's days, psychology has been fractured by a fault line which no one wants and which any number of theoreticians have repeatedly tried to bridge. Perhaps it must even be acknowledged that much theory formation in psychology occurs today at Western universities, outside of the so-called psychological institutes. In striving for scientific objectivity and prestige, mainstream psychology has mostly concentrated on the one pole of Wundt's research program: it naturalizes its object of study; its *modus operandi* is marked by de-subjectivization and de-contextualization. When orienting themselves according to this mainstream approach, large parts of psychology of religion run the same risk (cf. e.g. Brown 1987).

PSYCHOLOGY'S OBJECT: A PRODUCT OF CULTURE

Religiosity, as so many aspects characteristic of human beings, is a culturally constituted phenomenon. Decades ago psychologists like Vygotsky (1978) had already pointed out that the higher psychic functions have a double origin: first a cultural and, after appropriation, an individual one. All concrete phenomena belonging to the reality of the psychic are determined by cultural encadration. All knowing, experiencing, action, wanting and fantasizing can only be grasped in light of the individual's historico-cultural situatedness and mediation. Emotions, for example, are not irrational eruptions of purely natural and unavoidable reactions. In contrast to what is currently thought, they turn out rather to be characterized by convictions, evaluations, and wishes, whose content is not given by nature but determined by systems of convictions, values and mores of particular cultural communities. Emotions are socio-culturally determined patterns of experience and expression which are acquired and then expressed in specific social situations (Armon-Jones 1986). The various behavioral, physiological and cognitive reactions which belong to the syndrome which is a specific emotion are not necessarily emotional in and of themselves. Ultimately emotions are based on the same physiological processes which underlie all other behavior. But what makes a syndrome specifically emotional is the way in which the different responses are organized and interpreted within a certain context. To put it succinctly, emotions conform to pre-existing cultural paradigms: they are socially-construed syndromes, temporary social roles, which encompass an assessment of the situation by the person in question and are interpreted as passions instead of actions (Averill 1985). Further, in the course of the so-called civilization process (Elias 1978-82) which can be described for Western society, certain emotions, it turns out, are not only regulated but even created (Foucault 1977). Human subjectivity in its totality is always subject to specific historico-cultural conditions: there is no meaningful conduct that is not culturally constituted. It has to be understood in light of cultural contexts; and this not to find out how the postulated constant articulates itself again and again in different contexts ('cultural variation') but to trace how a specific cultural context made the specific action, knowledge and experience possible. Accordingly, psychology of religion, like history, anthropology and linguistics, is an interpretive science: it focuses its attention on meanings and searches out the rules according to which meaning originates in a cultural situation.

The Cultural-Psychological Approach

A psychology which seeks to study something as specifically human and entirely culturally determined as religiosity will therefore be well-advised to orient itself towards various hermeneutical psychologies (cf. e.g. Messer et al. 1988; Terwee 1989; Widdershoven & Boer 1990; Mooij & Widdershoven 1992) and consult recent developments like narrative theory, which are being used today to help explore the relation between culture and the human subject. Narrative psychology, for example, directs one's attention to the role which available leading stories play in the construction and articulation of identity. It tells us that humans think and act, feel and fantasize in accordance with narrative structures and shape their lives in conformity with stories (cf. Sarbin 1986). In this connection some psychologists, inspired or not inspired by Ricoeur (1992), go so far as to view the "self" — the object of much discussion in anthropology and psychology — as a "story" (Schafer 1983).

It goes without saying that we are here not, out of reaction, interested in denying that physical or psychophysical factors play a role in human subjectivity. On the contrary, in the historical-hermeneutic school of psychology now evolving there is plenty of room for the body which is a human being. In line with such divergent seminal thinkers as Portmann (1951), Gehlen (1961), but also Lacan (1966), the physical is here conceived as a complex of potentialities which need a complement of cultural care and regulation in order to become the basic material from which the psychic can originate. Further, it is pointed out in this psychology — along the lines of Merleau-Ponty (1962) — that the body, belonging as it does to a certain life form and shaped by its practices, possesses an intentionality of its own (Merwe & Voestermans 1995). One must not underestimate the cultural-psychological perspective referred to here; it is still tricky enough to think through its implications. It cuts across numerous ideas which in the last few centuries have come to be common to Western thought.

Its point is not only that human action, cognition and experience have consistently assumed variable forms in different cultures. Its viewpoint is more radical than that. It stresses that human subjectivity *as a whole* is culturally constituted. Somewhat aphoristically this perspective can be found articulated in the work of Clifford Geertz, an anthropologist who has had considerable influence in the psychology of culture: "There is no such thing as human nature independent of culture" (1973, p. 49). The implications of this position are *(inter alia)* that psychology must attempt, much more forcefully than it has up until now, to recover and understand how by their culture human beings have become who they are. A psychology which does not study the human being on the analogy of a mechanism but seeks to understand the almost infinite plasticity of human subjectivity, inquires into the effects of culture. It seeks to find out how a given culture incarnates itself, how it takes possession of the subject and shapes his (second; Boer 1983) nature.

In other words, whenever a person wishes to undertake a psychological study of a specific religiosity, he will have to re-situate it in a specific (sub-)cultural segment which, by a certain mode of treatment, i.e. by the way it speaks to and treats people, passes down the frameworks for individual experience and expression. In contrast to what is usually done in the natural sciences, the investigator, if he or she wants to make a psychological study of any form of meaningful life whatever, should as much as possible approach the subjects in their ordinary everyday reality (Voestermans 1992). In contemporary research, common techniques like experiments, tests and questionnaires are ill-adapted to this reality and are abandoned in the psychology of culture in favor of so-called 'experience-friendly' methods like the interview, participatory observation and self-confrontation. Cultural psychology argues for modesty: "the search for stable patterns and long-range predictions in human psychological phenomena would probably not be the proper goal of the science. The role of the psychologist as a knowledgeable person would be to help in understanding, reading and interpreting behavioral episodes within the culture, and informing people about the potentialities of action within the range of possibilities in the culture. Thus the research would be a co-participant in the joint construction of reality, rather than an authority to control and predict the future of a person" (Misra & Gergen 1993, p. 237; Hermans & Kempen 1993).

THE HISTORICITY OF HUMAN SUBJECTIVITY

Cultural psychology consists in a synchronic and a diachronic variant. The synchronic variant, studying primarily contemporary subjects, has a natural ally in disciplines like sociology and anthropology. Especially when dealing with non-Western subjects or when making comparisons between subjects from various countries, it is sometimes, rather incorrectly, referred to as "cross-cultural psychology" (Berry 1992; Bouvy 1994; Grad et al. 1996; Moghaddam et al. 1993): the latter approach usually takes existing Western psychological constructs and tests for their presence in other cultures, while cultural psychology is inclined to ground theoretical categories in terms of the specific cultures from which they are derived (Much 1995). Leaving this synchronic variant aside for now, I want to try to elaborate a little more on the preceding thoughts with the aid of the much less known diachronic variant of cultural psychology. But first we should realize that the historical variant is a logical necessity because of the *historical nature* of psychology's object.

In striving to understand religiosity, a hermeneutical psychology always meets the subject at an intersection of corporeality and a complex of cultural meaning. Usually it encounters a human being at a time when the latter has already completed a certain stage in her life's journey. When it asks the traveler about her identity, the person she is, it inquires into her history, into the maturation process the individual has undergone to become the person she is. The relation between a human being and (her) culture, after all, is not a natural but a historical one. A hermeneutical psychology is continually confronted by history, since, on the one hand, a human being is shaped by a culture which has reached a certain (historical) stage of its development and, on the other, every individual is the outcome of a process of becoming, of a history within a particular historico-cultural context. To function as a human being and not to become a Kaspar Hauser, the individual after all must more or less harmoniously fit herself into a specific culture. In the case of the study of contemporary subjects it is also of lasting importance to conceptualize this historical character of the relation between culture and the body which every human being is.

In so doing one can take either the culture or the individual body as starting point. Thus structuralist-inspired psychologists of culture have tried to grasp the way in which the culture takes possession of the individual subject. In the history which every human being undergoes, socialization is set in motion by social definitions which existed prior to the birth of the individual and which assign him his place in the human cultural order into which the subject, saying "I", will later insert himself. These definitions are continued, strengthened and confirmed by the corresponding (social) treatment of the individual and are transformed into a quasi-naturalness. The "habitus" (Bourdieu 1990), which thus originates as a product of history, starts then producing its own history and that in conformity with the schemes engendered by history. In that way it insures the active presence of past experiences which have crystallized in the form of schemes of perception, thought and action. The past, thus present, guarantees that a person becomes the bearer of the culture which produced him.

Psychoanalysis is of course another and perhaps more familiar example of conceptualizing the relation between culture and individual which takes its starting point in the body. Its reflection on the vicissitudes of the 'drive', this boundary concept between soul and body, offers important contributions by fixing its attention on the very earliest experiences of the human child and by reminding that subjectivity, in all of its manifestations, also inevitably bears the marks of vulnerable moments in the individual's life history, of a relation to dynamic tension implying the possibility of failures which may later, in an extreme way, come to expression in the various forms of pathology known to psychology. With respect to every act and experience, therefore, one can and must raise the question concerning the place it occupies in the individual life story, in the life history of the person in question (Jütteman & Thomae 1987). Accordingly, in psychotherapy and other practical psychologies which, in contrast to academic psychology, were never devoid of hermeneutic inclination (Strien 1986), the authors usually understand by 'meaning' the particular significance which can only be grasped from within the history of the individual. Thus Freud defines the meaning of a psychic process as "the intention it serves and its position in a psychical continuity. For most of our researches we can replace 'sense' by 'intention' or 'purpose'" (1917, p. 40), that is to say, by terms which convey an intentional connection.

THE DOUBLE PERSPECTIVE: HISTORICAL *AND* CULTURAL

In such a historicizing approach, whether one proceeds from the culture or the body is a difference in accent. Ultimately psychology's aim is to understand something that has taken shape at the point of intersection between the two. For a psychological understanding of meaningful action and experience it is therefore necessary to apply a double perspective: the perspective of the meaning shared by a cultural community in general as well as that of the personal meaning which can only be understood in terms of the individual life history. Even a deviation, understood as symbol (in the sense of Lorenzer 1977), can thus be interrogated as to its meaning, since in deviating from the surrounding order it can be a manifestation of the underlying psychic conflict. I deliberately say "can be" since not every deviation points to psychopathology and, on the other hand, the (apparent) absence of conflict need not indicate psychic health. Psychology cannot say a thing in advance about a person's health and sickness and will only make statements about them after it has examined a concrete individual against the background of his culture and life history.

To a very large extent, therefore, psychology of religion is a historicizing science. Hermeneutical psychologists and historians also frequently resemble each other in the concrete ways in which they operate: they favor attending to the concrete and specific, the individual and qualitative aspects of the person. In his exposition of the so-called "indication paradigm" Ginzburg (1989) puts both groups of practitioners of the *ars individualisandi* in the same category as Sherlock Holmes. Psychology and history, however, not only follow a frequently similar way of working but may also go hand-in-hand materially. On some of the ways in which this may happen I want to comment in just a moment.

VARIANTS OF A DIACHRONIC CULTURAL PSYCHOLOGY

I will set aside possible combinations like 'a psychology of history' and 'the history of psychology'. As can be surmised by now, I consider a psychology of history problematic: psychology can no more make history as such the object of investigation than it can explain religion or culture. Psychology does not explain history; the reverse, rather, is true: history may account for (rise and decline of varieties of) psychology. Obviously, the historiography of psychology is a natural place of encounter between psychology and historical science. It has, however, grown into a special discipline all by itself, with its own organizations and publications.

Let us rather turn briefly now to (a) historical psychology, (b) psychological historiography, and (c) so-called psychohistory, and consider their relation to psychology of religion. All three can be regarded as belonging to a continuum between psychology and history or to an area where psychology and historiography overlap. Historical psychology is still mainly the business of psychologists; psychological historiography the business of historians; while psychohistory is a kind of natural intersection between the two.

(a) historical psychology

Historical psychology is not 'dated' psychology: that kind of psychology belongs to the history of psychology. Historical psychology is a modern psychology: it comes into being when the cultural-psychological perspective is expanded diachronically, not synchronically or cross-culturally; it is a natural part of cultural psychology. Just as subjects differ to the extent that they live in different cultures, so they also differ in their subjectivity in each successive historic era of the same culture. But in psychology people in general still consistently proceed on the assumption that 'in essence' human beings were always and everywhere the same. In the meantime a sufficient number of studies have been made which invalidate this assumption. In historical psychology it has been adequately demonstrated that even if one remains within a single culture, the phenomena which psychologists so eagerly study — phenomena like cognition, emotion, personality, identity, mental illness — are historically determined (Peeters 1974, 1993; Hutschemaekers 1990). And this is true not only in the trivial sense that in earlier times people thought, desired or felt somewhat differently than they do today, but in the more radical sense that in earlier times people thought, desired or felt in a different way. The course of life, cognitive development, the memory — each of them was different and used to function differently in earlier times (Olbrich 1986; Ingleby & Nossent 1986; Huls 1986; Sonntag 1990; Carruthers 1990). For a psychology which considers itself scientific to the degree that it attempts to uncover unchanging laws, this is hard to swallow. For this psychology, culturally and historically determined variability in human conduct and experience is actually only disturbing, an error in measurement for which compensation must be made in the analysis. It is fearful of the conclusion which Gergen (1973) drew from these considerations for his own discipline: social psychology, according to him, is the historiography of the present, the recording of how a thing is at the moment of investigation. The facts with which it operates are historical and do not permit generalization. Historical psychology for that reason calls for relativization and modesty: it raises the question whether present-day psychological concepts can be applied at all in a context different from that in which they were developed.

It may be considered characteristic for historical psychology that it has its starting point in present-day psychology. It has a mild as well as a critical variant: the mild variant believes it is able, by means of historical research, to arrive at an additional validation of (present-day) psychological knowledge (Runyan 1982, 1988). The critical variant, in contrast, continually points to the limited validity of such knowledge. Like a bug in the fur of established psychology, it keeps alive the critical awareness that as an academic enterprise psychology is just as much a historical product as the object for which it wants to be the science. Its point of entry reminds the historiography of psychology that it describes the construction of psychological objects, not the history of discoveries.

(b) psychological historiography

Clearly related, of course, but still different is the somewhat older psychological historiography or the history of mentalities (Vovelle 1990). Being as a rule but little concerned with the systematics and nomenclature of any twentieth-century psychology whatsoever, historians such as Huizinga, Ariès, Fèbvre, Le Roy Ladurie and Le Goff focus their attention on psychologically relevant phenomena such as anxiety, hate, smell, hearing and visual perception (Anders 1956; Ariès & Béjin 1985; Corbin 1986; Delumeau 1990; Kamper 1977; Lowe 1982; Schivelbusch 1979). They describe and analyse how in earlier times these phenomena were different both in form and in content, and how they have changed over the course of centuries. If these authors were read more by psychologists, they would see in them constant reminders of the 'hodiecentric' character of present-day psychological investigation. This psychological historiography has been the primary source of inspiration of historical psychology. Since the psychology of religion is a part of (more) general psychology, it is understandable that there exists no historical psychology of religion: the theoretical and methodological instrumentarium of the psychology of religion, after all, is that of psychology in general. In contrast to what has often been implied by older psychologists of religion (e.g. Rümke 1952), who conceptualized religiosity by analogy with a natural or biological drive, there are no specifically religious psychic functions, functions either religious in themselves or only found in religious people; consequently, no specifically psychology-of-religion concepts or methods exist. (By calling his recent volume a *dictionary*, Dunde (1993) therefore runs the risk of creating an anachronistic misunderstanding.) On the other hand, a historiography dealing with the same themes as psychology of religion does in fact exist, though it hardly refers to our discipline: fine studies have been published on the psycho(patho)logical aspects of spiritual and religious themes. Just think of such works as those of Fèbvre (1942), Keith Thomas (1971), King (1983), Cohen (1986), Demos (1988), Rubin (1994).

(c) psychohistory

Concerning psychohistory, the third and most interdisciplinary form of a possible relation between psychology and history to which I wish to draw attention, there are a number of prejudices and misunderstandings, not the least place of course due to the existence of bad examples and to the pretentious conduct of someone like DeMause (1982). To focus on these examples in forming a judgment seems unfair. Let me try to correct a couple of these misunderstandings. In general, psychohistory can be defined as the systematic use of scientific psychology in historical investigation. In all its unpretentiousness this definition nevertheless does call attention to a potential advantage of the psychohistorical *modus operandi*: one who turns to the past, after all, always uses one or another psychology, and certainly when reviewing themes relevant to this field. Now, instead of doing this altogether uncritically, or mindlessly applying the homegrown common sense one happens to have inherited, psychohistory attempts to follow a carefully thought-out procedure. Though not a guarantee of infallibility, such a considered attempt is nevertheless preferable over unreasoned psychological dilettantism. In the same way that disciplines such as sociology or economics can be integrated with historiography (cf., e.g., Burke 1980) and yield an additional perspective, so can this also be done with psychology. Here it is also the case that psychohistory and the psychology of religion share a similar fate: they are accused of reductionism, of explaining history or religion in terms of psychology. This representation of the state of affairs is obviously incorrect; it has already been sufficiently refuted above. Contrary to what could still recently be stated in a professional journal of psychology, psychohistory is *not* "the most extreme representative of the assumption that much of culture is shaped by the psychodynamics of the individual psyche" (Gadlin 1992, p. 888). Far from being reductionistic, psychohistory, as presented for example by Erikson, may be considered exemplary in its attempt to recognize the individual intertwinement of an instinct-driven body and the symbolic order. A good psychobiography requires triple-entry bookkeeping. The individual under study needs to be understood on three complementary levels: a) the body and all that constitutionally comes with it; b) the ego as idiosyncratic synthesis of experience, and c) the social structures within which the individual life history is realized and whose ethos and mythos shape the subject and, in the case of exceptional individuals, is shaped by the subject.

SOME FURTHER REFLECTIONS ON THE PSYCHOHISTORICAL APPROACH

Psychohistory, for that matter, in no way needs to limit itself to the genre of biography and to the utilization of psychoanalysis. These are additional misunderstandings which need to be rejected. Although the lion's share of psychohistorical production is still made up of biographical and psychoanalytical studies, there is no logical necessity for this. It does have to be recognized, however, that psychoanalysis in its reflection on the interpretive process in therapy offers a valuable instrumentarium for helping in the analysis of the interpretive work of the historian (Röckelein 1993). The number of studies in which an attempt is made to conduct other than exclusively biographical investigations with diverse forms of psychology is growing. In two ways, heuristically as well as hermeneutically, one can also employ, say, personality theory, social or developmental psychology, in historical investigation. The views developed in these branches of psychology can draw the attention of historians to certain themes which would probably otherwise remain un- or underexposed. In the second place, psychological theories or viewpoints may furnish additional possibilities for the interpretation of sources. I will be the last to sing the praises of the attainments of academic psychology, but it seems hard to deny that it has produced some knowledge of motivation and emotion, social interaction, decision behavior, human development and personal life stories which, for all their limitations, exceed the level of common sense. To deny that these and many other psychologically namable processes have played a role in the lifes of past individuals, groups, organizations, institutions, also *in religiosis*, would seem a rejection of historical science as such because the latter, also being only partial, adds no knowledge either to what we already know about the past.

On the other hand, we must indeed practice modesty and not forget Fèbvre's critical question: what could a psychology developed in and in response to the twentieth century contribute to the study of the past? As pointed out earlier, this is a question which historical-psychological research raises. Between psychohistory and historical psychology, both of which assume the historicity of the psyche, there exists therefore a tension-filled relation of which psychohistory can in any case take account and from which it can profit. Historical psychology can keep psychohistory continuously alert to the boundaries of its competence. Just as psychohistory can keep a historian who is interested in psychic phenomena from an unreasoned application or assumption about an equally anachronistic common sense psychology, so historical psychology can keep psychohistory from flatly applying present-day psychological categories — categories which though scientifically developed are nevertheless often of only limited validity — to phenomena in the past. Historical psychology prompts hermeneutic reflection. The history of human consciousness, furthermore, remains important for psychohistory by calling attention to things such as folk culture and ordinary people. Why, after all, would psychology of religion study only the lives of the mighty and noble? Are there so many mystics among them? From the perspective of spiritual development, for example, those who remain under psychiatric care could be as interesting as or even more interesting than the inhabitants of an equally total institution (Goffman 1961) like a monastery. On the other hand, experiences and actions of many who are not known as patients but as 'spiritual heroes' are often so bizarre that they are likely to raise the difficult but intriguing question of the demarcation between mental health and pathology. What to think, for example, of the bolemia that sometimes came over Ramakrisna, of Francis of Assisi's desire to kiss leprosy patients, of Margarete Ebner, who breast-fed a statue of Jesus, or of 'reclusen', medieval women who had themselves walled in for many years? Devoted adoration seems just as misplaced as premature pathologizing. It will be more instructive to try to understand something of the dynamic relations between life history, religious culture and spiritual experience.

PSYCHOHISTORY AS AN EXAMPLE OF INTERDISCIPLINARY RESEARCH

Numerous attempts at exploring religiosity have already been made from a psychohistorical viewpoint. There is even striking historical kinship between the psychology of religion and psychohistory. Stanley Hall, one of the founders of the present-day psychology of religion and founder and publisher of the first professional journal in this field, attempted to make a psychohistorical study of Jesus Christ, an attempt which did not gain a following (Hall 1917). Usually, however, psychohistory is viewed as having started with Freud's study of Leonardo da Vinci (1910). And it is well-known that Freud is also considered the patriarch of the psychoanalytic psychology of religion. The era of steady growth in contemporary professional psychohistory begins with a study which at the same time became one of the most popular classics in the psychology of religion, viz. *Young man Luther* by Erik Erikson in 1958. It would seem that there is some sort of psychic kinship between the psychology of religion and psychohistory: both great and small in the psychology of religion have made psychohistorical contributions. Just consider Pfister's studies on Zinzendorf (1910) and Sadhu Sundar Singh

(1926); the work of Sundén (1966, 1987); his pupils (Källstad 1974, 1978, 1987; Wikström 1980; Holm 1987) and many other Scandinavian colleagues (Geels 1980; Åkerberg 1975, 1978, 1985; Hoffman 1982); Vergote's (1988) study of Teresa of Avila and other mystics, Meissner (1992) on Ignatius, and the many psychological studies of Augustine (Capps & Dittes 1990). As examples of the psychohistorical psychology of religion which does not confine itself to the study of one individual we can mention Freud (1913), Pfister (1948) and Carroll (1986), while Festinger et al. (1956) offer an example that also employed something other than a psychoanalytic instrumentarium.

I do not suggest that each of these examples can claim paradigmatic status in a kuhnian sense (Kuhn 1962). Nor do I want to suggest that contemporary cultural psychology, in both its synchronic and diachronic variants, is a modern legitimation of this kind of previous work. I would like to suggest, however, that theories and methodology as they are developed in cultural psychology will presently be an impetus to any psychology that strives for studying an evasive and variable phenomenon like religiosity. Acknowledging that psychological phenomena are developing products of historico-cultural constitution is something else and something more than combining psychology with an interest in religious phenomena from other times and places (as, e.g., with Jung (1938) who — quite the opposite of cultural psychology — searched for the same psychological archetypes in various places). It is also different from carrying a psychological interest into the study of the history of religions, as with admittedly great authors such as Van der Leeuw (1926), Söderblom (1908) or Andrae (1932). Some kind of progress could be achieved if psychologists of religion would no longer just confine themselves to commenting (from their 'armchairs', as it were) on research previously conducted — by others — as in most of the studies just mentioned. They should rather turn into interdisciplinary workers. Collaborating with anthropologists, synchronic cultural psychologists of religion might, for example, modify their research instruments in order to apply them to or develop alternative ones for other than western populations (cf. Herdt & Stephen 1989). Evidently, such a procedure is impossible for a diachronic cultural psychology of religion. Here, as pointed out earlier, psychological questioning and hermeneutics can be combined with thorough empirical historical research of primary sources (e.g. Geels 1989; Meissner 1992). Both these suggestions are but examples, yet they would present a step forward in comparison with the 'mere' (and all too easily forgotten) awareness that all data and interpretation in psychology of religion are limited by time and culture. Both would be expressions of seriously trying to take into account that the objects of psychology (of religion) are historical and cultural phenomena that require new approaches in psychological research.

Thus taking up Wundt's seminal suggestion in a new and reflected way, psychology of religion will enlarge its foundations, competence and applicability, and will make a contribution to a truly human scientific psychology. Moreover, after so many complaints that much of academic psychology in its analytical-statistical branch is 'boring', this strategy will make its results relevant and interesting to an even broader audience of scholars and general public. Quite a number of psychologists of religion have been on this track already: they usually are to some extent aware of the cultural and historical make-up of the phenomena they investigate — probably more than psychologists in general and perhaps precisely because of their often being located in an academic department with historians, anthropologists and philosophers. To them, contemporary historico-cultural psychology is an encouragement. To other psychologists of religion, it should — for the sake of their own object! — be a challenge to start collaborating with scholars from neighboring disciplines. Only this time, preferably, not with neuroscientists and mathematicians, but with anthropologists and historians.

REFERENCES

Åkerberg, H. (1975). *Omvändsele och kamp: en empirisk religionspsykologisk undersökning av den unge Nathan Söderbloms religiösa utveckling 1866-1894.* [Conversion and struggle: an empirical psychological study of the religious development of the young Nathan Söderblom 1866-1894] Ph.D. diss., University of Lund, Sweden (*Studia Psychologiae Religionum Lundensia, 1).*

Åkerberg, H. (1978). Attempts to escape: a psychological study on the autobiographical notes of Herbert Tingsten 1971-1972. In: T. Källstad (ed.). *Psychological studies on religious man* (pp. 71-92). Stockholm: Almqvist & Wiksell.

Åkerberg, H. (1985). *Tillvaron och religionen: psykologiska studier kring personlighet och mystik.* [Existence and religion: psychological studies in personality and mysticism] Lund: Studentlitteratur.

Anders, G. (1956). *Die Antiquiertheit des Menschen: über die Seele im Zeitalter der zweiten industriellen Revolution.* München: Beck.

Andrae, T. (1932). *Die Frage der religiösen Anlage religionsgeschichtlich beleuchtet.* Uppsala: Universitets Årsskrift.

Ariès, Ph. & A. Béjin (eds.) (1985). *Western sexuality: practice and precept in past and present times* (transl. A. Forster). Oxford: Blackwell. (orig. publ. 1982)

Armon-Jones, C. (1986). The thesis of constructionism. In: R. Harré (ed.). *The social construction of emotions* (pp. 32-56). Oxford: Blackwell.

Averill, J.R. (1985). The social construction of emotion: with special reference to love. In: K.J. Gergen & K.E. Davis (eds.). *The social construction of the person* (pp. 89-109). New York: Springer.

Berry, J.W. (1992). *Cross-cultural psychology: research and applications.* Cambridge: Cambridge University Press.

Boer, Th. de (1983). *Foundations of a critical psychology* (transl. Th. Plantinga). Pittsburgh: Duquesne Univ. Press. (orig. publ. 1980)

Bourdieu, P. (1990). *The logic of practice* (transl. R. Nice). Cambridge: Polity Press. (orig. publ. 1980)

Bouvy, A.-M (ed.) (1994). *Journeys into cross-cultural psychology.* Lisse: Swets & Zeitlinger.

Brown, L.B. (1987). *The psychology of religious belief.* London: Academic Press.

Burke, P. (1980). *Sociology and history.* London: Allen & Unwin.

Capps, D. & J.E. Dittes (eds.) (1990). *The hunger of the heart: reflections on the Confessions of Augustine.* West Lafayette, IN: Society for the Scientific Study of Religion.

Carroll, M.P. (1986). *The cult of the Virgin Mary: psychological origins.* Princeton: Princeton University Press.

Carruthers, M.J. (1990). *The book of memory: a study of memory in medieval culture.* Cambridge: Cambridge University Press.

Cohen, C.L. (1986). *God's caress: the psychology of puritan religious experience.* New York: Oxford University Press.

Corbin, A. (1986). *The foul and the fragrant: odor and the French social imagination* (transl. A. Montaigne). Leamington: Berg. (orig. publ. 1982)

Delumeau, J. (1990). *Sin and fear: the emergence of a western guilt culture, 13th-18th centuries.* New York: Saint Martin's Press. (orig. publ. 1982)

DeMause, L. (1982). *Foundations of psychohistory.* New York: Creative Roots.

Demos, J. (1988). Shame and guilt in early New England. In: C.Z. Stearns & P.N. Stearns (eds.). *Emotion and social change: toward a new psychohistory* (pp. 69-86). New York: Holmes & Meier.

Dunde, S.R. (ed.) (1993). *Wörterbuch der Religionspsychologie.* Gütersloh: Gütersloher Verlagshaus Gerd Mohn.

Elias, N. (1978-82). *The civilizing process* (2 vols.) (transl. E. Jephcott). Oxford: Blackwell. (orig. publ. 1976)

Erikson, E.H. (1958). *Young man Luther: a study in psychoanalysis and history.* New York: Norton.

Fèbvre, L. (1942). *The problem of unbelief in the sixteenth century: the religion of Rabelais* (transl. B. Gottlieb). Cambridge, MA: Harvard University Press, 1982.

Festinger, L., H.W. Riecken, & S. Schachter (1956). *When prophecy fails.* Minneapolis: University of Minnesota Press.

Foucault, M. (1977). *Discipline and punish: the birth of the prison* (transl. A. Sheridan). London: Lane. (orig. publ. 1975)

Freud, S. (1910). Leonardo da Vinci and a memory of his childhood. In: *The standard edition of the complete psychological works of Sigmund Freud, vol. 11* (pp. 63-137) (transl. & ed. J. Strachey). London: Hogarth, 1964[2].

Freud, S. (1913). Totem and taboo. In: *The standard edition of the complete psychological works of Sigmund Freud, vol. 13* (pp. 1-161) (transl. & ed. J. Strachey). London: Hogarth, 1964[4].

Freud, S. (1917). *Introductory lectures on psycho-analysis. (The standard edition of the complete psychological works of Sigmund Freud, vol. 15)* (transl. & ed. J. Strachey). London: Hogarth, 1971[5].

Gadlin, H. (1992). Lacan explicated [review J. Scott Lee. *Jacques Lacan*]. *Contemporary Psychology, 37* (9), 888.

Geels, A. (1980). *Mystikerna Hjalmar Ekström 1885-1962.* [Mystic Hjalmar Ekström 1885-1962] Malmö: Doxa.

Geels, A. (1989). *Skapande mystik: en psykologisk studie av Violet Tengbergs religiösa visioner och konstnärliga skapande.* [Creative mysticism: a psychological study of Violet Tengberg's religious visions and artistic creations] Löberöd: Plus Ultra.

Geertz, C. (1973). *The interpretation of cultures.* New York: Basic Books.

Gehlen, A. (1961). *Anthropologische Forschung zur Selbstbegegnung und Selbstentdeckung des Menschen.* Hamburg: Rowohlt.

Gergen, K.J. (1973). Social psychology as history. *Journal of Personality and Social Psychology, 26* (2), 309-320.

Ginzburg, C. (1989). *Clues, myths, and the historical method* (transl. J. & A.C. Tedeschi). Baltimore: John Hopkins University. (orig. publ. 1986)

Goffman, E. (1961). *Asylums: essays on the social situation of mental patients and other inmates.* Chicago: Aldine.

Grad, H., A. Blanco & J. Georgas (eds.) (1996). *Key issues in cross-cultural psychology.* Lisse: Swets & Zeitlinger.

Hall, G.S. (1917). *Jesus, the Christ, in the light of psychology.* New York: Doubleday.

Herdt, G., & M. Stephen (eds.) (1989). *The religious imagination in New Guinea.* New Brunswick/London: Rutgers University Press.

Hermans, H.J.M. & H.J.G. Kempen (1993). *The dialogical self: meaning as movement.* San Diego, CA: Academic Press.

Hoffman, D. (1982). Der Wege zur Reife: eine religionspsychologische Untersuchung der religiösen Entwicklung Gerhard Tersteegens. Ph.D. diss., University of Lund, Sweden (*Studia Psychologiae Religionum Lundensia, 3)*

Holm, N.G. (1987). *Joels Gud: en religionspsykologisk studie.* [Joel's God: a study in psychology of religion] Åbo: Åbo Akademi.

Huls, B. (1986). Historische veranderingen in geheugenprocessen bij kinderen. [Historical changes in children'n memory processes] In: H.F.M. Peeters & F.J. Mönks (eds.). *De menselijke levensloop in historisch perspectief* [The human course of life in historical perspective] (pp. 139-153). Assen/Maastricht: Van Gorcum.

Hutschemaekers, G.J.M. (1990). *Neurosen in Nederland: vijfentachtig jaar psychisch en maatschappelijk onbehagen.* [Neuroses in the The Netherlands: 85 years of psychical and societal discomfort] Nijmegen: SUN.

Ingleby, D. & S. Nossent (1986). Cognitieve ontwikkeling en historische psychologie. [Cognitive development and historical psychology] In: H.F.M. Peeters & F.J. Mönks (eds.). *De menselijke levensloop in historisch perspectief* (pp. 122-138). [The human course of life in historical perspective] Assen/Maastricht: Van Gorcum.

Jüttemann, G. & H. Thomae (1987). *Biographie und Psychologie.* Berlin: Springer.

Jung, C.G. (1938). Psychology and religion. In: *The collected works of C.G. Jung, vol. 11* (pp. 3-105) (eds. H. Read, M. Fordham & G. Adler). Princeton, NJ: Princeton University Press, 1969[2].

Källstad, T. (1974). *John Wesley and the bible: a psychological study.* Uppsala: Acta Universitatis Upsaliensis.

Källstad, T. (1978). *Psychological studies on religious man.* Stockholm: Almqvist & Wiksell.

Källstad, T. (1987). *Levande mystik: en psykologisk undersökning av Ruth Dahlens religiösa upplevelser.* [Living mysticism: a psychological investigation of Ruth Dahlen's religious development] Delsbo: Åsak.

Kamper, D. (ed.) (1977). *Über die Wünsche: ein Versuch zur Archäologie der Subjektivität.* München/Wien: Hanser.

King, J.O. (1983). *The iron of melancholy: structures of spiritual conversion in America from the Puritan conscience to Victorian neurosis.* Middletown, Conn.: Wesleyan University Press.

Kuhn, T.S. (1962). *The structure of scientific revolutions.* Chicago: University of Chicago Press.

Lacan, J. (1966). *Écrits.* Paris: Seuil.

Leeuw, G. van der (1926). Über einige neuere Ergebnisse der psychologischen Forschung und ihre Anwendung auf die Geschichte, insonderheit die Religionsgeschichte. *Studi e Materiali di Storia delle Religione, 2,* 1-43.

Lorenzer, A. (1977). *Sprachspiel und Interaktionsformen: Vorträge und Aufsätze zu Psychoanalyse, Sprache und Praxis.* Frankfurt am Main: Suhrkamp.

Lowe, D.M. (1982). *History of bourgeois perception.* Chicago: University of Chicago Press.

Meissner, W.W. (1992). *Ignatius of Loyola: the psychology of a saint.* New Haven: Yale University Press.

Merleau-Ponty, M. (1962). *Phenomenology of perception* (transl. C. Smith). London: Routledge & Kegan Paul. (orig. publ. 1945)

Merwe, W.L. & P.P. Voestermans (1995). Wittgenstein's legacy and the challenge to psychology. *Theory & Psychology, 5* (1), 27-48.

Messer, S.B., L.A. Sass & R.L. Woolfolk (eds.) (1988). *Hermeneutics and psychological theory.* Brunswick, NJ: Rutgers U.P.

Misra, G. & K.J. Gergen (1993). On the place of culture in psychological science. *International Journal of Psychology, 28* (2), 225-243.

Moghaddam, F.M., D.M. Taylor & S.C. Wright (1993). *Social psychology in cross-cultural perspective.* New York: Freeman.

Mooij, A.W.M., & G.A.M. Widdershoven (1992). *Hermeneutiek en psychologie: interpretatie in theorievorming, onderzoek en psychotherapie.* [Hermeneutics and psychology. Interpretation in theorizing, research and psychotherapy] Meppel: Boom.

Much, N. (1995). Cultural psychology. In: J.A. Smith, R. Harré & Luk Van Langenhove (eds.). *Rethinking psychology* (pp. 97-121). London: Sage.

Olbrich, E. (1986). De levensloop in de moderne tijd: historische perspectieven en levenslooppsychologie. [The course of life in modern time: historical perspectives and psychology of the course of life] In: H.F.M. Peeters & F.J. Mönks (eds.). *De menselijke levensloop in historisch perspectief* (pp. 84-100). [The human course of life in historical perspective] Assen/Maastricht: Van Gorcum.

Peeters, H.F.M. (1974). *Mensen veranderen: een historisch-psychologische verhandeling*. [Man changes: a historical-psychological essay] Meppel: Boom.

Peeters, H.F.M. (1993). Mentaliteitsgeschiedenis en psychologie. [History of mentalities and psychology] *Nederlands Tijdschrift voor de Psychologie, 48* (5), 195-204.

Pfister, O. (1910). *Die Frömmigkeit des Grafen Ludwig von Zinzendorf: ein psychoanalytischer Beitrag zur Kenntnis der religiösen Sublimierungsprozesse und zur Erklärung des Pietismus.* Leipzig: Deuticke.

Pfister, O. (1926). *Die Legende Sundar Singhs: eine auf Enthüllungen protestantischer Augenzeugen in Indien gegründete religionspsychologische Untersuchung*. Bern: Haupt.

Pfister, O. (1948). *Christianity and fear: a study in history and in the psychology and hygiene of religion.* London: Allen & Unwin. (orig. publ. 1944)

Portmann, A. (1951). *Zoologie und das neue Bild vom Menschen: biologische Fragmente zu einer Lehre vom Menschen*. Basel: Schwabe.

Ricoeur, P. (1992). The question of proof in Freud's psychoanalytic writings. In: J.B. Thompson (ed. & transl.). *Hermeneutics and the social sciences* (pp. 247-273). New York: Cambridge University Press. (orig. publ. 1977)

Röckelein, H. (ed.) (1993). *Biographie als Geschichte.* Tübingen: Diskord.

Rubin, J.H. (1994). *Religious melancholy and protestant experience in America.* New York: Oxford University Press.

Rümke, H.C. (1952). *The psychology of unbelief.* London: Rockliff. (orig. publ. 1939)

Runyan, W. (1982). *Life histories and psychobiography: explorations in theory and method.* New York: Oxford University Press.

Runyan, W. (1988). *Psychology and historical interpretation.* New York: Oxford University Press.

Sanders, C. & J.F.H. van Rappard (1982). *Tussen ontwerp en werkelijkheid: een visie op de psychologie.* [Between design and reality: a perspective on psychology] Meppel: Boom.

Sarbin, T.R. (ed.) (1986). *Narrative psychology: the storied nature of human conduct.* New York: Praeger.

Schafer, R. (1983). *The analytic attitude.* New York: Basic Books.

Schivelbusch, W. (1979). *The railway journey: trains and travel in the 19th century*. New York: Urizen Books. (orig. publ. 1977)

Söderblom, N. (1908). *Studier av religionen.* [The study of religion] Stockholm: Diakonistyrelsen.

Sonntag, M. (ed.) (1990). *Von der Machbarkeit des Psychischen.* Pfaffenweiler: Centaurus.

Strien, P.J. van (1986). *Praktijk als wetenschap: methodologie van het sociaal-wetenschappelijk handelen.* [Practice as science: methodology of social-scientific action] Assen: Van Gorcum.

Strien, P.J. van (1993). The historical practice of theory construction. *Annuals of Theoretical Psychology, 8*, 149-227.

Sundén, H. (1966). *Die Religion und die Rollen: eine psychologische Untersuchung.* Berlin: Töpelmann. (orig. publ. 1959)

Sundén, H. (1987). Saint Augustine and the Psalter in the light of role-psychology. *Journal for the Scientific Study of Religion, 26* (3), 375-382.

Terwee, S. (1989). *Hermeneutics in psychology and psychoanalysis.* New York: Springer.

Thomas, K. (1971). *Religion and decline of magic: studies in popular beliefs in 16th and 17th century England.* London: Weidenfeld & Nicolson.

Vergote, A. (1988). *Guilt and desire: religious attitudes and their pathological derivatives* (transl. M.H. Wood). New Haven/London: Yale University Press. (orig. publ. 1978)

Voestermans, P.P.L.A. (1992). Cultuurpsychologie: van cultuur in de psychologie naar psychologie in 'cultuur'. [Cultural psychology: from culture in psychology to psychology in 'culture'.] *Nederlands Tijdschrift voor de Psychologie, 47,* 151-162.

Vovelle, M. (1990). *Ideologies and mentalities* (transl. E. O'Flaherty). Cambridge: Polity Press. (orig. publ. 1982)

Vygotsky, L.S. (1978). *Mind in society: the development of higher psychological processes* (ed. & transl. M. Cole). Cambridge, Mass.: Harvard University Press.

Widdershoven, G.A.M. & Th. de Boer (eds.) (1990). *Hermeneutiek in discussie* [Hermeneutics in discussion]. Delft: Eburon.

Wikström, O. (1980). Kristusbilden i Kristinebergsgruvan: historiska och religionspsykologiska aspekter. [Figures of Christ in Kristineberggrave: historical and psychological aspects] *Kyrkohistorisk Årsskrift, 80*, 99-112.

Wundt, W. (1900-1909). *Völkerpsychologie: eine Untersuchung der Entwicklungsgesetze von Sprache, Mythos und Sitte.* Leipzig: Engelmann.

THE HERMENEUTICS OF LIFE HISTORY
A PLEA FOR A HERMENEUTICAL PSYCHOLOGY OF RELIGION, EXEMPLIFIED BY THE WORK OF ERIK H. ERIKSON

T.H. Zock
University of Leiden (The Netherlands)

PREVIEW[1]

In this chapter, I will advocate the use of hermeneutical approaches in psychology of religion, presenting the psychology of Erik H. Erikson as an example.

Part I contains some methodological implications of combining psychology with hermeneutics. First I will go briefly into the questions: what exactly are 'hermeneutical approaches'?, and how can they be justified? I will further draw attention to the growing interest in hermeneutical approaches in psychology — there is even a tendency to consider these approaches as the only appropriate ones. Subsequently I will present my own view: hermeneutical approaches are not only justified, but may even be preferred in the study of religion. Finally, I will sketch the outlines of the debate on the status of psychoanalysis, the psychological current to which Erikson belongs — is it a scientific or hermeneutical discipline?

Part 2 is an analysis of the hermeneutical characteristics of Erik H. Erikson's psychological approach to religion: his holistic and contextual approach; the distinction between originology and teleology, and between factuality and actuality; the link between religion and actuality, which asks for a hermeneutical approach; and Erikson's contribution to philosophical hermeneutics according to Jerald Wallulis. The last section contains some brief conclusive remarks.

I: HERMENEUTICS AND PSYCHOLOGY — METHODOLOGICAL PRELIMINARIES

HERMENEUTICAL VERSUS SCIENCE-ORIENTED APPROACHES

The title of this volume, *Hermeneutical approaches in psychology of religion*, sounds like a programmatic statement and a *cri de coeur*. For although it may not be clear at first what exactly 'hermeneutical approaches' are, one thing is certain: they do not represent the dominant trend in academic psychology, which is generally characterized as 'scientific' (in the sense of: oriented towards the natural sciences), or even in a polemical way as 'scientistic'. What is more important, hermeneutical approaches are looked upon with suspicion or dismissed with straightforward rejection, as they are assumed not to conform to the strict standards of scientific objective knowledge. Yet there are few psychologists today who view strictly empirical-inductive research as only respectable and would like to see psychology gain the status of a natural science. Even A.D. de Groot, the famous advocate and methodologist of empirical research, did not take such a view (Groot 1961, pp. 315-316). The discussion has moved to the question of in what way the social sciences may claim the prerogative of being scientific, in the sense of producing objective, intra-subjectively verifiable knowledge.

This change has, however, not settled the dispute in social sciences, as is expressed in the way methodical approaches are still classified in opposite (though not necessarily mutually exclusive) pairs: idiographic versus nomothetic, qualitative versus quantitative. As far as 'hermeneutical' (or 'interpretative', 'phenomenological') is concerned, its opposite is usually formulated in terms of 'empirical'. Hanford (1975, p. 219) speaks of 'empirical' versus 'phenomenological' approaches; the main distinction between the two is the assumption of knowledge being reducible or not reducible to sensory experience such as observation. Others specify empirical as empirical-analytical (Strien & Rappard 1990, pp. 232-234[2]; Terwee 1989, pp. 1-4), or as statistical-empirical (Wulff 1991, p. x), using the term 'empirical' in the broader sense of "grounded in experience as opposed to speculation" (Wulff 1991, p. 38), and contrary to a narrowly conceived 'empiricism'. In my view, hermeneutical approaches too are 'empirical' in this latter, broader sense. One may add to the foregoing extension of 'empirical' by broadening the term as not only referring to 'observation' as visual but also to observation as listening to and talking with somebody, or as reading somebody's written reports, stories, diaries etc.

In a methodological respect, social sciences have always been oriented towards the humanities as well as towards the natural sciences. The same goes for the psychology of religion: Hanford (1975) sees two traditional research orientations — the empirical and the phenomenological one, studying religion respectively from the inside and on the outside. He pleads for a broad synoptic orientation. Wulff (1991) orders the diverse approaches in psychology of religion in 'objective' and 'subjective' approaches. "The perspectives considered here are organized in terms of two large classes: the *objective*, which treats religion as publicly observable behavior to be explained scientifically in terms of cause and effect; and the *subjective*, which views religion as primarily an inner process to be understood emphatically in terms of its meaningful structure" (Wulff 1991, p. 39). The subjective approach seems to have been more favoured in the psychology of religion, maybe because one of its roots was the history of religions — a typical humanities discipline.

Because the terms 'scientific' and 'hermeneutic' are used in various confusing and sometimes contradictory ways, for the sake of terminological clarity I propose to speak of 'science-oriented approaches' alongside 'hermeneutical approaches'. I will now make a hazardous attempt to suggest a working definition, without any pretence of originality or comprehensiveness (cf. Messer et al. 1988; Terwee 1989; and Wulff 1991). *Science-oriented approaches* 'reduce' (in a non-normative sense) reality to abstractions which can be grasped in formalized language and rational models, with quantitative and standardized methods; they look for general laws and correlational-causal relations, and aim at explaining, predicting and controlling reality. *Hermeneutical approaches* try to stick as closely as possible to reality as experienced in everyday life, take into account the standpoint of the 'objects of research' — how human beings, using language, talk about and view themselves — and render their research results as far as possible in everyday language rather than in abstract terminology. Hermeneutical approaches look for the meaningful structure of human reality, and thus consider man as an intentional, conscious and meaning-giving being. A being, moreover, anchored in history and culture (human life cannot be understood outside history and culture), and presenting itself as an active agent in this context. Hence man is an 'object' of research who, as a subject, interferes with the research. Moreover, the personal involvement of the investigator is acknowledged as instrumental in, and contributing to the research (as opposed to the natural sciences, where the ideal is to standardize methods as much as possible, and to minimize the role of the investigator as much as possible). The contextual nature of knowledge is acknowledged.

In order to define a position in this methodological debate and justify the choice of appropriate methods, one decisive question must be answered: What is the best way to get sight of 'human reality', including *individual* as well as *collective*, socio-cultural, human phenomena? We must realize that an answer to this question always has a normative ring, because basic assumptions about the nature of human reality — a view of man and a world view — play a role.

A STRATIFICATIONAL VIEW ON HUMAN REALITY — A JUSTIFICATION OF THE USE OF HERMENEUTICAL APPROACHES

Sanders and Rappard (1982) introduced the concept 'level of structuring' in a stratification theory of human reality. Their theory is based on and fits in with similar theories about the stratification of reality, for instance that of Shotter (Strien & Rappard 1990, p. 34). All agree in distinguishing three levels of structural complexity in human reality, which are hierarchically ordered, higher levels presupposing lower ones. The choice of method to study human reality now depends on the structural level with which one is dealing. First there is the *mechanistic* layer, on which human beings are viewed in as far as they are determined by external influences, causal relations, and natural forces. The second is the *organistic* layer, which results from considering human beings as an organism, i.e. as a dynamic, coherent whole, which grows and is transformed in a constant interaction with the environment, continually adapting to and at the same time modifying the environment. Then finally there is the *personalistic* (or 'humanistic') layer, representative of human beings seen as persons: beings gifted with intentionality, consciousness, continually giving meaning to and interpreting their own life and world, behaving as active agents in a socio-cultural context.

So the higher the level, the greater the role of meaning giving and interpretation, and the greater the variance of meaning. The higher the level, the more we move away from strictly scientific knowledge and experience, and the more we take into account the complexity of everyday life. On the personalistic level, due to the variance of meaning, it is not possible to strive for general knowledge, formulated in laws; the individual plays a more important role, and it is more the common structures, patterns, types that one must search for. As Runyan (1982) incessantly emphasizes, the impossibility to formulate general laws does not mean, as is frequently thought, that no systematic, reliable, intersubjectively verifiable scientific knowledge is possible. Special rules have to be formulated for the orderly study of this personalistic dimension of reality.

It is clear that science-oriented approaches may do to examine the lower structure levels. But if one wants to gain insight into the highest, personalistic level, then hermeneutical approaches are required, and even seem to be the most appropriate ones. On the whole, the method to be used depends on the structural level on which one focuses. A stratification theory of human reality at least justifies the use of both science-oriented *and* hermeneutical approaches.

THE TIDE HAS TURNED — A GROWING INTEREST IN HERMENEUTICAL APPROACHES AND THE DISCOVERY OF THE NARRATIVE STRUCTURE OF HUMAN REALITY.

The 'scientific' approach has long been prevalent in academic psychology and psychology of religion, although an undercurrent of hermeneutical approaches has always been present. However, Clifford Geertz stated in 1980 that a turning point had seemed to be reached: dependent on the cultural shift in "the way we think about the way we think", he sees a shift in social sciences from "a laws-and-instances ideal of explanation to a cases-and-interpretations one" (Geertz 1980, pp. 165-166). "[...] a challenge is being mounted to some of the central assumptions of mainstream social sciences. The strict separation of theory and data, the 'brute fact' idea; the effort to create a formal vocabulary of analysis purged of all subjective reference, the 'ideal language' idea; and the claim to moral neutrality and the Olympian view, the 'God's truth' idea — none of these can prosper when explanation comes to be regarded as a matter of connecting action to its sense rather than behavior to its determinants" (Geertz 1980, p. 178). Geertz draws attention to the root-metaphor which emerges, namely text and narrative representing human reality. This metaphor asks for hermeneutical, interpretative approaches. Geertz' words may be seen as prophetic, for indeed, since 1980, terms like 'text', 'narrative', 'interpretation' and 'hermeneutics' have been turning up everywhere: in the Faculties of Arts, of Theology and of Social Sciences. The tide has clearly turned.

In psychology, this change even resulted in the rise of a new sub-discipline: 'narrative psychology' (cf. Messer et al. 1988; Sarbin 1986; Ankersmit et al. 1990; Terwee 1989; Packer & Addison 1989). Narratives, it is argued, are important in psychology, because human beings use narratives to clarify and order their experience and to form and protect an identity. It is the way of narratives, by telling stories, that an identity is constructed. "The narratory principle guides thought and action" — and, I would like to add: experience. (Messer et al. 1988, p. 11).

If interpretation plays such a central role in the constitution of human reality, if we are constituted to a large extent by our self-interpretations, this apparently has important methodological consequences in the field of psychology. Our self-interpretations are always embedded in culture and history. So to understand human beings, you must always take 'the horizon of understanding' (Gadamer) into account: the socio-cultural context, and thus the role of human subjectivity in the enterprise of interpretation itself. Hence psychology can no longer work with a concept of fact as neutral, objective, positioned in a value-free, transhistorical, epistemological arena (Messer et al. 1988, pp. 24-25). Facts are inextricably interwoven with theory and with the socio-cultural context of the investigator. The narrative nature of human reality demands a hermeneutical approach.

But what about other approaches? Here we come across the important methodological problem (discussed by Messer et al. 1988) of the 'ontological' status of texts, narratives and interpretations. Does, somewhere behind the narratives, a 'reality' exist, which can be reached by way of the narratives, but has nevertheless an ontological status of its own? Do narratives offer an access to an otherwise inaccessible reality, or are they reality itself? Some psychologists go as far as considering psychological theories themselves as a kind of narrative interpretation — hereby taking a postmodernist, relativistic position, and denying every 'objectivist' knowledge-claim of psychology (cf. for instance the work of Kenneth J. Gergen and Donald Spence). In this debate, I do not take the position that human reality is completely textual, narrative, and can thus be understood adequately *only* with the help of hermeneutical methods. It is the great merit of narrative psychology to have drawn attention to the narrative structure of human reality, but, as argued in the previous section, I think other strata of human reality justify the use of other methods too.

THE PERSONALISTIC LAYER IS CENTRAL IN RELIGION — HERMENEUTICAL APPROACHES ARE TO BE PREFERRED IN PSYCHOLOGY OF RELIGION

The conclusion up to now is that hermeneutical approaches have a place in their own right within psychology, because of its object: human reality, which has (at least *also*) a personalistic layer, in which 'meaning' plays a central role. I will now argue that hermeneutical approaches are not only justified, but are even to be preferred when studying religion, because of the specific nature of human *religious* reality.

I will not go into the endless, often confusing and distressing discussions about the definition of religion, but propose to approach religious behaviour and experience with the help of the stratification theory of structural levels. In doing this, it seems clear that religious conduct — although it also belongs to the sphere of convention and determination — to an important extent takes place on the personalistic level. It is a specifically human personalistic conduct: neither machines nor other living organisms can be religious. Smith's (1979) concept of 'faith' as a human capacity is useful in this respect. Faith is "one's orientation or total response to oneself, others and the universe. It reflects 'the human capacity to see, to think, to feel in terms of a transcendent dimension', to perceive meaning that is more than merely mundane" (quoted from Wulff 1991, p. 4). Faith is expressed in concrete forms of 'cumulative traditions'. Faith now presupposes the typical *human* capacities of self-reflection, (self-)consciousness, and symbolic vision and behaviour. So religion has to do with the human capacity to find meaning and give meaning, individually and collectively. Concrete religious traditions involve a highly symbolic structure, offering a view on life, proposing a way to live, to order one's own life into a meaningful coherence. Religious traditions are culturally specific phenomena (presented in texts and symbols), which have to be understood, interpreted and appropriated by each individual. They appeal to the human person who is actively looking for a coherent view on life, and striving to integrate a specific tradition in its own life. Religious traditions appeal to personalistic capacities. They presuppose there is a person, a subject who — more or less consciously — has appropriated a religious tradition. Being religious involves the human being especially in his/her personalistic aspects: as a conscious, active, intentional being, approaching reality in a symbolic way.

There is another argument for the desirability of hermeneutical approaches in psychology of religion. We are now seeing, at least in Europe, the fragmentation and waning influence of concrete religious traditions. Religious conduct is less and less linked with and anchored in concrete traditions, and is becoming more and more the result of a conscious, individual search for and of an individual design of a meaning system, a proper way of ordering life and giving meaning to life. Religious conduct is becoming more and more the result of an active, individualized, conscious way of constructing a religious identity, and thus it demands personalistic qualities.

My conclusion is that, although other structural levels also play a role in religion (remember that the levels are hierarchically ordered, so the personalistic level presupposes the preceding ones) the personalistic layer must be considered as central. So it is high time to pay more attention to hermeneutical approaches in psychology of religion!

Finally, I have a more pragmatic reason to plead for hermeneutical approaches, an argument closely linked with my personal situation as a psychologist of religion with a theological-educational background, teaching in a theological department. This is a situation typical for the Netherlands: at all universities but one psychology of religion is institutionally housed in a Faculty of Theology (which in the Netherlands usually is a combination of 'divinity school' and 'department of religion'). Here the climate of education and research is dominated by the interests and mentality of the humanities. Students learn mainly hermeneutical approaches and methods; emphasis is on the literary-historical study of religious 'texts', texts in the broadest sense of the word (i.e. all products of the religious imagination). In secondary education they mostly followed a typical humanities curriculum. Now in my view, a social sciences department in a Department of Theology should seek to join in with this mainstream of hermeneutical approaches, for the sake of academic integration and fruitful interdisciplinary cooperation.

PSYCHOANALYSIS — A HYBRID DISCIPLINE

In order to be able to situate Erikson's psychology as a kind of hermeneutical psychoanalysis in Part II, I will briefly go into recent discussions about the status of psychoanalysis. Here the methodological debate — science oriented or hermeneutical approaches? — is fought still more fiercely than in the other psychological disciplines (cf. Zwaal 1990; Terwee 1989; Messer et al. 1988). From the early beginnings of psychoanalysis, the hybrid character of the discipline was noticed: on the one hand, there is Freud the clinician, who discovered that psychic complaints and symptoms express meaning — hidden meaning, which has to be discovered by interpreting the symptoms, dreams, associations and stories of his clients. Psychoanalysis was primarily a 'talking cure', interpretation being its most important instrument. On the other hand, there is Freud the theoretician, who has undeniably scientific claims: in his metapsychology he offered a causal, mechanistic model to explain human behaviour, by referring to forces (the drives), psychic instances (unconscious/conscious; ego, id, superego), and mechanisms (suppression, transference).

But which is the real Freud? More and more authors, following the classic studies of Ricoeur and Habermas, consider psychoanalysis, to a greater or lesser extent, as a hermeneutical discipline.[3] In early ego-psychology and in later object-relations psychology and self psychology, a paradigm shift can be discovered: the emphasis is no longer on the drives as objective, autonomous forces, which determine behaviour, but on the attempt of a subject to relate to and integrate specific objects; object and subject cannot be separated (cf. Jones 1991; Zwaal 1990). We are not only the products of the causal forces of our past, but also the product of our subjective, narrative structure.

All narrative approaches in psychoanalysis — however different they may be — focus on interpreting life histories, and reject a logical-positivistic ideal of science. Donald Spence (1987) for instance, argued that Freud's concepts were originally meant as metaphors, but became mistakenly reified — due to the dominant scientific paradigm of Freud's time. There is, however, 'truth' in the essentially narrative discipline of psychoanalysis: 'narrative truth' instead of 'historical truth': psychological facts have an interpretative nature.

In this debate on psychoanalysis, the problem of the 'ontological' status of narratives, mentioned above, emerges in a discussion about the status of psychoanalytic interpretations. The critical and main point of discussion here can be formulated as follows: is a psychoanalytical interpretation a reconstruction or a construction? Does it represent or rather present reality? Is it a reconstruction of the past, a re-covery of a structure which lies beneath the stories, dreams and symptoms — a reality which really exists, and lays hidden until it is revealed and re-constructed by interpretation? In this view interpretations reveal underlying structures, and thus lead to formulation of a theory about these structures. Or is a psychoanalytic interpretation a construction rather than a re-construction? "The verbal construction that we create not only shapes (our view of) the past, but, indeed, a creation of the present, it *becomes* the past" (Spence 1982, p. 11).

This is no academic debate, given the recent fierce struggle, fought out in the *New York Review of Books*[4], concerning the use of psychoanalytic interpretations in legal cases of incest. It is alleged that repressed memories of incestual violence may be revealed during psychoanalytic treatment — they may be 'dug up', to use Freud's image of the psychoanalyst as an archaeologist — and thus can be allocated as evidence in court. The presupposition is that the psychoanalytic interpretation renders a past reality. If, on the other hand, the psychoanalytic interpretation is — wholly or partly — a construction of a meaningful pattern in individual life, a way to give meaning to life and make sense of one's experiences, then the psychoanalytic interpretation must be rejected as reliable evidence of what actually happened in the past.

Another way to characterize the two positions is the following: is the psychoanalyst an archaeologist, discovering, laying bare facts about psychic life, or is he/she someone who helps clients to get a meaningful view on their life, and, we must add, on their religious experience and behaviour? Erikson, as we will see, takes a middle position.

II: ERIK H. ERIKSON'S CONTRIBUTION TO A HERMENEUTICAL PSYCHOLOGY OF RELIGION

In the second part of this paper, I will argue that Erik H. Erikson's psychological approach to religion is an outstanding example of a hermeneutical approach. Erikson, who died recently (in 1994), was educated as a traditional psychoanalyst in the ego-psychological circles around Anna Freud, but developed a psychology very much of his own, which in my view must be characterized as 'existential' and 'hermeneutic' (cf. Zock 1990). Here I take the outlines of his life-cycle theory — which is seldom absent from survey works on personality development — to be common knowledge.

Just as there seem to be two Freuds, there seem to be two Eriksons: the Erikson of the life-cycle theory and Erikson the psychohistorian. The life-cycle theory, which indicates the structures and patterns underlying human development, offers a general psychological model to explain individual and collective human behaviour, and claims to be universally valid. The theory is clearly psychoanalytically inspired, its basic assumption being the libidinal foundation of development. In this respect Erikson resembles the scientific Freud.

But on the other hand, there is Erikson the psychohistorian, the involved commentator of modern society, who wanted to focus on 'life history' instead of on 'case history' and wrote psychohistorical biographies of great religious figures. The life-cycle theory gains a different status in this psychohistorical work: it functions not so much as a general theory, but rather as an interpretative paradigm, with no general, timeless claims; it evolves in the course of Erikson's psychohistorical work, influenced by his concrete objects of study as well as by his personal involvement. This second Erikson orients himself towards the hermeneutical Freud, and is the more important one. The survey works on personality development, while focusing on the life-cycle theory as general theory, show a mutilated Erikson.

I will now discuss various aspects of Erikson's psychology which justify his characterization as a hermeneutical thinker.

SOMA-EGO-ETHOS: ERIKSON'S VIEW ON THE STRATIFICATION OF HUMAN REALITY — A HOLISTIC APPROACH

Erikson argues time and again that if human reality is to be understood, it must be considered as a whole: a dynamic, growing, developing process, in which the various part-functions are interdependent. Consequently, he advocates a holistic approach. You cannot just take human reality apart, and look at the various parts in isolation, as you can a machine. So in his view it is impossible to consider human behaviour on one level only — be it the mechanistic, organistic or personalistic one. But all the same, within this one and indivisible whole, various dimensions can and must be distinguished.

Already in his early work, while still developing the life-cycle theory, Erikson distinguishes three interdependent, continually interacting part-processes, three organizational levels in human life: *soma*, *ego* and *ethos*:

> There is, in whatever order, the biological process of the hierarchic organization of organ systems constituting a body (*soma*); there is the psychic process organizing individual experience by ego synthesis (*psyche*); and there is the communal process of the cultural organization of the interdependence of persons (*ethos*) ... in the end, all three approaches are necessary for the clarification of any intact human event" (Erikson 1982, pp. 25-26).

Soma stands for the biological substrate of human reality, which is viewed by Erikson as libidinal: human bodily reality is libidinal reality. In this description of the soma level, we come across physical processes, anchored in 'scientific' psychoanalytic thought: Erikson speaks of bodily spatial modes which are linked with the three Freudian psychosexual stages (incorporation, elimination, intrusion), about drives which have a certain intensity, and about psychosexual needs — all being determinants of behaviour — as being influential in a mechanistic way. Yet Erikson never maintained that a specific bodily state (Luther's obstipational problems, for instance) is 'the cause' of a specific behaviour (his anal-obsessive coloured defiance of the devil and the pope). Rather, he points at parallel patterns in bodily and psychic/spiritual modes; in Luther's case the development of the bodily mode of elimination predisposes him to mold his creativity in a specific way.

Soma — a bodily constitution, libidinal patterns — may be the basis of human reality, the material human reality is made of, but it is not yet *human* life: the somatic aspects become part of human reality, only because they get a specific *meaning* in a socio-cultural context, and in a particular individual life history. Societies try to synthesize their ideals and values in a coherent design for living, and transmit this design by giving specific meaning to the bodily and interpersonal experiences of their children. Take for instance the way the infant's oral needs are met. In the act of feeding children and taking care of their needs, a world view, a way of experiencing the world is transferred. As Erikson shows in his studies of Northern-American Indians in *Childhood and society*, care of children differs from culture to culture. The members of one tribe let their infants cry for some time before feeding them, in order to let them know that feeding is a serious matter, and that food is not easily available: that you have to do something to get it, and that it must be accepted gratefully — just like life in general. In another tribe food is delivered immediately on demand and in abundance, thus making clear that it is a matter of course and may be enjoyed — just like life in general. Differences in child rearing say much about the diversity of cultural meanings.

Now this interaction between soma and culture results in individual *ego* development (i.e. psychic, personality development). Thus in Erikson's view ego development does not (only) consist in the unfolding of inner potential, but is always dependent on a specific socio-cultural environment: the direct attendants of the child (the parents), the family, anchored in a specific culture. Here we come to the dimension of *ethos*. Every individual identity is anchored in a collective identity, and thus cannot be understood apart from a specific socio-cultural context. That is why Erikson calls his life-cycle theory a schema of psycho*social* development, and speaks of psycho*social* identity as the only possible identity. Yankelovich and Barrett (1971, p. 141) concisely summarize Erikson's approach, by saying that his object of study is 'the indivisible person in his world'.

We may conclude that in Erikson's view somatic processes constitute the potential and the boundary conditions of development. In this sense they have a determining, albeit seldom direct causal force. In any case they can only be understood in so far as they assume 'meaning' in a sociocultural and individual context. So in understanding human reality, one always comes across meanings which have to be interpreted; consequently, an abstract, objectifying approach in terms of causal and correlational interdependencies is not adequate. 'Human reality' is always a reality in which 'meaning' plays a role, and thus it requires an interpretative approach.

The three processes of soma, ego and ethos are intricately interwoven, and cannot finally be studied separately. This led Erikson to create the new genre of *psychohistory*: he looks at individual (somatic and psychic) development in the context of a specific familial background, of a certain culture and a time in history. The psychohistorian has to look at "the individual's stage of development, his personal circumstances, and political, historical and cultural processes" (Erikson 1964, p. 165). In *Young man Luther*, for instance, he continually shows how a specific problem of Luther must be understood against the background of his libidinal and somatic development and problems, his stage of ego development, his specific capacities (for instance the gift of the word), the relationship with his parents, and the greater socio-cultural developments, i.e. late medieval society, the mining milieu, and the crisis in the Roman Catholic church.

Let us take a closer look at one aspect of Erikson's Luther interpretation which is often misunderstood: the role of the harsh, cruel beatings of the young Luther by his parents and at school. Erikson emphasizes that these beatings must have led to anal-obsessive problems, a bad conscience, and a lack of trust. But not in the way of a direct causal sequel! First of all, one has to look at the cultural meaning of 'beating children' — the ethos aspect. In Luther's time, beating was an accepted educational measure. Why then, some critics ask, did beating have such a disastrous effect on young Luther, when all the boys around him were also beaten regularly? Erikson argues that besides the ethos aspect, there is also the influence of soma: obstipation might have aggravated the way the beatings emotionally affected Luther, and the beatings might have aggravated obstipation. Further, there is the ego-aspect: personal developmental conflicts could confer a different meaning to the beating: in Luther's case, he was beaten by a father, who in this act expressed his high ambitions and consequently great frustrations with regard to his son, and at the same time ventilated his own repressed aggressivity. One therefore also has to look at individual, interpersonal relationships. Lastly, as a *homo religiosus* Luther was constitutionally sensitive to the existential character of these and other human situations: to the precariousness of human identity, the finiteness of existence, the limits of human possibilities and choices, the negative side effects of human interaction — in short, to the human condition. Erikson's interpretative approach consists of analyzing the inherent connection between all these factors, thus exposing the (overt and hidden) meaning of Luther's behaviour.

Originology and Teleology — Erikson's Hermeneutical View on Psychoanalysis

Erikson considered himself a psychoanalytical thinker — "I am primarily a psychoanalyst; it is the only method I have learned" (Evans 1967, p. 81) — but he certainly did not embrace the whole of psychoanalysis (Zock 1990, pp. 47-51). He was always very critical of the scientific current in psychoanalysis, and rejected its materialistic and deterministic point of view and its use of physicalistic and mechanistic concepts and models. Erikson clearly feels more at home with what he calls the "phenomenological, literary" Freud, who deals with the meaning of human phenomena: " [...] the discerner of verbal and visual configurations which revealed what consciousness wanted to enlarge upon, and what it attempted to disguise — and revealed" (Erikson 1975, pp. 39-40). This Freud was erroneously overlooked and neglected by most of his followers, and that is how mainstream psychoanalysis became 'scientistic' in Erikson's view.

Proposing his own psychology, Erikson wanted to complete scientific psychoanalysis by elaborating on this phenomenological trend in Freud, thus introducing the human factor in "the physicalistic and mechanistic wording of psychoanalytic thinking" (Erikson 1982, p. 19).

An undue emphasis on the scientific aspects of Freud's psychoanalysis was attacked by Erikson as "the originological phallacy", or "originological thinking" (cf. Erikson 1975, p. 160; and Zock 1990, pp. 56, 123-126, and 155-156). Originological thinking implies considering human reality only with regard to its (often traumatical, pathological) origins; it is orientated towards the past, searching the past for causes of present behaviour. The present is seen as almost pre-empted by its own origins (Erikson 1975, p. 160). It is not a wrong way of thinking, but a one-sided one. Important aspects of the human reality are thus overlooked: the orientation towards the future, the possibility of renewal and creative solutions — in short: progression, man as a conscious, intentional being, to a certain extent free, not completely determined by what has happened in the past. A psychology which focuses on these aspects may be called 'teleological': orientated towards 'telos' — intentions, the future — instead of towards 'origins'.

A second feature of an originological approach is the neglect of the ethos dimension. This leads to what Erikson calls "case history", the reduction of historical processes to individual psychopathology. A concrete life, concrete human behaviour is lifted out of history and out of the socio-cultural environment. The task of psychology is rather to examine the interesting process of how a concrete human case becomes part of a historical event. What Erikson aims at is not case history, but *life history*: viewing human behaviour in its cultural context, anchored in the past while at the same time open towards the future. So interpretation is required.

To get the teleological aspects in view, Erikson adds a psychic instance to the tripartite Freudian structure of id, ego and superego: the 'I', the centre of consciousness and (self-)awareness, the dynamic, integrating centre of the personality. It is the conscious, subjective counterpart of the (for the greater part) unconscious, objective ego. It is the capacity of self-reflection and self-consciousness: the 'I' is aware of a 'me'. According to Erikson, both I and ego aspects were originally present in the German term 'Ich' used by Freud, but the subjective aspect escaped the attention of many of his followers.

With the introduction of a teleological way of thinking in his psychology, Erikson abandons a purely causal explanatory model, and adopts a more hermeneutic approach. But good psychoanalysis should encompass both orientations at the same time. This view on psychoanalysis bears a striking resemblance to Ricoeur's Freud interpretation.

FACTUALITY AND ACTUALITY — ERIKSON'S VIEW ON REALITY AND ITS CONSEQUENCES FOR THE STATUS OF KNOWLEDGE[5]

The distinction between originology and teleology is directly linked with a particular *view on reality*, and it is here that the hermeneutical character of Erikson's psychology reveals itself most clearly.

Already during his psychoanalytic training, Erikson wondered about the artificial separation of 'outer' and 'inner' world in traditional psychoanalysis (Erikson 1982, p. 22). In ego-psychological circles, however, inner and outer reality were seen as closely connected, and it is this view that Erikson adopts in his emphasis on the intrinsically psycho*social* nature of identity and development. He speaks of the separation of inner and outer world as an ideological division, "a Cartesian strait jacket we have imposed on our model of man" (Erikson 1964, p. 163). This view — originating in the psychoanalytic emphasis on the individual in conflict with his or her environment — finally resulted in a reduced view of reality as 'factuality': "a consensually validated world of facts" (Erikson 1975, p. 103), "the world of phenomenal experience perceived with a minimum of distortion and with a maximum of customary validation agreed upon in a given state of technology and culture" (Erikson 1964, p. 165).

There is, however, another aspect of reality implied in Freud's term '*Wirklichkeit*': '*Actualität*' — actuality, the immediate world of participation as experienced by an active subject who continually interacts with the environment. It is the world in its '*Wirkung*' aspects: in how individual and environment mutually affect each other; it is the world judged by its effectiveness. "Actuality is the world of participation, shared with other participants with a minimum of defensive maneuvering and maximum of mutual activation" (Erikson 1964, p. 165). Actuality thus refers to the dynamic interplay of inner and outer world, of the various levels of reality: soma, ego and ethos. 'Actual' is what furthers individual and collective development. Actuality presupposes human beings who have an active, conscious I and a teleological orientation. As he phrases it in *Gandhi's truth* (p. 396): factuality is what is demonstrably true, actuality is what feels effectively true in action.

During his work, Erikson became gradually convinced that psychology must take both factuality and actuality into account. In *Young man Luther* he states, still somewhat hesitatingly: "psychoanalysis...often occupies a position on the borderline of what is demonstrably true and of what demonstrably *feels* true" (Erikson 1958, p. 21). Hence a specific human behaviour can only be understood in what Erikson calls its "relativity": looking at the interrelatedness of an individual's stage of development, his or her personal circumstances, and the socio-cultural context.

The inseparability of factuality and actuality — both being 'real' — has epistemological consequences. We need, Erikson argues, a broader concept of fact. Because reality always implies factuality and actuality, and because inner and outer world cannot be separated, purely 'objective' knowledge — in the sense of 'brute facts' — is not possible. The same human behaviour must be judged differently in different contexts. A 'fact' in this broader sense always plays a role in an 'act'.

All knowledge is relative, in the sense of inherently related to specific (individual and collective) circumstances and human interactions. Yet Erikson's view on knowledge is not relativistic; to a certain extent, 'factual' knowledge is possible: there are things which can be *demonstrated* to be true, especially in the field of natural science (with regard to human reality, for example, this is the case for insight in somatic structures and patterns). But the more the specifically human aspect of actuality comes into view, the more knowledge gains a relative character.

Erikson's specific concept of fact has given rise to much misunderstanding, especially with respect to his psychohistorical work. For instance, a main criticism of *Young man Luther* has been that the interpretation of Luther was based on uncertain facts — derived from unreliable sources like (half) legends and (auto)biographical material. Erikson, however, argues that 'psychological truth' — reality viewed from a psychological point of view, encompassing the actuality aspect — is a different thing than 'historical truth'. For instance, it may be not literally, factually, true that Luther was beaten by his mother because he had stolen a nut (a famous memory), but this fact does tell us something about Luther's relationship with his parents *as he experienced it*; and thus we learn something about what influenced his development. So this fact reveals psychological truth. In a similar way, Luther's autobiographical writings may be a useful source for getting to know Luther's self image and his evaluation of his past.

"We are thus obliged to accept half-legend and half-history, provided only that a reported episode does not contradict other well-established facts; persists in having a ring of truth; and yields a meaning consistent with psychological theory" (Erikson 1958, p. 37).

But Erikson goes further than propagating a broader concept of fact. The actuality aspect of reality also leads to looking at the *interaction between researcher and his/her object of research*. The personal situation of the researcher influences what he/she knows of reality. The role of the research in the life of the researcher, his/her personal circumstances and socio-cultural context determine what the researcher notices in reality. So there is a subjective element in every research — most clearly in the humanities, but also in the natural sciences. The researcher can never completely leave aside his or her own subjective involvement and the role of knowledge, technology and science in his/her culture. In Erikson's view, this is the only way to an adequate knowledge of reality, for leaving aside the relativity of the researcher leads to a distorted view on the actuality aspect of reality.

Lastly, where can we situate Erikson in the reconstruction-construction debate? On the one hand, he presupposes the possibility of discovering facts (in the factual sense of the word), and thus a certain degree of reconstruction is possible in a psychological interpretation. But on the other hand, he accords a greater importance to the relativity of truth and to the subjective involvement of the researcher. Here, the construction aspect of knowledge and interpretation comes to the fore. So all truth is relative, but nevertheless there are facts to be discovered.

The tension between actuality and factuality comes to the fore in the claims of universality inherent in the life-cycle theory. Erikson pretends, no more and no less, to indicate developmental tasks, stages and functions which are universally human — 'facts' underlying development. But critics pointed out that Erikson's view on personality development with its emphasis on autonomy and individual identity is representative of a Westerner's development only, and of male development at that. However, Erikson himself acknowledges the relativity of his life-cycle theory. He emphasizes that no theory can encompass the whole of reality, but in his view this does not mean that no general structures and functions can be discovered at all. In the successive psychological theories, for instance, different general structures of human reality come to the fore. So in the Vienna of the turn of the century Freud could discover the importance of the unconscious and repressed drives, and it was in the USA during the sixties, with its collective societal crisis (Vietnam etc.), that the importance of identity development could be discovered. Moreover, Erikson's own diffuse identity background (a stepson as well as a Germanic looking Jew with Danish/German/American identity elements) made him the right person to formulate a theory of identity.

The tension between the claim of universal validity inherent in the life-cycle theory, and the acknowledgement of its relativity, seems a fruitful one to me, as long as the theory is open to revision.

RELIGION AND ACTUALITY

If a hermeneutical approach is necessary to grasp human reality in its actuality, the same goes for *religious* reality. After all, no dimension of behaviour can be isolated from the whole. But there is another reason why especially religious behaviour should be examined in a hermeneutical way: actuality itself is, according to Erikson, a religious process. Peter Homans states about Erikson's view on personality development: "[I]dentity, like the fully-functioning self, self-actualization, and propriate striving, constitutes a psychological effort to delineate the dynamics of that sector of personal existence claimed as the proper territory of theology" (Homans 1968, p. 74).

In Erikson's work, actuality and religion are intricately connected. He develops his ideas about actuality in and during his studies of great religious figures. It was Luther's religious development in particular which led him to discover the existential part of identity development, which he came to call 'actuality' in *Gandhi's truth*. But it is in *Young man Luther* that he states for the first time that the psychologist has to deal not only with "what demonstrably is true", but also with "what demonstrably feels true" — which is a first characterization of actuality. Religion now belongs to the latter category, because it "elaborates on what feels profoundly true even though it is not demonstrable" (Erikson 1958, p. 21).

Erikson considers the I — the actualizing, integrating centre of personal identity development — as an essentially numinous, religious phenomenon (cf. Zock 1990, pp. 100-103). The I emerges in interaction with all kinds of 'others', of whom the primal, maternal other is the most important. But the basis of all these encounters is the encounter with an "Ultimate Other" — "the I's only true counterplayer" (Erikson 1968, p. 220). In this encounter the I emerges and the foundation of identity development is laid. Existential nothingness can be conquered, and from 'nothing' man can develop a vertical existential identity, an anchor in eternity, and only thus a horizontal psychosocial identity in a specific socio-cultural space-time perspective can be developed. The encounter with the Ultimate Other gives courage to constitute an identity, it activates the process of actualization and mutual activation.

The role of religion in the actualization process is clearly illustrated in *Young man Luther*. Here Erikson shows how Luther's theological solution of his religious crisis (which was also a collective crisis) parallels the solution of his identity crisis and the process of ego recovery: "The characteristics of Luther's theological advance can be compared to certain steps in psychological maturation which every man must take: the internalization of the father-son relationship; the concomitant crystallization of conscience; the safe establishment of an identity as a worker and a man; and the concomitant reaffirmation of basic trust" (Erikson 1958, p. 213).

The new way to relate to God — by introspection, emphasizing the inner encounter with God, "the rediscovery of the passion of Christ in each man's inner struggle" (p. 229) — fits the needs for autonomy, responsibility and action of Luther himself, and of Renaissance man. The actualizing experience of God was the trigger for a sound identity development.

Actualization is basically a religious process, because every *real* actuality — i.e. leading to a maximum of actualization and mutual activation — is anchored in an encounter between I and Ultimate Other (cf. Erikson 1969, pp. 396-399). However, in Erikson's view actuality is not necessarily achieved in an *explicit* religious way. The universally human structural core of religion, discovered by Erikson in the process of actualization — a dynamic relationship between I and Ultimate Other — can, for instance, also be realized with the help of secular ideologies. Therefore Erikson mostly uses 'religious actuality' and 'actuality' synonymously. But on the other hand, religion is more than just one way to actualize: Erikson's conceptualization of actuality is coloured by the very substances of the religious traditions which revealed to him its structure (especially Lutheran Protestantism and Gandhian Hinduism). So the content of these traditions serves as a criterion to determine what real (= religious) actuality is.

Whatever the precise role of religion in Erikson's psychology, in his view religion has to do precisely with those aspects of human reality which require a hermeneutical approach. But not exclusively: every human reality involves factuality besides actuality, and therefore other approaches, focusing on factuality may be necessary. Let us take another look at Luther's anal-obsessive problems in theologicis (his preoccupation with sin and the devil). These problems may not only be seen as part of an existential struggle to find a solid basis to stand on, to develop an identity, but also as determined by general human structures, functions and modes: especially the bodily modes of elimination and retention, and their importance for the development of the ego quality autonomy and its negative counterparts shame and doubt. Further, there is the factual background of Luther's relationships with his parents and the socio-cultural situation of his time. It is only by taking all these bodily and historical facts into account that the psychologist can start the interpretative search of how these facts gain a specific meaning in the course of Luther's life history: how Luther, with this factual past was able to creatively develop ways to be and act in the future — how Luther was 'actualized'. So the psychologist needs, besides interpretative skill, factual knowledge, *and* the methods to amass factual knowledge — or at least to be able to judge facts amassed by other researchers.

JERALD WALLULIS — ERIKSON AND PHILOSOPHICAL HERMENEUTICS

Several authors have noticed, to a greater or lesser degree, the hermeneutical orientation in Erikson's work (cf. Hanford 1975; Coles 1970; Johnson 1977; Capps 1977, 1978). Recently, the affinities between Erikson and hermeneutical thinking has been set forth systematically by Jerald Wallulis (1990), to whom I owe the title of this paper, in: *The hermeneutics of life history*. In his view, Erikson's approach to life history is exemplary of what he calls "hermeneutically informed and hermeneutically situated social science" (p. 94). Moreover, he considers Erikson's work as an important complement to philosophical hermeneutics.

Summarizing: in Erikson's work Wallulis sees a good balance between a regressive and a progressive view. There is on the one hand the insight of Gadamer that man is 'historically effected' — a product of the past; the emphasis is on the 'situatedness' of human events in collective history and personal life history. Human events have a *happening structure*. In short, Erikson displays a '*wirkungsgeschichtliches Bewusstsein*'. So to understand human events, you have to look at the past, to what effected a specific individual or collective identity.[6] In this sense, Wallulis states, Erikson's view on identity is a correction of Habermas' theory, who overemphasizes the progressive side of identity: man's cognitive abilities to project a rational identity to the future.

But man is not only a product of his past. Human events also have an *action structure* — and here, according to Wallulis, lies the most important point of Erikson's approach, and a useful complement to the hermeneutics of Gadamer. Wallulis' notion of 'action structure' covers Erikson's notion of 'actuality'. Wallulis argues that in his psychology Erikson integrates man as an 'actor', as initiator and accomplisher of his own life history. Therefore, human events are not just *happenings*, but personal, active *achievements*. Individuals have an active role in accomplishing their own life history, besides being a product of their past. (So Erikson does not lose sight of historical situatedness). What you are in the present is not effected by the past. Rather, the past *enables* you to achieve. This involves a change of consciousness in the present: The consciousness is not that of 'having been effected', but of 'having been enabled' to achieve.

Wallulis sees the action structure of human events most clearly elaborated in Erikson's view on play:

> I propose the theory that the child's play is the infantile form of the human ability to deal with experience by creating model situations and to master reality by experiment and planning. It is in certain phases of his work that the adult projects past experience into dimensions which seem manageable. In the laboratory, on the stage, and on the drawing board, he relives the past and thus relieves leftover affects; in reconstructing the model situation, he redeems his failures and strengthens his hopes. He anticipates the future from the point of view of a corrected and shared past. No thinker can do more and no playing child less... (Erikson, quoted in Wallulis 1990, p. 129).

So play is a way to creatively master the future, while at the same time integrating the past. This contention "...makes the life cycle into a historical process for the individual with both preservation and development, renewal and creativity, a 'truth' that both continues and changes" (Wallulis 1990, p. 131).

In short: Erikson looks for a "balance between being situated within the biological, social and historical processes of development and being actors within that same process" (Wallulis 1990, p. 94). Man is formed by the past, dependent on tradition and social structures, but is to a certain extent also free: it is possible to actively recreate the past by a preservation of past positive experience and the acknowledgement of continuity between life periods. A personal, active appropriation of life history is possible. This does not involve a restitution of the original past as much as a reconstruction of immature development, as well as a functional integration of the past in present life (Wallulis 1990, p. 133).

In my view, Wallulis shows excellently the intrinsically hermeneutical character of Erikson's psychological approach. Yet his particular focus — philosophical hermeneutics — restricts his view on

Erikson. In the first place, he does not notice the important role of religion in Erikson's psychology (although he is not the only one who makes this mistake). Secondly, he pays too little attention to the generalistic, universalistic claims of the life-cycle theory, although he is right in characterizing this theory as a "hermeneutics of life history" rather than as a "theoretics of individual development" (Wallulis 1990, p. 132), or as a "generalized psychological theory" (Wallulis 1990, p. 7). I agree that in the course of Erikson's work the life-cycle theory becomes more and more an interpretative instrument. Yet the factual structures of soma and ego (which may and have been empirically validated, cf. Ochse & Plug 1986) have always remained the basis of the theory. It is, however, with the introduction of ethos (and thus the actuality aspect — the dynamic interaction between individual and environment) that the factual structures are no longer of value in themselves, but become hermeneutical keys in the service of interpretation.

CONCLUSION

It is beyond question that Erikson's psychological approach of religion is best characterized as 'hermeneutical'. With his life-cycle theory, he offers a contextual, holistic way of examining human reality. In his view, 'meaning' always plays a role in the construction of human reality, and thus we cannot do without an interpretative approach. By focusing on teleology and actuality, he views man not only as determined by mechanistic processes, but also as an intentional, conscious and meaning-giving being. Therefore, a hermeneutical, interpretative approach is indispensable in psychology.

Yet, in spite of his emphasis on actuality, factuality originally was, and has always remained the starting point of his psychology. Actuality is always embedded in factuality. There are some facts about the psychic life that can and must be established as universal/general and non-contextual. The life-cycle theory is a clear example of this double focus. On the one hand, it describes the basic structure and elements of development which are of universal value (although a cultural context always determines which universal aspects of development come to the fore). On the other hand, by introducing the dimension of actuality (with concepts like 'I' and 'ethos') it becomes clear that we need a hermeneutical approach to study how a concrete individual develops, how the 'facts' of a life turn into 'acts'. In this way the character of the life-cycle theory changes: its factual basis is no longer a goal in itself, but serves as a hermeneutical key to interpret actuality.

In my view, it is the great merit of Erikson to have shown that the various levels of human reality are intrinsically linked with each other. To understand human phenomena, it is never sufficient to look at one level, whether it be the personalistic or the mechanistic one. Erikson's psychology presents an interesting approach to combine both factuality and actuality. This complex approach, however, illustrates the tension between science-oriented and hermeneutical approaches. One problem, for instance, is determining where factuality ends and where actuality begins. Therefore, his approach cannot be easily applied. But I think it is worth trying.

Finally, Erikson's work shows that the psychology of religion has an important contribution to make to psychology in general. By linking religion with the I and the integrating process of actualization, he situates religion in the centre of the psychic life. It is only by understanding the (religious) process of actuality that we can really understand the process of personality development. So we need psychology of religion if we want to understand human reality as such.

Notes

1. I would like to thank prof. dr. C.A.J. van Ouwerkerk for his helpful comment on an earlier version of this article.
2. Strien & Rappard distinguish 'empirical-analytical' science — oriented towards the logical-positivism developed in Vienna in the twenties, trying to discover general laws and causal relations in order to explain, predict and control reality — from a 'hermeneutic approach', trying to analyze the meaningful structure of reality.
3. Cf. Schafer (1992), Spence (1982; 1987), and in the Netherlands for instance A.W. Mooij and P.C. Kuiper. Adolf Grünbaum (e.g. 1984) is a tireless adversary of hermeneutical conceptions of psychoanalysis.
4. Cf. the articles which appeared in 1994 and 1995 titled: Making monsters: False memories, psychotherapy, and textual hysteria. *41* (19), p. 54 ; *41* (20), p. 49; *42*, p. 20 ; *42*, p. 667. And further: Matthew Hugh Erdely & Frederick Crews. Freud and memory: An exchange. *42* (5), p. 65.
5. Cf. Erikson (1964), pp. 161-215, and Zock (1990), pp. 70-72 and 233-239.
6. Erikson's life cycle theory has "a hermeneutical relevance, that is essential for comprehending the historical dimensions, including the contents of tradition, that have contributed to the development of — and produced — the personal and social identities that we as a matter of fact have" (Wallulis 1990, p. 94).

References

Ankersmit, F., M.C. Doeser, & A.K. Varga (1990). *Op verhaal komen: over narrativiteit in de mens- en cultuurwetenschappen* [On narrativity in human and cultural sciences]. Kampen: Kok Agora.

Capps, D. (1978). Psychohistory and historical genres: the plight and promise of Eriksonian biography. In: P. Homans. *Childhood and selfhood: essays on tradition, religion and modernity in the psychology of Erik H. Erikson* (pp. 189-228). Lewisburg, Pa.: Bucknell University Press.

Capps, D., W.H. Capps, & M.G. Bradford (eds.) (1977). *Encounter with Erikson: historical interpretation and religious biography.* Santa Barbara, California: Scholarpress for the American Academy of Religion, and the Institute for Religious Studies.

Coles, R. (1970). *Erik H. Erikson: the growth of his work.* Boston: Little, Brown & Co.

Erikson, E.H. (1958). *Young man Luther: a study in psychoanalysis and history.* New York:. Norton.

Erikson, E.H. (1963). *Childhood and society.* New York: Norton. (orig. publ. 1950)

Erikson, E.H. (1964). *Insight and responsibility: lectures on the implications of psychoanalytic insight.* New York: Norton.

Erikson, E.H. (1968). *Identity: youth and crisis.* New York: Norton.

Erikson, E.H. (1969). *Gandhi's truth: on the origins of militant nonviolence.* New York: Norton.

Erikson, E.H. (1975). *Life history and the historical moment.* New York: Norton.

Erikson, E.H. (1982). *The life cycle completed: a review.* New York: Norton.

Evans, R.I. (1967). *Dialogue with Erik H. Erikson.* New York: Harper & Row.

Geertz, C. (1980). Blurred genres: the refiguration of social thought. *The American Scholar, 49,* 165-179.

Groot, A.D. de (1961). *Methodologie: grondslagen van onderzoek en denken in de gedragswetenschappen.* 's Gravenhage: Mouton. [Transl.: *Methodology: foundations of inference and research in the behavioral sciences* (transl. J.A.A. Spiekerman). The Hague: Mouton, 1969]

Grünbaum, A. (1984). *The foundations of psychoanalysis: a philosophical critique.* Berkeley: University of California Press.

Hanford, J.T. (1975). A synoptic approach: resolving problems in empirical and phenomenological approaches to the psychology of religion. *Journal for the Scientific Study of Religion, 14,* 219-227.

Homans, P. (1968). *The dialogue between theology and psychology.* Chicago: University of Chicago Press.

Johnson, R.A. (ed.) (1977). *Psychohistory and religion: the case of Young man Luther.* Philadelphia: Fortress Press.

Jones, J.W. (1991). *Contemporary psychoanalysis and religion: transference and transcendence.* New Haven: Yale University Press.

Messer, S.B., L.A. Sass & R.L. Woolfolk (1988). *Hermeneutics and psychological theory. Interpretive perspectives on personality, psychotherapy and psychopathology.* New Brunswick: Rutgers University Press.

Ochse, R. & C. Plug (1986). Cross cultural investigation of the validity of Erikson's theory of personality development. *Journal of Personality and Social Psychology, 50,* 1240-1253.

Packer, M. & R. Addison (eds.) (1989). *Entering the circle: hermeneutic investigation in psychology.* Albany, NY: State University of New York Press.

Runyan, W.M. (1982). *Life histories and psychobiography: explorations in theory and method.* New York: Oxford University Press.

Sanders, C. & J.F.H. van Rappard (1982). *Tussen ontwerp en werkelijkheid: een visie op de psychologie* [Between design and reality: a perspective on psychology]. Meppel: Boom.

Sarbin, Th.E. (ed.) (1986). *Narrative psychology: the storied nature of human conduct.* New York: Praeger.

Schafer, R. (1992). *Retelling a life: narration and dialogue in psychoanalysis.* New York: Basic Books.

Smith, W.C. (1979) *Faith and belief.* Princeton, NJ: Princeton University Press.

Spence, D.P. (1982). *Narrative truth and historical truth: meaning and interpretation in psychoanalysis.* New York: Norton.

Spence, D.P. (1987). *The Freudian metaphor: toward paradigm change in psychoanalysis.* New York: Norton.

Strien, P.J. van & J.F.H. van Rappard (1990). *Grondvragen van de psychologie: een handboek theorie en grondslagen* [Basic questions in psychology: a handbook of theory and foundations]. Assen: Van Gorcum.

Terwee, S.J.S. (1989). *Hermeneutics in psychology and psychoanalysis.* Amsterdam: Centrale Drukkerij Universiteit van Amsterdam.

Wallulis, J. (1990). *The hermeneutics of life history: personal achievement and history in Gadamer, Habermas, and Erikson.* Evanston, Ill.: Northwestern University Press.

Wulff, D.M. (1991). *Psychology of religion: classic and contemporary views.* New York: Wiley.

Yankelovich, D. & W. Barrett (1971). *Ego and instinct: the psychoanalytic view of human nature — revised.* New York: Random House.

Zock, H. (1990). *A psychology of ultimate concern: Erik H. Erikson's contribution to the psychology of religion.* Amsterdam: Rodopi.

Zwaal, P. van der (1990). Het narratieve paradigma in de psychoanalyse [The narrative paradigm in psychoanalysis]. In: F. Ankersmit, M.C. Doeser & A.K. Varga. *Op verhaal komen: over narrativiteit in de mens- en cultuurwetenschappen* (pp. 36-62). Kampen: Kok Agora.

The Obsessional Episode in the Conversion Experience of Ignatius of Loyola
A Psychobiographical Contribution

J. Corveleyn
University of Leuven (Belgium)

Psychoanalysis, Psychobiography and 'Sanctity'

The masterly *Psychology of a saint* by W.W. Meissner (1992) is not a hagiography of Ignatius, nor is it an apologetic demonstration by an insider of the Company. With respect for Ignatius' personality and in the spirit of a great connoisseur of the theology and history of Ignatius' epoch, Meissner tries to illuminate as a psychologist the whole personality of the great man. He does not have the - scientifically unsound - ambition to *explain* psychologically what theologians and religious believers call sanctity. As a good clinician and full experienced psychoanalist, he tries to *understand* Ignatius' personality in both his weaknesses and greatness. His greatness is beyond doubt for Meissner but, as he demonstrates very well, even this holy greatness is understandable only when one takes into account the very humaneness of Ignatius and thus, his weaknesses.

Religiosity and Psychological Understanding

If psychology can contribute to the understanding of exceptional religiosity, it does so only by throwing light on the very personal set of psychological components that characterize the human particularity of the 'holy' subject. Holiness is not explained by psychology. Psychology can only excavate a part of the hidden intelligibility of this exceptional phenomenon. If this human science does its job by showing that the exceptionality is among other things constructed with common and very ordinary - or even with very imperfect - psychological building blocks, it neither blames the great personality nor diminishes its perfection, but only shows that human greatness and 'perfection' is possible only - as is underlined by Rita Levi-Montalcini in her book *In praise of imperfection* - because of man's *imperfection*, which is the base of human creativity (see Levi-Montalcini 1988).

PSYCHO-BIOGRAPHY

Meissner describes the task of the psychobiographer as follows: "His work consists in bringing to bear an interpretive schema, based on his clinical knowledge and experience and drawn from psychological theory - in this case psychoanalysis - to yield hypotheses that will add a significant dimension to the understanding of the subject's personality and behavior in the course of that individual's life" (Meissner 1992, p. xvi). Further on he underlines that the specific concern of the psychoanalyst is with "personal meaning and motive" (op.cit., p. xxii): those of consciousness, which can be very misleading and concealing, and those of the unconsciousness, which most of the time remain concealed. It is typical for the point of view of the psychoanalyst that he considers these meanings and motives to be causal factors, i.e. belonging to a domain of causality in its own right, and thus to be differentiated from other kinds of causality (organic, sociological, historical, etc.) which can be scientifically understood. Meissner does not give an explicit definition of this psychic causality.

In his *Guilt and desire*, A. Vergote (1988) devotes a lot of attention to the elaboration of a refined definition of *psychic causality*. I believe that the psychoanalytically inspired circumscription he produces fits very well with the approach of our Ignatian author. Vergote first explains "that the psyche is shaped in the juncture between the instincts and the symbolic forms and meanings of culture" (Vergote 1988, p. 22). The psyche is not only shaped by its interiority; the psychic 'apparatus' is not the psyche in its totality. The psyche is the 'result' of the interaction between the interiority of the subject and the 'outside' symbolic cultural world which is to the subject a 'given' transmitted to him through the mediation of language. This interaction between interiority and exteriority, between "the instinctual body and cultural significations comprises a *cumulative history* that leads back to the very origins of each individual" (op.cit., p. 22; our emphasis). This personal history is at the kernel of Vergote's definition of 'psychic causality'. He states that "this determination of the psyche by our archaic history" is "psychic causality because the historical past present within us circumscribes the actual possibilities open to us as well as the limits that bind us" (op.cit., p. 24).

Meissner is very conscious of the many risks and pitfalls of the psycho-biographic enterprise. The problems concern data collection and selection, hypothesis and pattern building, as well as the strictly interpretive aspects of the job: over-interpretation, psychologizing, "underemphasizing aspects that do not fit the putative hypothesis" (Meissner 1992, p. xvi), etc. As a consequence of these risks, he proceeds in his work with great caution. He never abandons the hypothetic style in the formulation of his interpretations, never tries to put forward a 'definitive' truth, and always respects the criteria of "correspondence" between data from different sources and "coherence" of meaning dimensions (op.cit., p. xxi).

MEISSNER'S PSYCHOANALYTIC APPROACH

With Pine (1988), one can map the psychoanalytic landscape as being composed of four perspectives: the psychology of drives, the psychology of the ego, the psychology of object relations and the psychology of the self. Meissner mainly operates with the tools of classical Freudian drive psychology and with those of the ego-psychological approach. Taking into account the abovementioned difficulties of the psychobiographical enterprise and agreeing with all the precautions which one must respect, as Meissner does, I do not share the experience of one of this book's reviewers. She mentions her "sense of deprivation, missing the fluent interpersonal subtleties of object-relations theory (especially in the short, sparse handling of Ignatius' very early life), and having to learn as I went along to make vital use of the rather ponderous concepts of early one-person psychology" (Coltart 1993, p. 1281).

First of all, with regard to the sparseness of Meissner's handling of Ignatius' very early life, our author is indeed rather 'sober' with his interpretations of Ignatius' origins and early childhood. One must not forget that the subject under study dates from a pre-autobiographical era, if one may forge this term. This means that trustworthy data about this period are very rare. And in this case, the psychoanalytical psychobiographer must also be cautious. He must avoid one of the biggest pitfalls of psycho-biography, namely the "so-called genetic fallacy" or, as Meissner says with E. Erikson's words, the "originological fallacy" - in other words, "explaining current behavior by appealing to its origins in the past" (Meissner 1992, p. xix). But the data about precisely those origins are very limited, so that adopting the explicit object-relational perspective would in this case certainly lead to psychologizing and to over-interpretation.

Secondly, I do not see in what way the perspectives used by Meissner can be considered old-fashioned one-person psychology. The fact that he does not use the (object-)relational vocabulary does not necessarily imply that he does not take into account what is at stake in the interpersonal field. Indeed, Meissner does try to illuminate Ignatius as an exceptionally religious man by throwing some light on his (personal) motivational life. But on every page, so to speak, he also mentions the social field with which Ignatius is in interaction. He does not approach his subject as an isolated atom. He always adopts the interactionist perspective, as should be done, even in a 'classical', Freudian psychoanalytic approach. He demonstrates convincingly how Ignatius is in continuous 'concert' with his 'environment': his family and the spirit of its traditional way of life, the religion of his time, the profane and the religious literature that greatly influenced his world of thinking, the pious women in his company at Manresa, the influence of his confessors and spiritual leaders, the importance of his first companions, etc. ... This is not a 'one-person psychology'.

PSYCHODYNAMIC FINDINGS

In the chapters on Ignatius' origins (family, his evolution from childhood until young adulthood), on his conversion and on the Manresa period, Meissner gives arguments for and illustrates at least three capital psychodynamic patterns that can be considered possible sources of pathology in the case of Ignatius. In this sense his psychobiography is at the same time a pathography.

These psychodynamic problem fields are well known: Ignatius' narcissism, his tendency to depression linked with early maternal deprivation (his mother died on the occasion of, or shortly after his birth) and his (obsessional) scrupulosity in the middle of his post-conversion, mystical evolution at Manresa (cf. Beirnaert 1957; Vergote 1988, pp. 174-179 for Ignatius' mystical and visionary experience).

In this article I will focus on the obsessional aspect of Ignatius' conversion episode and in his post-conversion mystical period at Manresa (May 1521 - February 1523). And, more precisely, I will limit myself to a close reading of that part in Ignatius' autobiographical text (Ignatius 1962) which is relevant for this period and of some specialized historical and biographical commentaries. In a future article I will complement this approach by a re-reading of some of his other texts that are pertinent to this perspective, namely the well-known *Spiritual exercises* (Ignatius 1991) and the so-called *Discernment log-book* (Ignatius 1987). To document Ignatius' obsessional personality traits as expressed in these texts, I will focus attention on some formal characteristics of the text, as well as on some aspects of its content. In making this interpretation, I will not add any really new insights or new facts to the already known *psychobiographical* constructions, but only will try to show more clearly than has been done before how these personality traits or problems remain visible, or better, 'readable' in some classical, 'sacred' Ignatian texts.

In doing this I agree completely with Freud's restrictions and admonitions concerning the psychological or the pathographical research into "the greatest of the human race" (Freud 1910, p. 63).

THE LIMITS OF PATHOGRAPHICAL DESCRIPTION

In fact, there are two 'movements' in Freud's attempt to analyze the greatest of the human race. On one hand, he always emphasizes the strict limitations of the possibilities of psychoanalytic and, *mutatis mutandis*, pathographical research into sublime human realizations, be it works of art or other great achievements of sublimation.

The achievements in themselves, the greatness of cultural creations and the nature of an exceptional artistic, political or religious talent, are not explicable by psychoanalysis. As Freud formulates it in his Leonardo study: "Pathography does not in the least aim at making the great man's achievements intelligible." (op.cit., p. 130). In the synthetic overview of his own creation, psychoanalysis, elaborated in his *Autobiography*, he applies this limitation specifically to the question of artistic talent. "It [psychoanalysis] can do nothing towards elucidating the nature of the artistic gift, nor can it explain the means by which the artist works, [namely the] artistic technique" (Freud 1925, p. 65; see also Freud 1928). In this perspective, psychoanalysis certainly does not aim to "blacken the radiant and drag the sublime into the dust, [... and ... to narrow] the gulf which separates the perfection of the great from the inadequacy of the objects that are its [psychiatry] usual concern" (Freud 1910, p. 63), on the contrary. Psychoanalysis does not explain talent by an operation of psychological reduction of the sublime to the earthly.

On the other hand, psychoanalytic understanding leads to the narrowing of another kind of gulf, namely the 'gulf' that commonsense psychology presupposes between so-called normality and what is psychologically exceptional (pathology or excellence). These are not two separate realms of human existence, as if normality stems from another psychological world than the exceptional. On the contrary, we learn about psychic normality by studying the pathological or exceptional ways of being. This opinion has been eternalized by Freud in his *New Introductory Lectures*, where he explains the relationship between psychological normality, on one hand, and psychopathology, on the other hand, by means of the metaphor of the broken crystal (Freud

1933, pp. 58-59). In the final remarks of his Leonardo study, Freud applies this vision by saying that:

> Leonardo - [with all due respect, we could just as well read 'Ignatius' here J.C.] - himself, with his love of truth and his thirst for knowledge, would not have discouraged an attempt to take the trivial peculiarities and riddles in his nature as a starting-point for discovering what determined this mental and intellectual development. We do homage to him by learning from him. *It does not detract from his greatness if we make a study of the sacrifices which his development from childhood must have entailed, and if we bring together the factors which have stamped him with the tragic mark of failure* (Freud 1910, pp. 130-131; emphasis added).

This does not reduce the 'great' achiever, or the hero to a particular psychopathological category, be it neurosis or psychosis. We may not forget, as Freud himself emphasizes already in 1910, that:

> we no longer think that health and illness, normal and neurotic people, are to be sharply distinguished from each other, and that neurotic traits must necessarily be taken as proofs of a general inferiority. Today we know that neurotic symptoms are structures which are substitutes for certain achievements of repression that we have to carry out in the course of our development from a child to a civilized human being. We know too that we all produce such substitutive structures, and that it is only their number, intensity and distribution which justify us in using the practical concept of illness and in inferring the presence of constitutional inferiority (op.cit., p. 131).

THE SCRUPULOSITY PERIOD AT MANRESA

Let us turn now to the obsessional element in Ignatius' post-conversion episode (Manresa, March 1522 — February 1523).

The specific scrupulosity episode at Manresa is well known. We refer to Ignatius' own words for a succint description:

> "But at this time he had much to suffer from scruples. Although the general confession he had made at Montserrat had been entirely written out and made carefully enough, there still remained some things which from time to time he thought he had not confessed. This caused him a good deal of worry, for even though he had confessed it, his mind was never at rest" (Ignatius 1962, n° 22).[1]

THE WHOLE 'CLINICAL' CONTEXT

To understand this episode and its - from a clinical point of view - apparently good outcome, it is necessary to situate it in the context of the whole history of the Manresa conversion period. We may not forget that the obsessional episode is a fragment of a very eventful period, lasting only a short time in the middle, or more correctly, at the beginning of the very complicated evolution that Ignatius went through, transforming his life from that of a proud and ambitious *hidalgo* to that of a mystic pilgrim (see for this particular aspect, Beirnaert 1983) on the road of the *Imitation of Christ* - or that of a *"fool for Christ's sake"*, as Saward puts it (1980) - and to that of a proud soldier in the army of Christ engaged in the battle against evil for the glory of God.

From a clinical point of view the very *succession* of Ignatius' experiences in that first period in Manresa is interesting.

I do not agree with Beirnaert's (1957) presentation of this period. Although he deals with the whole Manresa period as an integrated sequence, namely as "the founding experience from which Ignatius (has) received his *Spiritual exercices*", he clinically presents the elements of this episode as parts of "an evolution which is characterised by strange events" (Beirnaert 1957, p. 112), as if these events, strange as they may well be, form an esoteric clinical cocktail and were not parts of a psychodynamically understandable, 'integrated' evolution. He then enumerates the events: first there is an "enigmatic" hallucinatory vision (that of the serpentlike 'thing'), then comes hesitation about the sense of the asceticism in which he forces himself to live; this is followed by sudden alternations between depression and states of serenity, and then, again suddenly, an obsessional phase begins, followed by the "decision" not to come back on the confession of his past sins. This decision leads to the "permanent liberation" of his scruples and to the beginning of a period in which he receives numerous visionary intellectual illuminations (cf. Beirnaert 1957, pp. 112-113).

I have two questions here. How justifiable is it to look at the different steps in this period as so many separate experiences rather than considering this period an integral clinical and psychodynamic unity? I will treat this question first. The other question concerns Beirnaert's thesis, namely that Ignatius "was liberated for ever from his scruples" (Beirnaert 1957, p. 113). In my clinical reading of Ignatius' account of his scruples I will show that this thesis is questionable in its generality. Meissner also speaks of a 'liberation', but with more nuances; he says that "what is significant is not the ultimate course of action but the fact that his ego was able to achieve a deeper insight and to proceed to the organization and direction of its energies, and finally to a course of action" (Meissner 1992, p. 78). And Meissner states on the basis of his reading of the *Autobiography* that Ignatius "found himself delivered from his scruples" (cf. Ignatius 1962, n° 25) with the aid of a "transference cure", namely Ignatius' relationship with his confessor (Meissner 1992, p. 80).

OBSESSIONALITY AS PART OF THE 'CLINICAL' HISTORY

To correct Beirnaert's (1957) picture of the Manresa period in the evolution of Ignatius, I go back to one of his great biographers, namely Dudon (1934; to be preferred to the all too succinct Rahner 1955), and try to integrate the historical approach into the 'clinical' story. I will use mainly the time-schedule Dudon elaborates in detailed discussion with his colleague-historians. For these historical details I refer the reader to this very interesting and accurate biography. I will focus on the Manresa period, during which the most intense episode of scrupulosity took place and I will localize this period in the broader context of the conversion history. In my overview of this episode, I will bring into the foreground all details that seem psychodynamically relevant in the context of the obsessional structure.

From Loyola to Manresa

Begin March 1522

In the beginning of March 1522, Ignatius decided to leave his family home at Loyola with the intention of making a pilgrimage to Jerusalem. Before going, as it was planned, to see his sister at Onate, he went first to the Basque sanctuary devoted to Mary at Arantzazu. He persuaded his brother Pedro Lopez who, together with two servants, accompanied him, to pass the night in vigil at the shrine of Our Lady.

According to Rahner, it would have been there, immediately after he left his family's house, that Ignatius made a vow to Mary of permanent *chastity*. "Because he knows his weakness", Rahner explains (Rahner 1955, pp. 105-106), and then adds the following quotation - of which he does not specify the origin - from a confidence to a friend: "As he left his homeland to go to Montserrat, he was more afraid of being overcome by the sin of the flesh than by any other burden; it had occasioned him many a struggle and defeat" (Rahner, quoted in Meissner 1992, p. 60).

By placing this psychologically important anecdote so early in Ignatius' pilgrimage, Rahner very heavily (too heavily?) accentuates the topic of chastity. But perhaps he is right.

Let's put together the important data that are available about this first move of Ignatius after his convalescence in the Loyola castle:

1. Although he situates this vow at another moment, Dudon also stresses the importance of the topic of the chastity in this early period. He places the vow episode after the visit to his sister and after Ignatius' visit to the duke of Navarrete. "And because he had been beaten many times by the demon of lust, he made the vow of permanent chastity to God through the mediation of Mary, somewhere on his way, at a place and on a day we do not know" (Dudon 1934[2]).

2. In the context of the sexual problem, Dudon (1934) stresses another anecdote. All other (psycho-)biographers I have been able to consult (Rahner 1955; Vergote 1988; Meissner 1992), put the same accent, namely on the well-known scene with the Moor Ignatius met on the royal road to Montserrat. They fell into conversation, and the Moor:

> admitted that the Virgin had conceived without man's aid, but could not believe that she remained a virgin after once having given birth, and for this opinion submitted the natural reasons which occurred to him. For all the arguments which the pilgrim gave against this opinion, he could not refute it... There gave rise to emotions that brought on a feeling of discontent in his soul, as he thought that he had failed in his duty. This in turn led to indignation against the Moor, as he thought that he had done very ill to allow a Moor to say such things against our Lady, and that he was obliged to defend her honor. Hence a desire arose to go in search of the Moor and give him a taste of his dagger for what he had said. This battle of desires lasted for some time with the pilgrim quite doubtful at the end as to what he ought to do. The Moor, who had gone on ahead, had said that he was going to a place, which was on the same highway, a litte further on... Tired out from this examination as to what it would be good for him to do, and not being able to come to any clear decision, he thought of letting the mule decide, and gave her a free rein up to the spot where the road divided. ... But it was our Lord's will that, although the village was only thirty or forty steps away, and the road to it broad and even, the mule took the royal highway and passed by the village road (Ignatius, quoted in Meissner 1992, pp. 61-62).

It is clear that this episode reflects an internal conflict between the ideals of the chivalrous knight "who feels that he must fight to defend the honor of his queen" and the ideal of the pilgrim "which would not permit this course" (Meissner 1992, p. 62). But most striking is that "the argument was about sexuality" (ibid.) ànd that Ignatius devotes so much of his dictation time with da Camara, his secretary, to telling precisely this story in full detail. Meissner explains:

> The Moor had cast aspersions on the virginity of the idealized Mother, who had become the sublimated vessel for Inigo's repressed [already?] and conflicted libidinal impulses. The impulse to kill him who would sully and make sexual the idealized Mother can hardly elude the implications of oedipal

determinants and origins. The oedipal struggle is cast against repressed incestuous wishes that are projected onto the Moor, who can then be effectively punished and destroyed as the bearer of such dangerous sentiments (Meissner 1992).

And Meissner concludes that "however repressed, Inigo's sexual wishes remained a vital force in his psychic economy and a source of continuing conflict" (ibid.).

3. While reading the different versions of this episode, I was struck by a rather *mysterious reference*. After the visit to his sister, Ignatius went directly to the duke of Navarette whom he formerly had served as a knight and soldier (cf. Dudon 1934, pp. 68-70; and Ignatius 1962, n° 13). Arrived at Navarrette, he does not present himself directly to the duke, but contacts the duke's treasurer. What can be the significance of this strange connection with money? Let us first read what Ignatius himself says about this. It seems very curious that he gives so much attention to something that seems so unimportant in the context of his 'great' pilgrimage. This money story almost covers the entire 13th paragraph of the second chapter of the *Autobiography*:

> And while it came back into his mind that the house of the duke owed him a small number of ducats, it seemed to him that it would be good to have them and with that aim he wrote a note to the treasurer. And the treasurer informed him that there was no money left. The duke heard about it and said to him that there could be a lack of money for everybody except for a Loyola, whom he wanted to pay for his services. And he received the money and *he gave a part of it to certain persons to whom he felt obliged* and with the other part he contributed to the restauration of a statue of Our Lady which was very deteriorated (Ignatius 1962, n° 13; italics added, J.C.).

To whom in Navarrete had he to pay a debt, to whom was he obliged? Might this be someone who had played a role in his sinful life when at the duke's service? We know from the context that the sin probably referred to here, be it only in an indirect way, is of sexual nature: the vow of eternal chastity as one of the first things he cares for after he left Loyola; "he had been beaten many times by the demon of lust" (Dudon 1934, p. 70); and, concerning the vision of Our Lady with the Child, occuring in the first phase of his conversion at Loyola (about August the 15th of 1521 (cf. Dudon 1934, p. 61)), he reports that

> "from that vision on he received a very special inner motion and he felt himself such *disgust* at his entire former life and specifically at the *things of the flesh*, that it seemed to him that different kinds of images painted in his soul were torn out of it. It is in this way that from that hour on until August

> 1553, the time at which this is being written, he never has again had even the slightest consent to the things of the flesh" (Ignatius 1962 n° 10; italics added, J.C.).

And finally, we remember here the very violent affective reaction he had after the meeting with the Moor who had been doubting about the virginity of the Lady.

Some final remarks must be added. From a formal, discursive point of view *four characteristics* are striking in the way in which he tells the money story:
1. the *amount of words* he spends on this seemingly futile peripetia;
2. the *insistence* with which he seems to report the *details* of how he spent the money, nevertheless leaving the reader in uncertainty about the person to whom he payed the first part of the money - he who is always so accurate, open and frank in telling his history;
3. he *starts* virtually the entire story of his move away from home, his 'pilgrimage' to Jerusalem after which he wished to begin a life of penitence (cf. Ignatius 1962, n° 12), with this story of getting money and repaying "certain persons to whom he was obliged" (op.cit., n° 13), and
4. there is a *curious narrative turn* in Ignatius' account of this story. I refer here to the following observations:

4a. In his account of this episode Dudon stresses that Ignatius did not consider the visit to the duke very important: "he thought the trip was useless" (Dudon 1934, p. 68). He gives only *conjectural* reasons for this opinion, or suffices with simply quoting the text of the *Autobiography*. This is something he never does in other contexts; elsewhere he always tries, as a good historian, to fill in the open places with historical facts deduced from historical documents and archives. He hypothezises that "the little town" with its fortresses no longer interested Ignatius - except perhaps the old collegial church in which so many kings and princes were buried - and that he "perhaps had only to say to the duke: *Sic transit gloria mundi*". And, Dudon freely adds: "Certainly he would not have lacked the courage to say this; but he wanted to keep secret his decision to begin a new life" (Dudon 1934, pp. 68-69).

Why, one could ask, would he want to be so secret towards his former lord? Rather than seek an explanation for this, Dudon presents as his evidence that Ignatius "found it sufficient to transmit via the house personnel [not mentioned in Ignatius' account; Dudon's addition] a note to the treasurer of the duke in which he claimed his pay" (op.cit., p. 69). And he adds, inventing more facts, that "Inigo less than ever thought about earthly fortunes; he wanted only to be the soldier of Christ. In a letter, or via the messenger who gave him the duke's money, he undoubtedly thanked the duke for his goodness" (ibid.). Dudon finishes this passage by merely quoting Ignatius' text about his distribution of the ducats.

4b. But most curious of all concerning this anecdote is the *internal contradiction* in Ignatius' own account. At the end of the chapter preceding the one on the period between Loyola and Manresa, he recounts how he tried to convince his eldest brother Martin Garcia to allow him to leave Loyola. One day, "probably at the beginning of March 1522", "he decided that it was time to go and he said to his brother: "Sir, the duke of Najera, as you surely know, has been informed about the fact that I am doing well. It would be good that I go to Navarrete", and he adds between brackets: "(The duke was there at that moment)" (Dudon 1934, p. 64). At this point precisely da Camara, Ignatius' secretary, adds the following footnote: "His brother was suspecting, like others in the house, that he was planning to make a great change in his life" (Ignatius 1962, n° 12). His brother then tried to convince him to stay at home, saying to him that everyone admired him and that many people had placed great hope in him. "But the answer was such that, without being contrary to the truth - concerning which he already had a great scruple - he could, by hiding his intentions, escape from his brother" (ibid.). This is the first time the term 'scruple' is used in Ignatius' autobiographical text. Truth is of utmost importance for him; and he had just told his brother that he intended to go to the duke at Navarrete. And then, in the immediately following paragraph, he says that he did not address himself to the duke, but only the treasurer. *Where is the 'scruple' ?*

And, looking at this same sequence, why is he so secretive towards his brother? He, who, in the time between the vision of Our Lady with the Child and his final - but already well prepared - decision, "used the time he shared with the people of the house in speaking about the matters of God in order to be fruitful to their souls" (Ignatius 1962, n° 11), and he who openly sent a servant for information about the Chartreuse of Sevilla (op.cit., n° 12). *What is the secret he is in fact hiding from his brother?*

It is possible that all this is only the expression of his holy intention to begin his new life, the expression of his "immovable decision", and it is possible that "... for months the projects of the wounded convert had been firmly designed" and that "nothing in the world interested him anymore, and that the brillant future about which his brother was speaking to him was nothing but folly to the reader of the *Vita Christi* and of the *Flos Sanctorum*" (Dudon 1934, p. 66). *It is possible.*

But *why the contradiction in the text and, what to do with the convergence of significant text data in the direction of a real fault, a secret ?* Is it so that the obsessional period that begins shortly after the month of March 1522 was only a temporary neurotic phase or an element of a depressive reaction?. Or does the secret concern something more and other than the need to keep his pilgrimage project hidden (if it was so, taking into account his conversations with his family) from his eldest brother? Were the later scruples only the expression of an obsessional character structure which remained covert until then and that manifested itself only, using the contemporaneous religious language about the sinfulness of men, under the pressure of his very intense religious concerns - or were the scruples, among other things (the neurotic characteristics), also the expression of concerns and sadness with a 'real' inextinguishable fault ? We do not know, and it will probably remain so, but the lines of convergence of meaning in the direction of this latter hypothesis do not seem unimportant.

21 March 1522

I will be brief about the few, but very important, days Ignatius spent in Monserrat (between March 21st and March 25th; cf. Dudon 1934, p. 72, 76). Before he arrived at Montserrat he bought in Igualada the rough tissue of which a pilgrim robe can be made. Upon arriving at Montserrat, he looked for a confessor. "We know with utmost certainty that he went to Fray Juan Chanones" (Dudon 1934, p. 73), a French priest to whom he made a general confession in writing (Ignatius 1962, n° 17). This operation took three days. At the end of those days he obtained *general absolution.* And he passed the night of Monday 24th to Tuesday the 25th of March (Annunciation-day) in vigil before the shrine of Our Lady of Montserrat (Dudon 1934, p. 75). "Ignatius has always kept secret the mystery of that sacred night. None of his confidants, not even Father Gonzalès da Camara, has ever learned anything about this experience" (ibid.). The only information we have is, according to Dudon, the Annunciation meditation in the *Spiritual exercices.*

Regarding this long confession we evidently do not have further information from other sources, except the near certainty about the name of the confessor (Dudon 1934, pp. 73-76; Meissner 1992, pp. 63-65). And except the fact, reported by Ignatius himself, that this general confession was later at the origin, and became the core of his scruples at Manresa (Ignatius 1962, n° 22).

He left behind his arms in *ex voto*, in the morning gave his beautiful nobleman's clothes to a beggar and, departing in the direction of Barcelona on that morning of the 25th, passed through Manresa, where he stayed nearly a year. The long stay at Manresa was totally unplanned: "He wanted to stay there for a couple of days in the hospital, with, among other things, the intention of making some notes in his notebook which never left him and which was of great consolation to him" (Ignatius 1962, n° 18).

25 March 1522 — February 1523

Regarding this period, I only will recall here only the main 'clinical' steps. After a first *period of mystic enthousiasm* without any sign of anxiety, doubt or sad feelings (Dudon 1934, p. 81) and in which he starts a life of severe asceticism, a hallucinatory vision, the vision of the many-eyed, serpent-like 'thing' comes to him. This vision brings him much pleasure and consolation, but finally leaves him in sadness when it disappears.

Then follows a *period of "affective instability"* (Vergote 1988, p. 175) or of great fluctuations in his basic mood. In his own words: "great changes in his soul" (Ignatius 1962, n° 21).

This *instability* had been initiated by a "*sour and violent thought*". From a clinical point of view it seems important that Ignatius gives a precise determination of the moment in which this thought came to his mind. It came to him "during the days that the vision was taking place or", as he adds to this stipulation, immediately amending himself, it came to him "a little time *before* the vision began" (op.cit., n° 20). Thus the succession of these important experiences has been: first the sour and violent thought, the doubt, (during or just before the, at first sight, consoling vision) and then, the alternations in his affective state, alternations in which the depressivity stood in the foreground. The succession was not: depressivity first, and then the beginning of doubt about his vocation. That the doubt could have been coming even before the vision is, in my opinion, very interesting. It leads to the psychodynamic interpretation of the vision as a kind of compensation, a momentary consoling ideation that was at first of some help to combat the doubts. But it also shows that the affective disturbance was not the first psychic hindrance in Ignatius' incipient religious life, as it would have been in the life of a person weakened by a constitution for an affective disease and thus, easily suffering from a depression. But even if the other alternative (the doubt coming *during* the days of the vision) had been the case, the fact remains that the doubt came first and that the affective disturbance came afterwards as a reaction to these doubts.

The *clinical hypothesis* that can be proposed on the basis of these considerations is that Ignatius was not primarily suffering from a mood disorder but from doubtfulness that became obsessive (cf. the later on beginning "scruples") and led to a depressive reaction. At this point, it is important not to forget the sometimes very close relationship between obsessionality and constitutional depressivity (cf. Tellenbach 1961).

Let us now go into more detailed consideration of the content of the "sour and violent thought" and Ignatius' reaction to it. "It was as if someone said to him in his soul: 'How will you be able to stand a life like this for the following seventy years of your existence?'" (Ignatius 1962, n° 20). But he fought this "temptation" ("he understood that the question came from the ennemy" (ibid.)) coming from an inwardly posed 'counter-question': "You poor creature ! Are you able to promise me even one hour of life?" (ibid.). In that way he was momentarily victorious against that temptation. But, only a little while later, "great alterations in his soul" began to harass him (op.cit., n° 21).

The dominating state of his mood is a *depressive* one, characterized by *abulia* and the loss of any enjoyment. He describes this negative subjective experience in very clear words: "He found himself in a state of such a distaste that he found no desire in himself to recite prayers or to hear the Mass, or to deliver himself to intense inner prayer." (Ignatius 1962, n°21). He also speaks of "sadness and desolation" (ibid.). But, a while later, these depressive states suddenly disappeared; he had the impression that those sad feelings "were taken away like one removes a cloak from someone's shoulders" (ibid.). These depressive states are not followed by truly positive feelings, enjoyment or euphoria. He 'simply' returns to his usual devotional life, his daily prayers and his usual sacramental practices; but at the same time he begins regular conversations with "spiritual persons who trusted him and who desired to speak with him" (ibid.). What impressed and frightened him most of all were "those alternations (of his mood) which he never had experienced before" (ibid.).

From a close reading of this passage (Ignatius 1962, n° 21), I obtain the impression that Ignatius does not simply undergo those alternations. Especially the beginning of the post-depressive phases are not passive experiences, as if they were automatic mood changes induced by a constitutional factor as is the case in an affective disease. He reports neither a return to the *status quo ante*, as is the case in unipolar affective disease, nor the classical alternation of depression and euphoria, as is the case in bipolar affective disease. On the contrary, although he first speaks of the removal of the heavy depressive mood as if "a cloak is taken away from his shoulders" (a passive experience, one could say), immediately afterwards, so he reports, he begins to make personal *efforts*: he "perseveres" (op.cit., n° 21) in his devotional life, he is tempted by the doubt "What is this new life that we [sic] start at present?" (ibid.), and he engages in conversations with spiritual persons. Those spiritual persons are themselves seeking conversation with him ... as if they are worried about him. When reporting this, he insists on the fact that he demonstrated much fervour in these conversations and in his "great willingness to make progress in the service of God" (ibid.). I hypothesize that these persons probably were worried about Ignatius. For this hypothesis I refer to the example Ignatius gives of one of those persons who approached him: an old woman of great piety - for which she was well-known in many regions of Spain and "whom the Catholic King once called in order to communicate some things to her" (Ignatius 1962, n° 21). "This woman one day spoke with the new soldier of Christ and said to him: 'Oh! That it may please to my Lord Jesus Christ to appear to you one day'" (ibid.). Let us not forget at this moment the exact picture that we must keep in mind in trying to understand psychologically Ignatius' situation: the pitiful image of a young nobleman who arrived in Manresa coming from Montserrat, and immediately adopted a very ascetic life (no meat, no wine, fasting everyday, eating only on Sundays and, as a "perfect fool for Christ's sake" (cf. Saward 1980), neglecting his outer appearance), who lived in a hospital among the poor and the sick and spent a lot of time in all the holy places of this little town. It is very understandable that he didn't pass unremarked and, in fact, caused some concern among the pious persons of that place. It can be hypothesized that those persons had noticed his depressive state in reaction to his doubts and that they tried to encourage him. It was visible to them that he needed help.

To the old lady's well-meant encouragement - or was it already visible to her that a future great Saint was there sitting before her? - he reacts fearfully with the words "Why should Jesus Christ appear to me?" (Ignatius 1962, n° 21).

CONCLUSION

Still, in spite of all his *efforts* to combat his doubtful ideas and his "sadness and desolation", and in spite of his "perseverance in practicing weekly confessions and communion" or, precisely as an aggravation of all these efforts, "a lot of suffering came on him by the fact of his scruples" (Ignatius 1962, n° 22).

The center of these scruples is the general confession he made at Montserrat some weeks before. "Although he had made his general confession at Montserrat with great diligence and entirely by writing, it nevertheless sometimes seemed to him that he had not confessed some things and this caused him much affliction. Although he confessed anew, he remained unsatisfied" (ibid.). I will not go into further detail about this wellknown episode. There is ample evidence in this story for the clinical hypothesis of an obsessional disturbance in Ignatius cured only by the positive transference he made toward his confessor (cf. Meissner 1992, pp. 79-80). I have tried to find more evidence for this hypothesis in those parts of the story that have been less studied in this perspective.

In a further study I would like to investigate the question of the probable vestiges of Ignatius' obsessionality in his later life. According to Freud's 'principle of the broken crystal' it must be so that such an important structural personality trait such as obsessionality should express itself in the later course of life, even if this problem had been overcome in an earlier life period. I think, that the nature of the formerly neurotic conflict and the structure of the solutions found for it, remain present in the personality structure, even in that of a recognised saint. This must find its expression in the works of that person. In the case of Ignatius this obliges us to study his writings. Most of all I think here of the *Spiritual exercices* (Ignatius 1991) and of his *Discernment log-book*, his "Spiritual Diary" (Ignatius 1987).

Notes

1. I translate from this critical French edition and, from time to time, I find inspiration for making translations in Ignatius (1956).
2. p. 70 and p. 70, n. 3 in which he discusses the timing of this, agreeing with Polanco, who places the vow before the meeting with the Moor and, disagreeing with Ribadeneyra, who places the vow some days later, just before his entrance in Montserrat.

References

Beirnaert, L. (1957). L'expérience fondamentale d'Ignace de Loyola et l'expérience psychanalytique. *La Psychanalyse*, *3*, 111-137.

Beirnaert, L. (1975). Une lecture psychanalytique du *Journal Spirituel* d'Ignace de Loyola. In: L. Beirnaert. *Aux frontières de l'acte analytique: La bible, Saint Ignace, Freud et Lacan* (pp. 205-218). Paris: Seuil, 1987.

Beirnaert, L. (1982). La règle ignatienne de l'agir. In: L. Beirnaert. *Aux frontières de l'acte analytique: La bible, Saint Ignace, Freud et Lacan* (pp. 219-227). Paris: Seuil, 1987.

Beirnaert, L. (1983). Ignace de Loyola, fin ou transformation du pèlerinage. In: L. Beirnaert. *Aux frontières de l'acte analytique: La bible, Saint Ignace, Freud et Lacan* (pp. 199-204). Paris: Seuil, 1987.

Coltart, N. (1993). [Review of W.W. Meissner, *The psychology of a saint*]. *International Journal of Psycho-Analysis*, *74*, 1281-1283.

Dudon, P. (1934[3]). *Saint Ignace de Loyola.* Paris: Beauchesne.

Freud, S. (1910). Leonardo da Vinci and a memory of his childhood. In: *The standard edition of the complete psychological works of Sigmund Freud, vol. 11* (pp. 63-137) (transl. & ed. J. Strachey). London: Hogarth, 1964[2].

Freud, S. (1925). An autobiographical study. In: *The standard edition of the complete psychological works of Sigmund Freud, vol. 20* (pp. 1-75) (transl. & ed. J. Strachey). London: Hogarth, 1964[3].

Freud, S. (1928). Dostoevsky and parricide. In: *The standard edition of the complete psychological works of Sigmund Freud, vol. 21* (pp. 177-194) (transl. & ed. J. Strachey). London: Hogarth, 1964[2].

Freud, S. (1933). New introductory lectures on psycho-analysis. In: *The standard edition of the complete psychological works of Sigmund Freud, vol. 22* (pp. 5-182) (transl. & ed. J. Strachey). London: Hogarth, 1964[2].

Ignatius of Loyola (1956). *St. Ignatius' own story* (transl. W.J. Joung). Chicago: Loyola University Press.

Ignatius of Loyola (1962). *Autobiographie* (transl. & ed. A. Guillermou). Paris: Seuil.

Ignatius of Loyola (1987). *Inigo: discernment log-book. The spiritual diary of saint Ignatius Loyola* (transl. & ed. J.A. Munitiz). London: Inigo Enterprises.

Ignatius of Loyola (1991). Exercices spirituels. In: *Ecrits* (pp. 45-255) (transl. & ed. M. Giuliani). Paris: Desclée de Brouwer.

Levi-Montalcini, R. (1988). *In praise of imperfection: my life and work* (transl. L. Attardi). New York: Basic Books. (orig. publ. 1987)

Meissner, W.W. (1991). Psychoanalytic hagiography: the case of Ignatius of Loyola. *Theological Studies*, *52*, 3-33.

Meissner, W.W. (1992). *Ignatius of Loyola: the psychology of a saint.* New Haven: Yale University Press.

Pine, F. (1988). The four psychologies of psychoanalysis and their place in clinical work. *Journal of the American Psychoanalytic Association*, *36*, 571-596.

Rahner, H. (1955). *Ignace de Loyola.* Paris: Desclée de Brouwer.

Saward, J. (1980). *Perfect fools: folly for Christ's sake in Catholic and Orthodox spirituality.* Oxford: Oxford University Press.

Tellenbach, H. (1961). *Melancholie: zur Problemgeschichte, Typologie, Pathogenese und Klinik.* Berlin: Springer.

Vergote, A. (1988). *Guilt and desire: religious attitudes and their pathological derivatives* (transl. M.H. Wood). New Haven, CT: Yale University Press. (orig. publ. 1978)

A Reader's Guide for Interpreting Texts of Religious Experience
A Hermeneutical Approach

J.M. Day & M.H.L. Naedts
Université Catholique de Louvain (Louvain-la-Neuve, Belgium)

We have for some time been interested in how religious experience might be best understood. Informed by research and practical work in developmental and clinical psychology, and nurtured in environments where religious experience has been valued and cultivated, we have sought to understand how it is that people talk about religious experience, make sense of it, know themselves in relation to it, and make decisions in light of it.

Immediate to any effort of the kinds we have undertaken is the question of interpretation. The very act of defining terms such as 'religious', 'experience', 'make sense', 'know themselves', and 'make decisions', is fraught with problems of an epistemological kind. How do we 'know' anything? What kind of account is to be trusted? How do the nature of the research process, the instruments involved, the context(s) in which the research occurs, and the stance of the researcher(s) concerned contribute to understanding or obscuring our comprehension of the phenomenon in question?

In wrestling with these matters, we have contributed to and been much influenced by the developing paradigm that we call a *narrative approach* to understanding the human subject, the meaning of language, and related implications for psychological research. In these terms, we have tried to work out a research method that takes seriously what we call the *dialogical nature of the self*, that permits *multiple interpretations* of interview *texts*, and which is *sensitive to culture and context* as important factors in how it is people talk about themselves. We think that the factor of *gender* is particularly interesting where context is concerned, because of the ways in which it touches upon cultural norms, psychological development, and the *performative as well as informative nature of language* in research processes (Day 1993, 1994a; Day, Naedts & Saroglou in press; Day & Naedts 1995; Day & Tappan 1995, in press).

In this paper we hope to show how the method we propose accomplishes the aims we have defined for our work, how problems of interpretation are both underscored and managed in it, and how classical questions of validity and reliability might be addressed in light of this kind of work.

SOME IMPORTANT CONCEPTS

It now behooves us to say something, in brief, about the meaning of the terms 'voice', 'narrative', 'text', and 'gender', we privilege in conducting our research and interpreting interview material.

On our view, it makes sense to discuss religious experience in terms of *voice* because of the inclusiveness of this term for understanding the irreducible relatedness of cognitive, connative, and affective dimensions in religious experience. We join a number of authors whose use of 'voice' expresses similar concerns. (Brown & Gilligan 1991; Brown et al. 1989; Tappan 1989, 1990, 1991a, 1991b):

> To speak of someone's religious *voice* is to speak of something living, embodied, incorporative, and constative as well as representative and expressive, of something that is multidimensional, that may not always sound the same, that is simultaneously engaged in acts of persuasion as well as information, which tells stories in order to place itself and to give meaning to the reasons it offers, and which echoes the sounds and styles and vernaculars of other voices. The use of "voice" permits an appreciation of the richness of religion as it is lived by its speaker. Religion as belief, ritual, symbol, social practice, moral code, myth, as discourse about the ultimate meanings of life, about the composition and workings of the cosmos, and about God(s) or first principles, are all present in the voices of those who describe themselves as religious, and who tell us what this means to them (Day, Naedts, & Saroglou in press).

We assume in our work that persons are *dialogical*, that mind is fundamentally *conversational*, and that it is impossible to think of what a person says apart from the fact that it is said *discursively* — in terms of an engagement with another person. Thus, when we encounter a person in a research interview, or must come to terms with the text that is the record of such an encounter, we are engaged in a process of conversation with a text that is dialogical, and which forms an account of some of the kinds of dialogues in terms of which the research subject operates in the world, including the part of her world that is pertinent to her and our definitions of religious experience.

We also take as important the "paradigm of the text" (Ricoeur 1981) as a constitutive element in our work. We agree with Ricoeur, following Dilthey (1900) that scientific methodology is engaged in procedures akin to *Auslegung* or "text interpretation" (Ricoeur 1981, p. 197). In so doing, we explicitly acknowledge the interpretative stance of the researcher as reader, admit that a variety of readings of interview texts are possible, and take for granted that a text may reveal more than one story, more than one voice, more than one set of purposes. We think it best to assume that texts are read properly when they are read responsively; when they are read and reread, when more than one reader makes explict the terms of his reading and rereading, and when the plurivocality of an author's representation in a text is not only permitted but made explicit in the process of analysis and interpretation of a text. To engage a text as a vehicle of voice means, furthermore, that the researcher must take into account his part in the process of authoring; he must read and reread in an effort to understand how it is that the text in question represents a relationship in-the-making between the researcher and the researched. He must thus come to grips with the ways in which the text in question includes his voice as well as that of the research subject (see also Brown & Gilligan 1991).

A number of authors have by now been influential in contributing to a *narrative approach* to understanding human behavior and psychological research (see e.g. Bruner 1986; Freeman 1991; Gergen & Gergen 1986; Packer 1989, 1991; Sarbin 1990; Tappan 1989, 1990, 1991a, 1991b, 1992; Tappan & Brown 1989). When we speak of narrative, we wish to emphasize that when people account for themselves, or when they describe experience, they often do so in story form. They speak in terms of plot, time, and character. Indeed, we would argue that the employment of narrative strategies is not incidental or secondary, but is instead essential in making a self possible and meaningful. To assess an interview in terms of elements that leave the narratory principle aside, is to miss much of what it is a person has to say, and is to ignore the social importance of how it is the person uses language not only to describe reality, but to make it. It may be difficult to take the processive nature of interview discourse, including how it is that story-making figures in such behavior, into account when interpreting an interview text. We think it necessary, and useful, to do so.

The psychological literature is by now replete with references to *gender* as an important feature of how it is people behave and make sense of experience. We are particularly interested in how gender figures in the ways people have, speak about, and otherwise make sense of religious experience. We argue that to speak of ourselves as though gender were immaterial would be ridiculous; it would be as ludicrous as speaking of ourselves as though we were other than human, physical, and sexual, as though we were ahistorical and noncontextual.

In thinking about gender as a factor related to our interest in voice, text, and narrative, we have been influenced by the work of Gilligan and colleagues (e.g. Brown & Gilligan 1993; Gilligan 1977, 1982). Gilligan has argued that moral experience is spoken of in two major ways; in terms of concerns with "justice" and "care". According to Gilligan, all persons are subject to two primary disadvantages both potential and real:

> disadvantages of oppression and of abandonment. They are thus necessarily concerned with the distribution of power, or rights and justice, and with the maintenance of relationship and connection with others. On this view, everyone contends with two principal moral anxieties: fear of powerlessness and fear of abandonment (Gilligan & Wiggins 1988).

Because male and female identity are socially constructed in different ways *vis-à-vis* independence and connection, separateness and relationship, Gilligan and her colleagues argue, they are also configured differently with regard to experiences of oppression and abandonment, justice and care, as the central features of moral concern. While the two concerns outlined by Gilligan are not gender exclusive, they are gender preponderant and characteristic. Men characteristically speak of self as separate. They speak predominantly in terms of individuality and independence. They talk about rights and justice when they talk about morality, an ethic of equality dominates their moral speech. Women speak of self in terms of relationships with others, and talk about morality with a greater attention to issues of care, connection, and an ethic that all be preserved from harm (Gilligan, Ward & Taylor 1988).

Gilligan is not alone in claiming that women and men speak differently about themselves and their behaviors; Tannen (1991) for example, has argued, on the basis of research in linguistic anthropology, that men and women speak different languages of self, friendship, love, and the meaning of work. Similar differences have been noted in other domains (Youngman 1993).

We do not claim that there is an exclusive correlation between gender and voice, but are interested to understand how particular accents come to characterize the speech of a person in relation to her gender.

Our own, initially anecdotal, observations of similar differences in talk about religion prompted the enquiry represented in this chapter. As we will attempt to illustrate in the paragraphs that follow, we tested the hypothesis that women speak of religious belief and practice in terms of relationship and affective value (what we call a *relational religious voice*), while men speak of belief in terms of principles and intellectual assent (what we call a *principled religious voice*).

RELIGIOUS EXPERIENCE: DEFINITIONS, DESCRIPTIONS, AND DECISIONS

At this point, we wish to turn to the questions that most centrally interest us in this chapter: How is it that an *interest* in voice, text, narrative, and gender in relation to religious experience, becomes translated into a program of research, analysis, and interpretation? How are our concepts related to our methods of conducting research, collecting data, and interpreting the texts that result?

In reply to these questions we turn first to a series of historical precedents; to answer as though we were not historical, that we did not have a kind of 'road' to hermeneutics, to a shared set of consternations, fascinations, and commitments with regard to an explicitly interpretative research approach, would be inconsistent with what we have thus far asserted.

Given a background that sensitized us to the importance of interpersonal variables in the conducting of interviews we developed the habit of thinking about *interviews* in terms of *relationships*: in order for certain kinds and qualities of information to be obtained, a certain climate of relationship was ordained. We have become increasingly convinced that to think about information obtained in such interviews apart from the relationships in which the information is produced is short-sighted.

These convictions have, in turn, seemed at odds with some of the reductionistic aspects of the research projects in which we were engaged: how it was that relationship could matter so much to information, but that the relationship was excluded from analyses of the 'data', escaped our understanding. In this vein, we have come to view as problematic the well-known efforts of Kohlberg, Oser, and adherents to their paradigms of interview work, efforts which on our view reduce the whole of an interview text to the structural components — in strictly cognitive-developmental terms — of the reasoning of the subject.

Our initial efforts to compensate for the oversights of such structuralist reductionism were to complement the structuralist paradigm with a more explicitly constructionist, or narrative, one (Day 1987, 1991a, 1991b, 1991c, 1993, in press a, in press b; Day & Naedts 1995). This involved efforts to interview research subjects who had responded to classical questionnaires and interview formats in the domains of moral and religious development, in such a way as to permit the same subjects to speak more 'freely' in the terms they wished, to concepts such as 'self', 'moral experience', 'religious experience', 'moral and religious judgment', 'dilemmas' and 'decisions'. We continue to regard these efforts as pertinent to a multi-paradigmatic program of research in which traditional cognitive-developmental paradigms hold a central place. At the same time, we are increasingly convinced of the integrity of our originally intended 'complementary' efforts in their own right, as we describe more fully below.

From these efforts the questionnaire used in the study reported on here, was developed.[1] As the reader will note, the questions in this interview invite the research subject to define the terms as he wishes to define them. The subject is asked whether a term is meaningful to him, and is then requested to elaborate how, if at all, it is so. The task of the interviewer is to make as much room as possible for the subject to talk freely about his own experience, and to ask questions in such a way as to amplify the response of the subject.

From the earliest efforts to make use of these interview formats, we found that research subjects very easily and richly responded to them in terms of stories which reflected, among other things, the historical, cultural, and embodied situations in which they found themselves; thus accounts of moral decision-making turned on the uncertainties involved in conflicting principles, multiple relationships, divided loyalties, a variety of voices which the subjects reported hearing and speaking to in order to make sense of the questions with which they were grappling. Likewise, accounts of religious experience were inseparable from what it was to have such an experience as a man or woman, husband, wife, son or daughter, working professional, and other such roles and contexts in the lives of the subjects as they reported them.

The following excerpts from two interviews illustrate some of the richness, and the challenges, inherent in the kind of interpretative project we have undertaken. The subjects have been asked questions from the Moral Experience Interview (hereafter referred to as the MEI) including questions as to the subject's own definition of self and identity (drawn from Lyons 1983, 1988) and three questions about religion; these questions touch upon the subject's definitions of religion, descriptions of religious experiences, and of religious decisionmaking. The reader will note that we use these initial excerpts for the purpose of illustrating how it is that our intentions, interview strategy, and interpretative inclinations cohere. In the next section of this chapter, we explain in greater detail how subject selection occurred and procedures were established in the research project from which these interview excerpts are taken.

Identity Questions
How would you describe yourself?
What can you tell me about yourself as a person?
Questions Concerning Religion:
I wonder if the term 'religion' means anything to you. If so, can you tell me what that means?
Now I wonder if the terms 'religious experience' mean anything to you, and if so, whether you can explain what that means to you.
I wonder if you have ever made what you would call a 'religious decision'. If so could you tell me about that, and what a religious decision would be to you?

The subjects' first responses to the questions about identity and religious experience follow, with brackets used to mark statements for coding purposes.

> **S1: Identity** What kind of a person am I, if that's your question then I'd say I'm a seeker of the truth, that is very, very important to me.][I study everything I can get my hands on, and to try to make sense of things in terms of enduring principles or truths][I was always like this, ever since I was a boy, which is probably where my interest in religion comes from].[I could never understand it that some people just seemed to live and not be preoccupied with the meaning of their lives].[And you can't just rely on feelings, from day to day, all that stuff that changes, to figure those things out].[So in my case, I went to the library, I borrowed books from friends and other people][I took philosophy courses in college][I really went about it in a systematic way, looking at things objectively, as objectively as I could][so I guess you could say I'm a seeker of the truth and I only feel good when I feel I understand things correctly].[I guess this is real tied up with my whole point of view about living].[There is a truth that can be found that is embodied in the teachings of Christ which are completely consistent with all the best philosophy][and your task as a human is to stand there, and kind of take it all in, and look at the world out there and say, hey, what does this all add up to?][You've got to use your God-given capacity to think and reason, and then you're going to find, if you're honest with yourself, that there's a truth that's eternal and has immediate implications for your life]. [So I guess we're talking identity here].[I'm a religious person, who seeks the truth, who wants to understand things, and who doesn't rest until I do][. And I think I've found that, quite objectively and empirically, in the Christian religion, everything that's true is in there].

> **S1:Religious Experience** [That one's pretty clear and pretty simple for me]. [Religious experience I would say is the experience of being convicted of the truth, being shown the way to what's real, in the empirical sense]. [You're out there struggling, all alone,][all the while in your struggle, maybe unbeknownst

to you, getting closer to the truth][, and, man, it hits you that you are getting onto something][, that the truth is going to be found][you can kind of feel your brain working closer to it][and the world is going to show you what is true][if you apply the right questions and experiments you are going to pass your test and get there].[And then, on the other side, there's the joy of religious faith that is a kind of religious experience][when you discover in living even more how true that truth was that you found in all your searching].[That's a kind of confirmatory experience][based in living out what you've found to be true, and finding out that the consequences of that truth you found philosophically work out very practically].[So religious experience as to do with the truth, going after it, finding out, and getting that confirmation for all your hard work].

S2: Identity [Who I am as a person?][I guess that would be pretty hard to talk about apart from the relationships I'm in], [I mean, the other people in my life, the people I am close to]. [I can define myself in terms of roles and competencies attached to those roles, I suppose] [but if I think about who I am I have to say that is where I am, interpersonally somehow], [which is in my relationships with the other people in my life], [I just can't think of myself apart from the people to whom I am relating any given moment]. [So then I would have to think about how I feel about those people][because my identity is all wrapped up in that][and that means that I am a person in terms of those I love][and about whom I have other feelings].[I'm someone who cares deeply about the others in my life][and who tries to be a good listener][who tries to understand other people in their own terms][and who tries to provide for them in a way that lets them grow].[I guess I'd say I'm a person who strives for a balance in my life][between what it is I need to do for myself, as a person in my own right][and meeting the needs of others who are in need of me].[That sense of myself as involved with others in order to know and be a self at all][is inseparable from the the sense I have of mission, of action, of what I have to do].

S2: Religious Experience[I would have to say that for me religious experience is both specific, I mean you can point to some cases, and very diffuse, or general; something that is always there as a part of life in all its aspects].[There have been moments, mostly in prayer, where I have felt, sure, of that presence of God,which weaves everything together], [which makes life what it is — umm — a series of connections], [in which everything has its place but is really, umm, all tied together.] [And so for me, I would say yes, that kind of a melding of things between myself and that presence I can only call God],[that kind of merging but you don't really lose yourself]; [a deep kind of connecting that places all the other things in their proper context, their connection is made clear].[But, I don't know if this makes sense], [but, you know, if you see it that way, if you feel that kind of connection, umm, with God I mean], [then, well, you could say kind of that every day is, well, a kind of religious experiencing], [in that that connection of things once you've felt it stays always there]. [You can't look at anything, and not feel it as, as, the thing it is in connection], [in connection to God and all other things], [and so

> the sacred kind of dimension, the ultimate connection of things in that thing], [is something you feel, you kind of see, in a certain way of seeing]. [You see your child being born, and your husband there], [you see how that presence of life itself is there in the face of your baby], [and the love that is there flowing all between you], [or you see your friend, her face, you see her face through the eyes of love], [you just see God in everything, you see a plan, a way things are connected]. [That's it for me — a kind of plural it, if you see what I mean, where the boundaries are kind of in question]. [But I don't know if that qualifies as religious experience], [but it's what it means to me when I think of that word].

READING AND REREADING THE TEXTS

In our efforts to make sense of such texts, we engage in at least four readings . In all of the readings, subjects' responses to the questions are read 'blind', in so far as the reader can be 'blind' under these circumstances. The texts of subjects' responses are mixed so that different coders read different texts randomly, and the names and other relevant data (including the sex of the respondent) are obscured from view. Thus, only the content of the subjects' responses are available to the reader. Readers do their work, at this stage of the reading process, independently of one another.

We are aware that it might strike some readers of this chapter as contradictory to stress context, responsiveness, and the irreducible importance of factors such as gender when conducting interviews and reading texts, on the one hand, and then, on the other to insist, as we do here, that readers follow, at one step in the reading process in such a way as to be 'blind' to the interview data's particulars in this regard. To some degree, the dilemmas one might detect in this apparent contradiction will be, we hope, resolved as we enter into a fuller discussion of the steps we take in the whole of our reading process. We think it important to observe, in addition, that this apparent contradiction represents part of our struggle to learn how explicitly hermeneutical methods, which endeavor to explicate otherwise neglected aspects of interview texts, make sense in relation to the rigours of positivist scientific methods, whose aim is to make it likely that facile theses are carefully tested and dispensed with if they cannot be operationalized and examined as working hypotheses. We would like to think of ourselves as working carefully and critically at the interface of these two 'inclinations', each of which has scholarly merit and which might be more fruitfully employed when they can be worked 'at' side by side, step by step. The reader will note on this account, as we describe in the following paragraphs, that initial 'blind' procedures move to a much more explicit grappling with the contextual richness provided by the interview texts and the dynamics of the readers who work with them, at a later stage in the process we employ in the reading, analysis, and interpretation of interview texts.

Readers are asked to read the subjects' responses and to underline in different colors the statements they read according to the relevant coding category. The use of color highlights the fact that different readers may read the same texts differently, underscores that where differences of reading occur, such differences are interesting, and provides a kind of map to a joint re-reading of texts once the original coding procedures have been completed, so that the fullest possible discussion of reading processes, reactions, and remarks concerning the texts can occur.

It should be said here that one option open to the readers is to leave statements uncoded. Such an option allows us to falsify, if necessary, the hypothesis that subjects' voices can be characterized in terms of the categories we propose, and requires us to be attentive to other possible ways of reading the texts to which we become increasingly related through our engagement with them.

In the first reading, the subject's response to the 'identity' question is coded according to Lyon's scheme for reading for 'separate' and 'connected' presentations of self (Lyon 1983, 1988). Readers are asked to turn to Lyon's coding scheme in order to employ the categories of 'connected' and 'separate' identity presentations which derive from her own efforts to establish coding criteria relevant to the notion that both men and women typically speak in terms of separateness and connectedness when they talk about themselves, but that one of these two modes of self-description and self-presentation will be predominate according to the person's gender.

When this stage of the reading process has been concluded, readers turn to the coding categories developed for the coding of responses to the questions about religion. The readers again read the pertinent texts in random order. Thus, a given subject's responses to the questions about religion, are mixed with all of the other subjects' responses to these questions. A given reader will then read in random order the subjects' responses to different ones of the questions about religion, and these responses will not follow from a given subjects' responses to the question about identity. The aim here is to assure independence of coding, between coders, and across texts.

In this second reading the subjects' responses to the 'religious' questions are similarly treated, employing our scheme for coding 'principled' and 'relational' voices in religious orientation (Day 1994b).

The constraints imposed upon us in this chapter do not easily permit us to show how coders might differently read the texts we encounter, let alone the texts we have excerpted from interview documents here.

In the following paragraph, though, we show how one reader made sense of one of the texts we noted earlier in the chapter: In this first paragraph, underlined passages denote the coder's choice of 'separate', while **bold** passages denote the coder's selection of 'connected' to describe the mode of presentation engaged in by the subject regarding the question of identity.

> **S2:Identity [Who I am as a person?]**[I guess that would be pretty hard to talk about apart from the relationships I'm in], [I mean, the other people in my life, the people I am close to]. **[I can define myself in terms of roles and competencies attached to those roles, I suppose]** [but if I think about who I am I have to say that is where I am, interpersonally somehow], [which is in my relationships with the other people in my life], [I just can't think of myself apart from the people to whom I am relating any given moment]. [So then I would have to think about how I feel about those people][because my identity is all wrapped up in that][and that means that I am a person in terms of those I love][and about whom I have other feelings].[I'm someone who cares deeply about the others in my life][and who tries to be a good listener][who tries to understand other people in their own terms][and who tries to provide for them in a way that lets them grow].**[I guess I'd say I'm a person who strives for a balance in my life][between what it is I need to do for myself, as a person in my own right]**[and meeting the needs of others who are in need of me].[That sense of myself as involved with others in order to know and be a self at all]**[is inseparable from the the sense I have of mission, of action, of what I have to do]**.

As the reader will note, the coder coded all of the statements as fitting one or the other of the categories proposed for coding, found that the subject in question spoke in both 'separate' and 'connected' ways about self, and coded a majority of statements as conforming to the criteria for the 'connected' mode. As we have observed, another coder might have coded differently. As we take up in our discussion of analysis of coded texts, we try in several ways to take such differences into account before drawing conclusions about our categories of analysis and the hypotheses to which they are related.

The next paragraph illustrates how another coder coded the other subject's response to a question about religious experience: *Italics* mark statements coded as *principled* descriptions, while CAPITALS mark statements coded RELATIONAL descriptions by the same coder.

S1:Religious Experience [THAT ONE'S PRETTY CLEAR AND PRETTY SIMPLE FOR ME]. [*Religious experience I would say is the experience of being convicted of the truth, being shown the way to what's real, in the empirical sense*]. *[You're out there struggling, all alone,][all the while in your struggle, maybe unbeknownst to you, getting closer to the truth][, and, man, it hits you that you are getting onto something][, that the truth is going to be found][you can kind of feel your brain working closer to it][and the world is going to show you what is true][if you apply the right questions and experiments you are going to pass your test and get there]*.[AND THEN, ON THE OTHER SIDE, THERE'S THE JOY OF RELIGIOUS FAITH THAT IS A KIND OF RELIGIOUS EXPERIENCE][WHEN YOU DISCOVER IN LIVING EVEN MORE HOW TRUE THAT TRUTH WAS THAT YOU FOUND IN ALL YOUR SEARCHING].[*That's a kind of confirmatory experience][based in living out what you've found to be true, and finding out that the consequences of that truth you found philosophically work out very practically]*.[*So religious experience has to do with the truth, going after it, finding out, and getting that confirmation for all your hard work]*.

In this paragraph the coder left some statements uncoded, and coded the majority of statements as conforming to the criteria for 'principled' speech about religious experience. No statements conforming to the relational mode were found by this coder employing the criteria from our guide. We include this excerpt not only to show how one interviewee responded to a question about religion, but to show how, in practice, a variety of options are open to the coder.

In the third of the readings we propose, we ask coders to check the 'alignment' of the subject's presentation of self in the subject's responses to both the identity question and the questions about religion. This is coherent, we think, with our attention to narrative. Given that subjects offer narrative representations of self in both the 'identity' and 'religion' domains, we want to track how it is that these representations of self are similar or different between and across domains. Can the 'separate' or 'connected' voice of the subject as speaker be found in the different areas where she speaks, or does her voice change according to the kind of domain in question and the kind of story employed to speak to it. We think this also allows us to ask interesting questions about how it is that identity and religion — as definition, experience, and realm of decision-making and problem-solving — are related. Do some speakers align consistently with one mode of self-presentation, while others do not? Are there consistent variations across domains and across subjects? Does gender identity shift across domains in relation to the alignment of self that can be read? All of these questions, and of course more, are at issue in this reading of the texts.

In the fourth reading we 'open the door' to further themes that emerge from the texts and which do not conform to our coding criteria. We stand to learn much from our subjects about domains in which we are not yet formulating and testing hypotheses, and these can fruitfully be discussed in terms of this fourth reading.

Analyzing the Coded Texts and Questions of Validity and Reliability

We have already noted that texts are coded independently and without prior knowledge of any pertinent characteristics of the subjects, including gender. After the texts are read, we tally numbers and percentages of non-codable and codable statements by category, and then compute ratios for separate/connected and principled/relational statements coded. We tabulate units of analysis within subjects, within responses to specific questions, across subjects and across questions. We then assess correlations between the content areas separate/connected and principled/relational and respondents' genders. Our analyses very consciously are designed to allow for overlapping categories (e.g. separate to connected and principled to relational, separate to relational and connected to principled, etc.).

In the study documented here, we drew texts from a previous study of moral experience in the lives of six young adult subjects, subjects thus interviewed before the principled and relational categories and related gender-associated hypotheses were developed. The original research had as its objective the refinement of the MEI and replicated portions of a larger study (Day 1994, in press a, in press b) of various factors influencing and related to moral judgment in a sample of forty young adults at or about the age of 30 years. Thus, categories generated for the development of the readers' guide were applied to texts which came from MEI questions asked in a study with an objective other than that of measuring gender as a primary distinguishing factor in talk about religion. It is probably worth remarking here that the subjects did not conform to stereotypical notions of gender in at least one important domain: career. Two of the women were military officers. Two of the men were in 'caring' professions.

In all, six subjects, each of whom responded to questions about identity, definition of religion, religious experience, and religious decisionmaking, had been interviewed using the MEI. The texts produced from their responses to these questions were then submitted to the reading procedures we describe here. Three coders, one who developed the criteria, and two who were for the first time exposed to the categories and criteria at the time they first read the coding manual included here, were involved (two initially trained coders and one highly trained coder). Thus, each reader read a total of 24 (6 subjects by 4 questions) separate texts, producing a total of 72 (24 texts by 3 readers) codings.

Our preliminary research corroborated Lyon's findings (1988) that self-presentational strategies in the realm of personal identity could be coded in terms of separate and connected voice categories, that both voices were present in most subjects' presentations, and that such voice categories are predominated by gender. We were also able to confirm our hypotheses that participants' definitions of religion, descriptions of religious experience and religious decision-making could be read and coded in terms of principled and relational voices, and that these also would be jointly present in most subjects' accounts and would be predominated by gender. We argue that it is possible to find significant correlations between voice categories and gender, between response categories (identity and religion, identity and religious experience, and identity and religious-decision) within and across participants and within and between genders. We summarize these findings as follows: that women spoke predominately in terms of connection and relationship in identity and religion, and that men spoke predominately in terms of separateness and principles, respectively. Where a given subject spoke of self as separate in identity, he also spoke of religion in terms of principles. Where subjects spoke of identity in connected terms, they also spoke of religion in relational ones. Subjects were consistent within and across domains, and their alignments of self did not shift markedly when talking about different themes; they were remarkably consistent in their presentations of self, even if this consistency included a marked variety of self-positionings within and across domains. Thus it might have been, that what was consistent about a subject, was the way in which she moved back and forth between the voice categories we coded for, and the way in which she did so across all of the questions we posed.

It is of course important to ask the question whether our methods are valid and reliable. Given that our system of reading and coding permits readers to make individual determinations about how a subject's texts should be coded, and that we do not specify a fixed number of units which must be coded, and that we do not force an 'either/or' choice for coders about every unit of analysis, the validity question here focuses on whether texts can be coded at all, and whether there is a logical correspondence between ways in which our texts are coded and the ways in which other related researchers have coded texts using the same criteria.

Where reliability questions are concerned, we report moderate to excellent inter-rater agreement in coding for presence of voice, predominance of voice, within categories, across categories, within subjects, and across subjects, and between subjects and categories. We assert then that despite the enormous latitude given readers, it is possible using the coding criteria we propose to arrive at remarkably coherent profiles of how subjects talk with us about matters of identity and religion in their lives; profiles in which different interpolations of voice are present, and in which gender matters.

If we were at this time to take research concerning our method a step further, we would begin by making a text of the readers' reactions and discussions of similarities and differences across their readings of the official text before them. In such a step we would be concerned to understand how coding could occur as a function of particular features of coders' contexts (age, gender, religious affiliation, to name a few we take to be of interest) and of the interaction of the coders with the texts. In the case of the data and coders we report here, we only very initially began this process, when we asked whether coder agreement was a function of gender. In this case, of three coders, one of whom was female and two of whom were male, inter-rater agreement was consistently higher across subjects, and domains, between one female reader and one male reader than between the two male readers or the other male reader and the female reader. Thus it could not be concluded that male readers coded more often in terms, say, of principled categories, or that the female reader coded more often in terms of, say, relational categories. We would certainly think it vital in the further development of the method we propose to undertake research on reader-text, reader-category, and reader-reader relationships. In the first of these domains, we would want to know more about how particular readers would produce different accounts of the texts they would read in common. In what ways would the individual reader's interests, training prior to or additional to their training as a reader in our method, and personal-contextual factors (such as gender, for example), interact with the text at hand in such a way as to produce the particular reading she or he would make. In the second of these domains, we would think it important to understand how it is the reader appropriates the furnished descriptions (principled or relational, for example) for coding categories in applying them to the coding of texts. In the third of these areas, we would want to know how relationships between and among readers influence the way in which they read differently or similarly the texts that are before them; how might they collude or collaborate in excluding or accentuating details that are present in the texts they have to read, how does their being together when they reach the point of discussing texts in common modify conclusions they might have drawn previously about the content, meaning, and detail of a text, the appropriation of coding categories and their employment as strategies of analysis and interpretation. How, when they are together in discussion, do the factors they hypothesize to matter when thinking about the person who is the research subject in the text, also matter between or among them in the act of reading, coding, and interpreting it?

INTERPRETATION AND BEYOND

It has already been observed that we engage in a fourth reading of our texts that offers us a chance to reread what we have already encountered for other trends, which in turn, we read again in terms of the gender of the subjects. As readers, we read and reread, and convene in order to discuss our observations.

What follows are some of the observations that have been most striking to us in the course of reading the interview texts of our subjects.

First of all, we note that the subjects' responses to the question about identity vary according to gender. Women repeat the question, or echo it, and then engage in a process of self-questioning as to whether what they are talking about makes sense, conforms to the expectations of the interviewer, or somehow departs unacceptably from what is expected of them. This can be read as an invitation to dialogue, to communication, to relationship with the interviewer. We propose that female subjects 'actualize' their relational identity in the very *Dasein* of the relationship between the interviewer and interviewee. Their question is already an affirmation that makes them be present to the other.

Another observation concerning the resonses of both men and women to the identity question is that "they are not talking so much about who they are as who they would like to be. They speak about themselves in terms of what they are reaching for, searching for, trying to do." (Day, Naedts, & Saroglou in press). We would argue that they seem to be using the interview format to present the ideal of self which they self-consciously realize they have not yet attained. There is a sense in which they are posing the question of identity even as they answer it: am I capable of being the self which I think I should be or would like to be? How can I become that self whom I regard as ideal? The interview itself becomes a forum for stating and questioning the self-ideal, and for asking whether such an ideal is attainable.

We observe that men and women describe religion differently not only in terms of relationship or principle, but also in terms of how they refer to religion in relation to the question of identity. When women talk about religion they use considerably more personal pronouns; they seem at once to act as though they are subjects of religion and as though they 'make' what religion is to them. Men, meanwhile, are more impersonal in talking about themselves *vis-à-vis* religion. Their phrases are marked by 'one', 'we', 'you' pronouns, in contrast to women's use of 'me', 'myself', 'I think', 'to me religion is', 'for me'.

Likewise, descriptions of religious experience are different not only in terms of the principled and relational categories for which we code, but also in terms of what we call the 'horizons' of religious experience in terms of which the subjects recount their experiences. In the male subjects, religious experience makes sense as an *experience of limits*, and the search for something bigger, behind, underlying, beyond; an experience of emptiness punctuated by the longing and active search for something trancendent, sure, lasting, reliable, true. By contrast, the experience of women is an *experience of fulfillment, abundance, and plenitude*. God is reveals 'him'self by 'his' very nature — God is relational in his being God, and no particular effort is required by the human subject to find 'him'.

Women say, for example: "Someone who is there to whom I am speaking", "I'll be accompanied"; "surrendering control to God"; "that kind of melding of things between myself and that presence I can only call God"; "that kind of merging but you don't really lose yourself"; "the love that is there flowing between you"..., while men say: "You face the endpoint of your wisdom and then resolve to do the best you can"; "that God will see you in the light of your best effort"; "religious experience is the experience of being convicted of the truth, being shown the way to what is real"; "you are out there struggling, getting that confirmation for all your hard work"; "the self is forced to see its relation to the whole".

Religious decisions are also framed differently by women and men. For women, most of the time, a religious decision is a decision in which the principal factor of decision is *how to do certain things*, in what spirit should they take a decision affecting everyday life. A woman subject said: "I prayed that Christ might fill my heart..., to guide me to be with her in the right kind of way..., to see her as a sister ...". Men's religious decisions resemble explicitly 'moral' decisions: How do I act in conformity to my principles, in light of my principles. "You do what you have to do because it is right". "Am I going to do the thing that I have to do in the situation". "I prayed for God to guide me to live up to what it was I had to do...".

We are keenly interested in the differences we note here, and are struck by how important the open-endedness of the interview methods we propose is to the kinds of results we have obtained. We would also underscore the importance of all of the steps of reading we propose in arriving at the kinds of observations we make in stating the conclusion that much more work needs to be done in order to fully appreciate the importance of context, and especially gender, in the religious experience of women and men.

Acknowledgements: We wish to thank our colleagues Jacob Belzen, Jozef Corveleyn, Dirk Hutsebaut, Jean-Denis Moerman, and Vasilis Saroglou, for their critical reviews, at different stages of our work.

We owe a particular debt to Lyn Mykel Brown and Mark Tappan, who have influenced our thinking about the reading of interview texts. Their work (See especially Brown et al. 1989) has run very much parallel to related efforts on our parts, and since 1989 they have generously shared their insights, questions, and work products with us on a regular basis. Without their development of a reader's guide to reading texts of moral dilemmas and choices, we would have been less likely to produce the guide we used in the research related to this chapter.

We also owe a special note of gratitude to Professor Jean-Marie Jaspard for the liberty to work unhindered in the Center for the Psychology of Religion, of which he is director in Louvain-la-Neuve. We acknowledge our invaluable debt to the National Science Foundation of Belgium and the Funds for Scientific Development of the Universite Catholique de Louvain and the French-speaking community of Belgium for the funds which made Myriam Naedts' presence possible at the Center.

NOTES

1. Copies of the *Moral Experience Interview-Revised* (MEI-R) (Day 1992) and *A Scheme for Coding Questions about Religion, Religious Experience, and Religious Decisions* (Day 1994b) may be obtained from Professor James M. Day, Université Catholique de Louvain, Centre de Psychologie de la Religion, Unité de Psychologie du Developpement Humain, Place Cardinal Mercier 10, 1348 Louvain-la-Neuve, Belgium.

REFERENCES

Brown, L., M. Tappan, C. Gilligan, B. Miller & D. Argyris (1989). Reading for self and moral voice: a method for interpreting narratives of real-life moral conflict and choice. In: M. Packer & R. Addison (eds.). *Entering the circle:*

hermeneutic investigation in psychology (pp. 141-165). Albany, NY: State University of New York Press.

Brown, L. & C. Gilligan (1991). Listening for voice in narratives of relationship. In: M. Tappan & M. Packer (eds.). *Narrative and storytelling: implications for understanding moral development* (pp. 43-61). San Francisco: Jossey-Bass.

Brown, L. & C. Gilligan (1993). *Meeting at the crossroads: women's psychology and girls' development*. Cambridge: Harvard University Press.

Bruner, J. (1986). *Actual minds, possible worlds*. Cambridge: Harvard University Press.

Day, J. (1987) *Moral development in laboratory learning groups*. Ann Arbor, Michigan: University Microfilms.

Day, J. (1991a). The moral audience: on the narrative mediation of moral 'judgment' and moral 'action'. In: M. Tappan & M. Packer (eds.). *Narrative and storytelling: implications for understanding moral development* (pp. 27-42). San Francisco: Jossey-Bass.

Day, J. (1991b). Narrative, psychology, and moral education. *American Psychologist*, *46*, 167-168.

Day, J. (1991c). Role-taking reconsidered: narrative and cognitive-developmental interpretations of moral growth. *The Journal of Moral Education*, *20*, 305-317.

Day, J. (1992) *The Moral Experience Interview-Revised*. (unpublished manuscript).

Day, J. (1993). Speaking of belief: language, performance, and narrative in the psychology of religion. *The International Journal for the Psychology of Religion, 3* (4), 213-230.

Day, J. (1994a). Narratives of "belief and unbelief" in young adult accounts of religious experience and moral development. In: D. Hutsebaut & J. Corveleyn (eds.). *Belief and unbelief: psychological perspectives* (pp. 155-175). Amsterdam: Rodopi.

Day, J. (1994b). *A scheme for coding responses to questions about identity and religion from the moral experience interview-revised*. Unpublished manuscript.

Day, J. (1995). Sviluppo, educazione, e personalita morale. *Pedagogia et Vita, 53* (1), 31-49.

Day, J. (in press, a). Knowing the good and doing it: moral judgment and action in young adult narratives of moral choice. In: D. Garz, F. Oser & W. Althof (eds.). *Der Kontext der Moral*. Frankfurt: Suhrkamp.

Day, J. (in press, b). Exemplary sierrans: stories of the moral. In: R. Mosher, D. Connor, J. Day, K. Kaliel, M. Porter & J. Whiteley. *Character in young adulthood*. San Francisco: Jossey Bass.

Day, J. & M. Naedts (1995). Moral judgment and religious judgment: theoretical, methodological, and practical considerations. Paper presented at the International Conference on Moral Development and Education convened at the Katholieke Universiteit Nijmegen, The Netherlands. (To be published as a chapter in W. van Haaften (ed.). *Moral development and education: advances in theory and research*.)

Day, J. & M. Tappan (1995). Identity, voice, and the psycho/dialogical: perspectives from moral psychology. *American Psychologist, 50* (1), 47-49.

Day, J., M. Naedts & V. Saroglou (in press). Reading interview texts for gender, self, and religious voice. *The International Journal for the Psychology of Religion.*

Day, J. & M. Tappan (in press). From epistemic subjects to moral selves: toward a narrative approach to moral development. *Human Development.*

Dilthey, W. (1900). The understanding of other persons and their expressions of life. In: *Descriptive psychology and historical understanding* (transl. R. Zaner & K. Heiges). The Hague: Nijhoff, 1977.

Freeman, M. (1991). Rewriting the self: development as moral practice. In: M. Tappan & M. Packer (eds.). *Narrative and storytelling: implications for understanding moral development* (pp. 83-101). San Francisco: Jossey-Bass.

Gergen, K. & M. Gergen (1986). Narrative form and the construction of psychological science. In: T. Sarbin (ed.). *Narrative psychology: the storied nature of human conduct*. New York: Praeger.

Gilligan, C. (1977). In a different voice: women's conceptions of self and morality. *Harvard Educational Review*, *47*, 481-517.

Gilligan, C. (1982). *In a different voice: psychological theory and women's development*. Cambridge: Harvard University Press.

Gilligan, C., J. Ward & J. Taylor (eds.) (1988). *Mapping the moral domain: a contribution of women's thinking to psychological theory and education*. Cambridge: Harvard University Press.

Gilligan, C. & G. Wiggins (1988). The origins of morality in children's early relationships. In: C. Gilligan, J. Ward & J. Taylor (eds.). *Mapping the moral domain: a contribution of women's thinking to psychological theory and education*. Cambridge: Harvard University Press.

Lyons, N. (1982). *The manual for analyzing responses to the question: how would you describe yourself to yourself?* Unpublished manuscript, Harvard Graduate School of Education.

Lyons, N. (1983). Two perspectives: on self, relationships, and morality. *Harvard Educational Review*, *53*, 125-145.

Lyons, N. (1988) Two perspectives: on self, relationships, and morality. In: C. Gilligan, J. Ward & J. Taylor (eds.). *Mapping the moral domain* (pp.71-91). Cambridge, MA: Harvard University Press.

Packer, M. (1989). Tracing the hermeneutic circle: articulating an ontical study of moral conflicts. In: M. Packer & R. Addison (eds.). *Entering the circle: hermeneutic investigation in psychology* (pp. 95-118). Albany: State University of New York Press.

Packer, M. (1991). Interpreting stories, interpreting lives: narrative and action in moral development research. In: M. Tappan & M. Packer (eds.). *Narrative and storytelling: implications for understanding moral development* (pp. 63-82). San Francisco: Jossey-Bass.

Ricoeur, P. (1981). The model of the text: meaningful action considered as a text. In: *Hermeneutics and the human sciences* (pp.197-222). Cambridge: Cambridge University Press.

Sarbin, T. (1990). The narrative quality of action. *Theoretical and Philosophical Psychology*, *10*, 49-65.

Tannen, D. (1991) *You just don't understand: women and men in conversation.* London: Virago.

Tappan, M. (1989). Stories lived and stories told: the narrative structure of late adolescent moral development. *Human Development*, *32*, 300-315.

Tappan, M. (1990). Hermeneutics and moral development: interpreting narrative representations of moral experience. *Developmental Review*, *10*, 239-265.

Tappan, M. (1991a). Narrative, authorship, and the development of moral authority. In: M. Tappan & M. Packer (eds.). *Narrative and storytelling: implications for understanding moral development* (pp. 5-26). San Francisco: Jossey-Bass.

Tappan, M. (1991b). Narrative, language, and moral experience. *Journal of Moral Education*, *20*, 243-256.

Tappan, M. (1992). Texts and contexts: language, culture, and the development of moral functioning. In: L. Winegar & J. Valsiner (eds.). *Children's development within social contexts: Metatheoretical, theoretical, and methodological issues*. Hillsdale, NJ: Erlbaum.

Tappan, M. & L. Brown (1989). Stories told and lessons learned: toward a narrative approach to moral development and moral education. *Harvard Educational Review*, *59*, 182-205.

Youngman, D. (1993) *Moral development in older adults.* Ann Arbor, Mi.: University Microfilms.

Psychology of Religion as Hermeneutical Cultural Analysis Some Reflections with Reference to Clifford Geertz

U. Popp-Baier
University of Amsterdam (The Netherlands)

Introduction — Cultural Perspectives in Psychology

In an article about cultural sociological research, Grathoff and Knorr Cetina (1988) called cultural anthropology the classical place for cultural analytical discussions. In recent decades concepts of culture which can be used in empirical research and are relevant to the social sciences have been developed in cultural anthropology. Sociology itself, says Knorr Cetina, has not developed many 'operational' concepts of culture, but it has formulated cultural perspectives which include, above all, analytical preferences and methodical orientations. In this way these perspectives are comparable to anthropological cultural analyses. In this context Knorr Cetina mentions the so-called interpretive sociologies and the analyses of symbolic practices as they were presented by Foucault or by Bourdieu.

Since the beginning of psychology we have been able to recognize 'cultural perspectives'. Within these cultural perspectives human thinking, feeling, experiencing and acting were considered and studied in the context of their specific historical and socio-cultural conditions (cf. Stern 1920; Wundt 1900-1920). The debate of recent decades in German literature about the conceptualization of a cultural psychology was above all concerned with the methodical orientations regarding the purposes of psychological research and the problems of a psychological research which is to be relevant to everyday life (cf. for example Leithäuser & Volmerg 1979; Aschenbach 1984; Werbik 1986; Zitterbarth 1987; Keupp 1988; Jüttemann 1991).

With reference to Wittgenstein, the usual criticism was that in psychology problems and methods 'lie askew' to each other, and therefore the scientism in psychology, i.e. the aspiration to conceptualize psychology as a science according to the model of the natural sciences, was seen as responsible for this misalignment. Cultural psychologists wanted to establish a new orientation. Regarding the analytical preferences, cultural psychologists wanted to abandon 'behaviour' as the analytical preference of behaviourism and 'cognition' as the analytical preference of cognitivism. They preferred the concept of 'action' as the new analytical perspective and claimed a reference to the perspective of the actors by analysing human actions psychologically. And with reference to Wittgenstein's concept of the 'life pattern' (*Lebensform*) (cf. Wittgenstein 1971) some authors understood individual and social actions as 'participation in a life pattern', so that a cultural psychological analysis of actions has to consider such life patterns by understanding in the right way the aspects of meaning and dimensions of sense of human acting. Accordingly in cultural psychology the concept of science espoused by the *Wiener Kreis* and his successors was completed or even substituted by hermeneutics as a starting point for methodological considerations.

CLIFFORD GEERTZ' INTERPRETIVE CULTURAL ANALYSIS

Clifford Geertz' conceptualization of cultural analysis is considered one of the main streams of 'symbolic anthropology', ranking above all with Victor Turner and David M. Schneider.[1] The starting point for further considerations shall be Clifford Geertz' conception of culture as he developed it in his article "Thick Description: Toward an Interpretive Theory of Culture" in 1973: "Believing, with Max Weber, that man is an animal suspended in webs of significance he himself has spun, I take culture to be those webs, and the analysis of it to be therefore not an experimental science in search of law but an interpretive one in search of meaning" (Geertz 1973, p. 5). Geertz calls this concept of culture 'semiotic'. In considering this concept we first of all have to mention three aspects. Firstly, Geertz introduces his concept of culture with a definition of man, so that culture becomes a basic anthropological concept and is regarded as belonging to the nature of man. Secondly, culture is regarded as the result of intentional acting, and thirdly it is thereby regarded at the same time as the context of meaning, in which human acting is always situated, in which human acting is already entangled.

Geertz explicitly differentiates this concept from a mental concept on the one hand and a structural concept on the other. Firstly, he distinguishes his concept from the concept of culture contained within cognitive anthropology, according to which culture is in the minds and in the hearts of men — as Goodenough has formulated it. This point of view would give culture the ontological status of the mental. But culture, as Geertz formulates it, is public because the meaning is public in the sense of intersubjective. On the other hand Geertz limits his concept of culture to the concept of structural anthropology. He agrees with this concept when considering the semiotic concept of culture, but his understanding of semiotic is different from that of structural anthropology. Whilst the structural anthropologists consider culture as a system of symbols whose aspects of meaning are to be grasped through analysing underlying structures, Geertz conceives the task of cultural analysis that of studying the informal logic of actual life. And this calls for an actor-centred analysis.[2]

According to Geertz cultural forms can only find articulation through the flow of social action. Of course various sorts of artefacts also belong to culture, but these artefacts draw their meaning from the role they play in the ongoing patterns of life and not from any intrinsic relationships they bear to one another.[3]

The next question we have to answer in this context is which concept of meaning is used by Geertz. In my opinion the underlying concept of meaning in Geertz' essays is the concept which is most pregnantly formulated by Searle in his book *Intentionality*. According to Searle

> 'Meaning' is a notion that literally applies to sentences and speech acts but not in that sense to Intentional states. It makes good sense to ask, for example, what a sentence or utterance means, but it makes no sense to ask in that sense what a belief or a desire means. ... Meaning exists only where there is a distinction between Intentional content and the form of its externalization, and to ask for the meaning is to ask for an Intentional content that goes with the form of externalization. Thus it makes good sense to ask for the meaning of the sentence "Es regnet", and it makes good sense to ask for the meaning of John's statement, i.e., to ask what he meant; but it makes no sense to ask for the meaning of the belief that it is raining or of the meaning of the statement that it is raining: in the former case because there is no gulf between belief and Intentional content and in the latter case because the gulf has already been bridged when we specify the content of the statement. (1983, p. 28)

When we conceptualize cultural analysis as meaning analysis in this sense, then we have to analyse the kinds of articulations of intentional states. These can be various forms of articulations, for example linguistic, pictorial or mathematical forms. Also compatible with this concept of meaning is the analysis of more complex unities concerning represented intentional states, as for example actions, processes of actions, institutions, cultural artefacts etc. According to Geertz, such representations can generally be called 'symbols', and therefore we can also call the interpretive analysis of meaning which is combined with Geertz' semiotic concept of cultural 'symbol analysis'.

The most important aim of cultural analysis is, according to Geertz, the enlargement of the universe of human discourse. The task of cultural analysis is to make accessible the imaginative universe of the studied subjects within which their acts are signs, so that we can talk to them — in the broad sense of the term. In this way cultural analysis has a preparatory or a propedeutic function: It serves as a preparation to dialog. At the end of his essay Geertz once again emphasizes that the essential vocation of cultural analysis is not to answer our deepest questions, but to make answers given by others accessible to us and thus to include them in the consultable record of what man has said. "Anthropology, or at least interpretive anthropology, is a science whose progress is marked less by a perfection of consensus than by a refinement of debate. What gets better is the precision with which we vex each other" (Geertz 1973, p. 29).

Following Gilbert Ryle, Geertz appoints the method of 'thick description' as the appropriate method for cultural analysis, considering the object mentioned (webs of significance man himself has spun) and considering the formulated task (preparation for dialog). The meaningful dimensions of social actions are only accessible by thick description. Thick description, according to Geertz, is the intellectual effort which defines the whole enterprise of cultural analysis. We explain this 'method' by using an example. According to Ryle, "P contracts the left eyelid" is a thin description compared to the thick description "P winks to give a conspiratorial signal to a friend" or "P is parodying the winking of O", etc. These thick descriptions consist of our interpretations of the way other people interpret their own actions and those of other people speaking and acting in the context of everyday life. Therefore we can say that these thick descriptions always presuppose a meaningful context within which they can be intelligibly, that is, thickly described. The analysis of thick description cannot go beyond this factual situation. There is no 'basic observation' possible, on which we can methodically construct further interpretations. We are already members of an interpreted world when we begin to develop interpretations in the context of social scientific studies.

A further important aspect of cultural analysis as thick description is that cultural analysis is to be carried out from the perspective of the actor: "Nothing is more necessary to comprehending what anthropological interpretation is, and the degree to which it is interpretation, than an exact understanding of what it means — and what it does not mean — to say that our formulations of other peoples' systems must be actor-oriented" (Geertz 1973, p. 14). That our descriptions have to be 'actor-oriented' means, that for example

> the descriptions of the Berber, Jewish, or French culture must be cast in terms of the constructions we imagine Berbers, Jews, or Frenchmen to place upon what they live through, the formulae they use to define what happens to them. What it does not mean is that such descriptions are themselves Berber, Jewish or French — that is, part of the reality they are ostensibly describing; they are anthropological — that is, part of a developing system of scientific analysis. They must be cast in terms of the interpretations to which persons of a particular denomination subject their experience, because that is what they profess to be descriptions of; they are anthropological because it is, in fact, anthropologists who profess them (Geertz 1973, p. 15).

The problem is clear. It is the question of the perspective of the interpretations in a cultural analysis and, combined with this question, the question of the adequate level of speech. A consistent interpretation of Geertz' ideas seems to me the following: The structure of the interpretations must be constituted in such a way that they can be seized by the actors of the culture being studied to describe and interpret their own experiences. That does not mean that the 'interpretive constructions' have to be formulated in the everyday speech of the actors, that is, that only such constructions can be used which the actors actually use to communicate with each other. The anthropological interpretations can also consist of scientific (professional) terms. But these professional terms have to be 'constructions of a second degree' which are attached to the 'constructions of the first degree' of the actors (cf. Schütz 1971).

Clifford Geertz further describes aspects of his concept of cultural analysis with reference to the concept of text: doing ethnography can be compared to reading a manuscript. "Doing ethnography is like trying to read (in the sense of 'construct a reading of') a manuscript — foreign, faded, full of ellipses, incoherences, suspicious emendations, and tendentious commentaries, but written not in conventionalized graphs of sound but in transient examples of shaped behaviour" (Geertz 1973, p. 10). The thick description of meaning analysis can also be conceptualized as the construction of a way of reading a text, i.e. a text-analogous. Here Geertz refers explicitly to Ricoeur. I propose to call this concept of cultural analysis 'hermeneutical cultural analysis', because Geertz' semiotic concept of culture implies a hermeneutical concept of text as it is developed in the philosophical hermeneutics of Heidegger and Gadamer. I want to explain this concept in the following considerations.

TOWARD A HERMENEUTICAL CONCEPT OF TEXT

With Heidegger (1927) hermeneutics as a theory of understanding becomes a fundamental ontological conception. Heidegger conceptualizes 'understanding' neither on the level of epistemology nor on the level of methodology but on the ontological level. His extension of the concept of understanding to an existentiale, that is to a fundamental categorical determination of human existence (as the way in which the Being-of-mankind as *Dasein* is always Being-in-the-world) led to an important expansion of the hermeneutic question. Dilthey has already formulated the universal claim of this philosophical hermeneutics in remarking that understanding and interpretation come into play not only in expressions of life that are fixed in writing, but they also concern the general relation of people to one another and to the world. This fundamental understanding, in which *Dasein* understands itself in its Being and in its world, is not a way of acting toward definite objects of knowledge, but is rather the carrying out of Being-in-the-world itself. With this the hermeneutical doctrine of method transforms itself into a hermeneutics of facticity, which was guided by the inquiry into Being. The description of this fundamental relation as a hermeneutical circle (I am always trying to understand something that I have already understood in a certain way and this way of understanding always includes self-understanding) allows the overcoming of subject-object bifurcation on the ontological level and thereby a turning away from the philosophy of the subject as fundamental to the building of comprehension (*Verständnisbildung*). Heidegger no longer conceptualizes hermeneutics as an epistemology or a methodology for human studies but as a methodical explication of the ontological structure of understanding. This concept of understanding relates to the interpretation by the way that 'the world', which has already been understood, comes to be interpreted. Understanding as a fundamental existentiale contains in itself the possibility of interpretation, i.e. the appropriation of what is already understood. "Not only is interpretation a derivation of fundamental understanding — it is also directed by the latter in respect to the 'in-order-to' which has the structure of something as something" (Bleicher 1980, p. 101).

Heidegger called the thematic predicative sentence a sort of interpretation of understanding, a linguistic articulation of understanding, which primarily — pre-predicatively — appears in perceiving and acting. According to Heidegger understanding in everyday life remains almost unexplicated. Heidegger calls the structure of this understanding 'as-structure', because we always understand something as something, whereby the 'as' designates an unexplicated way of acting of the *Dasein* in its world.[4]

With Heidegger we can perhaps say that the ontological interpretation of understanding leads to its pragmatic foundation.

With the further explication of this ontological understanding by Gadamer (1960), understanding is explicitly bound to language: being which can be understood is language. But this concept of understanding does not contradict Heidegger's demonstration of the pre-predicative structure of understanding because Gadamer does not conceive language predicatively as a system of propositions. Gadamer conceives language, above all, as dialogue, as a connection of communication and interaction, to which understanding always belongs. According to Gadamer language does not take place in propositions but in dialogue (discourse; talking). Understanding is always the understanding of language, that is — more precisely — dialogical understanding.

Looking at Gadamer's 'dialogical principle' of understanding, two aspects are especially relevant: firstly Gadamer claims the limits of propositional logic, in which the proposition constitutes a unit of meaning which can be sufficiently comprehended without further additions or complements. Gadamer points out that the comprehension of a proposition cannot separate this proposition from the context of motivation, that is, from the dialogue in which the proposition is embedded and only through which it attains meaning. In this context Gadamer speaks of a 'hermeneutical logic of question and answer' which sees understanding as participation, as participation in a context of meaning, in a tradition, in a dialogue at least. In this dialogue there are no propositions, only questions and answers, and the answers always demand new questions.

Gadamer designates the fact that there is no possible proposition which cannot be understood as an answer to a question and that every proposition can only be understood in this way as a primeval phenomenon (cf. Gadamer 1983).

The second aspect which Gadamer worked out was that the dialogical character of language locates the starting point in the subjectivity of the subject, even that of the meaning-directed intentions of the speaker. "What we find happening in speaking is not a mere reification of intended meaning, but an endeavor that continually modifies itself, or better: a continually recurring temptation to engage oneself in something or to become involved with someone. But that means to expose oneself and to risk oneself" (Gadamer 1986, p. 383). Our dialogical experiences show us that beyond the communality of meaning we build up in conversation something else takes place which Gadamer calls "the potentiality of otherness" (*die Potentialität des Andersseins*) (Gadamer 1983, p. 336). According to Gadamer these are the two characteristics of each 'true' conversation: the communality of meaning and at the same time the impenetrability of the otherness of the other. That is why Gadamer considers linguisticality (*Sprachlichkeit*) both a bridge and at the same time a barrier: a bridge over which one communicates with the other and builds "sameness over the flowing stream of otherness" (Gadamer 1986, p. 385), and a barrier that limits our self-abandonment and that cuts us off from the possibility of ever expressing ourselves completely and communicating with others.

In the framework of this formulation of language and conversation the concept of the text presents a special sort of challenge.

> How does the text stand in relation to language ? ... How has the concept of the text been able to undergo such a universal extension? It is obvious to anyone who watches the philosophical tendencies of our century that more is at stake in this theme than reflections upon the methodology of the philological sciences. Text is more than a title for the subject matter of literary research. Interpretation is more than the technique of scientifically interpreting texts. In the twentieth century, both of these concepts have acquired a new importance in the role that they play in our view of knowledge and the world (Gadamer 1986, p. 385).

According to Gadamer the concept of text first constitutes a central concept in the structure of linguisticality starting from the concept of interpretation:

> ... indeed, the special mark of the concept of the text is that it shows itself only in connection with interpretation and, from the point of view of interpretation, as the authentic given that is to be understood. This is true even in the dialogical process of coming to an understanding insofar as one lets the disputed statements be repeated and thereby pursues the intention to a binding formulation, an event that culminates in reification of communication by way of a transcript. In a similar manner the interpreter of a text asks what is really in the text. This too can lead to a biased and prejudicial response to the extent that everyone who asks a question (like this) tries to find a direct confirmation of his own assumptions in the answer. But, in such an appeal to that which is in the text, the text itself still remains the first point of relation over and against the questionality, arbitrariness, or at least multiplicity of the possibilities of interpretation that are directed towards the text (Gadamer 1986, p. 388).[5]

Gadamer emphasizes that from the hermeneutical point of view the text is a mere intermediate product, a phase in the event of understanding, which, as such, certainly includes a definite abstraction, namely the isolation and reification of this very phase. "In every case, whether spoken or written, the understanding of the text remains dependent upon communicative conditions that, as such, reach beyond the reified meaning content of what is said. One can almost say that if one needs to reach back to the wording of the text, that is, to the text as such, then this must always be motivated by the peculiarity of the situation of understanding" (Gadamer 1986, p. 391).[6] And — we can perhaps add — this must also be legitimated by the peculiarity of the situation of understanding.

In the dialogical process this abstraction is necessary when there are difficulties in communication, whereby the simplest form of such a construction of a text is the word-for-word repetition of what is expressed in conversation and what is disputable. Such a procedure culminates in the recording of such utterances as propositions. In this case something linguistic is constructed as something whose written record provides a common basis for the disputable questions involved in the correct understanding of something. In any case we have to keep in mind that a text, that is, the construction of a text, is a methodical intermediate step in the dialogical process of understanding. The text is created as an independent entity of meaning by abstracting from its communicative and interactive relations, in short, from its pragmatic conditions. But this pragmatic reduction allows for semantic amplification by using elaborate strategies of interpretation for demonstrating a variety of alternatives of the meaning of the text, whereas only the text can be used as a parameter for its own interpretations.

The Consequences of Text Interpretation in the Social Sciences and Humanities

The above mentioned qualities of the text and their consequences for research in the social sciences and the humanities are discussed by Ricoeur (cf. for example 1981). In his essay "The Model of the Text: Meaningful Action Considered as a Text", Ricoeur uses Austin's and Searle's speech act theory to demonstrate which aspects of a discourse as a speech-event can be transcribed to which degree and which aspects of a discourse cannot be fixed in writing. Comparing the inscription of a discourse to the discourse as a speech-event we have to admit that written discourse cannot express all the processes by which spoken discourse supports itself in order to be understood — intonation, delivery, mimicry, gestures. But Ricoeur points out that this ‘weakness’ of written discourse, of a text, is at the same time its strength: the spirituality, that is the specific plurivocity of the text, allows for a variety of interpretations. This spirituality of a discourse manifests itself through writing by freeing us from the visibility and limitation of situations, from the narrowness of the factual dialogical situation to the openness of the world of a text which allows for a variety of interpretations, a variety of alternatives of meanings. In later essays Ricoeur tries to reflect on the relation between the written language, the text, and the ‘co-textual’ spoken discourses and actions. As a guideline for exploring the mediation between time and fictional narrative Ricoeur (1984) develops the distinction between three moments of mimesis which he named mimesis I (prefiguration), mimesis II (configuration) and mimesis III (refiguration). With mimesis I Ricoeur describes the ‘before’ of the narrative, the prefiguration of the practical field, with mimesis II he describes the process of narration, the configuration of the plot, that is the narrative self and with mimesis III Ricoeur describes the ‘after’ of the narrative, its refiguration through the reception of the work.[7]

With reference to these distinctions we have to discuss the following doubtful points when we are interpreting ‘texts’ in the framework of hermeneutical cultural analysis: the question about the prefiguration of the texts is a question about everyday reality, the everyday context of communications and interactions to which the texts are attached. Supposing that those texts are transcripts of oral narratives, a hermeneutical cultural analysis of those texts has to undoubtedly make a difference between two types of prefiguration, namely between the everyday events about which stories are told and between the framework of research in which the stories are told. In considering those two types of prefiguration we have to discuss in what respect and to what extent the texts, that is the transcripts, are prefigured through the corresponding everyday frameworks or through the corresponding research frameworks. Accordingly we have to differentiate between the ‘textimmanent’ and the ‘texttranscendent’ interpretation of the texts. In the textimmanent interpretations of the text only the text is the parameter for its interpretations. The claims to validity of such interpretations only refer to internal relations in the text, that is, these interpretations only consider the configurations of the text, the mimesis II. The texttranscendent interpretations, however, consider the external relations of the text, the prefigurations of the texts, the mimesis I. In interpretive psychological research, for example, such interpretations are theoretically reflected or justified by amongst other things social anthropology, biography theory, depth psychology.

And last but not least we have to discuss the 'after' of those texts — in this case not the refigurations of the texts but the refigurations of the interpretations of the texts. This means we have to discuss what use will be made of the interpretations of the texts, how they can be reclaimed by everyday communications and interactions of storytellers, how these interpretations can eventually be refigured in the everyday world of storytellers.

According to Ricoeur (1981) the text can be used as a paradigm for the object of human sciences and text interpretation as a paradigm for the methodology in human sciences in general because the object of human sciences, the so-called meaningfully oriented behaviour (*sinnhaft orientiertes Verhalten*, Max Weber), has a 'readability character'.

> My claim is that action itself, action as meaningful, may become an object of science, without losing its character of meaningfulness, through a kind of objectification similar to the fixation which occurs in writing. ... This objectification is made possible by some inner traits of the action which are similar to the structure of the speech-act and which make doing a kind of utterance. In the same way as the fixation by writing is made possible by a dialectic of intentional exteriorisation immanent to the speech-act itself, a similar dialectic within the process of transaction prepares the detachment of the meaning of the action from the event of the action (Ricoeur 1981, pp. 203-204).[8]

According to this basic assumption the interpretation of actions in the human sciences can be done according to the methodology of text interpretation and accordingly shares its 'weakness' and its 'strength' in comparing everyday understanding within the framework of a dialogue or of another social interaction (cf. above).

One of the main methodological problems in interpretive psychology for me is that this difference between 'text' and 'reality', as I want to say here (or between the three moments of mimesis as Ricoeur says), is not recognized and therefore not sufficiently reflected in the methodological and methodical implications involved in doing qualitative (or quantitative) research.[9]

OUTLINE OF A RESEARCH PROJECT IN THE PSYCHOLOGY OF RELIGION AS HERMENEUTICAL CULTURAL ANALYSIS

At the end of my paper I want to sketch briefly my research project, "Religious Orientations of Women in the Charismatic-Evangelical Movement", which I have conceptualized as a hermeneutical cultural analysis. My study is concerned with religious orientations in the everyday life of women who participate in a Christian women's group in a German city. The women's group is part of Aglow, an international organization of Christian women. The organization belongs to the so-called charismatic movement, but based on the religious orientation of this movement it is better to call it a charismatic-evangelical movement as it shares many characteristics with the evangelistic movement — for example the following theological characteristics:

a) a literal interpretation of the Bible as the inspired Word of God and

b) special emphasis on pneumatology and especially on the charismas such as glossolalia (speaking in tongues), prophecy and healing.

"The primary object of the movement is to change individuals in such a way that they have a living relationship with (God or) Jesus Christ and consequently lead a 'holy' life in conformity with the norms and values of the bible. The movement can be looked upon as a revitalization movement. It is not merely a conservative movement which tries to maintain the 'old-time-religion' but it is a movement which thinks to renew and awake the 'fundamentals' of the Christian belief" (Vellenga 1991, p. 305). Relating this movement to the basic characteristics of modern western society, it can be typified partly as a protest movement, actively resisting the cultural and moral aspects of this society but accepting the economic and technological aspects of the modern society (cf. Vellenga 1991).

In the eighties the charismatic movement numbered 80 million Christians worldwide (cf. Drehsen et al. 1988). Aglow belongs to the charismatic lay movement and is the name of the organization specifically open to women. It shows women how they can have a living relationship with God and Jesus Christ, and it helps them understand the everyday opportunities and responsibilities that come with leading a 'holy' life. In the German city X where I carried out my study, the structure of the Aglow group featured a monthly evening session, where the women prayed and sang together. Part of every session was also a lecture by a female speaker who told a story about her own life and how she has changed under the influence of God.

The aim of my study is the above mentioned preparation for dialogue. In this case I am oriented towards three types of dialogue: of psychological and psychotherapeutic counselling, pastoral counselling and intercultural dialogue. For constructing the corresponding texts I used three methods:

1. Participant observations of the evening sessions of the Aglow group and of other sessions (for example of divine healing services, sessions of private prayer groups, etc.). The notes from these participant observations were worked into 'texts'.

2. Biographical-narrative interviews[10] which I conducted with some women from the Aglow group in X and which were recorded on tape and later transcribed according to the rules worked out in conversation analysis.

3. A collection of life stories recorded on tape which were taken from various group sessions of Aglow and other documents such as journals, books, etc. from the charismatic movement.

The basic material for my text interpretations consists of the transcripts of my biographical-narrative interviews and of the life stories on tape. Thus regarding the moment of mimesis II, the configurations of the texts were central in analysing and interpreting the texts. That means that I first asked which sort of religious orientations I can 'discover' in the texts and not what are the religious orientations the interviewed women really have in their everyday life. But nevertheless the last question, the moment of mimesis I, was also an object of reflection informed by theoretical considerations.

The method of text interpretation I have used is the method of comparative analysis according to the analytical model of the so-called grounded theory (cf. Glaser 1978; Glaser & Strauss 1967; Strauss 1987; Strauss & Corbin 1990). Grounded theory is a general methodology whose main purpose is to develop theories which are grounded — generated and developed through interplay with data collected during research projects. It was argued that this type of theory would contribute toward "closing the embarrassing gap between theory and empirical research" (cf. Glaser & Strauss 1967). The grounded theory can be used as a general methodology for qualitative modes of research. "A grounded theory is one that is inductively derived from the study of the phenomenon it represents. That is, it is discovered, developed, and provisionally verified through systematic data collection and analysis of data pertaining to that phenomenon. Therefore, data collection, analysis, and theory stand in reciprocal relationship with each other" (Strauss & Corbin 1990, p. 23). I began my analysis with two case studies in which I tried to identify and to describe the related religious orientations on a concrete thematic level.[11] In further comparative analysis with other texts I 'discovered' one main thematic field: the concepts and experiences of healing.[12] In developing a typology of *healing concepts* by further comparative analysis I also looked for the actions which play an important role in the field of healing. These actions are the different ways of praying. Therefore on the level of actions I developed a typology of different *kinds of prayer* which are related in the interviews. These forms of actions also play a role in thematic fields other than the field of healing concepts. Therefore I tried to find a description on a more abstract level of the main situations which are related to the interviews in which prayer plays an important role, and called these situations 'situations of contingency'. Further I developed a typology of patterns of orientations and actions of the 'treatment of contingency' (*Kontingenzbewältigung*).

With another analytical perspective — a temporal instead of a structural perspective — I emphasized the temporal dimensions of the narratives and focused the related *conversion* on developing a typology of the temporal structuring of the different life stories and the related changes in these stories.

And at the end of my text interpretation I tried to combine the various comparative analyses and their results to develop a 'grounded theory' about the *religious experiences of women* who are oriented toward the charismatic-evangelical wing of the Christian faith.

NOTES

1. Ortner (1984, p. 128) shows in her historical study of the "Theory in Anthropology since the Sixties" that symbolic anthropology was a label for a number of rather different trends. There were, for example, important differences between Geertz' concept and that of Turner: Geertz was primarly influenced by Max Weber (via Talcott Parsons) and Turner was primarly influenced by Emile Durkheim. Schneider emphasized above all the systematic aspects of culture, to which Geertz never paid much attention.
2. With that Geertz also rejects cognitive anthropology which he blames for mentalism that is psychologism, as well as structural anthropology, which he blames for schematicism: "There is little profit in extricating a concept from the defects of psychologism only to plunge it immediately into those of schematicism" (Geertz 1973, p. 17).
3. Whereas Geertz (1973, p. 17) draws a radical conclusion and totally rejects structural analysis, I prefer a moderate solution: structural analysis can be accepted as a methodical intermediate step when it is related to the analysis of actions. In spite of his rejection of the structural approach Geertz also admits

that important theoretical insights took place in ethnology in the framework of the structural approach.
In social sciences the importance of structural concepts from different specialities for empirical research is recognized (cf. for example, Tillo 1993b). It is thereby demonstrated that the analysis of structures and the analysis of actions can be combined. For example the semiotic approach of Tillo (1993a, 1993b) in the sociology of religion can be called a structural one. But this approach also allows for the interpretive analysis of actions.

4. For a sufficient outline of Heidegger's concept of understanding we also have to explicate the moment of temporality of understanding. But in this context I can only mention some important aspects of the concept of temporality. According to Heidegger (1927) temporality is the Being of the *Dasein* which understands Being. Temporality is the unseparable unity of the ecstases of temporality, i.e. the phenomena of the future (*Zukünftigkeit*), of having been (*Gewesenheit*) and of the present (*Anwesenheit*), by which *Dasein* is defined as primordial. In this framework understanding as the 'executive form' of *Dasein* is also defined as primordially 'temporal' and Heidegger locates this temporality in the 'fore-structure' of understanding, in its moments of foresight (*Vorsicht*), fore-conception (*Vorgriff*) and fore-having (*Vorhabe*) by methodically working out the structure of understanding.
5. With the history of the word 'text' Gadamer demonstrates that beyond the classical fields of theology and music from which the concept of 'text' has entered modern speech, the word 'text' has found a wider extension in cases where a thing resists integration in experience, and where a return to the supposed given would provide a better orientation for understanding. "Thus, we find the hermeneutical return to the text at work whenever we encounter resistance to our primordial assumption of the meaningfulness of the given. The intimacy with which text and interpretation are entangled is thoroughly apparent insofar as even the tradition of a text is not always reliable as a basis for an interpretation. Indeed, it is often interpretation that first leads to the critical restoration of the texts. There is therefore a methodological advantage to be gained in making this inner relation of interpretation and text clear. The methodological advantage, which results from this observation made about language, is that here 'text' must be understood as a hermeneutical concept" (Gadamer 1986, p. 389).
6. According to Gadamer there are also vanishing points (*Schwundstufen*) for the text, for example the written scientific communication, which is not a 'text' for the scientific colleague but only becomes one for the historian of science. According to Gadamer we also cannot speak of the 'text' of a letter. A letter then becomes a 'text' when someone reads it with a special interest, for example with the interest of a social scientist who analyses letters as personal documents.
7. Ricoeur's thesis in *Time and Narrative* is that the very meaning of the configuration operation constituting emplotment is a result of its intermediary position between the two operations mimesis I and mimesis III. Ricoeur wants to demonstrate that mimesis II draws its intelligibility from its faculty of mediation which leads from the one side of the text to the other. In this context

Ricoeur also makes a distinction between 'semiotics' and 'hermeneutics'. According to Ricoeur it is characteristic for a semiotics of the text that a science of the text can only be established upon mimesis II and may only consider the internal laws of a work of literature without any regard of the two sides of the text. "Hermeneutics, however, is concerned with reconstructing the entire arc of operations by which practical experience provides itself with works, authors, and readers. It does not confine itself to setting mimesis II between mimesis I and mimesis III. It wants to characterize mimesis II by its mediating function. What is at stake, therefore, is the concrete process by which the textual configuration mediates between the prefiguration of the practical field and its refiguration through the reception of the work". (Ricoeur 1984, p. 53)

8. This is also the basic assumption — rather implicit than explicit — of participant observation as a qualitative research method in the social sciences.
9. Ricoeur's concept of text is different from the concept of text by Gadamer to the extent that Ricoeur emphasizes the difference between 'text' and 'dialogue'. Ricoeur proposes and describes two different models, the model of the speaking-hearing-relation and the model of the writing-reading-relation. In contrast Gadamer emphasizes the continuity between 'text' and 'dialogue' by conceptualizing the text as specific phase (stage) of the dialogue. Considering the normative destination of interpretive, that is hermeneutical, cultural analysis as a dialogical science, I find Gadamer's concept of the text to be the more suitable concept for this aim.
10. In this method of interviewing (cf. Schütze 1977, 1992; Rosenthal 1993) the autobiographical narrators were asked, by means of an initial opening question, to give a full extempore narration of events and experiences from their own lives. The ensuing story, or 'main narrative', is not interrupted by further questions but is encouraged by means of nonverbal and paralinguistic expressions of interest and attention, as 'mhm'. In the second part of the interview — the 'period of questioning' — the interviewer initiated, with narrative questions, more elaborate narrations on topics and biographical events already mentioned. In addition the interviewer asked about issues that had not been addressed (Rosenthal 1993).
11. I try to describe the process of analysis without the professional and technical concepts of Glaser, Strauss and Corbin, otherwise I have to describe the concept of the grounded theory methodology more in detail.
    Prior theories, theoretical models, results of other research reports can also be used in this inductive approach but only as so-called sensitiving concepts. I have also used theoretical concepts in this way but I do not want to describe the procedure in this context.
12. The word 'healing' means many things to women. They make a distinction between 'outer healing' and 'inner healing'. Getting a new job, for example, they call an example of 'outer healing'.

REFERENCES

Aschenbach, G. (1984). *Erklären und Verstehen in der Psychologie: zur methodischen Grundlage einer humanistischen Psychologie*. Bad Honnef: Bock & Herchen.

Bleicher, J. (1980). *Contemporary hermeneutics: hermeneutics as method, philosophy and critique*. London: Routledge & Kegan Paul.

Drehsen, V., H. Häring, K.-J. Kuschel & H. Siemers (ed.) (1988). *Wörterbuch des Christentums*. Gütersloh: Benzinger.

Gadamer, H.-G. (1960). *Wahrheit und Methode: Grundzüge einer philosophischen Hermeneutik*. Tübingen: Siebeck.

Gadamer, H.-G. (1983). Text und Interpretation. In: *Hermeneutik II: Gesammelte Werke, vol. 2* (pp. 330-360). Tübingen: Mohr, 1986.

Gadamer, H.-G. (1986). Text and interpretation. In: B.R. Wachterhauser (ed.). *Hermeneutics and modern philosophy* (pp. 377-396). Albany: State University of New York Press.

Geertz, C. (1973). Thick description: toward an interpretive theory of culture. In: *The interpretation of cultures*. London: Fontana, 1993.

Glaser, B. (1978). *Theoretical sensitivity*. Mill Valley, CA: Sociology Press.

Glaser, B. & A. Strauss (1967). *The discovery of grounded theory: strategies for qualitative research*. Chicago: Aldline.

Grathoff, R. & K. Knorr Cetina (1988). Was ist und was soll kultursoziologische Forschung? *Soziale Welt, 6* (Sonderband), 21-36.

Heidegger, M. (1927). *Sein und Zeit*. Tübingen: Niemeyer.

Jüttemann, G. (ed.) (1991). *Individuelle und soziale Regeln des Handelns: Beiträge zur Weiterentwicklung geisteswissenschaftlicher Ansätze in der Psychologie*. Heidelberg: Asanger.

Keupp, H. (1988). *Riskante Chancen: das Subjekt zwischen Psychokultur und Selbstorganisation*. Heidelberg: Asanger.

Leithäuser, Th. & B. Volmerg (1979). *Anleitung zur empirischen Hermeneutik: psychoanalytische Textinterpretation als sozialwissenschaftliches Verfahren*. Frankfurt: Fischer.

Ortner, S.B. (1984). Theory in anthropology in the sixties. *Comparative Studies in Society and History, 26*, 126-166.

Ricoeur, P. (1981). *Hermeneutics & the human sciences*. Cambridge: Cambridge University Press.

Ricoeur, P. (1984). *Time and narrative, vol. 1*. Chicago: University of Chicago Press.

Rosenthal, G. (1993). Reconstruction of life stories: principles of selection in generating stories for narrative biographical interviews. In: R. Josselson & A. Lieblich (eds.). *The narrative study of lives, vol. 1* (pp. 59-91). Newbury Park: Sage.

Schütz, A. (1971). *Gesammelte Aufsätze, vol. 1: Das Problem der sozialen Wirklichkeit*. Den Haag.

Schütze, F. (1977). *Die Technik des narrativen Interviews in Interaktionsfeldstudien. Arbeitsberichte und Forschungsmaterialien* Nr.1 der Universität Bielefeld, Fakultät für Soziologie.

Schütze, F. (1992). Pressure and guilt: war experiences of a young German soldier and their biographical implications. *International Sociology, 7*, 187-208.

Searle, J.R. (1983). *Intentionality: an essay in the philosophy of mind.* Cambridge: Cambridge University Press.

Stern, E. (1920). Probleme der Kulturpsychologie. *Zeitschrift für die gesamte Staatswissenschaft, 76,* 267-301.

Strauss, A. (1987). *Qualitative analysis for social scientist.* New York: Cambridge University Press.

Strauss, A. & J. Corbin (1990). *Basics of qualitative research.* Newbury Park: Sage.

Tillo, G.P.P. van (1993a). Naar een semiotische godsdienstsociologie [Towards a semiotic sociology of religion]. In: W. Smeets & G.P.P. van Tillo (eds.). *Religie als systeem van tekens en symbolen* [Religion as system of sighns and symbols] (pp. 48-63). Heerlen: Universitair Centrum voor Theologie en Pastoraat.

Tillo, G.P.P. van (1993b). *Onder tekens van macht en schijn* [Under signs of power and appearance]. Amsterdam: Edmund Husserl-Stichting.

Vellenga, S.J. (1991). *Een ondernemende beweging: de groei van de evangelische beweging in Nederland* [An enterprising movement: the growth of the evangelical movement in the Netherlands]. Amsterdam: VU Uitgeverij.

Werbik, H. (1986). *Existenz-Psychologie.* (Vortrag am 35. Kongress der Deutschen Gesellschaft für Psychologie, Universität Erlangen, Institut für Psychologie) (Memorandum Nr.22).

Wittgenstein, L. (1971). *Philosophische Untersuchungen.* Frankfurt: Suhrkamp.

Wundt, W. (1900-1920). *Völkerpsychologie: eine Untersuchung der Entwicklungsgesetze von Sprache, Mythos und Sitte (10 vols.).* Leipzig: Engelmann.

Zitterbarth, W. (1987[4]). Kulturpsychologie. In: R. Asanger & G. Wenninger (eds.). *Handwörterbuch der Psychologie* (pp. 382-386). Weinheim: Beltz.

MYSTICAL EXPERIENCE AND INTERPRETATION
A HERMENEUTICAL APPROACH

A. Geels
Lund University (Sweden)

We all know that religious mysticism is a vast and complex area of research. There are mystical dimensions within all the religions of the world. Some traditions, like Taoism, Zen and other types of Buddhism, as well as Hindu traditions like Kashmir Shaivism, Vaishnavism and Advaita Vedanta, are basically mystical in the sense that they all strive for transcendence from this world of multiplicity. In the West there is a growing interest in Christian mysticism and its relation to other traditions like Zen and Theravada meditation. Sufism still belongs to the popular expressions of Islam, all the way from Marocco to Indonesia, and offers an alternative to fundamentalism. Finally, in the Jewish world there is an increasing interest in the mystical Kabbalah.[1]

The scholarly study of mysticism is a phenomenon that probably runs parallel to the increasing popularity of the subject among the general public. Naturally, the scholar has to peruse earlier studies in order to increase his knowledge of this complex phenomenon. In these studies three problem areas can be discerned. Firstly, there is the problem of definition. Secondly, we repeatedly encounter the problem of the relation between mystical experience and interpretation. Finally, there is the question regarding types of mystical experience. In this article the focus will be on the second problem area, which, I intend to show, has implications for the problem of typology. The question of definition will only be discussed shortly as an introduction.

DEFINITIONS AND DIMENSIONS OF MYSTICISM

As early as 1899 the English scholar and dean William Ralph Inge wrote that the concept 'mysticism' is even more misused than the word 'socialism' in the English language (Inge 1899, p. 3). In an appendix, Inge presented no less than twenty-six definitions of mysticism and mystical theology. However, when we study classical definitions of mysticism it is striking that what scholars usually define is the mystical *experience* (see for example Pratt 1920, p. 337; Leuba 1925, p. 1; Clark 1958). All three classical studies referred to here state that the mystical experience is not related to perception. The three scholars rather regard it as a non-rational, intuitive experience. In my opinion this is an *obscurum per obscurum* procedure; in the definition of the problematic object new obscure concepts are introduced, putting a veil, so to speak, over the subject area.

The concept of mysticism, however, covers more than just the special types of experiences reported by mystics. The concept is just as general as the word religion. For that reason we could apply the five dimensions of religion presented by Glock and Stark (1965) to the area of mysticism. These are, first, the *experiential* dimension of mysticism, i.e. the mystical experiences, the core of mysticism. These personal experiences can be described as the presence of a Power greater than oneself, as a state of unity, or as visions and voices, or a combination of them. Scholars discuss whether a common denominator, a universal core, can be discerned, while others analyse the same descriptions of mystics and come to the conclusion that they should be divided into two, three, or more categories.

Secondly, there is the *ritual* dimension, i.e. different techniques used in order to reach beyond the world of multiplicity. I am referring for example to techniques of isolation, meditation, contemplation and prayer. Through contemplative devotion and attention (*kavvanah*) and meditative prayer the Jewish mystic approaches the divine; Theresa of Avila describes the seven stages of prayer in her *El castillo interior*. A special type of repetitive prayer occurs not only in the Greek Orthodox tradition (the Jesus prayer) but also in 'Pure Land Buddhism' in Japan, as well as in mystical Islam, where dervishes monotonously repeat the prayer *La ilaha illa llah* ('there is no god but God') and other divine names.

The third dimension is the *intellectual*, i.e. the cognitive processing of the mystic, presented in his or her texts. An apparent paradox is the fact that although most mystics declare that the experience is ineffable, they nevertheless devote considerable time to the description and systematic analysis of their own experiences. This dimension is closely related to the fourth, *ideological* dimension, i.e. the tradition to which the mystic belongs, for example branches of the Jewish Kabbalah, or the Sufi tradition, Zen, Vedanta, etc. These traditions not only influence the experiences itself, but they also colour the descriptions presented by the mystics. It should be added, however, that there are persons who could be called mystics but do not confess to belonging to any tradition (see below).

The fifth and final dimension is the *consequential* one, i.e. the different ways in which the mystic is influenced by the experience. This important and somewhat neglected dimension of mysticism will be commented upon below.

My own definition of mystical experience is based on a study by Robert S. Ellwood (1980, p. 29), but with several additions, here marked in italics:

> (1) Mystical experience is experience in a religious *or a profane* context (2) that is immediately or subsequently interpreted by the experiencer as an encounter with *a higher or* ultimate divine reality (3) in a direct, *according to the subject* nonrational way (4) that engenders a deep sense of unity and of living during the experience on a level of being other than the ordinary. (5) *This experience is accompanied by far-reaching consequences in the individual's life.*

A short commentary on the five elements of this definition is necessary. Concerning the first statement it is clear that most mystical experiences occur within the context of a religious tradition. Within these traditions mystics not infrequently are regarded as religious radicals, drawing on the profound consequences of their personal, intensive, transforming experiences. In some cases this leads to serious disputes with representatives of the orthodox faith. The martyrdom of al-Hallaj in Islam, executed in Baghdad (922) for his extravagant utterances, is well-known. He was far from the only mystic who was being accused of heresy,[2] especially during the period up to al-Ghazzali (d. 1111), when Sufism became consolidated with the orthodox faith. Jewish Kabbalists have always been regarded with a certain suspicion, and Chassidim have been condemned on several occasions (Scholem 1941; 1974). Christian fourteenth-century mystics like Eckhart and Ruusbroec had to defend themselves for using certain phrases which were seriously suspected of being pantheistic; a number of Eckhart's statements were condemned in a bull in 1329, two years after his death. Cases like those mentioned above were probably in the mind of W. R. Inge, who in one of his last studies of mysticism, after nearly half a century of research, wrote that "institutionalism and mysticism have always been uneasy bedfellows" (1947, p. 21).

However, mystical experience does not have to occur within the more or less secure or threatening context of a religious tradition. There are many examples of experiences which could be regarded as mystical that took place in a profane context (Laski 1961, Maslow 1973). In addition, sociologists of religion in England, the United States and Finland, have convincingly shown that every third or fourth American, Englishman or Finnish person responds positively to questions like "Have you ever felt as though you were very close to a powerful spiritual force that seemed to lift you out of yourself?" (quoted in Hay 1985, p. 137). For several years I corresponded with a Swedish writer who wrote in a popular magazine about a type of experience he frequently had, especially when cycling on the small island where he lived. Let me quote a few lines from this article:

> I am not religiously inclined, but I often feel a mystical communion with nature, presumably in the sense of an *all-encompassing feeling* reported by mystics. Almost independent of the time of the year and outer circumstances I often have a feeling that everything is right, that everything is related to all else, or rather that all is one.

The Swedish author subsequently refused to interpret his experiences. Although his knowledge of the Christian mystical tradition is considerable, the only interpretation he mentioned in his letters to me was that his 'body fluids were in total balance'. We now touch upon the second aspect of the definition. Experiences can be interpreted instantly or retrospectively, sometimes years later; and interpretations can be put into a religious or a profane frame of reference. One of my colleagues told me that in his teens he was very interested in ornithology and that he spent many hours and days in nature, equipped with binoculars and a notebook. During this time of observation he frequently had a sense of unity with nature, intense feelings of absorption, of being part of a larger whole. At that time he did not give it much thought. A few years later, when he started to study religion, he came across *The varieties of religious experience*, the famous classic by William James. Then he understood that his experiences were not all that common. Moreover, he gained a language with which he could interpret his experiences retrospectively.

The third aspect of the definition, the direct, non-rational encounter with a higher reality, underlines the fact that most people report that the experience comes suddenly, that they were both surprised and overwhelmed by it. However, there can be a long and arduous preparation prior to the experience, which, according to the reporting person, is non-rational. That does not prevent the scholar from observing rational factors involved.

The fourth aspect emphasizes the dimension of unity, one of the most common characteristics of the mystical experience. According to Walter T. Stace this is "the one basic, essential, nuclear characteristic, from which most of the others inevitably follow" (1960, p. 110). It is of course not surprising that such an experience of unity in a world of multiplicity is understood as coming from another dimension of reality. Although the experience itself may last only minutes, life will never be the same again. After these transforming minutes the mystic usually re-evaluates his or her life, dividing it in a 'before' and an 'after'. One of my informants dated her letter to me the third of March in the year 0003, three years after the overwhelming experience.

This is the fifth and final aspect of the mystical experience, an aspect which I think is important to underline. The mystic's personality now has a new centre. Around this nucleus, the experiential *axis mundi*, a more or less sophisticated conceptual web, can be woven. The complexity of the web, as well as its boundary transgressing qualities, are partly dependent on the degree of loyalty towards a certain tradition, through the medium of a *guru* or otherwise. When there is a low degree of loyalty, then continuous re-interpretation of the original experience can be expected. After all, the experience is ineffable, and the mystic, out of the intensity of his or her emotion and the ambition to express the inexpressible, will use any language system that serves the goal. The boundaries of the language system, limited as it is, will constantly be explored and stretched, leading to poetical metaphors, daring paradoxes, and condensed expressions like the anonymous Javanese mystic exclaiming: "Oh, you guide of the perplexed, let my perplexity increase!"

MYSTICAL EXPERIENCE AND INTERPRETATION — PHILOSOPHICAL PERSPECTIVES

It is striking that the scholarly study of mystical experience and its interpretation is dominated by philosophers of religion. A short review of their work will be presented below. Then I will introduce my model which I hope will provide a better understanding of this problem from the viewpoint of the psychology of religion.

Since the beginning of the 1960's there has been a clear distinction between a mystical experience and, in the words of W.T. Stace, "the conceptual interpretations which may be put upon it" (Stace 1960, p. 31f). This distinction can be compared to the relation between perception and interpretation. By interpretation Stace means "anything which the conceptual intellect adds to the experience for the purpose of understanding it, whether what is added is only classificatory concepts, or a logical inference, or an explanatory hypothesis". Stace admits, however, that it is difficult to reach 'pure' experience. We could possibly gain something, he continues, by introducing different levels of interpretation. When someone says: "I see red paint", this could be called a 'low level interpretation', while the physicist's theories about light waves of the same colour can be regarded as 'high level interpretations'. In a similar manner the mystic's description of his experience in terms of 'undifferentiated distinctionless unity' is of the low level type, while descriptions like 'mystical union with the Creator of the universe' are of a high level type. The latter presupposes both an assumption about the beginning of the world and a belief in a personal God (Stace 1960, p. 37).

Regardless of what we may think of his analysis it can be said that Stace's book has been inspirational for many scholars. Ninian Smart developed the above mentioned levels of interpretation by introducing the concept 'ramifications', i.e. theological concepts having a certain meaning within a specific tradition. The rather wide definition of the concept of interpretation is more narrowly defined by Smart: "the use of relatively ramified concepts in describing the experience" (Smart 1962, p. 20). In a later article he asserts that a description containing many ramifications is further from the original experience than descriptions with few ramifications (Smart 1965). If I understand Smart correctly, then the following quotations can be regarded as comprising many and few ramifications:

> And thus they (good men) are united with God through Divine Grace and their own holy lives. (Jan van Ruusbroec)
> When the spirit by the loss of its self-consciousness has in very truth established its abode in this glorious and dazzling obscurity. (Heinrich Seuse)

The concept of ramification is problematic in my opinion. If references to an empirical world are being used based on the mystic's own experience (concepts like 'light', 'darkness', 'abyss', 'desert', etc.), then this does not necessarily mean that the description contains few ramifications. The concept 'light' could be a ramification if it were being used in, for example, Iranian Sufism, which developed a mysticism of light. In other words, concepts referring to an empirical reality can be theologically based in certain traditions. The conclusion is that the road suggested by Smart is a blind alley.

Another example of the philosophical analysis of the problem discussed is Peter G. Moore. In an article from 1973, Moore suggests three 'possible junctures at which interpretation could relate to experience'. Five years later Moore increased the distinctions to four, comprising firstly what he called 'retrospective interpretation', i.e. interpretations influenced by tradition and arising after the experience. However, Moore discussed neither the problem of time intervals nor that of intention, problems which from a psychological perspective are important. To whom is the text directed? Was there any censorship involved? Methods of literary criticism should be applied as well as knowledge from the psychology of memory and social psychology.

The second type Moore calls 'reflexive interpretation', that is spontaneous interpretations formulated during the experience or immediately afterward. When the mystic's own belief, his expectations and intentions influence the experience, then Moore speaks of 'incorporated interpretation', divided into two subgroups: 'reflected interpretation', ideas and images that are reflected in the experience in the forms of visions; 'assimilated interpretation', the experiential type which builds a phenomenological analogy to a belief or a doctrine. Finally, the last type in Moore's categorization consists of experiences which are supposed to be uninfluenced by the mystic's earlier belief, expectations or intentions. In such cases Moore speaks of 'raw interpretation' (1978, p. 198f).

The last category, I think, is a theoretical abstract. From a psychological point of view, the mystic's original experience is an unknown factor, a subjective experience which is studied primarily through the medium of the written word — the mystic's own descriptions. Scholars only work with interpreted experience. This last category of Moore coincides, as far as I can see, with that of 'reflexive interpretation'.

A systematic presentation of different philosophical approaches to the problem has been produced by Philip Almond (1982), who organized them in five different groups. The first group defends the thesis that all mystical experiences are the same, that there is a high degree of concordance among mystics of different cultures and ages. The group can be exemplified by a short quotation from one of its famous scholars, William Ralph Inge. After a presentation of a number of definitions of Christian mystical experiences, Inge wrote that the same "harmony is found, to a very remarkable extent, among mystics of all times, of all countries, and of all religions" (1947, p. 32).

The second group starts from the assumption that the mystical experience is essentially the same in all cultures, but interpreted within the frame of reference of the cultural tradition. The third group works with typologies, stating that there are types of mystical experience to be found across cultures. Here we encounter the well-known typologies of Ronald C. Zaehner (theistic, monistic and panenhenic experiences), Rudolph Otto (*Gott-Mystik* and *Seelen-Mystik*) as well as Nathan Söderblom (mysticism of personality and mysticism of infinity).

The fourth group asserts that there are just as many types of mystical experiences as there are paradigmatic expressions of them. Almond rejects all four of them and suggests a fifth model worth defending: "There are as many types of mystical experience as there are incorporated interpretations of them" (Almond 1982, p. 128). We recognize the terminology of Peter G. Moore. Incorporated interpretation includes the importance of the religious and socio-cultural tradition for the mystical experience.

Almond presents Steven T. Katz as "the leading exponent of model five." This point of view, nowadays called the constructivist approach, asserts that the mystical experience, in the words of Katz, "as well as the form in which it is reported is shaped by concepts which the mystic brings to, and which shape, his experience." Katz is convinced that "*there are NO pure (i.e. unmediated) experiences*" (1978, p. 26; see also Gimello 1978).

For a psychologist of religion the model five suggestion is insufficient. Let me give an example from a text written by Martin Buber:

> From my own unforgettable experience I know very well that there is a state in which the bounds of the personal nature of life have fallen away from us and we experience an undivided unity. But I do not know — what the soul willingly imagines and indeed is bound to imagine (mine too once did it) — that in this I had attained to a union with the primal being or the godhead. *That is an exaggeration no longer permitted to the responsible understanding.* Responsibly — that is, as a man holding his ground before reality — I can elicit from those experiences only that in them I reached an undifferentiated unity of myself without form or content. /-/ *This unity is nothing but the unity of this soul of mine, whose 'ground' I have reached...* (Buber 1961, p. 43; the italics are mine).

Buber refers to an experience of undifferentiated unity with the godhead, an interpretation later altered into unity within his own self. According to the model five approach Buber should not have had such an experience. But then the proponents of model five do not seem to allow for the possibility that the mystic can present boundary transgressing interpretations, leaving the secure borders of doctrinal interpretation. As mentioned above, this dimension can have an explosive potential, a power which sent al-Hallaj to the gallows. Almond touches upon this possibility in his model five approach: "A mystical experience may lead too to the creative transformation of a religious tradition. Mystical experience is capable of generating new interpretations of the tradition while yet remaining faithful to it" (Almond 1982, p. 168). But then again: some mystics do not remain faithful, at least in the eyes of those defending the orthodox faith.

A growing number of scholars have put forward their alternative to the constructivist view in a recently published book entitled *The problem of pure consciousness: mysticism and philosophy*, edited by Robert K.C. Forman. In his introductory essay, Forman convincingly criticizes the constructivist approach, stating that "the history of mysticism is rife with cases in which expectations, models, previously acquired concepts, and so on, were deeply and radically *dis*confirmed" (Forman 1990b, p. 19f).

Forman presents a number of arguments, all refuting the conservative stand of constructivism. Firstly, there are examples of 'untrained and uninitiated' neophytes who have mystical experiences, which only in the course of time, months or years later, were religiously interpreted. Forman mentions published reports of Richard M. Bucke (1900), and the more recent book of Bernadette Roberts (1985). In addition to these cases, Forman presents interview data, collected by himself, and examples of classical mystics, who most often report being surprised over their experiences (Forman 1990b, p. 19f).

Constructivism, Forman concludes, cannot account for the existence of reports of so called 'Pure Consciousness Events' (PCEs), defined as 'wakeful contentless consciousness', the existence of which has been established 'beyond a reasonable doubt' by the authors of the above mentioned book (Forman 1990b, p. 21).

There are aspects of the constructivist approach which might be considered valid from a psychological point of view. Man's view of reality, his *Weltanschauung*, is socially constructed and charged with personal, subjective meaning.[3] A strict behavioural analysis of the way in which information is processed is too mechanistic, however, and cannot account for descriptions of experiences which transgress all doctrinal boundaries. The analysis of human information-processing should include a dimension from depth-psychology. An eclectic approach of this kind has become rather common since the influential work of Ulric Neisser (1967). The heuristic value of such an approach, which takes into account the various dynamic, associative ways of handling emotionally charged information, can easily be demonstrated. It enables us to understand new or unexpected features in reports of religious experience, whether they be Old Testament prophets combining, in their visions, contemporary iconographic elements with verbal data, or Christian mystics like John of the Cross, using sensuous, erotic imagery in his poetry while simultaneously stating that the mystical adept has to reach levels beyond the senses. If we consider that undercurrent of primary process activity, expressed for instance in plastic, symbolic representations and verbal syncretism, a process which usually functions in dreams but can be activated under certain conditions (such as from the outside world), then we have a better hermeneutical tool for understanding combinations of motives originating from such diverse sources as contemporary popular literature, Dionysius the Areopagite and the Song of Songs, motives melting together in John's poetry and regarded as belonging to the classics of world literature (see Geels 1989a, pp. 197ff).

The conclusion of all this is that the constructivist point of view is untenable. Man constructs most of the time, but, as a boundary-transgressing being, not all of the time. It is the task of the psychologist of religion to describe those processes that lead to new and unexpected constructions of a world, which, most of the time, can be shared with other human beings.

Mystical Experience and Interpretation — A Psychological Perspective

Ana Maria Rizzuto belongs to those psychologists who make a distinction between the concept of God and the representation of God. The former refers to the God of the theologians and the philosophers, a God which can be discussed and verbally objectified. The latter, however, first and foremost evokes emotional commitment; it is a God who touches us and reaches far beyond a mere intellectual understanding.

Another point of departure for this model can be presented in the words of Almond, words which at the same time imply criticism of the constructivist approach: "to look upon the mystic as a mirror who accurately reflects the contents of his experience is to totally ignore the possible distortions of the experience in the mystic's interpretation" (1982, p. 147). It is the task of the psychologist of religion, rather than his philosopher colleagues, to analyse these 'possible distortions'. It goes without saying that for a psychologist it is far better to study living persons than ancient texts which tell us very little concerning chronology, censorship and other questions asked from the perspective of literary criticism.

As mentioned above, the mystical experience *per se* is subjective, transient, beyond the boundaries of language according to many mystics. This subjective, transient *level of experience* is an unknown factor to the scholar. It is possible to study the 'traces' in terms of consequences in the mystic's life, the interpretations and re-interpretations offered — in other words, to study the language system of the mystic. But we should never forget that the mystic usually states that language has very little — if anything! — to do with the experience itself. This is the category of 'raw experience' mentioned by Moore. However, the object of study is at best 'raw interpretation', that is verbal reports delivered as close to the original experience as possible. With increasing time intervals, there is an increasing possibility of the type of distortions mentioned above.

When this inexpressible experience is over, it has to remain a psychological reality to the mystic. The coding of the experience in memory is dependent on the type of experience, but it is almost always something more than or beyond language. A person having an intense experience of fire fell on his knees and remembered the words: "It is awful to fall into the hands of living God". The sentence was uttered by the well-known Swedish theologian Nathan Söderblom (1866-1931). The few words allude to at least three psychologically relevant categories: a strong emotional dimension, a visual content (fire) and a motor reaction (falling on the knees). All categories are forced, so to speak, into a linguistic dress which really does not fit properly. From this perspective it is not difficult to understand the mystic's perpetually repeated words that the experience is ineffable. But 'since name it we must', as the neoplatonist Plotinos said as early as the third century, the language system that is usually selected expresses the experience in terms of 'I' and 'Thou' simply because human relations are the most suited analogy for expressing the experience of God.

This is the level called *the representation of God*. Still at the subjective level, it comprises both emotional and/or visual and/or motor information as well as, sometimes, information originating from the language system. With this integrated information the mystic can imagine the God who now no longer is immediately present.

While reflecting on the absent God and the intensity and significance of the experience, the mystic feels a need to communicate the transforming moment, despite its ineffability, to his or her environment. The most common way of communication is to use language. But in the eyes of the mystic verbal expressions are nothing more than stumbling attempts to express the inexpressible. However, our psychological reality tells us that we are being trained from early childhood to use the linguistic medium. At the same time we are often painfully aware of the fact that language cannot cover all the dimensions of experienced reality. For the mystic as well as the 'ordinary' human being, language sometimes is an intolerable limitation. But this is the very same limitation the scholar encounters when studying texts! We now touch upon the third level of the model, the objectified level of (usually) the linguistic system. However, there are examples of mystics who choose complementary forms of communication, such as art or ritual behaviour. In an earlier study I analysed not only the poetry of a Swedish artist who had intense visionary and auditive experiences, but also her paintings, which contain fragments of her visionary experiences expressed in a symbolic way (Geels 1989b).

I suggest calling this third level *the image of God*, the characteristics of which are firstly that the subjective experience now has been communicated, usually through the medium of the written word. In addition, we can allow for the possibility of visual and/or ritual and/or motor communication. From a scholarly perspective the optimal situation is, of course, that the time interval between the original experience and the verbal report is as limited as possible. When it comes to the study of classical mystics, we all know that this is seldom the case.

Like Buber mentioned above, mystics are no different from other human beings in their tendency to revise their interpretations of earlier experiences. With reference to classical psychoanalysis, more specifically the book *Traumdeutung* by Sigmund Freud, I have called this fourth and final level a secondary revision of an earlier image of God. The analogy of dreams and their interpretation can be used to clarify this relation. We all know from our own experience of dreams that the emotional content of a nightmare decreases in the morning, when we wake up and try to remember the dream. From a psychoanalytical perspective, the dream, which has its own 'language' (that is primary process mechanisms like displacement and condensation), is revised according to the demands of the secondary process (that is a tendency to intellectualise, create order and coherence). In other words: the subjective experience of the dream is 'forced' into the dress of secondary process adaptation — and it does not fit. In time, the interpretation can be revised, adapting it to a new life situation.

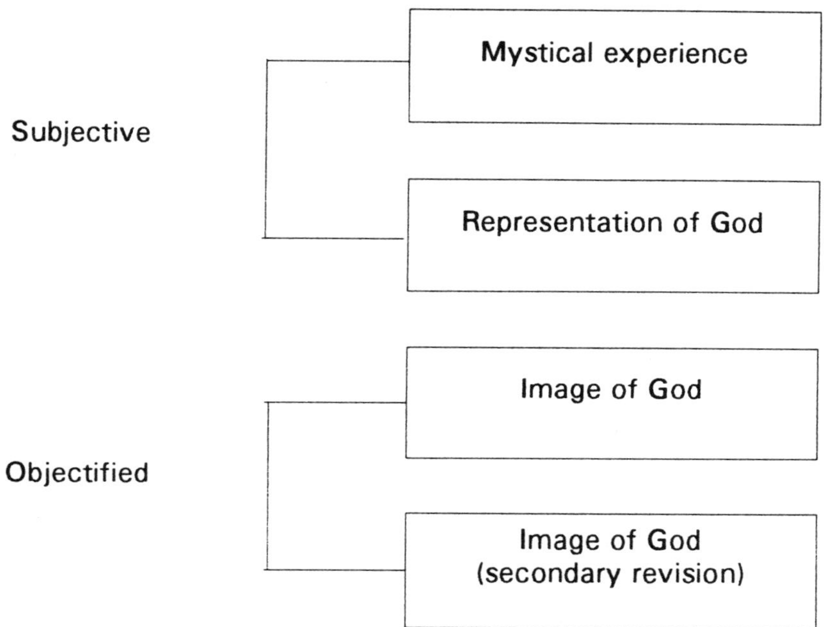

Fig. 1 Levels of interpretation

During the last decade I have devoted a great part of my research time to the study of persons now living and their predominantly visionary and auditive experiences. I have learned from them that they usually have very strong memories of their experiences, often decades back in time. An old lady wrote to me: "Tears are still running down my cheek when I write this, although it is more than fifty years ago". You hardly forget life transforming experiences. This means that it is possible to analyse different levels of interpretation. Informants often are aware of the 'possible distortions' mentioned above.

An example is the case of Eve, who was fifty years old when she had her first intense religious experience. It was a beautiful day in May. The sun was shining and Eve took a walk in nature, in the well-known surroundings from childhood. She had been working hard lately. Suddenly it started to thunder. Then the rain came and disappeared again just as suddenly. She wrote: "The sky turns blue, the sun is shining, birds are chirping. A wonderful rainbow, just like a heart, a double, shows up with powerful, pure colours". Then she had this experience:

> But suddenly nature changes. The rainbow disappears, the shadows disappear, the birds stop chirping, the sun turns into a fifteen watt lamp, it isn't able to shine. Everything becomes absolutely quiet. But a strong white light illuminates nature. On the verge of blinding. And I feel that I am in the centre of the universe and in the hand of God. Everything around me forms a unity, a whole. The meadow with its weeping birch, the pine forest, the grass, the sky, the hill. Light, silence, immovable. I am in active rest, observing, enjoying, heavenly happy. Anything could have happened then, but nothing could move me in my being. O God, how could I ever doubt your existence. Without you nothing would be. But that I could receive such a wonderful proof. I, a poor sinful person. I want to sing your praise.
>
> If eternity is a state beyond time, then I was there.

When I corresponded with Eve I asked her to sit back, close her eyes, and in her mind return to the natural scenery of her youth. Then I asked her about her interpretations. Immediately she was sure that words like being 'in the hand of God' were additions made at a later date, probably after a visit to a museum of a famous Swedish sculptor, whose piece of art called 'the hand of God' could have influenced her. Moreover, she added, the metaphor of the hand of God is rather common in the Bible. As one of the results of this overwhelming experience, Eve's concept of God was completely altered. Before God was like an eye, always persecuting her, giving her a permanent bad conscience; a punishing and judging God, frightening her. Afterward, God became a merciful, loving God, wiping away her bad conscience in one fierce stroke. Eve then decided to study for the ministry in the Swedish church. She is now a retired vicar living in Stockholm.

The conclusion we can draw so far is that the function of language for mystics seems to be that of a guide or a signpost, pointing in a certain direction, without equating the pointing finger with the object pointed at. We all are aware of the fact that the map is not identical with the territory, and we laugh when the sergeant says to his recruits: "If the map does not harmonize with the territory, then rely on the map." But in a similar way the scholar of mysticism identifies the text of the mystic with the experience.

The cognitive flexibility of the mystic is partly dependent on the degree of loyalty to a certain tradition. Let me give an example from the letters of the Swedish mystic and shoemaker Hjalmar Ekström (1885-1962). He was brought up in a religiously liberal environment, and as eldest in a family with eight children he learned to take responsibility and developed a certain measure of independence. Although trained as a deacon in the Swedish church, which he left when he was thirty, it took him about two decades to reach consolidation with the Christian tradition. He refused to go to church, even when a close friend visited him and served as a preacher in his local church. When I prepared my doctoral thesis about this mystic, I collected about five thousand pages of letters from his hand. In his letters Ekström sometimes describes the mystical experience, usually in answers to questions asked by the twenty people or so whom he corresponded with. It is obvious that his choice of words is influenced primarily by his consideration of the life situation of the addressee. Compare the following two quotations from his hand. The first is written to a handicapped woman, living alone in a small room in central Stockholm, hardly meeting any people. The second, written the very same day, was included in a letter to the eccentric Swedish linguistic genius Eric Hermelin, who spent about thirty-five years in a mental hospital in Lund because his aristocratic family didn't know how to handle his alcoholism. In time he developed a manic-depressive personality disorder. During his manic phases he translated a significant part of Persian Sufism, filling almost one meter on a bookshelf. Ekström corresponded with him for about twenty-five years. Now the two quotations about the mystic experience:

> The hand which then is stretched out to her and seizes her is infinitely mild and cautious; almost undiscernably, it takes care of her and pulls her forward on His road and into His life, in a way that is as mild as it is majestic, and this happens in a way that is often hidden from us.

> Yes, everything drowns in the clear stillness of god and becomes one in It: everything becomes transparent, everything turns into crystal.

The following quotation, similar to the second one above, was selected from a letter to a lawyer friend of Ekström:

> You are sort of absorbed, and drown in Him in heaven, in such a way that nothing remains but Him, nothing other than His will.[4]

The first quotation contains concepts referring to the personal life. The few lines allude to fatherly care and security, personal relations, in other words the social dimension lacking in the life of the handicapped woman. The second quotation, on the other hand, was sent to Hermelin, who 'associated' with Persian mystics, whose texts are loaded with abstract symbolism like the moth which is totally annihilated in the flame, or the drop that looses itself completely in the ocean. This, I think, illustrates the use of language by a modern mystic, choosing his words with consideration taken of the addressee. This can only be understood if the function of language is that of the pointing finger, enabling a certain flexibility of expression. It is therefore pointless to analyse the frequency of certain words pertaining to a personalistic or abstract category and then characterize the mystic in question as a representative of mysticism of personality or mysticism of infinity.

This last remark naturally leads to a criticism of earlier attempts to categorize mystical experience. The main point I wish to put forward is that those scholars, working with printed sources of the 'level four' type according to the model presented above, assumed that what I call secondary revisions of mystical experiences are correct verbal reflections of an experience. They disregarded the 'possible distortions' in the mystic's successive interpretations of their experiences. This means that typologies of the kind presented by Otto, Zaehner, and others, are psychologically unsound. The best way to study the complex relation between mystical experience and interpretation is to study persons now living. The results gained in such studies can possibly shed new light on historical data.

The attempts at categorization referred to have also been criticized from other perspectives. Ninian Smart wrote that we still are "in the early stages of any kind of refined classification of the varieties of religious experience, and unfortunately some writers, notably Zaehner, have mixed up classification problems with theological judgements" (1978, p. 13). The confessional and apologetic features in the research of Zaehner and others have been observed by a number of scholars.[5] The judgement of Frits Staal is short and clear: Zaehner's typology is nothing but a "reflection of his own belief" (1975, p. 75). Almond pointed at the confessional features in Zaehner's typology, constructed, as Zaehner openly confesses, "because I happen to believe it is true" (Zaehner 1967, p. xvi; Almond 1982, p. 38).

Summary and conclusion

As to the problem of definition, it is necessary to define different dimensions of the complex concept of mysticism. I suggested that the well-known dimensions of Glock and Stark, applied to religion, can be transferred to the area of mysticism. In this article the focus was directed on the experiential dimension. The main problem in the scholarly study of mysticism was identified as the relation between mystical experience and interpretation. Among different suggestions put forward within the philosophy of religion, perhaps the most fruitful one has been presented by Peter G. Moore. His categories are psychologically relevant. However, in order to analyse which parts of a certain interpretation are to be regarded as incorporated, reflexive, or retrospective — since combinations are not only possible but also plausible — we need to perform case studies, preferably of persons now living.

As to the problem of the 'pure consciousness event', an interesting area of research, there is a need to cooperate with psychologists. What does it mean to 'empty' consciousness? If that is possible, then what is it that is being emptied, and how is it possible that the mystic in question *remembers* the result of this process? These are philosophical and psychological questions, calling for interdisciplinary research.

In the psychological model suggested above, I made a distinction between the mystical experience, or the experience of the godhead, and the representation of God, both of which are subjective. In addition, I proposed to distinguish between these subjective levels and the objectified image of God, communicated to the environment. This image can be the object of single or multiple revision, for different reasons. In connection with the analysis of dreams I have labelled the alteration of interpretations as secondary revisions.

This model has been used firstly in order to criticize categorisations in earlier research on mysticism, and secondly in order to point to the possible psychological function of mystical language. The conclusion is that this language can be regarded as stumbling efforts, on the part of the mystic, to expressing the inexpressible, in the conviction that language works as a signpost, pointing in a certain direction, but only arbitrarily related to the object referred to. In the words of the famous semanticist Alfred Korzybski, discussing a number of 'silent, unspeakable levels' which precede the verbal fixation of an experience: "Statements are verbal, they are never the silent 'it'" (Korzybski 1951, p. 172f).

NOTES

1. I am referring especially to the work of Moshe Idel, who emphasized the importance of Ecstatic Kabbalah, which was of subordinate importance in the well-known studies of Gershom Scholem (see Idel 1988a; 1988b).

2. A number of similar cases, one of them a parallel to al-Hallaj, can be found in the Indonesian interpretation of Islamic mysticism. See Soebardi 1975, p. 35ff; Ernst 1985.
3. See e.g. the work of Berger & Luckmann 1966; Berger 1967.
4. Quotations from Geels 1980, p. 206ff. English rendering by the author.
5. See for example the following researchers in the relations between hallucinogenic drugs and religion: Masters & Houston 1966, p. 256; Solomon 1964, p. 152, p. 155ff; Aaronson & Osmond 1970, p. 189.

REFERENCES

Aaronson, B. & H. Osmond (1970). *Psychedelics: the uses and implications of hallucinogenic drugs*. London: Hogarth.

Almond, P. (1982). *Mystical experience and religious doctrine: an investigation of the study of mysticism in world religion*. Berlin: Mouton.

Berger, P. (1967). *The sacred canopy: elements of a sociological theory of religion.* New York: Doubleday.

Berger, P. & Th. Luckmann (1966). *The social construction of reality: a treatise in the sociology of knowledge*. New York: Doubleday.

Buber, M. (1961). *Between man and man* (transl. R.G. Smith). London: Collins.

Bucke, R.M. (1900). *Cosmic consciousness: a study in the evolution of the human mind*. New York: Dutton.

Clark, W.H. (1958). *The psychology of religion: an introduction to religious experience and behavior*. New York: MacMillan.

Ellwood, R.S. (1980). *Mysticism and religion*. Englewood Cliffs: Prentice Hall.

Ernst, C.W. (1985). *Words of ecstasy in Sufism*. Albany: State University of New York Press.

Forman, R.K.C. (ed.) (1990a). *The problem of pure consciousness: mysticism and philosophy*. New York: Oxford University Press.

Forman, R.K.C. (1990b). Mysticism, constructivism, and forgetting. In: R.K.C. Forman (ed.). *The problem of pure consciousness: mysticism and philosophy*. New York: Oxford University Press.

Geels, A. (1980). *Mystikern Hjalmar Ekström (1885-1962): en religionspsykologisk studie av hans religiösa utveckling*. [The mystic Hjalmar Ekström (1885-1962): a study of his religious development from the perspective of the psychology of religion] Malmö: Doxa.

Geels, A. (1989a). *Den religiösa människan: psykologiska perspektiv*. [Religious man: psychological perspectives] Vänersborg: Plus Ultra.

Geels, A. (1989b). *Skapande mystik: en psykologisk studie av Violet Tengbergs religiösa visioner och konstnärliga skapande*. [Creative mysticism: a psychological study of Violet Tengberg's religious visions and artistic creation]. Malmö: Plus Ultra.

Gimello, R.M. (1978). Mysticism and meditation. In: S.T. Katz (ed.). *Mysticism and philosophical analysis* (pp.170-199). London: Sheldon.

Glock, C.Y. & R. Stark (1965). *Religion and society in tension*. Chicago: Harper & Row.

Hay, D. (1985). Religious experience and its induction. In: L.B. Brown (ed.). *Advances in the psychology of religion.* Oxford: Pergamon Press.

Idel, M. (1988a). *Kabbalah: new perspectives.* New Haven: Yale University Press.

Idel, M. (1988b). *Studies in ecstatic Kabbalah.* New York: State University of New York Press.

Inge, W.R. (1899). *Christian mysticism.* London: Methuen.

Inge, W.R. (1947). *Mysticism in religion.* London: Routledge & Kegan Paul, 1969.

Katz, S.T. (ed.) (1978). *Mysticism and philosophical analysis.* London: Sheldon.

Katz, S.T. (ed.) (1983). *Mysticism and religious traditions.* Oxford: Oxford University Press.

Korzybski, A. (1951). The role of language in the perceptual process. In: R.R. Blake & G.V. Ramsey. *Perception: an approach to personality* (pp. 170-205). New York: Ronald.

Laski, M. (1961). *Ecstasy: a study of secular and religious experiences.* London: Cresset.

Leuba, J.H. (1925). *The psychology of religious mysticism.* New York: Routledge & Kegan Paul.

Maslow, A. (1973). *Religions, values, and peak-experiences.* New York: Viking Press.

Masters, R.E.L. & J. Houston (1966). *The varieties of psychedelic experience.* New York: Dell.

Moore, P.G. (1973). Recent studies of mysticism: a critical survey. *Journal of Religion and Religions, 3*, 146-156.

Moore, P.G. (1978). Mystical experience, mystical doctrine, mystical technique. In: S.T. Katz (ed.). *Mysticism and philosophical analysis* (pp. 101-131). London: Sheldon.

Neisser, U. (1967). *Cognitive psychology.* New York: Meredith.

Pratt, J.B. (1920). *The religious consciousness: a psychological study.* New York: MacMillan.

Roberts, B. (1985). *The experience of no-self: a contemplative journey.* Boston: Shambhala.

Scholem, G. (1941). *Major trends in Jewish mysticism.* New York: Schocken, 1971.

Scholem, G. (1974). *Kabbalah.* New York: Meridian.

Smart, N. (1962). Mystical experience. *Sophia, 1* (1), 19-26.

Smart, N. (1965). Interpretation and mystical experience. *Religious Studies, 1*, 75-85.

Smart, N. (1978). Understanding religious conversion. In: S.T. Katz (ed.). *Mysticism and philosophical analysis* (pp. 10-21). London: Sheldon.

Soebardi, S. (1975). *The book of Cabolèk: a critical edition with introduction, translation and notes.* The Hague: Nijhof.

Solomon, D. (ed.) (1964). *LSD, the consciousness-expanding drug.* New York: Putnam.

Staal, F (1975). *Exploring mysticism.* London: Penguin.

Stace, W.T. (1960). *Mysticism and philosophy.* London: MacMillan.

Zaehner, R.C. (1967). *Mysticism sacred and profane.* London: Oxford University Press.

BETWEEN MYTHOLOGY AND SYMPTOMATOLOGY THOUGHTS ON THE PSYCHOLOGY OF SYMBOLS

J. Scharfenberg
University of Kiel (Germany)

PREVIEW

Centered around a case study of the therapy of the son of a Nazi perpetrator in Germany, I try to show how strongly the mythological power of an ideology can be prolonged from generation to generation. Therefore, remythologizing our culture cannot be regarded as a solution. However, resymbolization is a creative possibility. Such a process of religious symbolization can be observed in the role of the former East German church and its leading role in a revolution without violence.

RATIONALIZATION AND MYTHOLOGIZING

During the last several decades the creative power of religious symbols has constantly been overlooked. The objective of this chapter is to prove that this is due to a particular rationalization, on the one hand, and to mythologizing on the other.

Rationalization is a very common defense mechanism. It is often used against the overwhelming power of affect. But it seems to have failed *vis-à-vis* anxiety. We know more and more about less and less, but the problem of anxiety seems to remain unsolved. The only thing to be done is to displace anxiety and fear where there is nothing to worry about (like the recent upwelling of hostility against foreigners in Germany), and to feel secure where there should be fear for the sake of the survival of mankind in an age of nuclear an ecological catastrophes. These mechanisms might be supported by a universal system of hidden meaning that can be constructed out of the leftovers of religious tradition. Such a thoroughly unhistorical repetition of that which prevents the return of repressed material might very well be called a *mythology* and should be distinguished from the creative use of religious symbols.

No doubt in ancient times mythology was a very fruitful and inspiring source of creative imagination. The Judæo-Christian tradition joined in this stream of thinking and expression, but after the Cartesian split into the sphere of 'objective reality' *(res extensa)* on the one side and an only 'subjective guessing' *(res cogitans)* on the other, the new developing sciences where striving for the exclusion of the subjective factor. Symbolic language became a subject of everlasting quandary. In order to get as close as possible to reality, the symbolic language that keeps together object and subject, as the corpus colossum does between the two hemispheres (Hoppe 1985), was even regarded as a kind of sickness of language. This, according to Hume (1757), was due to the inability of our ancestors to think clearly and to express themselves properly. Even in the field of theology, the disability of rationalism and symbolic expression can be observed. According to Karl Barth (1954) religion was regarded as a kind of original sin because of the effort to grasp the reality of God and objectify it. Rudolf Bultmann (1948) especially called the symbolic mythical expression in the biblical language a mischief (*Mißgriff*) because it tries to objectify the Eternal. In contrast, Paul Tillich (1962) was for a long time the only one in the field of theology who showed some appreciation for symbols and emphasized their importance as "the real language of religion". However, he suggested a tension in real language between the sacramental and the prophetic, which in any case should be maintained. Otherwise, if the constitutive element and the prophetic element split and separate, the first one will be bound to become heteronomous and demonic, the latter empty and sceptical. Symbols are representatively pointing in the direction of the Holy and Ultimate, which both is and is not present in reality at the same time.

The critique of religion of Feuerbach, Marx, and Freud made very clear that religious symbolism very often was misused in the sense of oppressing and exploiting people. Freud (1927) claimed that religion would "disappear with the inevitability of a natural process". But this prophesy, which was supported even by the German martyr and theologian Dietrich Bonhoeffer (1964), did not prove to be true.

In our times a new interest in religion (not necessarily connected to church membership) is growing. There is especially a new interest in ancient mythology, which to a certain degree may be called a remythologization of religion, and we have to find some criteria that will make it possible to differentiate between a creative use of religious symbols and its opposite. I claim that this may be possible by differentiating between remythologization and resymbolization, and will illustrate this with the help of clinical and political examples.

The Return of the Repressed

What can be called the most astonishing event in European history is the fact that, after almost 200 years of Enlightenment (which according to Kant is the "outlet out of self-imposed dependence"), the most powerful ideology that finally let Europe fall into ruins was created in the shape of a mythology.

Similarly, as in the antique mythology, which doubtlessly functioned to diminish the fear of the natural forces, the main ideologist of Nazi ideas, Alfred Rosenberg (1930), in his *The Myth of the Twentieth Century* planted into the mind of the masses the idea that externalization of terror into concrete objects would free man from the traumatization of terror within himself. This idea has been carried by an entire generation. Concentration camps, where people were locked up and then killed, provide a perfect example of 'fencing in fear'. In these camps the fascists placed people on whom they projected all of their own instincts that frightened them and that they were unable to acknowledge, all of those things regarded as inferior and parasitic. In this process, a comprehensive myth becomes linked with spiritual powers, the unacceptable becomes routine.

In order to survive this deeply frightening possibility of the "Hitler within us" (DeMause 1984), not only Germans, but all of humankind, have tried to adopt a means of repression. However, wherever repression exists, no true solution can occur. That which is repressed recurs. This is precisely what we are witnessing, in the second generation after Hitler, in such frightening detail. It shows up especially in the phenomenon of falsely placed anxiety, which again projects our anxiety on to innocent people and tries to erect totally illusionary defenses in the face of the real terror. When there is no symbolic expression of guilt by means of a superpower, as for example in the seventh chapter of Romans, the terror of one's own potential must once again be fenced off, as in the literal concreteness of the atomic and ecological holocaust.

Psychologists today have the unique opportunity of seeing the mechanisms of repression in the generation of the children of the perpetrators and victims. It is of course not possible to be totally objective in this observation. One must pay the price of discovering the frightening possibility of the Hitler within us.

Case Study

What I described above can be exemplified by a case history:

Mr. B., at the beginning of counselling, is a 37-year-old, slim, well-trained, athletic man of impressive stature, but with insecure, almost groping movements by which one immediately noticed that he tried to avoid eye contact. Even when he did achieve eye contact, he could not maintain it.

He was in a caring profession, and had already completed various therapeutic modalities. He presented himself with the problem of his fatherlessness. This was also expressed in a very smooth, a bit obsequious, establishment of contact. He was brought up in a household of women. His grandfather died during the first days of World War I, and the discharge document — which was drawn up and personally signed by Kaiser Wilhelm II — belonged to the family heirlooms. His father died in 1945. Mr. B. had no recollection of him personally, but his father was continually present throughout Mr. B.'s childhood through his picture above the piano and through his mother's stories. His mother provided for him and for his sister under the most difficult external conditions of deprivation. She made it possible for him to attend secondary school and to study the same subject as his father. However, he failed the doctoral exams, which he had taken for granted he would pass (as his father had done). Alone, he was unable to overcome this obstacle and lapsed into work mania which, until he began treatment, absorbed and ate away all of his life's expressiveness.

At the beginning of therapy, Mr. B. constantly fluctuated between ideas of inferiority and ideas of greatness. For him there was only work; all other activities he deliberately set aside. In the area of relationships there was only occasional sexual contact. Indeed, in his friendship with a woman, it appeared to be hardly possible for him to be in any sexual involvement. He did not enter into any social involvements and avoided any kind of social contact. He voted for the conservative Christian Democrat Party, but without conviction, and left the church. However, as he later realized, he had very strong religious ideas and feelings, even if merely in the loneliness of his own heart. He had never been sick in his life, but has a constant hypochondriacal awareness of his body.

His inner stability was assured through a distant camaraderie with colleagues and his girlfriend, through crisp but changing sexual relationships, through work (the more the better), and through his therapy. However, this therapy was not allowed to change anything.

When his girlfriend began hinting that she would like to have a child with him, he became panicked and horrified. Only the invariability of the present condition guaranteed for him security. In childhood, the Trinity of God, his dead father, and Jesus had done the same. In his normal life, the result was an increase in his work mania, and impotence with his new wife, his former girlfriend. Mr. B. accumulated a large fortune, but he could not do anything with it because he didn't allow himself to have anything.

At this point, if we ask ourselves how this tragic story comes out, in the background of the structural characteristics of the myth of 'fencing in fear', then we must come to the conclusion that it is not the absence of the mythical structure that Mr. B. keeps away from his life. Rather it is really the hypertrophy — or if you will, the perversion (as the negative of neurosis) of the mythical — that hinders him the most. His life appears to be a classical myth, an unhistorical repetition of the same. His very powerful father figure, who lacks any historical substance, hindered spreading into room for life. The polarity of genders determines all of life, but cannot be joined together into an integrated shape because women have a fatelike power at their disposal. Psychotherapy becomes a religiously excessive cult, a vicarious satisfaction for an unlived life.

How is the problem of overmythologizing all of life's functions, in the case of Mr. B., solved? The historical dimension returns when he makes inquiries, and turns out that his father, who 'fell on the fields of honour', actually was a supervisor of the concentration camp Dachau and was shot in 1945 by the liberating Americans.

The all-encompassing defense mechanism of repression breaks down. Only through the protection of religious and symbolic ideas can the question be formed, Can the father in heaven be human? It becomes clear how his mother, as keeper of the holy grail of the father complex, hinders and avoids grieving over dead men. In doing so, she avoids the debate and disassociation from the father. The question of the historical father that exists behind the mythical father threatens to break down the entire construction of Mr. B.'s ideas about life. The question is answered through a hard and bitter struggle with his therapist. Suddenly he discovers the weaknesses behind the idealization of communication with him as his mirror. A surge of ambivalent feelings occurs. On the one hand, as the therapist, I am seen as a repulsive liar who wants to soil his holy sacrosanct father. On the other hand, he wants to kiss my feet, and with tears in his eyes asks for a blessing with the sign of the cross, which will allow the expiation of guilt. He looks upon it as a repulsive temptation, replacing the motto 'work makes free' with the motto 'love makes free'. Slowly room can be made through 'reconciliatory work' between the different personality interests. In a dream he experiences himself as a truck that travels through a very wide piece of desert and finally comes to a golden city with shining towers, which is only reserved for trucks laden with guilt.

Some Political Observations

No doubt the power which the myth is able to exercise in our case history example is based on the repression of the historical truth about the father. The inability to manage a grieving period, which Alexander and Margarete Mitscherlich (1968) discovered in Germany's postwar history, means for an entire generation the avoidance of a confrontation with the actual perpetuated guilt, and the repression of the fear of one's own appalling possibilities. These are then passed on to the next generation, not only from the perspective of the children of the victims, but also from the children of the perpetrators.

Yet the moral indignation by which the whole world avoided the event reinforces the emotional mechanism of the outer projection. It continues further on a world scale and finds its eloquent expression in the internalization of a truly manufactured thing: the nuclear bomb. It is also in the just as bureaucratically planned and manufactured apocalypse of 'war games'. In contrast, the events of Fall 1989, which led to the collapse of a new mythological and political system erected in East Germany on the foundations of the suppressed Nazi mythology, may be called a resymbolization. What the participants in the Prayers for Peace in the Nicolai Church in Leipzig discovered was the fact that, if there is a free space in which sorrow and inner pain can be expressed and transformed into words, it may lead to a rediscovery of a creative use of traditional symbolism.

People who gathered in the church at that time were offered the possibility of lament. In an anonymous *Book of Lament* they could write down their personal and public mischief, and these were connected to the traditional form of litany and liturgy. In this context an old expression of mourning, like the poetry of the psalms, was connected to new meaning. This led to the rediscovery of the power of the symbol of the candle. Armed with nothing but candles, the people could develop the courage to leave the church and go out into the streets in demonstration. The candles were something to hold on to, to preserve the flames, and they were even used to build a wall (of candles) around the buildings of the hated enemies of state authority. This prevented the use of physical violence and aggression, and stimulated the creative invention of often even very humorous slogans, which were then picked up by the masses. According to Freud, humor is the inner triumph of the ego over the inconvenient compulsions of outer circumstances.

CONCLUSION

It is the suggestion of this chapter that the difference between a deeply unconscious mythology and the conscious use of creative symbols in masses is the same as that of the difference between symbol and symptom in individuals. I would like to illustrate this by a concluding case vignette, in which I myself am the case.

After the collapse of the Nazi ideology, which significantly influenced my growing up in Germany, I developed a symptom that, in spite of two psychoanalyses, could not be resolved. I always sensed the impulse to vomit when I noticed the flags in American churches, and in fact I had to surrender to that impulse several times. During the rise of the solidarity movement in Poland, I joined an open-air Mass where, on both sides of the altar, flags of the *solidarnocz* were held up by young girls. All of a sudden I remembered the longsuppressed fact that, as a little boy I had been selected to carry the flag myself. Through waves of shame came back to my memory the feelings I had had at that time, when we sang: "The flag is more than death". Only the process of this feeling becoming conscious had the power to resolve my symptom of vomiting and gave me back the possibility to join in the joyful expression of hope in the symbol of the flag, which for such a long time had been repressed by a demonic content. It may be that the creative power of religious symbols is hindered in its development as long as we do not discover the 'Hitler within ourselves', as suggested by the psychohistorian Lloyd DeMause (1984).

REFERENCES

Barth, K. (1954). *Die Kirchliche Dogmatik* (Vol. 6, Pt. 3.). Zurich: Evangelischer Verlag.

Bonhoeffer, D. (1964). *Widerstand und Ergebung*. München: Kaiser.

Bultmann, R. (1948). Neues Testament und Mythologie: das Problem der Entmythologisierung der neutestamentischen Verkündigung. In: H.W. Bartsch (ed.), *Kerygma und Mythos* (Vol. 1, pp. 15-48). Hamburg: Herbert Reich.

DeMause, L. (1984). *Reagan's America*. New York, NY: Creative Roots.

Freud, S. (1927). The future of an illusion. In: *The standard edition of the complete psychological works of Sigmund Freud, vol. 21* (pp. 5-56) (transl. & ed. J. Strachey). London: Hogarth, 1964[2].

Hoppe, K. (1985). *Gewissen, Gott und Leidenschaft*. Stuttgart: Hirzel.

Hume, D. (1757). The natural history of religion. In: E. Mossner, *An inquiry concerning human understanding and other essays*. New York: Washington Square Press, 1963.

Mitscherlich, A., & Mitscherlich, M. (1968). *Die Unfähigkeit zu trauern.* München: Piper Verlag.
Rosenberg, A. (1930). *Der Mythos des XX. Jahrhundert* (2nd ed.). Munchen: Hoheneichen Verlag.
Tillich, P. (1962). *Symbol und Wirklichkeit.* Göttingen: Vandenhoeck & Ruprecht.

Symbolic Experience: Transforming the Selfobject Relation
A New Symbol Theory Based on Modern Psychoanalysis

H. Wahl
University of Munich (Germany)

Why a New Symbol Theory?

It is not only in the fields of psychology of religion, but nearly in all anthropological and cultural sciences, including philosophy and theology, that we are confronted today with an exuberant and excessive use of the many-sided category 'symbol' which for the most time lacks any precise definition. The same is true for the use of the word 'symbol' in ordinary language, in the mass media and in esoteric literature. Very often the term is misused in the sense that everything people consider as not 'real' or 'not seriously real' is called 'symbol', 'symbolic' or, even worse, '*only* symbolic' (e.g. when we hear of a 'only symbolic gift' or of 'only symbolic military forces' dispatched to deter the enemy).

The result of this colloquial misuse of an ancient and venerable word designing a specific human potential of deep reality experiencing is its denudation of sense and devaluation of any concise meaning. Unfortunately, modern semiotics, literary criticism and philosophy of language cannot help us immediately, since they define 'symbol' either in a too narrow technical way (e.g. Peirce, Morris) or just dismiss it as inadequate and worn out. Very often they treat the symbolic dimension under different names and conceptions which still remain to be worked out in an intensive dialogue, which I have tried to engage in recently in a larger exposition (cf. Wahl 1994).

To rescue or to restore this nearly lost significance, my aims in this short essay must be very limited and modest:

(1) I would like to develop a working model of symbolic functioning which I call 'symbolic experience'. So the target is not the term 'symbol', seen as a fixed, isolated meaning to be grasped in itself and so often reified in an objectivating manner. Modifying a famous remark of Donald Winnicott (negating that there is 'such thing as a baby', without considering also his mother), I would like to propose my systemic issue as follows: There is no such thing as a 'symbol', there is only an *interaction* between a *person* (subject, self) experiencing a certain sign *as* something personally significant on the one hand, and this *sign* met by the self in a special manner (to be determined more exactly later) on

the other hand; this whole interactive process or happening I will conceive of as '*symbolic experience*'.

(2) The '*sign*', taken in a broad semiotic sense, e.g. a traditional myth, a religious ritual, a poem, painting or song, a biblical text etc., becomes in and through this process a potential '*symbol-sign*' for the self (subject) that meets with it; i.e. the *potentially* symbolic content of this sign will be *realized* in the symbolic experience the self is engaged in.

(3) In order to determine the specific and unique character of symbolic experience not only formally (as in most symbol theories), but strictly with regard to its inherent meaning (the 'contained' content), I will adopt the genetic and structural-functional stance of today's psychoanalysis. Using especially the concepts of '*selfobject*' (Kohut) and '*container-contained*' (Bion), I want to make evident both the individual and cultural development of the capacity to experience an occurring sign symbolically as a *transformation process* of basic selfobject experience, resp. of the communicative pattern of early 'container-contained' relationship.

(4) The usefulness of the new sight shall be illustrated very briefly by a fresh look at the religious phenomenon, respectively the 'symbolic form' (E. Cassirer), of praying seen in the light of modern selfobject psychology and under the point of view of symbolic experience.

THE BASIC MODEL: 'FITTING TOGETHER' OF SELF AND SELFOBJECT

Since Kohut's famous concept of 'selfobject'[1] — a scarcely exhausted anthropological tool for therapy, theology and psychology of religion — is still grossly misunderstood (even by psychoanalysts) as a regressive, pathological and immature psychic structure, I have to explain first why I shall use the term in a generalized, wide, and not pejorative, sense. The following traits are to be regarded as constitutive essentials:

(1) The term '*selfobject*' characterizes an 'object' (in the psychoanalytic sense of 'person') which is necessary to sustain the individual's self regulation — on all developmental levels during the whole life. Thus the central function of a selfobject consists in maintaining, transforming, and restoring the organisation of our basic 'sense of self'.[2]

(2) At the beginning of psychic life, a selfobject is experienced as a "part" of the self, as if it obeyed the self and could be controlled in a way similar to the adult's mastery of his body. But very soon this 'part experience' (not to be confused with a 'symbiotic merging' with the selfobject!) would transmute into a specific sort of '*parti*cipation', more

and more sensed and lived mutually: We have always to conceive not of a separate self supported by impersonal selfobject functions, but of the existing and developing self-selfobject relationship which is our unit of observation and research.

(3) Thus the developmental-psychogenetic *'model scene'* (the disclosing context) of any selfobject relation is the mother-infant pair or system. As soon as the late Kohut discovered that the resulting early 'narcissistic' patterns (like the grandiose self and its mirroring need, or the idealized parental figures and the need to merge with them) are not at all to be totally internalized and transmuted into inner psychic structures, he did acknowledge man's life-long need for supporting selfobjects in the outer world, too. Here I find and localize the birth-site or starting point of the new conception establishing and demonstrating the central content and form of symbolic experience as a highly condensed and transformed experience of early selfobject relations.

(4) It may remain open if we should speak of Kohut's 'self psychology' (nowadays better called 'selfobject psychology') as a totally new psychoanalytic and anthropological paradigm. The decisive point in my eyes is that it conveys the paradigmatic key for a new understanding of the symbolic (in the German sense of *Symbolik*) so long conceived of as a merely formal relationship between the symbolizing (the concealing sign) and the symbolized (the intended, but usually veiled 'true' meaning).

The failure of this impersonal view does not disappear, even when its dyadic-dualistic trait is widened and expanded into a triadic-triangular structure just by adding the 'symbol user'. Yet, speaking semiotically, we have to respect the pragmatic dimension not additionally and *besides* the semantic (and the syntactic) one, for the experiencing subject makes up a constituent part of, and thus necessarily belongs to, the occurring symbol experience itself!

(5) Regarding the limited volume of my essay, I cannot sketch the complex transformational lines of the developing selfobject relation between the infantile self and his selfobject caretaker (e.g. the mother) nor the corresponding transformation processes leading to the subsequent capacity to experience other figures, things, toys, rituals, ideas or works of art etc. symbolically, i.e. as various selfobject functions supporting ourselves during our lifetime.

(6) To mention only the central trait to be retained and developed in a transformed way, it is certainly the basic structure of emotionally 'fitting together', affectively 'being in tune' of the two partners and 'feeling connected with' each other: While the main function of every sort of selfobject is its emotional availability for the subject-self wholly

depending on this fulfilment of his neediness, the very peak of experiencing something symbolically likewise consists in meeting a potential symbol-sign offering a specific experience of deep *connectedness* transported and facilitated by the sign that is actually met. If the content contained by the sign 'fits' well the subject's present selfobject need, a new selfobjective experience becomes possible and actually is realized — now on a transformed, more differentiated symbolic ·level on which the old 'fitting together' is felt, sensed and relived immediately and sensuously.

(7) Of course, it is not exactly the old fitting experience itself that is symbolically met — neither in the way of 'transference' proper (which would work unconsciously) nor in the sense of an aesthetic representation (sign) to be consciously re-interpreted hermeneutically by a purely discursive translation ("that symbol stands for and means finally nothing else but..."). The relation of the old immediate and the new symbolic selfobject experience has to be considered strictly as an *analogy*, thus preserving the difference between the *then* and the *now* experiencing self which, in reliving the old scene, now makes a new, analogous experience! Otherwise we should clearly have to speak of unconscious transference which has to be interpreted.

(8) On the other side, the self does not need to know this 'symbolic difference' (as I name it) in a consciously reflected way; it is more like a 'tacit knowing' (Polanyi), an only implicit awareness, somehow like a playing child 'knowing' all the time that she/he is playing, and yet feeling totally and seriously involved in her/his playing world that is as much internal (psychic) as external, both aspects being undistinguishably 'real', as Winnicott made us see it.

The same is true, if for instance we attend a symphonic performance or look at a painting, and feel held, comforted, affirmed or elated: We need not know explicitly the aesthetic structure or intrinsic texture of the work of art (otherwise we would behave as art critics); it is enough to be implicitly aware of the *now* holding, or comforting, or affirming, or mirroring, or elating experience which proves — by its very psychic structure and functioning — to contain an aptly transformed, now again fitting selfobject experience of *then* having been held, comforted, affirmed, mirrored, or elated by a 'good enough' mother (Winnicott) or caretaker. In the end, this means that every selfobject relationship, and every symbolic experience likewise, is born out of and evolving out of rather complex interactional processes of bargaining, tuning, and testing out the best 'fit' between the two partners to be matched (mother-selfobject and infant; symbol-sign and self)! It will be an ongoing process during life-time, ended only by death, since we need such experiences of interchange and reciprocity as human beings.

(9) It would be absolutely misleading to assert that a symbol only *substitutes* the old selfobject function. For substitution never makes possible a structurally equivalent experience that is identical only by analogy (like in any true aesthetic-symbolic experience); substitution always connotes a failure or lack, it indicates something deficient, just calling for the well-known *reductionist* interpretation: "it's nothing else but...", which must (and does) destroy any relevance of the term symbolic.

(10) We've been concerned until now especially with the *pole of the self* and the vicissitudes of its selfobject needs. But when we conceive of the triadic process of symbolic experience as a bi-polar interaction *between* subject and symbol-sign, shaped on the 'original scene' of living interchange, fitting and tuning up between self and selfobject, then we have to ask ourselves: What about the *pole of the sign* that holds, as it were, the place of the original selfobject figures (e.g. the parents), 'vicarizing' (i.e. vicariously representing), not substituting them? Dealing once again with semiotics, we can state the following:

a) *Every symbol-sign is a sign* from the semiotic point of view: It shares its general traits and can, and must, be analyzed according to scientific criteria. On the contrary, *not every sign can pass for a symbol-sign*, because the latter represents a special case or sort of sign, defined by our symbol theory based on selfobject relation psychology. Its main criteria therefore cannot be limited to the scientific or logical discourse, but transcend it insofar as its underlying 'cognitive interest' (J. Habermas' *Erkenntnisinteresse*) is directed towards the genesis, structure, function, and transformations of human experience and practice in meeting potential symbol-signs, traditionally handed down and now being lived, used and scenically staged in a certain group or culture.

b) In the descriptive symbol theory I am proposing here, it does not make sense to separate the *form* (*Gestalt*) from the *content* (*Gehalt*) of a symbol-sign. For the symbol-sign itself is supposed to owe its origin to a historically earlier, genuine selfobject experience of people who eventually were able to transform this content into a new shape (mythical, religious, or artistic) that comprised the type or model of experience in such a valid and attractive manner that it became a general pattern for many other people, groups or generations. Of course, this should not be confused with C.G. Jung's concept of archetypes which reveals quite a different shape, and interest too.

c) On the individual's side, this cultural process must find its equivalent, by developing the *'capacity to symbolize'*, meaning here: becoming able to recognize relational (selfobject) experiences occurring in congruent figurative constellations of a highly personal, scenic quality conveying to the subject a structurally analogous selfobject experience!

FROM 'SELFOBJECT RELATION' TO 'SYMBOL THEORY'

To summarize, and to expand, these basic assumptions, drawn from the selfobject background of modern psychoanalysis, I suggest to retain the following tenets:

1) Freud (and with him traditional psychoanalysis, too) ends in a twofold impasse narrowing the symbol concept and actually rendering it nearly useless:

a) According to the classical psychoanalytic model of interpretation only that material (dreams, symptoms etc.) will be symbolized which had to be repressed or otherwise warded off; in the very sense of the word, it is substituted (see above) through a disguising representation that is less shocking to the censuring superego or ego ideal. Thus the whole symbolizing process would rest on impulsive conflicts requiring defenses that will render unconscious, disguise, and deform authentic experience. Consequently, on the symbolic level there is no discrimination between conscious, not veiled experiences and such rendered unconscious.

Since only the latter are generally considered to be, and therefore are called, "symbolized", all Freudian symbols are founded on repression. This view is fatal and deleterious for a theory of genuine symbolic experience, e.g. in the field of aesthetics or religion. Actually we should speak of the classical Freudian symbols as of individual or culturally determined *symptoms*, resp. in a less medicocentric language, of *dia*bols, representing the very opponents of true *sym*bols.

b) One of the most counterproductive consequences of this narrowed symbol concept consists in attributing fixed 'true' interpretations to each symbol, e.g. in the *Interpretation of dreams* (1900), leading into a hermeneutic impasse that evidently contradicts Freud's own and revolutionary interpretative pattern! The 'true meanings' rigidly ascribed to (mostly sexual) 'symbols' (e.g. every long-sized and sharp object 'means' the penis; every excavation signifies the vagina etc.) are given to the dreamer or patient in the service of undoing the 'symbolic distortion' and disguise. Yet, unfortunately it is the dream interpreter from outside who 'knows' all these translations, quite independently from the dreaming subject that creates and shapes his own dreams —

exactly in the same way the ancient dream-and-symbol books from Egypt and Greece would deliver their fixed interpretations.

In contradiction to his most important insights, Freud himself eliminates here the *subject's* irreplaceable interpretative capacity and the *relational context*, too, in which the interpretation or translation is to be worked out by both participants (e.g. the patient and his analyst)! We are confronted with a 'domination knowledge' (Scheler's *Herrschafts-wissen*) ruling over the 'true meanings' and often resulting in an 'expertocracy', revealing only the power of the symbol interpreters.

c) These critical remarks do not touch Freud's method to detect and to decode actually distorted contents rendered unconscious (in the sense of symptoms, resp. of cultural diabols, e.g. certain mythical contents). Therefore we should cease to call these *symptom*-signs or diabols symbols.

2) The new symbol theory based on the concept of transformed selfobject experience, on the contrary, is wholly centered on relationship and interaction as its main constituents.

a) The starting-point, to repeat the essential issues, is the specific quality of the earliest relation of an infant's evolving self with her/his mother facilitating this development. She is called her/his 'selfobject' since for the baby she represents neither an 'object', a distinctly separate *vis-à-vis*, nor is she perceived initially as a 'subject', a separate person with her own rights, interests and needs.

b) For the infant being aware of the good enough mother primarily available as a part of his rudimentary self, her selfobject function (holding, nursing, caressing, comforting, mirroring her baby etc.) is fundamental to her/his existence and her/his physical and psychic growth, even necessary for her/his survival in a literal sense! So everything depends on a person providing such an atmosphere and opening an area of full availability: the 'selfobject matrix' (Kohut) in which our self can develop and find its coherence, continuity, and identity.

We may compare this matrix of necessary selfobject support with the oxygen we need for breathing without normally being aware of it, or with the water the fish live in, briefly put: it is like something 'self'-evident we miss only when it is lacking!

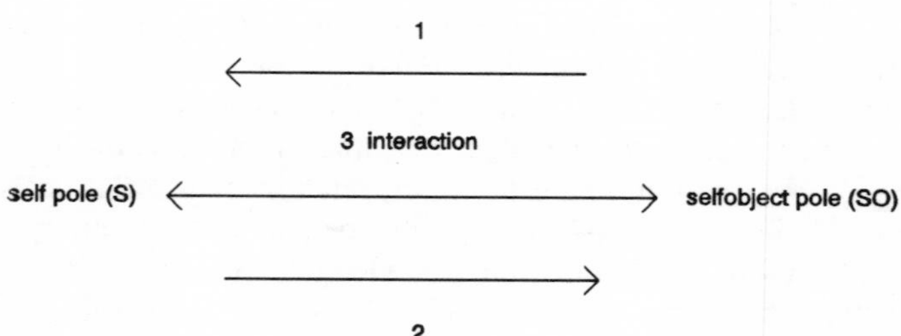

Figure 1.

c) These basic experiences are unfolding in infinite micro-steps of a reciprocal interaction process, transforming the primary (one-sided) selfobject relations and archaic needs into more and more reciprocal ones, but never dissolving them. As Kohut has taught us, the developmental track does not lead from immature, symbiotic dependency on 'objects' to mature autonomy, to separation, individuation and independence. So the need for selfobjects imposes itself as an everlasting anthropological structure of man's basic needs. Their aims and content will change, but the need to feel unconditionally accepted, admired, being held and comforted or encouraged by a loving, trustworthy *vis-à-vis* will endure during lifetime, no matter if it is a beloved person, a welcoming group or community, a work of art, a religious ritual, or a political ideal or faith that is able to exert for us this selfobject function.

d) One of the main traits of this developmental line, not yet mentioned, consists in the fact that the self supported by such a facilitating selfobject milieu or matrix will itself be gradually enabled to become a selfobject for the other (starting with the mother herself!); finally, the whole process can only be conceived of as thoroughly *reciprocal*.

3) A symbol theory built upon this base of lifelong mutual selfobject relations and their gradual transformations may therefore be characterized as follows:

a) When I meet and use a culturally handed down symbol (e.g. a mythical story, a religious ritual, a work of art etc.), this meeting must assume the cognitive-emotional quality and function of a historically transformed selfobject for me, resp. for the group I belong to. The potential meaning offered by and through this symbol, has to be experienced by me/by us as a meaning-for-me/for-us in a selfobjective way. Only in this case we would speak of a successful symbolic experience.

b) Since symbols, taken in the traditional sense, do not carry with them objectively their meaning, or simply cannot be interpreted to me by someone else, we would call this potential offer of meaning being signalized to the user of the sign, a *symbol-sign* in order to discriminate it from the ordinary language term symbol so frequently misused. Our brief illustration now is to be enlarged:

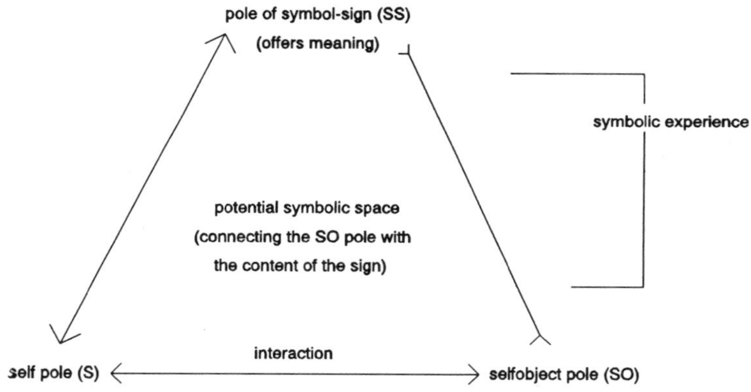

Figure 2.

c) It is the synchronized realization of experiencing *both* relationships (with the selfobject-pole and the symbol-sign) simultaneously that originates a true symbolic experience: We experience something (the particular content of a symbol-sign) *as* something (i.e. conveying its specific selfobject quality); therein we do not experience something *else*, but the same in a new way! Seen this way, every symbol actually 'gives to think' (Ricoeur), more exactly: it *gives to experience*, viz. its selfobject content offered by the sign. So we find again, in the very structure of the symbolic process, the early 'fitting together', the intimate 'connectedness' and 'tuning in an analogous shape', now linking the self and the content of the symbol-sign functioning as selfobject.

d) We might also discover and affirm the *specificity* of *symbolic* experience compared to various other forms of experiencing someone or something else: Not every experience of any (semiotic) sign automatically comes up to a symbolic one, even if we find it very often stated in this misleading way.

4) On the contrary, it is only in this simultaneously ongoing relationship *between* the self, the symbol-sign, and its selfobject quality

that we see unfold and spring up a space of living and experiencing, a triangularly structured 'intermediate area' (Winnicott)[3] in which a new meaning shines off for myself, resp. an old meaning is disclosed to me in a new manner.

5) Focusing on the pole of the symbol-signs, we have to recognize that usually we do not have to deal with isolated things or objects or actions, but of a whole interactional *scene*[4] we get involved in. Only in participating in such a symbolic scene, we can achieve a deep understanding and come to a corresponding action.

Take for example a mother praying with her child (to which I shall return later on; see below, part 4) or somebody reading or listening to a mythical story: Of course, we can see the mythical narrative as a symbol-sign dealing for instance with certain actions of 'gods' or 'God'. But what is important is the whole cultural and interactional scene the two participants are engaged and embedded in: Is it a possibly triadic space they are dwelling in, or will the reader (or listener) immediately be involved and swallowed into a relationship with the acting god(s) which is so magically loaded that he feels deeply influenced and cannot get any psychic distance from the events reported by the myth?

In my eyes the answer does not depend on the question if the reader himself believes in the myth. Even somebody believing in the mythical stories of his culture or religious group (e.g. certain mythical parts of the Hebrew Bible, as in Genesis etc.) should be capable (or get enabled by his culture — at least in our western post-enlightenment civilization!) to experience them symbolically, and not in the mythical, i.e. diabolic way I am referring to here. And this will depend on the way she or he has experienced as a child good (holding, soothing, comforting etc.) selfobjects, *and* how she/he likewise has experienced the image of God(s), e.g. as good parental figures, conveyed by the culture or religious group he or she belongs to.

In this case both interactive experiences can be fitted with each other and can come together in a symbolic experience of the mythical story presented: The reader, according to his developmental stage, and always selectively, will then be able to live the content of the myth, and eventually to experience it as a holding, supporting, and comforting, or even confronting selfobject configuration that he can address himself to with all his sorrows, needs, anxieties, and hopes while always implicitly knowing that he is dealing with a symbol-sign referring to, but not being identical with, the signified reality! Only in this case he would be able and free to realize also an eventually distorted selfobject experience contained in a certain myth or religious tradition; I am referring here to a capacity of 'myth criticism' of which also the believer in principal must dispose, at least in an implicit manner.

Being drawn into the mythical event itself without being able to maintain the indispensable symbolic difference would signalize that the individual's selfobject relationship has not been transformed into the level of symbolic capacity, and then we should expect — to mention only one possible event — that any cultural givings, like myths or work of arts etc., cannot be experienced symbolically, but get 'diabolized', i.e. distorted and destroyed, for example if the reader feels forced to act literally according to the mythical story in order to satisfy and to please an angry or vengeful almighty god-figure, so often representing a projected *negative* selfobject experience of parental (or tribal) figures.

In that case the two relational vectors SO and SS (see figure 2 above) would simply *coincide*, their potential for congruent 'fitting' and connecting thereby crashing down into a unifying merging so that the listener of the myth cannot discriminate between them any longer: Collapsing with the negative experience of selfobjects, the potential surplus of meaning of the sign (e.g. a selfobjective god-figure) would be dissolved into something threatening. The myth (for instance the biblical story of Paradise and Man's Fall) then has become a 'diabol' instead of becoming a potential symbol-sign!

And because of such disguised and distorted traits of many myths that are rendered unconscious and handed down to individuals by the "societal Unconscious" (M. Erdheim)[5], many myths first have to be properly interpreted by means of a special method I would call 'symbol criticism' or 'myth criticism' dealing with the diabolic distortion of potential symbol-signs. Here the aid of a critical psychoanalytic reading, interpreting and making conscious such material is indispensable, but we should not call this material itself symbolic!

BION'S MODEL OF 'CONTAINER-CONTAINED' AND ITS SIGNIFICANCE FOR A SYMBOL THEORY

W.R. Bion (1897-1979) was an analyst who greatly pushed forward the British School of Object Relations Theory initiated by Melanie Klein. Although he had undergone his personal analysis with her, he never considered himself to be a Kleinian. The central issue in Bion's creative thinking on psychic processes is "emotional experience" (Bion 1961, 1962). He is interested in its evolution and its vicissitudes, its transformations and connexions with thinking and speaking, but all this with permanent regard to its 'relationship to relation': "An emotional experience cannot be conceived of in isolation from a relationship" (op.cit., p. 42).

In its very core our mind evolves out of the processes of understanding the emotional experiences between infant and mother (the genetic-interactional point of view). The mother exerts psychic functions for her baby which the baby afterwards will learn to exert by himself once having internalized the whole 'understanding pair' (the structural-relational point of view).

Evidently, this reminds us of Kohut's selfobject function, although Bion explains his basic model in a rather concrete, bodily language following Melanie Klein's primary phantasies (good/bad breast getting introjected/projected etc.). I comprehend this mode of speaking rather as metaphorical way of illustrating the fundamental processes of our preverbal self-constitution. On a thoroughly somato-psychic level it would make no sense to separate them in terms of body versus mind. Yet, taken as metaphors, they may convey a working model, a narrative tool to imagine the development and functioning of our experiencing, thinking and symbolizing.[6]

Bion's basic pattern for the genesis and functioning of all inter- and intrapsychic processes is the relationship of *container* and *contained*. Its prototype refers (again) to the relation of the hungry and needy baby with a mother being primarily experienced as the breast. All the tormenting emotional experiences (like frustration, anxiety, confusion) which the baby cannot yet think by himself, viz. digest and work out psychically, are expelled, as it were, by the baby into this breast — serving as a "container" — in order to get rid of them.

This seems to look like a very archaic form of 'projective identification', as M. Klein would put it. But Bion enlarges this one-sided, defensive relation in a significant way: The mother has to exert *vicariously* the baby's lacking capacity to think, to imagine, to understand and to work out these violent feelings: She has to take over these tormenting parts of an emotionally overwhelmed self into her 'breast' and to 'contain' them in order to give them back to him in a transformed and 'detoxicated', decontaminated quality that now proves digestible. By this getting back the metabolized emotional material the baby is enabled to start thinking his experiences, of course rather inchoatively and dream-like.

The mother's part of receiving and taking in her baby's unbearable emotions Bion calls '*rêverie*'. But this paradigmatic receptive process is, in an analogous sense, as valid for any *adult* needing an own, internal or external, 'container' available to her/him, be it the analyst in a therapeutic session, or the partner in a successful interpersonal encounter. It is the dynamic relational process of 'containing' and 'being contained' that facilitates the development of the infant's so-called 'alpha-function' which I will not comment on further; briefly put, it means the decisive mechanism to transform sensuous impressions and emotional experiences into 'thoughts' the infant can 'think with' (phantasies, mental images, representations, ideas etc.).

The mother's *rêverie* is to supply the baby psychically with love, comfort, consolation and empathic understanding while nourishing her/him with milk and providing bodily care: In this way the baby's congenital proto-mental states of expectation (viz. of a good breast giving milk) which Bion calls 'pre-conceptions', are matched with the sensuous impressions of being nourished and satisfied, and by this 'realization' she/he becomes able to form conceptions and ideas. Here again we meet the important pattern of 'matching' or 'fitting together' in its fundamental meaning. The feeling of 'hunger' can by now gradually be differentiated as a mental representation (thought) from its sensuous realization.

But what will happen emotionally and cognitively when the breast is *not yet* there, and the infant has to wait? Bion pursues this question, since the baby does not record in a conscious way the satisfied need or drive, but the unsatisfied one, i.e. the frustration. Any further mental development will depend on whether the infant can *tolerate* this painful situation, respectively modify it, or has to avoid (and to evacuate) it. Only if the frustration tolerance is sufficient, the infant will learn to experience his need not as a present bad breast to be expelled, but to *think* it as an absent, good breast that is desired and needed! Here we are assisting at the birth of the first thought, as it were: 'no milk', 'no breast'.

In order to grasp the weight and range of this Bionian thesis for a symbol 'conception' (!) we have to realize that Bion in principle is preoccupied with processes of adult thinking, ranging from emotional experiences to ever higher forms of abstraction in which affection, cognition and interaction always are interwoven. The matching of a pre-conception with a realization of non-satisfaction ("no breast available") will be experienced by the infant totally different from a satisfaction, viz. as "not breast", or as an internal, absent and repudiating breast.

If there is enough capacity to tolerate the frustration of such a negative realization, the painfully felt "not-breast" inside (e.g. the absent mother) can be transformed into a thought proper, while simultaneously the capacity to think this thought can develop which later on also will be named: "I *wish* a breast for me". This proto-thought ('no breast', 'no milk') rests on the primary reality of lacking, of absence that can be transmuted only with the aid of a motherly 'container': a transformation to be followed by many others on the move to the 'depressive position' (M. Klein). The generalized wish for a correspondingly transformed, breast-like figure we might equate to the need for a selfobject figure which the adult utters.

"To have a thought" means then to be able to represent mentally the absent, the missed and, with regard to time, to think the *not yet* (a future experience), resp. the *not any longer* (a missed experience). On the other side, in the case of satisfaction, we would speak of the representation of *already*, of a past experience, viz. a positive realization of a pre-conception.

Both these sorts of representations, emotionally so different, have to be combined with each other in order to shape a true *symbolic* experience: Every symbolic representation does always (and has to) 'contain' not only need satisfaction (the 'already' got), but also the lacking, the absence of outstanding fulfilment 'not yet' sensed. The difference between the two, if emotionally elaborated and worked through, will constitute the 'contained'. Therefore a symbol can never be only a 'conception' or idea representing the Truth, or even the Whole; it is always the awareness of experiencing this difference, i.e. the lack and absence of the expected, that constitutes the symbolic structure.

Bion illustrates the functioning of the motherly-female 'container' by the typical events when the mystic bearing with him and bringing about a 'New Idea', crashes regularly with a societal establishment and its prejudices, or when a new Truth meets old beliefs, the latter proving not capable to receive and contain the former. Here we can observe the model of container-contained in its societal and cultural aspect: There is always a high tension between those who explore and reveal new realities (Bion's 'genius' or 'mystic'), and an existing society, between a new 'messianic' Idea and the Establishment. Very often the mystic's Idea (the 'contained', the content of the new, as yet Unknown which Bion calls 'O': ultimate reality) breaks up its 'container', the socio-cultural establishment that is unable to receive, to tolerate and to contain the new.[7]

Being himself in a way a genius or a mystic in the psychoanalytic establishment, Bion finally succeeds in expressing convincingly his often complex, abstract and highly condensed formulations in simple everyday language: Ending *Attention and Interpretation*, he has interwoven the central concepts of 'container-contained' and the interplay between the paranoid-schizoid and the depressive position (M. Klein) into two *basic attitudes* referring not only to the analyst in a session, but to everybody ready to engage really in and to meet the Unknown occurring in a significant interpersonal or psychic situation: these terms are '*patience*' and '*security*'.

To explain it more exactly what proves so important for any symbolic experience, too: It is just the permanent *oscillating* between both these attitudes, 'patience' thus corresponding to being ready to tolerate uncertainty. According to Bion this is an analogue to, and therefore is to be distinguished from, the 'paranoid-schizoid position', considered as a pathological outcome. The term 'patience' has been coined to retain its association with suffering (pati) and tolerance of frustration and to resist the popular urge to interpret instantaneously every occurring symbol-sign!

However, only if 'patience' can be retained and uncertainty be tolerated "without any irritable reaching after fact and reason" (J. Keats), a pattern will evolve. Now we find ourselves in a state of 'security' (connoting safety and diminished anxiety), which is an analogue to the 'depressive position'. Understanding and interpreting becomes possible only when both phases have been passed through — and then immediately another cycle of oscillating between both attitudes will start (cf. Bion 1962, p. 124.).

This 'inter-space' between patience and security embraces what I would call 'symbolic area' in which a new pattern of experiencing can evolve: Understanding a situation or scene *as* a new emotional experience, i.e. enduring the tension and oscillation between patience and security, between anxiety, uncertainty, pain, despair on the one hand, and safety, hope and calmness one the other, makes up true symbolic experience as a practice: a *transitional structure* (to enlarge Winnicott's famous term 'transitional object') between waiting patiently and feeling safe for a certain time.

Referring to J. Keats' 'negative capability', Bion thus describes (without naming it this way) a fundamental and central element of all true symbolic experience, "that is, when a man is capable of being in uncertainties, mysteries, doubts, without any irritable reaching after fact and reason" (op.cit., p. 125), linking up this way our symbol theory with the great mystic tradition of a negative theology.

To summarize and to enrich Bion's partial contribution to symbol theory:

1) The specificity of symbolic experience is founded on a lived relationship — genetically as well as, later on, structurally and functionally. The singular quality and shape of this sort of experience rests on the relation of *container-contained*, aesthetically speaking: on

the intrinsic, inseparable matching and fitting together of form (pattern, shape) and content.

2) The content ('contained') which continuously has to be transformed in ongoing history, consists basically of emotional experiences (primarily of emotionally sustaining selfobjects).

3) As well as with regard to the *selfobject-paradigm*, the main prerequisite of 'containing' is that it must be offered and facilitated *intersubjectively*, in an interaction; thus it depends thoroughly on the previous experience of holding selfobjects — even if they may work in an already internalized, intrapsychic mode. We need forever a 'selfobject matrix' (Kohut) *extra nos* which enables us to work out and to transform our intensive sensations and emotions. These *selfobject-containers* (as I would call them) will subsequently be organized on an ever more differentiated level.

4) In contrast to Kohut's selfobject concept, Bion stresses the role of *thought* and *thinking* evolving from transformations of basic sensuous and emotional experiences; in this sense Bion speaks of "learning from experience". It is of special importance that there will be no developing capacity of the self to distinguish and to link, to differentiate and to connect psychic contents without perceiving and tolerating the negative, i.e. the lacking, the needed but absent selfobject.

5) Following this Bionian line leading from emotional experience, formation of thoughts and the capacity to think them to symbolic experiencing, we have to retain that symbol formation or symbolizing is not identical with the general ability of forming inner representations containing imagos of the self or of outer objects. These capacities are constituting only the indispensable precondition that the self will not be overcome and overwhelmed by destructive attacks on truth, viz. those linkings (by love, hate and knowing) between ourselves, our inner reality, and the reality shared with other people.

In order to reach the symbolic level and its specific mode of experience, we should be able to dispose of all these psychic prerequisites for the functioning of our mind; otherwise it would prove impossible to approach that special path which Bion describes in an almost mystical way as 'becoming O': a way leading to a psychic truth to which we get access only by 'faith in O' (cf. Eigen 1985). Part of this must inhere in any true symbolic experience.

6) We have to keep in mind, however, one essential request: The whole cycle (starting with emotion and knowing and to be passed through in order to approach 'O', the Unknown, the psychic reality proper), while founding all symbolic occurrence, nevertheless makes up only an analogy or correspondence; the specific difference lies in the

request that in order to reach the symbolic matching of self and symbol-sign, this special mode of experiencing must transcend Bion's 'transformation of knowing into O' once more, thereby leading back to a new emotional, again *sensuously* mediated experience of the primary experience 'contained' and offered: symbolic experience in its very core thus means always *experiencing an experience*.

7) This whole process, while comprising the essence of true symbolic experience, resists getting wholly transformed into thoughts and, later on, into language and interpretation from outside. What resists, is the character of the sign itself referring to something Different being *present* in the content ('contained') of the sign ('container') only in the mode of *absence*, of lacking, being in want of: The 'old' content has been transformed, by this very process itself, into its own 'container'[8] — the experienced symbol therefore *is* its interpretation![9]

8) True symbolic experience means then the capacity not only to think something (in Bion's sense), but also — and again! — to live and experience something emotionally and sensuously *as absent* that becomes just in this way *symbolically present*! Seen in this Bionian perspective, a symbol in its full sense does not simply 'give to think' (Ricoeur) or 'to learn', but it does give 'to experience and to sense anew', and this giving is made up by any transformable selfobject which we meet always as something objectively coming from outside ourselves. Getting linked with it, we can live a new connectedness that then also will 'give to think', to form meaningful thoughts and images (vulgo: symbols).

9) Symbolizing thus can only mean the process of transforming generalizable emotional experiences into shared signs and handed down cultural ideas, artistically formed images and mental representations. Being externalized into such concrete objects, sensuous shapes or abstract signs, our ordinary language curtails and shortens these carriers of potentially symbolic meaning into so-called symbols (e.g. a flag ranking as symbol of the nation; a burning candle as symbol of devotion or enlightenment or resurrection etc.).

10) Contrary to this widespread popular (mis)use of the term 'symbol' I prefer to speak of *symbol-signs* in order to make clear that we are dealing with a cultural substratum which already must have been (or is to be) *formed*: it precedes any possible experience. The symbol-signs build, as it were, a new stratum of pre-conceptions culturally handed down and waiting, on the level of public signs, not only for their fitting sensuous 'realization' (to be transformed into thinkable thoughts), but mainly for a new subject to contain it.

Taken *as* signs, they refer to what they signify or mean: the experiential content 'contained' by them. Yet, as much as Bion's 'Idea' this content looks forward to subjects serving as new 'containers' that are able to decode the symbol-signs, to receive the thoughts carried on, *and* at the same time are able to re-liquefy the 'frozen' selfobject experience 'contained' in them in a transformed mode! Thus the content itself seeks, as it were, for subjects capable of symbolic experience. Here we assist the change of roles (of self and selfobject, container and contained) so typical and indispensable for any symbolic experience!

11) Wherever on the cultural level this specific *connexion of container-contained* happens, we can speak of true symbolic experience. And wherever the experiencing subjects listen, for example, to music not only acoustically or enjoy it sensuously, but at the same time live and go through it *as* something emotionally significant for them, we could speak of authentical *symbolic practice* (which the recipient does not feel forced to analyze rationally or to interpret hermeneutically).

12) What then is the gain of our relecture of Bion for a symbol theory? His basic figure of 'container-contained' (viewed not as a primitive defense, but as a prototype of interaction and communication) might sharpen and affirm our approach outlining the relational basis and the transformative structure of forming symbol-signs and of experiencing their content symbolically. The process consists in the continual transition and oscillation *between* emotion and thinking, sensuous-emotional realization and mental representation of the absent, consequently also *between* the paranoid-schizoid and the depressive levels, *between* anxiety of pain, persecution, loss and tolerance of doubts and uncertainty, *between* 'patience' and 'security'.

By the way this area of 'in-between' corresponds exactly to Winnicott's 'intermediate area' or 'potential space' of playing and creative 'illusion' in which our whole cultural (and religious) life is to be localized. And in Kohut's terms we might remember the 'selfobject matrix' so indispensable for the development of the self, its capacity for reciprocal interaction and for symbolic experience.

Finally I would like to illustrate these theoretical issues by some considerations regarding the potential symbolic significance of a religious phenomenon like praying.

A Short Illustration: Praying with a Child

This example is supposed to demonstrate very briefly two of my main topics:

a) It is only in a *triadic relation* occurring simultaneously *between* the poles of self and symbol-sign *in* its selfobject-quality that a fitting space of vivid symbolic experience will take rise in which for my self a new meaning springs up being disclosed anew by an old one.

b) Regarding the pole of *symbol-signs*, in most cases it is not a question of isolated things or actions or even persons, but in the last resort we have to do with a whole symbolic *scene* the sign user enters and gets involved in. It is only within this scene symbolically enacted that understanding and new action (praxis) become possible.

If we take for instance the scenic interaction of a mother praying with her child, what then will happen with the child's self on the level of symbolic experience? Certainly we would consider the formulated prayer as a potential symbol-sign, but the central issue concerns the whole relational scene. For only if the child has experienced in a benign way his mother as a holding selfobject and, moreover, also the image of God (e.g. as a 'good father' or 'mother') conveyed to him by the mother's correspondent daily conduct, both these relations — conceived of as lively felt interactions — can join and come together in a fitting manner in order to create a symbolic experience of the praying being done.

According to her/his developmental stage, and in a selective way, the child will sense the 'content' of the prayer by a silent, implicit knowing *as* something holding, supporting, sheltering to be worshipped with awe etc. which she/he can address with all requests, sorrows, troubles and wants. Of course the 'content' just mentioned means the specific selfobject quality being 'contained' in the sign 'containing' the wording of the prayer (for instance the Our Father) including its whole connotative semantic halo.

However, where these prerequisites are lacking in the mother-child relationship, there might happen — to point only to one possible outcome — not a symbolic experience, but a 'diabolization' of praying, i.e. its deformation and distortion into a sign being diabolically misused — for instance if a child is forced to pray by her/his mother who would otherwise be sad or disappointed with her 'bad' child.

According to our theoretical model (see figure 2 above) in this case two branches of the symbolic triangle would collapse and break down, fusing and melting in one line, the three-dimensional symbolic space thus being reduced to an exclusively dyadic relation; the indispensable difference gets lost, and the child cannot discriminate and differentiate any longer between the surplus of meaning contained in the prayer (the containing sign), for instance the 'good Father-God', and the allegedly good selfobject experience connected with this symbol use which in this case proves of extreme negative quality (the mother failing to be a good selfobject and conveying therefore a corresponding image of God). Coinciding with this malign selfobject experience of the mother, the potential symbolic surplus of the praying scene will dissolve into something threatening, and we might imagine how such a child will able to 'pray' as an adult.

NOTES

1. For the development of this term and of Self Psychology generally cf. Kohut (1977, 1984, 1985). See also Goldberg (1980, 1983). For a critical assessment of self psychology within the psychoanalytic theories of narcissism cf. Wahl (1985).
2. For the linkage of the developmental aspects of self psychology with the empirical observations of infant research by psychoanalytic 'baby watchers' cf. Lichtenberg (1983), Stern (1985), and Dornes (1993).
3. I cannot explain here the many links existing between the 'symbolic matrix' or 'selfobject milieu' (Kohut) and Winnicott's fascinating ideas on 'potential space' and the 'intermediate area' of playing and the origines of culture (religion, art etc.) in this creative play-room of necessary 'illusions' dwelling in the area exactly 'between' our subjective and objective world. For more details cf. Wahl (1994), pp. 161-197.
4. A scene, in the psychoanalytic sense of the word, means always a psychic product (*Gestalt*) created and shaped by the ego self experiencing and representing, or anticipating, an interaction, be it staged in the outer or the inner world.
5. Not to be confused with C.G. Jung's 'collective unconscious' containing the 'archetypes'! Erdheim (1982) is concerned with the production of concrete historical unconscious contents by the defensive interests of a certain society or culture.
6. If Bion, at the same time, tries to record and to note these psychic processes in highly abstract, mathematical terms and formulas, this may testify his need to counterbalance any too concretistic understanding.
7. In *Attention and interpretation* (1970, pp. 116-123) Bion refers this idea to Jesus and his relationship to his 'group', resp. society.
8. In semiotic terms: the signified (*significatum*) becomes its own signifier (*significans*)!
9. Only if there are grave "attacks on linking and thinking" (Meltzer 1986, p. 120), deforming and deteriorating thoughts and inner images into diabolic rags and parts, into lies and "bizarre objects", there is a need for interpreting and making conscious the unconscious motives of such destructive defenses.

REFERENCES

Bion, W.R. (1961). *Experiences in groups*. London: Tavistock.

Bion, W.R. (1962). *Learning from experience*. London: Marisfield, 1984.

Bion, W.R. (1970). *Attention and Interpretation.* London: Marisfield, 1984.

Dornes, M. (1993). *Der kompetente Säugling: die präverbale Entwicklung des Menschen.* Frankfurt: Fischer.

Eigen, M. (1985). Toward Bion's starting point: between catastrophe and faith. *International Journal of Psycho-Analysis, 66*, 321-330.

Erdheim, M. (1982). *Die gesellschaftliche Produktion von Unbewußtheit*. Frankfurt: Suhrkamp.

Freud, S. (1900). *The interpretation of dreams.* (*The standard edition of the complete psychological works of Sigmund Freud, vol 4 & 5* (pp. 1-621); transl. & ed. J. Strachey). London: Hogarth, 1964[4].

Goldberg, A. (ed.) (1980). *Advances in self psychology*. New York: International Universities Press.

Goldberg, A. (ed.) (1983). *The future of psychoanalysis: essays in honor of Heinz Kohut*. New York: International Universities Press.

Kohut, H. (1977). *The restoration of the self.* New York: International Universities Press.

Kohut, H. (1984). *How does analysis cure?* Chicago: University of Chicago Press.

Kohut, H. (1985). *Self psychology and the humanities*. New York: Norton.

Lichtenberg, J.E. (1983). *Psychoanalysis and infant research.* New York: Hillsdale.

Meltzer, D. (1986). *Studies in extended metapsychology: clinical applications of Bion's ideas.* Strath Tay: Clunie Press.

Stern, D. (1985). *The interpersonal world of the infant.* New York: Basic Books.

Wahl, H. (1985). *Narzißmus? Von Freuds Narzißmustheorie zur Selbstpsychologie*. Stuttgart: Kohlhammer.

Wahl, H. (1994). *Glaube und symbolische Erfahrung: eine praktisch-theologische Symboltheorie.* Freiburg: Herder.

Psychoanalytic Hermeneutics and Sacramental Theology

W.W. Meissner
Boston College (Chestnut Hill, MA, United States of America)

Introduction

The psychoanalytic effort to understand man's religious experience has had a checkered history. In this respect, Freud's brainchild got off on an unfortunate footing, largely due to his own religious attitudes, the product of his developmental experiences and prejudicial convictions (Meissner 1984). With the evolution of psychoanalytic perspectives in recent years, the psychoanalytic investigator is in a better position to approach the sensitivity and complexity of religious experience and render an account more faithful to the intentionality of the religious phenomenon. As Freud himself readily acknowledged, the resources of the psychoanalytic methodology were as open to the enrichment and faithful exploration of religious phenomena as to skeptical and destructive criticism. If the agnostic disbeliever could use the psychoanalytic tool for purposes of negative and destructive criticism, the faithful believer had available the same methods for more constructive and insightful understanding.

My purpose here is to bring some of the resources of the psychoanalytic method to bear on understanding sacramental experience, thus deepening and enriching theological understanding of sacramental experience in specifically human terms. The enterprise rides on certain suppositions deriving from a psychology of grace, specifically that sacramental action involves communication of grace, that its effects on the human soul are due to the operation of grace within the soul, that these effects must be congruent with the God-given nature of the soul, that effects of such sacramental grace cannot violate the conditions of receptivity of the soul, and that these effects that are specifically spiritual in nature but also involve psychological effects consistent with the nature of the human psyche and its inherent capacities (Meissner 1987).

Methodological Issues

In attempting this interdisciplinary exploration, we should remind ourselves of some important methodological principles governing the enterprise. The inquiry should make every effort to respect the autonomy, methodology, and specific characteristics of the respective disciplines. Psychoanalysis and theology do not speak the same language. They operate with different starting points, presuppositions, evidences, conceptual formulations, objectives, and criteria of intelligibility and truth-value. Meaningful dialogue stipulates that the inherent requirements and intelligibilities of the respective disciplines be maintained without crossing disciplinary lines and confusing respective orders of meaning. Theological reflection takes its origin from sources of revelation and brings the resources of intellectual discipline to bear in the effort to gain deeper understanding of the content of that revelation. The theological status of the revelation, however, has no pertinence for the psychoanalyst, for whom the data of revelation are no different than any data of human experience. His interest centers more on the parallels and resonances of revealed doctrine with other aspects of human psychological experience. The measure of intelligibility thus becomes correspondence with common sources of meaning in man's psychological experience rather than any religious implications of revelation.

In the context of faithful adherence to the revelation — determined in the Christian tradition, varying in degree and proportion in different church traditions and faith commitments, by an appeal to scripture and tradition — the theological emphasis falls on the reality of sacramental action exemplifying a concretization of divine salvific action in the world and the hearts of men. The meaning of the reality and its existential impact are variously interpreted, but emphasis falls on the objective and existent circumstances of the sacramental encounter. Whatever its symbolic resonances and implications, sacramental action is taken to involve a real action of God acting in and through the sacramental vehicle. The baptismal rite effects real change in the soul brought about by the conjunction of ritual with divine effect. The eucharist involves Christ's real, not simply metaphorical or restrictively symbolic, presence. This dogmatic emphasis on the real and objective — not necessarily on the physical reality — sets the stage for oppositional tension with psychoanalytic perspectives lacking any grounds for asserting or interpreting such objectivity. The psychoanalytic perspective is in this context inherently subjective; it has no scripture, no revelation, to serve as a basis for evaluating the reality of such claims. Thus the theology of sacramental action makes certain truth claims to which psychoanalysis has no access. These essential oppositional tensions provide the matrix for our efforts at dialogue.

I should emphasize that the fact that the psychoanalytic method prescinds from the special truth claims of the revelation in religious terms does not mean that it does or can deny the validity of such claims.[1] It simply has nothing to say on that score. Whatever meaning or meanings psychoanalysis can discern in exploring religious (here sacramental) phenomena, it has no resource or reason to assert or deny theological significance. The psychoanalytic approach can do no more than strive to illumine the intrapsychic and predominantly unconscious connotations of the religious content in question. Historically, this has been one of the stumbling blocks preventing more open and productive dialogue between psychoanalysis and religion in general. Freud, and many psychoanalysts in his wake, stumbled into the reductive error of thinking that if certain aspects of religious thinking could be interpreted in terms of unconscious dynamics — that is, as derivatives of unconscious motivational factors — they could be understood on a purely natural basis. Then understanding from a theological or supernatural perspective was to be rejected as false and misleading (Meissner 1991). It is easier in our day to recognize the fallacy in that reasoning and remain open to the interplay of various forms of understanding that can intersect to enrich our limited intellectual grasp of complex phenomena. No single approach or method exhausts the intelligibility of the matter under investigation. We have had to learn this difficult, and at times painful, lesson in many areas of scientific endeavor.

Our enterprise is, then, a subdivision of the dialectic between science and religion.[2] Psychoanalysis is a unique natural science with its own proper methodology and subject matter (Meissner 1981, 1985). It is not simply a positivistic science dealing with objective and observable subject matter, but a science of human subjectivity based on data of observation, empathic attunement, introspection, and interpersonal interaction. Its method is adapted to the requirements of the clinical setting of the psychoanalytic situation, so that, when it wanders from that setting and moves into areas of theological reflection, qualifications must multiply and the circumspection with which it draws its conclusions all the more telling.

But this is no reason to think that analysis has nothing to contribute to theological understanding. I would argue that, if the sacraments serve as channels of divine grace, they have an impact and influence on the human soul that has important reverberations in psychic terms (Meissner 1987). The counterpart to the theological understanding of the sacraments and their place in the economy of salvation is a deeper understanding of the psychological reverberations of these symbolic and grace-full actions and their meaning to the minds and hearts of the believers who receive and respond to them. Thus, a psychoanalytic reflection on this level of sacramental experience contributes nothing directly to the theological understanding of the sacraments themselves, but it can contribute significantly to the understanding of their psychic impact and the role they might play in the spiritual lives of believers.

Another salient consideration is that the enterprise of sacramental theology is more or less communally restricted. While the sacramental theologies of the Catholic tradition — Roman, Orthodox, and Eastern — are significant aspects of credal belief and cult, other religious traditions do not share this sacramental focus in the same degree. Thus any effort to develop a psychoanalytic hermeneutic of sacramental action and praxis is selectively relevant to some confessions and less so to others. If one attempts to focus on any specific aspect of religious belief or praxis, it is altogether likely to suffer from similar credal constraints.

I will focus my discussion here on the general concepts of sacramental action rather than on specific sacraments. There are unquestionably psychoanalytic issues and questions arising from reflection on the matter and substance of particular sacramental rites — particularly pertaining to matters of symbolic implication and meaning — that have been fertile fodder for analytic speculation since Freud's (1913) first expeditions into the religious realm. Psychoanalytically based speculations on the baptismal rite, with its symbolic references to water, birth and death (Beirnaert 1949, 1950), or the symbolism of bread and wine in the eucharist and its analogy to the totem feast (Freud 1913, 1939; Bergmann 1992; Jones 1974; Schuster 1970), have an established credibility, but the string on such speculations has more or less run out. The coin of such symbolic interpretation has been spent. Progress in deepening our understanding of the sacramental function and its faith impregnated experience may have to seek other directions of inquiry and look to other conceptual models of psychic implication.

The drift of these speculations is in some cases almost more anthropological in tone than psychological. The underlying hypothesis rests moreover on the somewhat questionable grounds of the fiction of the primal horde and the validity of assumptions regarding the return of the repressed. The guiding spirit in such reconstructions is the push toward connecting the phenomena under investigation to fundamental drives and their associated, usually infantile, and repressed mental contents. The intent of these psychoanalytic speculations is to explain aspects of the phenomena as derivatives of such unconscious and dynamic influences. As the discussion takes place at a distance from an individual data base, the enterprise becomes more precarious.

SACRAMENTAL ACTION — THEOLOGICAL PERSPECTIVES

The first step, in undertaking an effort to construct a conceptual approach that might provide foundations for a more meaningful and constructive integration of theological and psychoanalytic understandings to their mutual enrichment and development, is to examine some aspects of the theology of sacramental action. In its broadest connotation, sacramentality concerns the ultimate meaning of human existence, the idea of the saving presence of God, and a transformative effect on humans, whether individually or communally (Cooke 1990). Human existence is distinguished by its reflective self-consciousness. But sacramentality touches on the ultimate meaning of that existence as determined by the continuing presence of God resulting from a divine communication through His revealed word and the response to it through faith. Divine presence through self-communication to man changes the basic meaning of human existence. As human persons, the meaning of life is transformed by this divine-human relationship, embracing new values, goals, and a deepening of motivations through the agency of sacramental grace. Within this horizon, the Christian sacraments are 'sacred signs, instituted by Christ, to give grace'.

Within the Catholic theological tradition, the sacraments are seven in number — baptism, confirmation, eucharist, matrimony, penance, holy orders, and anointing of the sick. They are actions of the church conferring grace and sustaining men on the path to salvation. It is immediately evident that they intersect with the course of life at critical junctures — birth (baptism), death (anointing), at points of important life determining decision (matrimony, orders), and at times when special strengthening of the Christian is required to face life's pains and difficulties (confirmation, eucharist, penance). As Cooke (1990) notes, "All the basic experiences that comprise the fabric of people's lives — birth, growth into adulthood, sickness and suffering, love and friendship, success and failure, caring for one another, sin and reconciliation, and in a special way death — are meant to be transformed by what has happened in the life and death and resurrection of Jesus" (p. 1119).

But more than actions of the church, they are understood as actions of Christ, living and present as a vital force in his church, guiding, sustaining, supporting and strengthening the church and its members through sacramental grace. Thus an understanding of sacramental action includes not only an understanding of the meaning and function of grace in the economy of salvation, but a grasp of the implications of the relation of Christ to the church — in the pauline metaphor, Christ as head of the church joined to him as the mystical body, in which all members of the church are joined to Christ in a special and intimate union.

Scripture. Sacramental theology has evolved through the centuries, but rudimentary concepts of sacramental action can be identified in the early traditions. In the pauline church, baptism and eucharist were regarded as means of salvation (1 Cor 10: 1-22), and marriage was linked to these basic themes (Eph 5: 21-33). Comparable statements indicate the special role of other sacramental rites in the life of the early church.

Patristic development. Clarification of the implications of these cultic practices and the evolution of the doctrine of sacramental theology was a work of centuries, gradually emerging from the reflections of the Christian patristic dialectic to become common doctrine by the middle ages. Only gradually were individual sacramental rites included under the rubric of 'sacrament', so that sacramental theology actually evolved out of the development of thinking about separate sacraments and their interconnections. From a more general connotation of anything with a sacred character, reference was gradually restricted to a small number of specific rites as sources of grace and means to salvation — the now familiar seven sacraments. Throughout the course of this evolution, the tension between the emphasis on the physical aspects of the sacramental rites and their spiritual and symbolic significance, between physical reality and symbolic reality, has persisted and followed shifting patterns of accentuation and meaning.

With passing centuries, especially in the first millennium, the intimate sense of sharing in the mystery revealed in Christ was gradually attenuated (Cooke 1990). The participative meaning of the sacramental experience gave way to a more instrumental concept in which the cultic acts were taken to be divine means for giving grace through the mediation of an ordained minister. The role of the believer was as a recipient, a view abetted by their increasing exclusion from participation in the sacramental rite. This development was paralleled by diminishing understanding of the meaning of the sacramental mystery, resulting from social disruption, rudimentary religious instruction, and the prevalence of Latin as the liturgical language. The minister performed the sacred act, often at a distance from the faithful for whom it became a spectacle to be attended, rather than an expression of living faith. Sacramental liturgies became increasingly disengaged from the everyday significance of people's lives.

The growing identification of sacraments with the extrinsic rites led to confusion and ambiguity. The apparent decline of liturgical significance led to efforts at reform, but too little and too late to stave off the explosion of the Reformation. The Reformers drew attention to the place of personal faith and active liturgical participation, but also tended to disparage the sacraments in favor of scripture. The profound challenge to orthodox Catholic views of sacramental reality led to the response of the Council of Trent (Cooke 1990).

Trent. It was not until the Council of Trent, under the pressure from the doctrinal challenge from Reformers, that a more or less consistent teaching regarding sacraments was achieved. The council articulated the prevailing understanding in the following points (Schulte 1970):

1. While acknowledging sacramental elements in the Old Testament, sacraments of the New Testament are distinguished by their institution by Christ.

2. Sacraments are visible signs or symbols of invisible grace — instrumental causes containing and signifying grace which they elicit and channel *ex opere operato* — by reason of valid performance of the rite and not of the merits of either minister or recipient. This does not mean that the effects of this causality are automatic or mechanical, let alone magical, but depend essentially on the disposition of the recipient as a condition, that is, on faith and openness to the grace of the sacrament. Thus intentionality of the recipient is required, along with a corresponding intention of the minister to do what the church intends by the rite in question. This insistence on efficacy of the sacraments was opposed to the reform view that sacraments only promised salvation through faith without effectively communicating grace. While faith was a necessary disposition, the sacraments both signified and gave grace in virtue of saving power derived from the death of Christ. However, this efficacy is neither automatic nor independent of the faith and dispositions of the participants.

3. The grace of each sacrament corresponds to the symbolic signification of individual sacraments. The sacrament is an instrumental cause of grace, the principal and primary cause being God, specifically Christ as divine person and founder of the church. The grace conveyed by the sacrament is either justifying or contributes to the growth and development of justifying grace. For some sacraments, the nature of the grace (the sacramental 'character') is such that it cannot be repeated. The scholastic mentality viewed sacraments as objective realities, and posed its understanding in quasi-scientific terms establishing the nature, conditions and effects of sacramental action — that is, as actions of Christ.

4. The sacraments are essential for the salvific mission of the church as a whole and for each member of the church in personal and individual terms.

5. Since the sacraments are means for salvation instituted by Christ and entrusted to the church, valid administration requires authority either from Christ or the church. Valid and efficacious administration requires correct use of the materials ('matter') and verbal formulae ('form') and the proper intention. A correct intention in the recipient is required, but the terms of this intention can vary in different sacraments — none is required or possible in infant baptism, but rather the intentions of others than the recipient.

6. The number of sacraments is seven — no more, no less — but not all are equally necessary for salvation. Only exceptionally would a Christian receive all seven — usually marriage and orders are exclusive. The insistence on seven sacraments was intended to counter the Protestant claim that only baptism and eucharist were true sacraments.

The pronouncements of Trent are to be understood in the historical context to which they were addressed. In the face of the crisis of the reformation, these formulae are often onesided and stress one aspect of the sacramental reality. Criticism has been leveled at their limitations: e.g., lack of a sound ecclesiological base, emphasis on Christ's action understood as coming through instrumentality of the sacred minister rather than as Christ active within his church and people, inadequate understanding of the relation between word and sacrament, neglect of the role of the Holy Spirit, and failure to understand the theological significance of liturgical forms as expressions of the living faith of the church.

Current views. The progression of understanding in more contemporary settings has opened the way to revision of this theological perspective leading to a more evolved understanding of the meaning of sacraments and their role in the life of the church. Particularly as a result of deliberations of the Second Vatican Council, the sacramental life of the church has received increasing emphasis. Thus individual sacraments are conceived as actions of the church, united with Christ and acting in virtue of Christ's salvific action in and through the church. Through these concrete sacramental actions, the church serves as intermediary between Christ and the Christian. This renewed emphasis on the spiritual and symbolic reality of the sacramental life of the church opens the way to a more comprehensive understanding of the meaning of sacramental action in and on the individual believer.

The understanding of the meaning of 'sacrament' is embedded in its history, such that the continuing theological development of the meaning of sacramental efficacy takes place within parameters set by that historical understanding. Comparative study of individual sacraments reveals both their common characteristics and their considerable diversity. A common meaning that applies univocally or comprehensively to all sacraments is thus elusive. They share a common note as an unfolding of the graceful life of the church — in Rahner's terms, as "vital acts of the Church in the process of its self-realization as the primordial sacrament. In these acts the Church gives concrete form to its own essence, which is to be the eschatological, historical and social presence of God's self-communication to the world for the sake of individuals in the moments essential to their salvation" (cited in Schulte 1970, p. 381).

In the wake of Vatican II, a significant shift has taken place from a preconciliar scholastic and structural emphasis on the nature of the sacraments to a postconciliar emphasis on the mystery of Christ in relation to his church and to individual believers. The mode of discourse has moved from the more objective and scientific level of scholastic understanding to the more personal and phenomenological mode which shifts the basis for exploration of sacramental meaning closer to intrapsychic and personal spiritual terms and farther from objectivized philosophical accounts.

But in addition, the sacraments are not merely churchly actions, even as they pertain to individual members, but they are also acts of worship and gratitude to God for His saving grace and love. Seen in historical and ecclesial dimensions, sacramental grace is less a matter of the individual minister and the individual recipient, than a more authentically pauline sense of the vitality of the sacraments as concrete forms by which the spiritual life of the church increases and multiplies. They are in this sense concrete symbols expressing the communication and communion between God and man, of the flow of life-sustaining grace coming to man through God's Word and Spirit. Within the Christian tradition — with various credal variations — the concrete and specific intermediary of this presence of God's Word in the world is Christ. The eschatological salvation was achieved through the incarnation, death and resurrection of Christ. The sacraments are therefore related to the Christ-event and have become specific symbolic expressions of the reality of Christ's presence and action primarily within his church and secondarily within each individual believer. They are the concrete means by which church and believer come to share in the redemptive and salvific effects of God's salvific action wrought in and through the incarnational and sacramental presence of Christ.

The theological implications of the sacraments as forms of symbolic reality has its roots in this theological ontology and salvation history. But at the same time, a meaningful grasp of the significance of such symbolic reality presents its difficulties. From the side of the believing Christian, there is a basic need for self-expression in and through concrete actions and realities, particularly psychic or spiritual attitudes. These more intellective and spiritual dimensions of human experience only become real, personally meaningful and effective in words and gestures by which they are communicated to others. Such symbolic enactments are an integral part of concrete human experience, even in more mundane matters, but at certain telling points in human existence such concrete expressions take on special meanings, which are either performative or commemorative. Examples are births, deaths, marriages, family meals, and the creation of social structures with particular powers and functions. Sacramental actions tend to follow this natural patterning of life events and to echo their natural meaning by joining them to more specifically spiritual and supernatural movements. In this sense, the basic structures of human existence are joined to and become expressive of grace-informed, redemptive and salvific dynamisms.

Current postconciliar theology of the active presence of Christ in the church shifts the emphasis in sacramental meaning to that of a personal encounter between Christ and the believer. By implication, ". . . in replacing the "object model" of scholastic reflection with the more phenomenological and experiential model of "human encounter," he [Schillebeeckx] turned sacramental theology away from the extrinsic *quid pro quo* language of economic exchange (do this and receive grace) to the interpersonal language of relational human experience" (Fink 1990, p. 1109).[3] This paradigm shift introduced a new hermeneutical lens through which to understand the sacramental tradition — sacramental reality could be conceived as a form of saving dialogue between God and man, specifically God as man with his fellow men engaged in an interpersonal interaction of mutual presence. Thus, if scholastic theology had sustained the view that sacraments effect what they signify, Vatican II made it clear that sacraments must signify what they effect, since only through such signification do they become effective for those who participate in them.

Subsequent developments in sacramental theology have been searching out new models of sacramental meaning. Some of these developments have led to closing the gap between sacramental action and human experience, integrating sacramental experience with aspects of personality and psychic development (Cooke 1968; Powers 1973).

Sacramental action is geared to development of a mature Christian personality, and sacraments are regarded as possessing a formative or transformative function by which the soul is drawn closer to God along a path of self-transcendence. This transformation of consciousness invites the believer to a new level of self-realization marked by increasing freedom, hope, and the capacity for love (McCauley 1969). Some of these insights have found expression in liberation theology, closing the gap even more decisively between sacramental action and human realities (Segundo 1974).

Thus sacraments in this theological perspective are symbolic realities expressing the real, personal, and salvific presence of God communicating Himself to men in and through the sacramental life of the church. This aspect of the symbolic reality of the sacrament takes the form of the reality of the presence of Christ to the believer and of the believer to Christ — a relational and interpersonal dimension of the sacramental reality. Access of the believer to this salvific presence comes through faith — itself a gift of grace. The sacramental reality invites the believer to enter into and participate in this deeply relational and personally meaningful experience, intimately connected with the sacramental rite and geared to the spiritual enrichment of the believer in his belief, his openness to divine influence through grace, and his love of God. While the objective sacramental efficacy is a given aspect of the symbolic reality, the effectuation of any meaningful communicative experience is partly a function of the state of mind of the believer who receives the sacrament. The optimal disposition is different for each sacrament — stretching from the absence of intentional disposition in infant baptism to the full range of spiritual ecstasy and mystical transport of the spiritual heights. But these effects of grace cannot be achieved without the free response of the believer who enters the sacramental realm with the necessary openness and desire. This realization opens the way to a consideration of this psychic dimension of the sacramental experience and action.

The sacraments, then, the forms of Christ's gift of Himself, are taken as sources of reconciliation between men and God. In virtue of the resurrection and glorification, Christ transcends categories of time and space so that He is present when and where He wills (Suess 1969). This is understood as God's way of making Himself present to us, being present to us in a new way through Christ — a presence that is real, personal, sacramental, loving, forgiving, and comforting. The sacrament is thus connected to the mystery of revelation, the loving encounter with Christ as a real and living presence. It renews that reconciliation with God that Christ accomplished in the offering of the cross and the resurrection. Christ's giving Himself and conferring grace through the sacrament is a creative action which transforms the matter of the sacrament into something different — the water of baptism is no longer simply water, the bread of the eucharist is no longer simply bread, the absolution of sacramental forgiveness is more than a merely human exchange, the pledge of love and fidelity in marriage becomes more than an expression of merely human affection. The corporeal and natural has been transformed into the spiritual. The symbolic sacramental activity of Christ effects a change of being in which the material sacramental signs retain their place in the secular world governed by the laws of nature and corporality, but now assume a sacramental form. Christ becomes present in the sacrament as the Lord who gave Himself in death as an atonement for our sins and to return us to life-giving relationship to God. The sacrament becomes a sign of his presence, the real presence of Christ giving Himself to those who believe in him. The newer sacramental theology moves away from a merely physical or metaphysical orientation to an emphasis on the sacramental and spiritual presence of Christ not only in the sacramental species but in the community of believers and in the church.

Analytic Interpretations

I would like to turn to consider an interpretation of sacramental experience and probe the bases of meaning of sacramental action from a psychoanalytic vantage point. In so doing we enter an entirely different realm of discourse. Psychoanalytic formulations address issues of an entirely different order from theological inquiry, and they rest on a divergent set of suppositions and methodology. The psychoanalytic inquiry makes no assumptions regarding faith-orientation, truth-value, or revealed status of the data in question. Theological discourse in its classical expression directed its concern to the more or less ontological basis of real sacramental action and, despite contemporary refocusing, remains predominantly in the realm of objective reflection. In the psychoanalytic perspective, the frame of reference shifts to the subjective — the realm of intrapsychic meaning and subjective experience. Ultimately our interest is in the manner in which these disparate realms intersect and interact.

Moreover, ideas expressed in these formulations are applications of psychoanalytic perspectives to essentially nonanalytic material. This fact calls for a considerable degree of interpretive caution. This style of applied analysis is several stages removed from the proper realm of psychoanalytic inquiry — the immediate clinical psychoanalytic situation

— and thus constitutes a form of analytic speculation or conjecture. Such speculation has its limitations as well as possible heuristic interest. Further, the psychoanalytic focus falls on the human experience of sacramental participation. It concerns itself with the meanings and motives of such sacramental engagement, and has nothing to say about the nature of the sacrament itself. In this sense, the psychoanalytic inquiry lies closer to contemporary interests in sacramental theology than more classical concerns.

AN ANALYTIC REFLECTION

Any meaningful analytic reflection on the sacramental mystery requires a clear delineation between the realm of the symbolic and that of the real, between the objective dimensions of the mystery and the subjective. Any contribution it has to make will come in the contexts of subjective experience and symbolic meaning. It has nothing to say beyond that. The issues of reality and meaning come into play from the very first. The words of the sacramental rite use a language of identity or declarative efficacy — the eucharistic formula says: "This *is* my body", the baptismal rite: "I baptize thee". Dogmatic interpretation accepts this as a statement of something real. But the bread offers us nothing but the appearance of bread, common and familiar, the water is no different than any water.

The statements challenge our reality testing. Yet the claim of the faith perspective does not strain the credulity of the believer. Certainly if a communicant received the host and immediately began choking and vomiting because he believed he had eaten human flesh, we would have reason to question his mental condition. Communicants do not believe they are consuming human flesh. Whatever the doctrine means, it is *not* that. The reality in question has some other meaning. Similarly the water of baptism or the oils of anointing are not simply water or grease; their meaning is altered by the context and intentionality and the faith condition of their utilization. We can also accept that the language is mythic. Mythological usage does not say: "This bread stands for my body", or "This bread represents my body", not even "This bread is like my body". Mythic language says: "This *is* my body". No other expression will carry the weight of the mythic and symbolic significance intended. The church's teaching echoes this understanding by its insistence on the symbolic reality and efficacy of the sacraments.

The formulae of administration and the church's teaching convey a mystery that eludes human understanding. The mystery has both objective and subjective dimensions. Objectively, there is an assertion of certain spiritual realities accepted on the basis of faith and theological understanding; the doctrine asserts that Christ is really, personally, and meaningfully present in the sacrament, and that His presence brings with it graces contributing to man's spiritual life and salvation. Moreover, the sacrament is equivalently Christ's communication of Himself to believers in such a way that the believer is incorporated into Christ and becomes one with Him. The sacrament contains in addition a sacrificial aspect recalling and re-enacting the sacrifice of Christ on Calvary. The sacrament thus participates in the gift of Christ of Himself to the Father as the sacrificial victim expiating the sins of mankind and opening the way to salvation. It further asserts that these spiritual realities and effects are brought about through causality exercised by the Holy Spirit.

Subjectively, the symbolic and subjective impact is carried by the connotations of the matter and form of the sacramental rite — the eating and drinking of the bread and wine in the eucharistic meal, the use of water, chrism and salt in baptism, etc. Freud's association of the eucharistic meal with eating the totem animal reflected this aspect, along with other symbolic interpretations of material or formal symbolic aspects of the rites. That meaning may have considerable similarities in each of the relevant religious contexts as articulated by respective sacraments and their forms of symbolic expression.

TRANSITIONAL EXPERIENCE

An important contribution to conceptualizing one aspect of this kind of context of symbolic meaning came from Winnicott's analysis of the early experience of the child in the mothering context. Winnicott's genial contributions have spawned a revolution in psychoanalytic thinking about cultural phenomena. His ideas regarding transitional objects, transitional object relations, and transitional phenomena have exercised a tremendous influence on our thinking about broader human concerns — touching on questions relevant to the understanding of human cultural experience, on issues related to involvement with other human beings, and on man's place in a world that is not of his own making. One of the most important areas in which Winnicott's ideas have taken root and undergone significant evolution is in the psychoanalytic understanding of religious phenomena (Meissner 1984).

Winnicott's interest centered on the infant's developing experience of reality and the phenomenal stages through which the infant gained access to it. He approached the question through his analysis of the use of transitional objects as a childhood developmental phenomenon (Winnicott 1953). Various authors have discussed forms of transitional objects and stages of the evolution of transitional phenomena in the infant's experience, especially in the first two years of life (Tolpin 1971; Hong 1978).

This view of the child's early psychic development and the growth in his capacity to relate to other meaningful humans in his environment served as the initial platform on which Winnicott based his ideas concerning developmental aspects of play and the emergence of transitional space within which the play phenomenon took place, and which evolved into the locus of later transitional phenomena. My interest here, and the interest of this issue for religious phenomena, is in the contribution of the understanding of transitional phenomena to the area of illusion. Winnicott argued that illusion was an important aspect of human involvement in the world of experience, a capacity expressing itself in the creative shaping of a humanly meaningful environment and in facilitating in psychic terms the interlocking processes of accommodation and assimilation by which we adapt to the world around us — the world both of inhuman objects and other human beings.

In his analysis of the developmental contexts of transitional object experience, Winnicott argued that, in the optimal mother-child interaction, the 'good-enough mother' is sufficiently attuned to the infant's needs so that she is available and responsive at the very point at which the infant's need demands satisfaction. The conjunction of the infant's need and the response by the real object — mother — creates a situation of illusion in which, from the point of view of the child, he has the experience of creating the need-satisfying object. Thus, to the eyes of the external observer the response comes from the outside, but not from the point of view of the baby. But at the same time it does not come exclusively from within, that is, it is not a hallucination. As Modell (1991) recently commented:

> Within the illusion of the potential space the mother accepts and does not challenge the child's construction of reality; the question, whose reality is it?, does not arise. Winnicott generalized from the observation of infants to suggest that this potential space characterizes the mental process that underlies the shared illusions of aesthetic and cultural experiences. From the standpoint of an outside observer, this potential space is a space that belongs neither entirely to the subject's inner world nor to objective external reality; it represents the subject's creative transformation of the external world. (p. 234)

This area of the infant's experience is simultaneously subjective and objective. Winnicott (1971) thus stakes out an important dimension of human experience, over and above involvement in interpersonal relationships and the inner realm of intrapsychic experience and functioning. He articulates an intermediate area he designates as "experiencing" (p. 2), which lies at the intersection of psychic and external reality. He wrote, "It is an area that is not challenged, because no claim is made on its behalf except that it shall exist as a resting-place for the individual engaged in the perpetual human task of keeping inner and outer reality separate yet interrelated" (p. 2). The intermediate realm of experience, then, is neither subjective nor objective; it is both simultaneously.

ILLUSION AND CULTURAL EXPERIENCE

In Winnicott's view, the claims of illusion and of this intermediate realm of experiencing reach far beyond the developmental context. He (1971) commented:

> It is usual to refer to "reality-testing," and to make a clear distinction between apperception and perception. I am staking a claim for an intermediate state between a baby's inability and his growing ability to recognize and accept reality. I am therefore studying the substance of illusion, that which is allowed to the infant, and which in adult life is inherent in art and religion, and yet becomes the hallmark of madness when an adult puts too powerful a claim on the credulity of others, forcing them to acknowledge a sharing of illusion that is not their own. We can share a respect for illusory experience, and if we wish we may collect together and form a group on the basis of the similarity of our illusory experiences. This is a natural root of grouping among human beings. (p. 3)

In the course of development, the child's illusion of magical omnipotence and control over the transitional object gradually gives way to increasing degrees of disillusionment and optimal frustration, leading gradually toward accommodation to reality. This dialectic and tension between illusion and disillusion continues to elaborate throughout the whole of human life and experience. The process of gaining knowledge and acceptance of reality is never fully accomplished. Every human being is caught up in the tension and struggle of relating inner to outer reality. The relief and resolution of this interminable tension can be gained only within the intermediate area of illusory experience, which for the most part even in the life of the adult remains unchallenged, particularly as it finds expression in the arts and religion. Winnicott (1971) commented:

> Should an adult make claims on us for our acceptance of the objectivity of his subjective phenomena we discern or diagnose madness. If, however, the adult

> can manage to enjoy the personal intermediate area without making claims, then we can acknowledge our own corresponding intermediate areas, and are pleased to find a degree of overlapping, that is to say common experience between members of a group in art or religion or philosophy. (p. 14)

PLAY AS ILLUSION

The capacity for illusory experience develops and evolves into the play of the child and later the creative and cultural experience of the adult. Winnicott (1971) himself emphasized certain aspects of the playing experience that reflect its illusory character. The area of playful illusion belongs neither to the child's psychic reality, nor to the external world. Into this transitional space the child gathers objects (toys) that he invests with meanings and feelings derived from his subjective world. Play has an inherent excitement deriving not merely from instinctual arousal, but from the precarious interplay between the child's subjectivity and what is objectively perceived and received. Winnicott noted a direct development from the appearance of transitional phenomena to the capacity for play, from isolated play to shared playing, and from shared playing to the capacity for cultural experience. The child who plays well demonstrates a capacity for blending illusion and reality and reflects a relatively smooth integration of both libidinal and aggressive impulses. The capacity to utilize both libidinal and aggressive energy harmoniously is essential not only in the play of children but in more adult forms of creative activity.

RELIGIOUS EXPERIENCE AS TRANSITIONAL

The implications of the notion of transitional phenomena can be expanded to embrace more mature and adult forms of creative and cultural expression. Art in all its forms and religion are primary areas of transitional experience. The notion of transitional phenomena in this sense incorporates areas of human understanding in which the symbolic function plays a role. Symbols play a vital role not only in cultural phenomena but also in important areas of human social commitment and affiliation. Politics and religion are prime examples of where symbols play a central role.

Symbolism. The question in this consideration has to do with the extent to which Winnicott's understanding of transitional phenomena can serve as a meaningful model for analysis of religious experience and ideation. Analysis of culture in terms of transitional experience and the value of illusion stands in stark opposition to Freud's views. For Freud, the purpose and value of culture was instinctual restraint and a matter of the channeling intrapsychic conflict; for Winnicott, cultural dynamisms originate in the mother-child dyad and continually evolve in other interpersonal and social contexts as a matter of establishing and maintaining a sense of self. For Freud, civilization and culture are necessary evils resulting in neurotic adjustments; for Winnicott, they are indispensable sources of human psychic development and selfhood that keep the personality from slipping into schizoid isolation and despair. For Freud, religious beliefs were little more than vain wish-fulfillments; for Winnicott they were essential illusions answering to fundamental and ineradicable human needs (Gay 1983; Meissner 1984).

The infantile vicissitudes of transitional phenomena lay the basis for the child's emerging capacity for symbolism. In a sense, the piece of blanket symbolizes the mother's breast, but, as Winnicott (1971) suggested, its actual transitional function is as important as its symbolic value. He observed, "Its not being the breast (or the mother), although real, is as important as the fact that it stands for the breast (or mother)" (p. 6). The use of transitional objects, then, is more a step toward the development of symbolic function than itself a form of symbolism. When symbolism is achieved, the infant has already gained the capacity to distinguish between fantasy and fact, between internal and external objects, between primary creativity and perception, between illusion and reality. The use of symbols takes place within the intermediate area of experience that Winnicott designated as illusion.

By the same token, real external objects and experiences can become vehicles for the expression of similar subjective intentions and significances and can thereby take on an added, symbolic dimension. The symbolic quality of such experiences and objects participates in the intermediate realm of illusion, compounded from elements of external reality intermingled with subjective attributions expressing the human capacity to create meaning. The symbolic function comes into play at both conscious and unconscious levels. Consciously, we can express meanings by actions (gestures, behaviors) or by attributing meaning to external objects. Unconsciously, the meaning of the action or attribution is not immediately evident and can only be ascertained by interpretation within a broader social or historical context. An animal phobia expresses a fear, but the object of the fear is masked. As Godin (1955) remarked:

> These two levels of symbolic expression are closely linked and complementary to one another. The symbolic function is always exercised by an encounter between an interior urge, which results from the whole organization of a personality, and its actualization in exterior expressions of which most (but not

> all) are modeled by the surrounding culture, traditions and social conventions. The symbolic act, therefore, unites, not only several degrees of reality (matter and spirit), but several levels of human reality (conscious and unconscious, individual and social). (Godin 1955, p. 279)

This capacity for symbolic experience makes culture possible since it provides the matrix within which the cultural experience takes place. That experience is not merely subjective (as derivative of and determined by intrapsychic dynamics only), nor is it exclusively objective (as a reflection of extrinsic and objectively determined qualities of the object); it is compounded of objective qualities, as of a painting or statue or piece of music, and the subjective experience that the individual psyche brings to it. I will suggest that the same compounding of subjective and objective are characteristic of religious experience, in the first instance, and religious understanding (theology) in the second.

It is important to recognize the extent to which Winnicott's approach differs from Freud's (1927) view of illusion. Freud's emphasis on the distortion or contradiction of reality in the service of wish-fulfillment is basic to his view of illusion and consequently of religion. But what Freud saw as distortion and contradiction of reality, Winnicott saw as part of man's creative experience. What Freud saw as wish-fulfillment, in accordance with the pleasure principle and in resistance to the reality principle, Winnicott viewed as an inherent aspect of human creativity. In Winnicott's view, then, illusion plays a role in the developmental transition to reality: without the capacity to utilize transitional objects and to generate transitional forms of experience, the child's efforts to gain a foothold in reality will inevitably be frustrated. Further, without continuing access to and participation in illusory experience, human life becomes impoverished and withers, insofar as fundamental and vital human needs are deprived of appropriate nourishment and support. Thus illusion is not an obstruction to experiencing reality but a means of gaining access to it (Meissner 1984). In the same sense, the symbolic dimension of human understanding represents an attempt to see beyond the immediate, the material, the merely sensual or perceptual, to a level of deeper meaning and human, if not spiritual, significance. Religious symbolic systems are, at least in the Judeo-Christian tradition, derived from a twofold source that is at once subjective and objective. The subjective dimension comes from the dynamic constituents of human understanding and motivation, while the objective dimension is contributed by a revelation with the presumption of a divine presence and action behind it. Leavey (1986) articulates this dimension of religious belief systems as follows:

> Faith is by nature — human nature — presented symbolically, and religions are symbol systems. The believer, knowingly or not, owes his or her religious language to a revelation that is the spring of the tradition, coming from outside the believer's mind. The ultimate reference of faiths are not themselves products of regressive fantasies, but symbolic representations of ultimate truths. (Leavy 1986, p. 153)

It is within this dimension of religious experience that the psychological and the theological intersect, and it is likewise within this area of conceptualization that I have proposed transitional forms of understanding as providing the basis for bridging concepts that might facilitate dialogue between psychoanalytic and religious perspectives (Meissner 1990, 1992).

The Sacramental Experience

The problem arises in the interface between psychoanalytic and religious thinking. Each of these areas represents separate disciplines and ranges of discourse, each with its separate reference points, modes of conceptualization and symbolic connotation. Within the context of an accepted belief system and the record of revelation, religious thought addresses itself to a realm of conceptualization that it takes as having existential validity and substantial truth value. The meaning of the sacramental experience provides a test case for the manner in which the characteristic discourse of both psychoanalysis and theology intersect in the putative dialogue between them. The question is whether the above analysis and the notion of transitional conceptualization offer any basis for a deeper understanding of the sacramental mystery and its relevance to human psychology.

The doctrine of sacramental reality asserts the reality of Christ's action in and through the sacramental species and the symbolic connection of the material aspects of the sacrament with the giving and receiving of grace. It further asserts the union of Christ and the believer by reason of the believer's faithful reception of sacramental action and openness to grace. The given frame of reference for this theological conceptualization is the objective, existing and real world of human spiritual existence as guaranteed by the power of the Holy Spirit. On the opposite side of the conceptual chasm, psychoanalysis stakes its claim to an inner world of man's psychic experience, expressing itself in wishes and fantasies and more or less rooted in the subjective polarity of man's experience. In addressing human religious experience and conceptualization, psychoanalysis makes no commitments to a framework of existent or objective realities, but confines its focus and the implication of its arguments to the intrapsychic realm. It asserts no more than the subjective and the intrapsychic and at least prescinds from the objective or extrapsychic implications of its formulations. The business of psychoanalysis is psychic reality and nothing beyond. It has nothing to say about the sacramental reality.

In an effort to construct a conceptual bridge over this chasm between religious and psychoanalytic thinking, I have tried to adapt Winnicott's genial formulations regarding transitional phenomena to point toward a useful and potential conceptual space providing a medium for dialectical resolution of these tensions between subjective and objective. This analysis extends Winnicott's ideas regarding transitional phenomena and the area of illusion to include a form of conceptualization operating within the area of illusion — that as such is neither subjective nor objective in implication and lies open simultaneously to both subjective and objective poles of meaning without violation or exclusion of either (Meissner 1978, 1984).

All religions make use of religious symbols — the bread and wine of the eucharistic sacrifice, the water and chrism of baptism, the exchange of marriage vows, and so on, serve this function. As material objects or actions, they become the vehicles for expression of meanings and values transcending their physical reality. This symbolic dimension, however, in psychic terms, is not a product of the objects themselves; it can come about only by some attribution to them by the believer. Consequently, sacramental objects as religious symbols are neither exclusively perceived in real and objective terms nor simply produced by subjective creation in the manner of a fantasy or hallucination. Rather, they evolve from the amalgamation of what is real, material, and objective as it is experienced, penetrated, and creatively reshaped by the patterns of meaning attributed to the object by the believer — and, in the sacramental context, by the community of believers that is the church. Consequently, the object has its symbolic function only for the believer and his belief system. We are once again in the transitional space in which the transitional experience is played out in the context of religious illusion. Such symbols, even in their most primitive and material sense, serve the articulation and maintenance of belief that are important for the human experience of religious belonging and purpose.

As the believer approaches the sacrament, he brings with him all the residues of his life history and intrapsychic dynamics that psychoanalytic reflection addresses. They include the reverberations of his earliest feeding experience and the experience of union with the mother and her breast from the long forgotten depths of his infantile period, or infantile associations to washing and cleansing, or episodes of parental forgiveness and restitution after falling from grace. He brings these elements with him as he enters a special realm of transitional experience created by the ambiance of belief and ritual. In the process he creates out of the resources of his faith-determined creativity the experience of sacramental receptivity and symbolic realization. This statement needs to be immediately amended by a reassertion that the realm of transitional conceptualization is doubly derived — that is, both objectively and subjectively. The sacramental mystery is not simply the product of creative imagination.[4] In order to maintain conceptual clarity, the object — here the sacramental species — is not in itself a transitional object (like the infant's teddy bear) and is not intended as such. The experience and conceptualization of sacramental meaning is nonetheless transitional insofar as it remains open to both subjective and objective components or perspectives for the realization of the fullness of its sacramental meaning. With respect to the eucharist, for example, the meaning of oral incorporation, feeding, taking life-giving nourishment, and assimilation of the object as an integral part of oneself, is an essential part of the sacramental significance in the mind of the believer — consciously or unconsciously.

The details of that meaning may vary according to the conscious or unconscious associations they entail for the individual, but the essential associative contexts would involve the experiences of being fed and the related sense of dependency and attachment with respect to caregivers and feeders in the course of the child's developmental experience. For most people, the mother would have been the salient figure, but not exclusively so — fathers would have their place in the picture. The unconscious reverberations, therefore, involve not simply the echoes of the feeding experience itself, but include elements of the child's experience of significant and meaningful relations with the important objects and the quality of his relationships to them.

On the objective side, the belief system pre-exists the individual believer and is posed by an extrinsic, culturally determined and traditionally sustained declaration and imposition that asserts the real existence of the objects of belief. The sacramental doctrine is shaped and accommodated within a context of belief determined by the religious inspiration, traditions, originative mythology, and theological constructions by which the fundamental belief in the divinity of Christ and the validity of His sacramental promise are construed consensually within the religious group.

We might ask how the theological formulations explored above regarding the understanding of the sacramental mystery intersect with the psychoanalytically based view of transitional experience and understanding. The more traditional view, rooted in the insistence on the sacramental reality, focuses almost exclusively on the ontological dimension of the sacrament — a formulation that prescinds from, if not disregards, the intrapsychic experience of the communicant. That formulation, as far as I can see, is exclusively objective in intent and thus stands outside of the transitional realm. It offers nothing to the understanding of the communicant's experience, just as the reductive formulation from the exclusively subjective pole of psychoanalytic understanding of unconscious infantile motivations has nothing to say about the dogmatic truth-value of the theological statement.

Versions that emphasize questions of sacramental signification and symbolic action, giving a degree of priority to the issue of meaning and man's capacity to create meaning, bring the discussion closer to the transitional realm. It is man's capacity to create meaning and to enter a mode of symbolic experience that is essential to the transitional mode of experience. If the psychoanalytic understanding of transitional experience and conceptualization can be viewed as opening the way, or at least leaving the way open, to the real dimensions of man's symbolic experience in the realm of illusion, the shifts in theological perspective can also be said to open the door to the relevance of man's psychic experience to the fuller comprehension of the meaning of the sacramental mystery. If these degrees of rapprochement from both the theological and psychoanalytic sides do not effectively bridge the conceptual gap, they go a long way toward diminishing it.

I would stress, however, that in the realm of belief, neither the subjective nor the objective pole of this experiential continuum is ever altogether eliminated. For the naive believer (who probably comes closest to fulfilling Freud's caricature), whose faithful understanding of the sacramental experience is determined in large measure by concrete images of bread-as-body and wine-as-blood, or by images of cleansing or strengthening, and by transferential derivatives from parental figures, subjectively determined imaginings about sacramental action and effects are articulated within a community of belief in which the existential dimension adheres as an important aspect of the belief system. But the quality of his concept of the sacramental action may go little beyond the level of the immediate and concrete experience of reception. For the scientific theologian on the other hand, the theologically elaborated and derived conceptualization of the nature and meaning of the sacramental mystery is never so completely abstract as to remove himself from the correlated intrapsychic, even infantile, determinants that adhere — I might even say inhere — in the dogma.

NOTES

1. For a recent thrust in this direction, see Grünbaum (1993), especially his comments on theism, and my riposte in a review (Meissner 1994) and a subsequent article (Meissner 1995).
2. The recent discussion of this problem by Mooney (1991) provides a contextual statement for the present discussion.
3. We can note in passing the parallel shifts in theoretical perspective in psychoanalysis, from the more objective structural perspective of metapsychology to the more interpersonal, experiential and hermeneutic emphases in object relations theory, self psychology, and other postmodernist developments. See Leary (1994).
4. This faith-derived experience is not merely psychologically motivated, but operates under the impetus of grace and the activity of the Holy Spirit. See the discussion of grace and faith experience in Meissner (1987).

REFERENCES

Beirnaert, L. (1949). La dimension de la mythique dans le sacramentalisme chrétien. *Eranos Jahrbuch, 17*, 255-286. [Transl.: The mythic dimension in Christian sacramentalism. *Cross Currents*, 1951, *5*, 68-86.]

Beirnaert, L. (1950). Symbolisme mythique de l'eau dans le baptême. *Le Maison-Dieu, 22*, 94-120.

Bergmann, M.S. (1992). *In the shadow of Moloch: the sacrifice of children and its impact on western religions*. New York: Columbia University Press.

Cooke, B. (1968). *Christian sacraments and Christian personality*. Garden City, NY: Image Books.

Cooke, B. (1990). Sacraments. In: P.E. Fink (ed.) *The new dictionary of sacramental worship* (pp. 1116-1123). Collegeville, MN: Liturgical Press.

Fink, P.E. (1990). Sacramental theology after Vatican II. In: P.E. Fink (ed.) *The new dictionary of sacramental worship* (pp. 1107-1114). Collegeville, MN: Liturgical Press.

Freud, S. (1913). Totem and taboo. In: *The standard edition of the complete psychological works of Sigmund Freud, vol. 13* (pp. 1-162) (transl. & ed. J. Strachey). London: Hogarth, 1955.

Freud, S. (1927). The future of an illusion. In: *The standard edition of the complete psychological works of Sigmund Freud, vol. 21* (pp. 5-56).(transl. & ed. J. Strachey). London: Hogarth, 1964².

Freud, S. (1939). Moses and monotheism. In: *The standard edition of the complete psychological works of Sigmund Freud, vol. 23* (pp. 7-137) (transl. & ed. J. Strachey). London: Hogarth, 1964.

Gay, V.P. (1983). Winnicott's contribution to religious studies: the resurrection of the cultural hero. *Journal of the American Academy of Religion, 51*, 371-395.

Godin, A. (1955). The symbolic function. *Lumen Vitae, 10*, 277-290.

Grünbaum, A. (1993). *Validation in the clinical theory of psychoanalysis: a study in the philosophy of psychoanalysis*. Madison, CT: International Universities Press.

Hong, K.M. (1978). The transitional phenomena: a theoretical integration. *Psychoanalytic Study of the Child*, *33*, 47-79.

Jones, E. (1974). *Psycho-myth, psycho-history* (2 vols.). New York: Hillstone.

Leary, K. (1994). Psychoanalytic "problems" and postmodern "solutions." *Psychoanalytic Quarterly*, *63*, 433-465.

Leavey, S.A. (1986). A Pascalian meditation on psychoanalysis and religious experience. *Cross Currents*, *36* (2), 147-155.

McCauley, G. (1969). *Sacraments for secular man*. New York: Herder & Herder.

Meissner, W.W. (1978). Psychoanalytic aspects of religious experience. *Annual of Psychoanalysis*, *6*, 103-41.

Meissner, W.W. (1981). Metapsychology: who needs it? *Journal of the American Psychoanalytic Association*, *29*, 921-938.

Meissner, W.W. (1984). *Psychoanalysis and religious experience*. New Haven, CT: Yale University Press.

Meissner, W.W. (1985). Psychoanalysis: the dilemma of science and humanism. *Psychoanalytic Inquiry*, *5*, 471-498.

Meissner, W.W. (1987). *Life and faith: psychological perspectives on religious experience*. Washington, DC: Georgetown University Press.

Meissner, W.W. (1990). The role of transitional conceptualization in religious thought. In: J.H. Smith & S.A. Handelman (eds.). *Psychoanalysis and religion* (pp. 95-116). Baltimore: Johns Hopkins University Press.

Meissner, W.W. (1991). The pathology of belief systems. *Psychoanalysis and Contemporary Thought*, *15*, 99-128.

Meissner, W.W. (1992). Religious thinking as transitional conceptualization. *Psychoanalytic Review*, *79*, 175-196.

Meissner, W.W. (1994). Philosophy versus psychoanalysis — or how to bottle a cloud. *Contemporary Psychology*, *39*, 524-527.

Meissner, W.W. (1995). The pathology of beliefs and the beliefs of pathology. In: E. Shanfransky (ed.). *Religion and the clinical practice of psychology*. Washington, DC: American Psychological Association.

Modell, A.H. (1991). A confusion of tongues or whose reality is it? *Psychoanalytic Quarterly*, *60*, 227-244.

Mooney, C.F. (1991). Theology and science: a new commitment to dialogue. *Theological Studies*, *52*, 289-329.

Powers, J. (1973). *Spirit and sacrament: the humanizing experience*. New York: Seabury Press.

Schulte, R. (1970). Sacraments. I. The sacraments in general. In: K. Rahner et al. (eds.). *Sacramentum mundi: an encyclopedia of theology, vol. 5* (pp. 378-384). New York: Herder & Herder.

Schuster, D.B. (1970). The holy communion: an historical and psychoanalytic study. *Bulletin of the Philadelphia Association for Psychoanalysis*, *20*, 223-236.

Segundo, J.L. (1974). *The sacraments today. Vol. IV*. Maryknoll, NY: Orbis Books.

Suess, T. (1969). La présence du Christ: recherches protestants. *Revue des Sciences Philosophiques et Théologiques, 53*, 433-457.

Tolpin, M. (1971). On the beginnings of a cohesive self. *Psychoanalytic Study of the Child, 26*, 316-352.

Winnicott, D.W. (1953). Transitional objects and transitional phenomena. *International Journal of Psychoanalysis, 34*, 89-97.

Winnicott, D.W. (1971). *Playing and reality*. New York: Basic Books.

INDEX

Aaronson, B. 230
Addison, R. 133
Åkerberg, H. 121
Allen, S. 77
Allport, G.W. 86
Almond, P. 219-221, 229
Anders, G. 117
Anderson, H. 101, 102
Andrae, T. 121
Ankersmit, F. 133
Apel, K.-O. 40
Arbib, M. 54
Ariès, Ph. 117
Aristotle 11, 51, 95
Armon-Jones, C. 110
Aschenbach, G. 195
Atwood, G. 57
Austin, J.L. 203
Averill, J.R. 111

Baker-Miller, J. 59
Barbour, I. 58
Barrett, W. 140
Barth, K. 234
Bateson, G. 94
Batson, C.D. 89
Beirnaert, L. 158, 161, 162, 266
Béjin, A. 117
Belzen, J.A. 102
Berger, B. 230
Bergman, M.S. 266
Bernstein, R. 53, 57
Berry, J.W. 113
Bettelheim, B. 77, 79, 82
Billig, M. 8
Bion, W.R. 251-260
Black, M. 25
Bleicher, J. 200
Boer, Th. de 39, 44, 46, 48, 111, 112
Bonhoeffer, D. 234
Bourdieu, P. 114, 195
Bouvy, A.-M. 114
Brandchaft, B. 57
Brenner, C. 53
Brown, H. 54
Brown, L. 174-176, 190
Brown, L.B. 89, 110
Bruner, J. 8, 175
Buber, M. 220, 224
Bucke, R.M. 221
Bühler, K. 7
Bultmann, R. 234
Burke, P. 118
Butler, J. 65, 67

Capps, D. 88-90, 121, 148
Capps, W.H. 148
Caroll, M.P. 121
Carruthers, M.J. 116
Cassirer, E. 242
Castaneda, C. 19
Chasseguet-Smirgel, J. 75
Chaucer, G. 79
Chodorow, N.J. 59, 82
Clark, W.H. 88, 213
Coe, G.A. 88
Cohen, C.L. 118
Coles, R. 148
Coltart, N. 157
Cooke, B. 267-269, 272
Corbin, A. 117
Corbin, J. 207, 210
Corveleyn, J. 38, 102
Crews, F. 151
Crowley, H. 93

Danzinger, K. 100
Day, J.M. 103, 173, 174, 177, 182, 185, 188, 190
Delaney, C. 76
Delumeau, J. 117
DeMause, L. 118, 235, 239

Demos, J. 118
Deren, M. 67
Dewey, J. 51
Dilthey, W. 13-15, 56-58, 95, 174, 200
Dinnerstein, D. 82
Dionysius the Areopagite 222
Dittes, J.E. 86, 87, 121
Dornes, M. 260
Downing, M. 68
Dray, W. 44, 48
Drehsen, V. 206
Dudon, P. 162-168
Dunde, S.R. 117
Dulles, A. 94
Durkheim, E. 208

Eckhart 215
Edwards, D. 8
Eigen, M. 256
Eilberg-Schwartz, H. 65, 73, 74
Ekström, H. 227, 228
Eliade, M. 19
Elias, N. 111
Ellwood, R.S. 215
Erdely, M.H. 151
Erdheim, M. 251, 260
Erikson, E.H. 118, 120, 129, 136-154, 157
Ernst, C.W. 230
Esrock, B. 66
Evans, R.I. 141
Evans-Pritchard, E.E. 26
Eyre, D. 66

Fairbairn, W.R.D. 59, 60, 66
Faulconner, J.E. 85, 91, 92
Fèbvre, L. 19, 117-119
Fenichel, O. 53
Festinger, L. 121
Feuerbach, L. 234
Feyerabend, P. 40, 53
Fink, P.E. 272
Fletcher, F. 94
Forman, R.K.C. 221
Foucault, M. 96, 111, 195
Fowler, J.W. 20, 33
Francis, L.J. 87
Freeman, M. 175
Freud, A. 138
Freud, S. 15, 20, 24, 25, 28, 39, 51, 52, 57, 60, 61, 66, 67-73, 93, 114, 120, 121, 136-144, 224, 234, 238, 246, 247, 263, 265, 266, 276, 279-281, 285

Gadamer, H.-G. 96, 133, 148, 149, 199, 201-203, 209, 210
Gadlin, H. 181
Gay, V.P. 280
Geels, A. 121, 222, 224, 230
Geertz, C. 42, 112, 133, 195-199, 208, 209
Gehlen, A. 111
Gendler, M. 80
Gerben, M. 175
Gergen, K.J. 8, 97, 100, 101, 113, 116, 134, 175
Gerhart, M. 55
Giles, H. 87
Gill, M. 52, 53, 60
Gillet, G. 8
Gilligan, C. 59, 174-176
Gimello, R.M. 220
Ginzburg, C. 115
Giorgi, A. 7, 8
Glaser, B. 207, 210
Glock, C.Y. 88, 89, 214, 229
Godin, A. 86, 88, 89, 280, 281
Goffman, I. 120
Goldberg, A. 260
Goodenough, E. 196
Goodman, N. 54, 57
Goolishian, H. 101, 102
Gorsuch, R.L. 89
Grad, H. 113
Grathoff, R. 195
Greenson, R.R. 53
Groot, A.D. 42, 130
Grosz, E. 93
Grünbaum, A. 51, 151, 286
Guntrip, H. 59, 60

Habermans, J. 96, 100, 136, 148, 245

Hall, S. 88, 120
Hanford, J.T. 130, 148
Harré, R. 8, 101
Harris, D. 87
Hart, H.L.A. 43
Hay, D. 88, 216
Hegel, G.W.F. 60
Heidegger, M. 47, 96, 100, 199-201, 209
Herdt, G. 121
Herik, J. van 61
Hermans, H.J.M. 113
Hermelin, E. 227, 228
Hesse, M. 54
Himmelweit, S. 93
Hoffman, D. 121
Hoffman, L. 100
Holm, N.G. 121
Homans, P. 87, 146
Hong, K.M. 277
Hood, R.W. 88
Hoppe, K. 234
Houston, J. 230
Hubbs, J. 77
Huizinga, J. 117
Huls, B. 116
Hume, D. 234
Hunsberger, B. 87
Husserl, E. 35, 46
Hutschemaekers, G.J.M. 116
Hutsebaut, D. 102

Idel, M. 230
Inge, W.R. 213, 215, 219
Ingleby, D. 116
Ignatius of Loyola 121, 155-171

James, W. 18, 32, 86-88, 216
John of the Cross 221, 222
Johnson, M. 55, 57
Johnson, R.A. 148
Jones, E. 266
Jones, J.W. 53, 58, 60, 61, 92, 136
Josselson, R. 8
Jung, C.G. 31, 121, 245, 260
Jütteman, G. 114, 195

Källstad, T. 121
Kamper, D. 117
Kant, I. 32, 35, 38, 43, 45, 235
Katz, S.T. 220
Keats, J. 255
Keller, F. 59
Kempen, H.J.G. 113
Keupp, H. 195
Klein, M. 59, 66, 73, 77-80, 251-254
Knorr Cetina, K. 195
Kohlberg, L. 20, 177
Kohut, H. 52, 56, 242, 243, 247, 248, 252, 256, 258, 260
Korzybski, A. 230
Kuhn, Th. 40, 53, 121
Kuiper, P.C. 151

Lacan, J. 48, 93, 111
Lakoff, G. 55, 57
Lans, J. van der 87
Laski, M. 215
Leary, K. 286
Leavey, S.A. 281, 282
Leeuw, G. van der 121
Le Goff, J. 117
Leithäuser, T. 195
Lenk, H. 43
Le Roy Ladurie, E. 117
Leuba, J.H. 213
Levi-Montalcini, R. 155
Lichtenberg, J.E. 260
Lieblich, A. 8
Linschoten, J. 37, 40
Loewenthal, K. 87
Lorenzer, A. 115
Lowe, D.M. 117
Luckmann, T. 230
Lyddon, W.J. 94
Lyons, N. 178, 182, 186
Lyottard, J.-F. 96

Marx, K. 234
Maslow, A. 215
Masters, R.E.L. 230
McCauley, G. 273
McFarland, S.G. 89

Meissner, W.W. 61, 87, 89, 98, 121, 155-159, 162-164, 167, 170, 263-265, 276, 280-283, 286
Meltzer, D. 260
Merchant, C. 77
Merleau-Ponty, M. 93, 96, 111
Merwe, W.L. 112
Messer, S.B. 53, 57, 85, 96, 111, 131, 133, 134, 136
Miller, J.B. 59
Misra, G. 113
Mitchel, S. 57
Mitscherlich, A. 238
Mitscherlich, M. 238
Moddell, A.H. 277
Moghaddam, F.M. 113
Moi, T. 59-61
Molière 17
Mooney, C.F. 286
Mooij, A.W.M. 111, 151
Moore, J.A. 92
Moore, P.G. 218, 219, 220, 229
Morris, C.W. 241
Morris, J.E. 87
Much, N. 113
Mully, A. 66

Naedts, M.H.L. 173, 174, 177, 188
Neisser, U. 221
Needham, R. 26
Noble, D. 77
Nossent, S. 116

Ochse, R. 150
O'Collins, G. 94
O'Conner, K.V. 99, 102
Olbrich, E. 116
Olds, L.E. 92
Ormerod, N. 94
Ortner, S.B. 208
Oser, F. 177
Osmond, H. 230
Otto, R. 18, 32, 88, 220, 228

Packer, M. 133, 175
Palma, R.J. 87
Paloutzian, R.F. 98
Parsons, T. 208
Peeters, H.F.M. 116
Peirce, C.S. 241
Pellegrini, A. 66
Peters, R.S. 97
Pfister, O. 120, 121
Piaget, J. 20
Pine, F. 157
Plotinos 223
Plug, C. 150
Polanco, J. de 171
Polanyi, M. 244
Polkinghorne, D.P. 91, 92, 100, 101
Pope, A. 35
Portmann, A. 111
Potter, J. 8
Powers, J. 272
Pratt, J.B. 213
Pruyser, P.W. 86

Raab, K. 77
Rahner, H. 162, 163
Rahner, K. 271
Rappard, J.F.H. van 109, 130, 132, 151
Ricoeur, P. 35, 42, 45, 92, 96, 101, 111, 136, 143, 174, 175, 199, 203-205, 209, 210, 249, 257
Ribadeneyra, J. de 171
Rizzuto, A.M. 222
Roberts, B. 221
Röckelein, H. 119
Rokeach, M. 89
Rolston, H. 58
Rosenberg, A. 235
Rosenthal, G. 210
Rorty, R. 53
Royce, J.R. 87, 92
Rubin, J.H. 118
Rümke, H.C. 117
Runyan, W. 117, 132
Russel, A. 55
Russel, B. 42
Ruusbroec 215, 218
Ryle, G. 198

Sanders, C. 109, 132

Sarbin, T.R. 111, 133, 175
Saroglou, V. 173, 174, 188
Sartre, J.-P. 47
Saussure, F. de 15
Saward, J. 161, 170
Schafer, R. 101, 111, 151
Scheler, M. 247
Schillebeeckx, E. 272
Schivelbusch, W. 117
Schleiermacher, Fr. 32, 88
Schneider, D.M. 196, 208
Scholem, G. 215, 230
Schrag, C.O. 51, 92
Schuster, D.B. 266
Schulte, R. 269, 271
Schütz, A. 199
Schütze, F. 210
Searle, J.R. 45, 197, 203
Segundo, J.L. 273
Sense, H. 218
Shotter, J. 8, 132
Smart, N. 89, 218
Smith, W.C. 29, 33, 135
Söderblom, N. 121, 220, 223
Soebardi, S. 230
Solomon, D. 230
Sonntag, M. 116
Sorenson, R. 61
Spence, D.P. 53, 57, 101, 134, 137, 151
Spilka, B. 87, 89
Staal, F. 229
Stace, W.T. 216-218
Stanton, E.C. 68, 69
Starbuck, E.D. 88
Stark, R. 214, 229
Steenbarger, B.N. 102
Steiner, G. 41
Stephen, H. 121
Stern, D.N. 60, 260
Stern, E. 195
Stolorow, R. 57
Strauss, A. 207, 210
Strien, P.J. van 109, 114, 130, 132, 151
Strunk, O. 87
Suess, T. 273
Sundén, H. 121

Tannen, D. 176
Tappan, M. 173-175
Taylor, C. 97
Taylor, J. 176
Tellenbach, H. 168
Terwee, S.J.S. 37, 97-99, 111, 130, 131, 133, 136
Theresa of Avilla 24, 214
Thiselton, A.C. 96
Thomae, H. 114
Thomas, K. 118
Thouless, R.H. 87
Tillich, P. 234
Tillo, G.P.P. van 209
Tolpin, M. 277
Toulmin, S. 51
Turner, V. 196, 208

Vanhuyse, B. 20
Vellenga, S.J. 206
Ventis, W.L. 89
Vergote, A. 13, 14, 25, 86, 87, 89, 92, 94, 102, 121, 156, 158, 163, 168
Verwey, G. 38
Voestermans, P.P.L.A. 112
Volmerg, B. 195
Vovelle, M. 117
Vygotsky, L.S. 110

Wachterhauser, B.R. 95, 96
Waele, J.-P. 101
Wahl, H. 260
Wallulis, J. 129, 148-152
Ward, J. 176
Watts, F. 94, 98
Watzlawick, P. 94
Weber, M. 39, 196, 205, 208
Werbik, H. 195
Widdershoven, G.A.M. 111
Wiggins, G. 176
Wikström, O. 121
Wilde, P. de 20
Williams, M. 94, 98
Williams, R.N. 85, 91

Winch, P. 48
Winnicott, D.W. 59, 66, 241, 244, 249, 255, 258, 260, 276-283
Wittgenstein, L. 27, 38, 195, 197
Woolfolk, R.L. 101
Wright, G.H. von 38, 48
Wundt, W. 195
Wulff, D.M. 7, 130, 131, 135

Yankelovich, D. 140
Youngman, D. 176

Zaehner, R.C. 219, 228, 229
Zitterbarth, W. 195
Zock, T.H. 138, 141, 142, 146, 151
Zwaal, P. van der 136